Artists in the City
SPACE in '68 and

Published to mark the 50th anniversary of SPACE

SPACE, London 2018

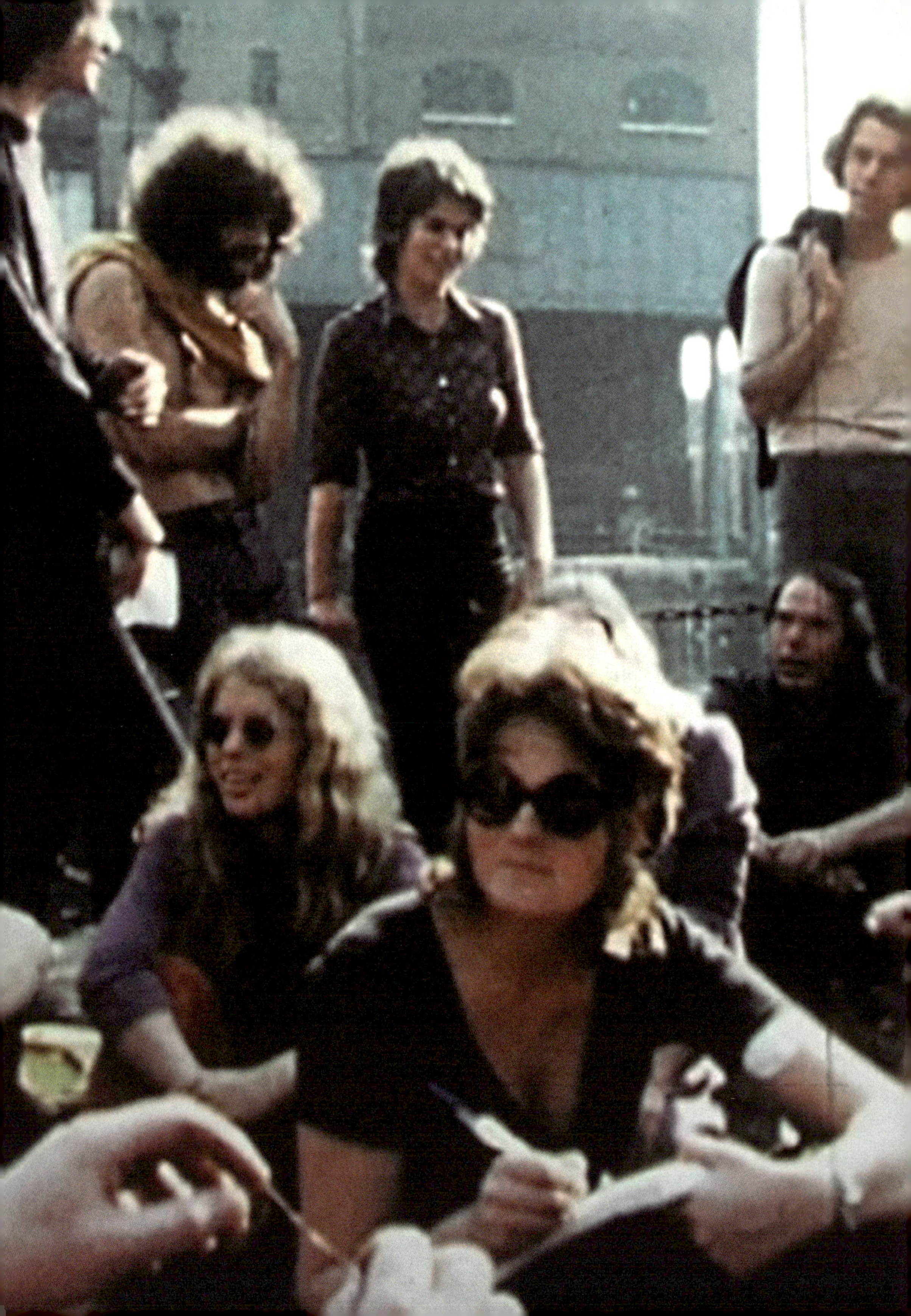

Introduction

Anna Harding

The history of an artist-run initiative would not be a history without a plan to break boundaries and overthrow the establishment. The history of SPACE has these ingredients. This book, published to mark SPACE's 50th anniversary, celebrates the contribution of the organisation to London. The focus is on 1968-75, the early years of SPACE and its sister organisation AIR. We were interested in how much is similar and how much has changed for artists in cities across the globe today facing challenges of working in ever-more expensive and congested cities.

It is hard today to appreciate the novelty of SPACE and why it caught the popular imagination to the extent demonstrated by the wealth of press listed in the bibliography. This may have been due, in part, to its iconic dockland premises, featured simultaneously in photo shoots and films by The Beatles and The Rolling Stones.

London is considered a hyper-successful city, a global capital of finance, culture and tourism, three facets that are closely intertwined. The synergy between creativity, DIY and entrepreneurialism was possibly as key to London in the late '60s as it is today. Visitors are attracted by the energy and inventiveness of London's creative communities and subcultures. The swinging '60s was arguably when this started.

The birth of SPACE in 1968 coincided with student protests and autonomous interventions in cities across Europe. Asserting rights to space was a theme common to student sit-ins, squatting and free festivals. The unique contribution made to the city by SPACE is that its founders, Bridget Riley and Peter Sedgley, negotiated vast amounts of space for creativity through legitimate means, and many have subsequently benefited from the example they set. Setting up a company, Riley and Sedgley persuaded authorities and landlords to lease them property to which artists could bring new life and creative uses. SPACE proved that artists could be trusted and were adept at taking on and managing risks. They envisaged and realised new uses for buildings at a post-war moment when new ways of thinking were much needed.

Artists meeting at St Katharine Docks to discuss the move to Martello Street and Stepney Green, still from SPACE Film, 1970 © SPACE

The founding artists have both written for this book, providing insights into their experience of setting up SPACE. It may be useful to understand the qualities that enabled them to convince authorities to allow them to take on huge premises at low rents for cultural use.

Peter, born in 1930, had studied architecture and worked for ten years in an architect's practice while developing his art. In 1968, ahead of his field in Op Art and Kinetics, the growing demands of his practice, particularly large-scale sculptural installations made with fibreglass, required bigger premises. Bridget, born 24 April 1931 was in 1968 one of the most influential artists of the day. That summer, she represented Britain at the Venice Biennale and won the International Painting prize. Her prominent position also involved her in debate around changes in art school education in 1967 and '68.

Bridget was adept at working her connections to set up SPACE. A series of letters to Henry Moore illustrate this.

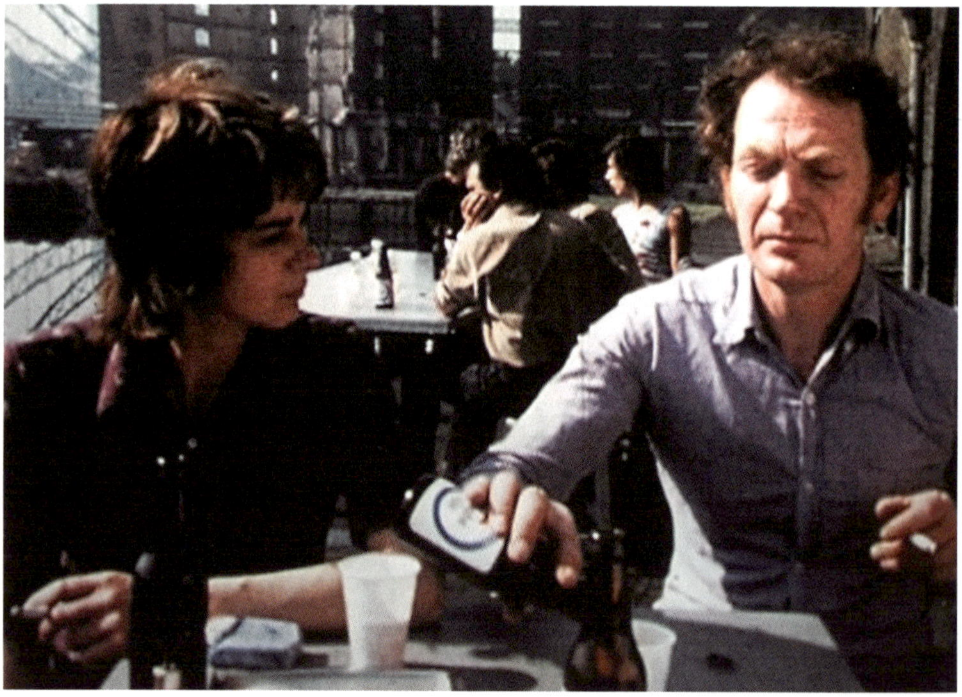

Bridget Riley and Peter Sedgley,
still from SPACE Film, 1970 ©SPACE

27 Nov 1968

Dear Henry Moore

I am haunted by your last remark when we met to visit Jennie Lee [Minister for the Arts in Harold Wilson's government], you mentioned the Erasmus Prize, which was so rightly awarded to you recently. If I remember correctly, a portion of this was set aside for a good cause, chosen by yourself. Have you given any further thought to this in relation to Space trust?

Since I last saw you - the Space trust is now legally formed as a non-profit making company, limited by guarantee and we shall have a site office in the Docks prior to the completion of the lease formalities, which we reckon will be during December. Plans for a press conference in January are going ahead and we will inform you of the date, hoping you will come.

Meanwhile, although we have nothing concrete as yet from Jennie Lee, we have had a message from her saying that we may quote her as being in favour of the scheme. Perhaps in order to keep the project fresh in Jennie Lee's mind, we could, as you suggested, take her down to see over the warehouse at St Katherines dock [sic]. Would you still be willing to escort her with one or two of the trustees? [...] Naturally we would fit in with any date convenient to you both.

On Sunday 4 January 1969, she followed this with a further letter:

Dear Henry Moore,

Here are the two carbon copies of the letters Jennie Lee suggested Professor West write to her concerning details of the scheme - your own letter will be of critical importance - it is extremely kind of you to be such an active sponsor.

The carbon copies attached were:

2 Nov '68
Rt Hon. Jennie Lee MP, Dept. of Education & Science

Dear Miss Lee

It was most kind of you to give us so much of your valuable time last Thursday.

May I give a brief outline of our problem and our plans.

There is a real need for studio workspace and most artists are working in extremely discouraging conditions. Although virtually no working studios as such are available or indeed are likely to become available, there are a number of existing buildings - such as industrial buildings awaiting demolition - which are capable of being used with relatively minor adaptions by persons working in the visual arts. The difficulty in putting them to such use is that as soon as they are occupied in this way, the rating laws would require them to be assessed at their most remunerative use - e.g. as industrial buildings, and this would put them out of the reach of the average artist who (even though he ordinarily supplements his earnings by teaching) is unlikely to be able to contribute more than two or three pounds a week towards running costs. This is particularly grievous as otherwise the buildings would remain empty and non-productive. Our main hope would be if the Borough Council concerned could give sympathetic consideration to the exercise of their discretionary power of rate relief. (our scheme is non-profit making our group is unlikely to be registrable as a charity for technical reasons and thus mandatory rate relief would not be available.)

If you could use your good offices in this respect, our scheme would be possible.

Signed Professor WA West, on behalf of SPACE

Professor West had been enlisted as a company director. A second carbon copy letter, from Professor West to Jennie Lee, set out the plans for SPACE, originally for the Marshalsea Prison site.

On 14 January 1969, Riley wrote again to Moore, requesting him to add his signature to a letter to The Times in support of SPACE. By way of persuasion, she included a list of the other art world figures invited to sign: Anthony Caro, Sir William Coldstream, John Hoyland, Barbara Hepworth, Jasper Johns, Bryan Kneale, Philip King, Robert Motherwell, Robert Medley, Sidney Nolan, Serge Poliakoff, Mark Rothko, Robert Rauschenberg, Tim Scott, Mark Tobey and Keith Vaughan. She enclosed the draft letter:

Sir,

The St Katharine's Docks [sic] are now on offer to developers. We hope that the GLC will consider turning the whole area into a centre for the arts, which would surely be a project unequalled anywhere in Europe.

The site and the buildings, as they are, present a unique working and exhibition environment. The proximity of the Tower and the beauty and peace of these internal pools, readily accessible by road, river and underground, would in addition enhance the tourist attractions of the area.

The buildings themselves are acknowledged significant examples of Victorian industrial architecture, and would seem to merit preservation in their own right.

We hope the GLC will give some of us the opportunity to present more detailed proposals for development on these lines.

Yours faithfully

On 6 July 1969 Riley wrote to Moore saying that they were 'delighted that the Erasmus Foundation had been in touch and had agreed to give half of Moore's prize money to SPACE'. The letter ended with a gentle but persistent reminder: 'We are still hoping that you will find time to visit St Katharine's Dock [sic]'. An entry in Moore's diary for 22 July 1969 reads '6pm Douglas Smith (SPACE film)', referring to Moore's appearance in a film commissioned by SPACE.

Riley wrote to Moore on 11 December 1969:

> The 'Space' directors have asked me to write to you and thank you for [your] so very generous contribution to the studios project. [...] We feel that this should be announced, even if informally, because news of your gift will help the scheme, and also I think that younger artists should know of your sympathetic understanding of their working problems, and your stalwart support of our efforts to alleviate these.
>
> A number of works have already been made which would not have been physically possible otherwise. The studios, though equipped, are Spartan, and yet people are working in a relaxed and busy atmosphere.

Riley's powers of persuasion and Moore's commitment to supporting younger artists are clear. This letter demonstrates a determination to expand SPACE to other sites: 'There are also six other affiliated warehouses scattered around London under the umbrella of "Space" which provide for another 170 artists. Yet we still have a waiting list of 250 names and so will be expanding'. Moore finally visited St Katharine Docks late in 1970, garnering further publicity for the SPACE cause.

The essays in this book are grouped into three sections. We are fortunate to have new texts by Bridget Riley and Peter Sedgley, describing why and how they set up SPACE. These are followed by some art historical context. Andrew Wilson focuses on the Arts Lab movement and the Antiuniversity as contemporaneous self-organising structures, and Courtney J Martin considers the work of SPACE artist Rasheed Araeen and the impact that his experience at St Katharine Docks had on his work.

Naomi Pearce describes the Art Information Registry (AIR), the sister organisation to SPACE, through the eyes of Letty Mooring, its first 'official' administrator. Robert Kudielka's text was originally published to coincide with the SPACE exhibition London Now in Berlin at the Akademie der Künste, Berlin, 1971. It explains the London art scene and SPACE to an international audience in a text that feels as vibrant and urgent now as it would have done then.

In section two William Fowler explores experimental practice at 10 Martello Street, a studio site which fascinates due to a grouping of artists working between performance, music, installation and film. Ana Torok examines the birth of the Artists Union, conceived in the early '70s by artists based at SPACE, considering its recent reincarnation and relevance today. Alicia Miller examines challenges faced by AIR and SPACE as the organisation experienced growing pains.

The third section is called Change and looks at key issues relevant to artist-run initiatives. The concept of DIY is examined by David Morris. The relationship between artist-led initiatives and the state in Scotland is considered, with Neil Mulholland identifying a DIY doxa and relating this to cultural devolution from 1967 to 2017. Larne Abse Gogarty explores debate around gentrification and the agency of artists and cultural workers. Mel Dodd presents a research project looking at SPACE's creative effect or agency. Rebecca Gordon-Nesbitt brings us up to date by examining how SPACE navigates urban development for artists through specific partnerships – with a local authority, a regeneration agency, a housing association and a private developer.

Artists in the widest sense have benefited from SPACE, through dozens of London studio locations and membership of an organisation providing community and advocacy. A symbiotic relationship between artists and the city has served London well for 50 years. But the challenge of affordable space for artists is more critical than ever. Lack of affordable living and working space for low-waged people in London is forcing many to reconsider their future in the capital. Increasing rents underpin the story of artists living and working in London, and the challenges of affording a studio and making work have worsened considerably. Practices, studio sizes and lifestyles have had to adjust to the challenge of living in a congested and increasingly expensive, yet stimulating, city. Vital resources, such as studio space and alternative arts venues, should not be taken for granted. Without them, London's pre-eminence as a creative city is at risk.

With nearly 800 artist tenants in SPACE studios today, illustrating the value of SPACE for art in London over 50 years cannot ever adequatley describe how artists have benefitted. We have attempted to provide a list of SPACE artist tenants, which amounts to around 3,000, but this is bound to be incomplete. More books could be written about AIR Gallery, SPACE's current gallery and programme at Mare Street, The White Building, or its learning programme with schools and local communities.

Images are as important to the story as texts, however cameras and photographic processing were prohibitively expensive for many artists in the early days of SPACE. Luckily a few photographers were around. As a student at Guildford School of Art, Andrew Tweedie photographed St Katharine Docks, as did Douglas Smith who was commissioned by SPACE. Shirley Read, SPACE studios manager from 1972 to 1975, photographed all the studio buildings for SPACE's London-wide Open Studios event in 1975. Chris Dorley-Brown, a SPACE tenant in the '80s has also generously provided some studio shots. Archival material reproduced in this book comes from SPACE's own archive, AIR and SPACE former staff Letty Mooring and Shirley Read, founder Peter Sedgley and many more.

Acronyms are used throughout the book. **SPACE**, always referred to in this way, stands for Space Provision (Artistic Cultural and Educational); **AIR** is Art Information Registry; **ASG** is Art Services Grants Limited, the umbrella company for AIR and SPACE since January 1974; **ACGB** is Arts Council of Great Britain; **GLC** is the Greater London Council and **GLA** is a later incarnation, the Greater London Authority.

Artist Rebecca Warren, a current SPACE studio tenant states in Tate Etc. magazine that 'The studio is where the mess coagulates into certain kinds of realities. Nothing else happens there, which makes a studio quite a strange place in the general run of the world'.* These hidden places can be a mystery to the outside world. This book shines a light on how such studios, vital to London as a creative city, came about and why they are valued by artists in the city today more than ever.

* Rebecca Warren interview with Laura Smith, *Tate Etc.* Issue 41, Autumn 2017, p. 54.

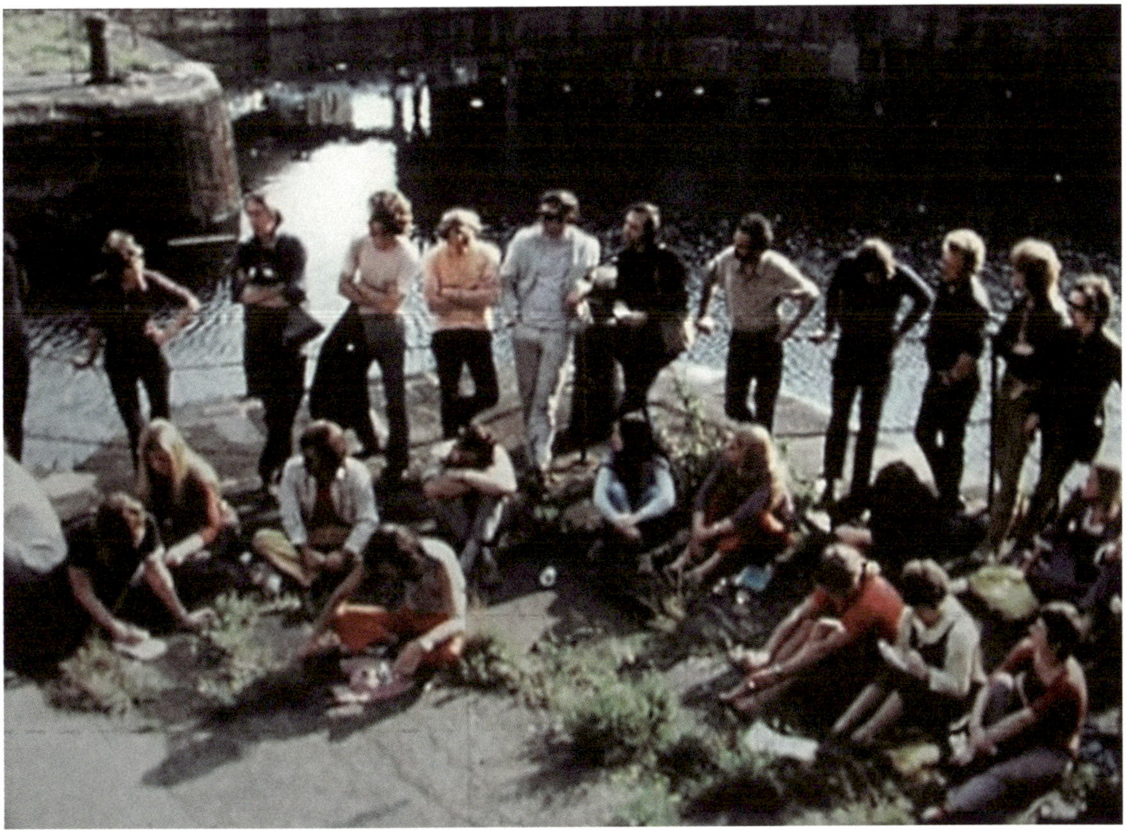

Artists meeting at St Katharine Docks to discuss the move to Martello Street and Stepney Green, still from SPACE Film, 1970 © SPACE

60s
AIR and SPACE

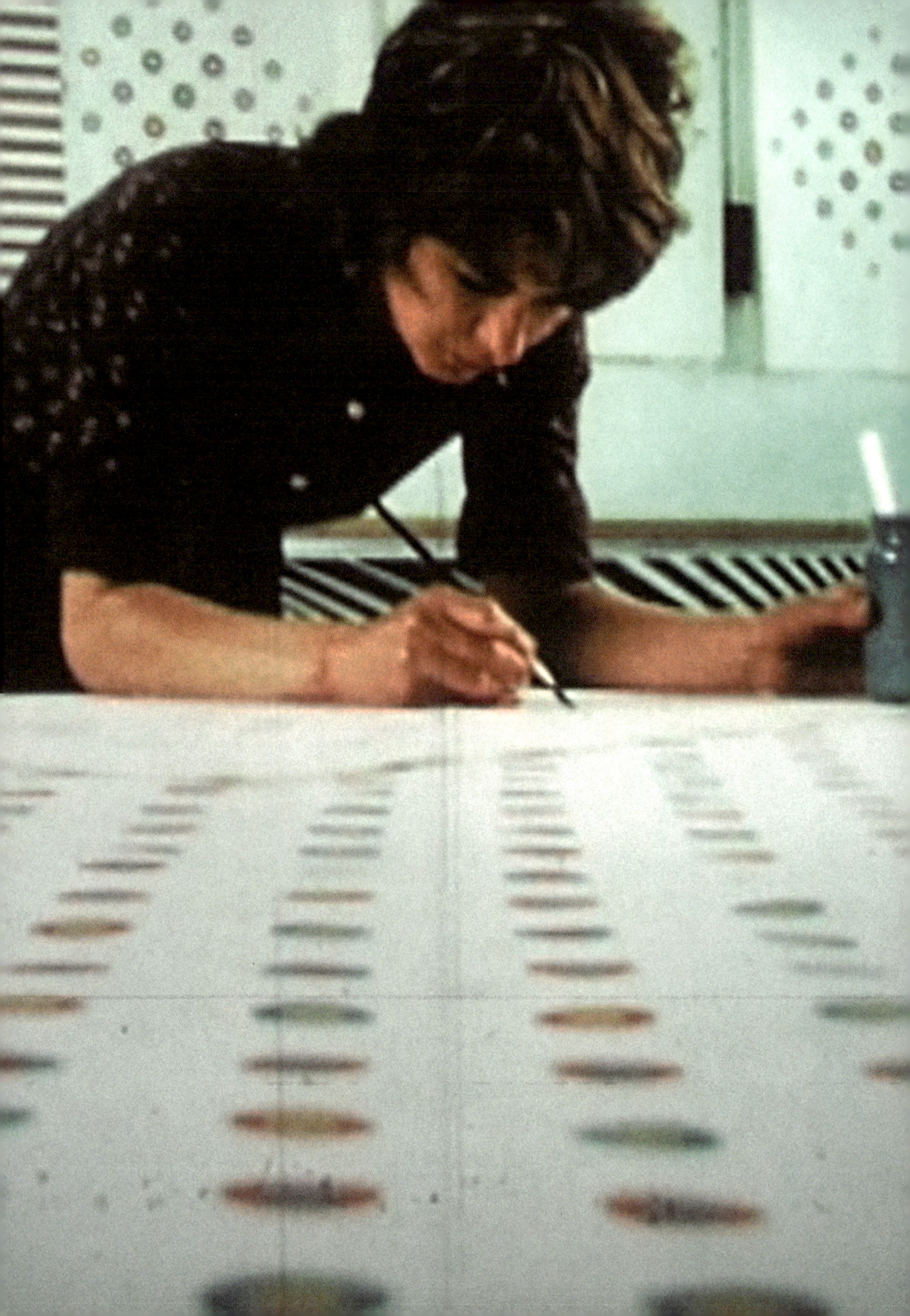

A dream of a studio in the South

Bridget Riley

In the spring of 1962, Gallery One put on an exhibition of my Black and White paintings. Victor Musgrave, who ran the gallery, told me that my work was being much discussed at The Queen's Elm in Fulham Road and suggested I went along to have a drink there. I met Peter Sedgley, and we talked about my work. Later he came to my studio in Warwick Road and looking around said, 'what you need is a proper working table'. The table that he made became, for many years, the model for all my tables.

That summer, I had been invited to stay with friends in the valley of Vaucluse, and, on an impulse, I asked Peter to come with me. We set off on a Lambretta across France. In the South, the light was dazzling. As Monet said, 'you would need a palette of diamonds here'. My friends pointed out a small abandoned farmhouse on a neighbouring hill, saying, 'That's your house, Bridget!' It had been empty for 40 years, but, if one stood on the terrace and looked across the valley, one could see the curves of Les Alpilles – painted many times by Van Gogh. At first, I resisted the temptation to buy the property, not wanting the responsibilities or distractions I knew it would bring. I was already working hard towards my second show at Gallery One, planned for the following year. Peter was thrilled by the potential of restoration and confident that the house could provide studio space. That won me over. My first exhibition had gone well, and as I could, in fact, afford to buy this little property, I did so.

After this initial trip, Peter returned to stay and work in the valley. Letters flew back and forth, and I visited whenever I could, using a small loft-like space as a studio. He began to dream of a community of artists working there, a dream of a studio in the South.

However, this dream was not at all easy to realise, and he returned to London more and more often. By the late '60s, he was working in a studio in London, but it was simply not big enough for the geodesic dome that he was planning to make. There were many painters in London who, like John Hoyland, had built studios in their gardens, which, although they served a purpose for a while,

Bridget Riley in her studio at St Katharine Docks,
still from SPACE Film, 1970 © SPACE

did not really meet the need to find independent working space outside the home.

Peter began to search for disused buildings which could be refashioned as artists' workplaces. One of the most memorable of these was Marshalsea Prison, a debtors' prison on the edge of the Thames, where inmates were tied to a post in the river to await the rising tide. The building was too far gone to rescue, and so Peter's search continued further along the Thames. Near Tower Bridge, he saw the gates to St Katharine Docks. We went to look through them together and saw the Ivory Warehouse, quite clearly a very firm, solid building and completely empty.

Bryan Robertson, a good friend since the New Generation shows at the Whitechapel Gallery, had introduced me to Irene Worth, the American actress, who at the time was working mainly in the West End. Both these friends took a great interest in this increasingly desperate search for workspace, knowing full well how important it is for artists. I told Irene what I had seen, looking through the riverside gates of St Katharine Docks, and it so happened that she was to dine with the Lord Admiral at Admiralty House at the other end of St Katharine Docks, of which he was in charge. She asked him about the warehouse, and he said that he had, just the day before, completed the sale to the Greater London Council (GLC), but he offered an introduction. This was 1968, the year that I had won the International Prize for Painting at the XXXIV Venice Biennale, and this helped. Irene explained the importance of a good letter, and together we wrote one to the GLC, asking if we might come to talk about a possible use for their newly acquired St Katharine Docks.

We rested our case on the grounds that, if temporary use of the warehouse for artists' studios was granted, we would safeguard the premises against vandalism; we would work but not live there; we would relinquish our squatters' rights and leave immediately when required to do so. This was agreed, and a peppercorn rent was charged. We left triumphant, and the great adventure began. A charitable company was being formed – Space Provision (Artistic Cultural and Educational) – SPACE. A friend of Peter's from The Queen's Elm, Professor West, who I believe taught Planning at university level; Peter Townsend, Editor of *Studio International*, and Tony Paterson, Bryan Robertson's accountant, were among the trustees. Plans were drawn up for the division of space.

Once we had the keys, a small party set to work cleaning out the warehouse. It had clearly been unused for many years. The pigeon shit was at least six inches deep throughout; the Boyle family, Bert Irvin, Peter and I shovelled much of it into bags. Having cleared up the space, the next need was for temporary partitions and lighting. We began a search for funds and applied to the Arts Council for a grant. Meanwhile, simply by word of mouth, over 90 artists applied for studio space. This was quickly allocated, and waiting lists were drawn up. Peter and I both had studios – on opposite sides of the warehouse. SPACE Studios was well and truly launched and on its way.

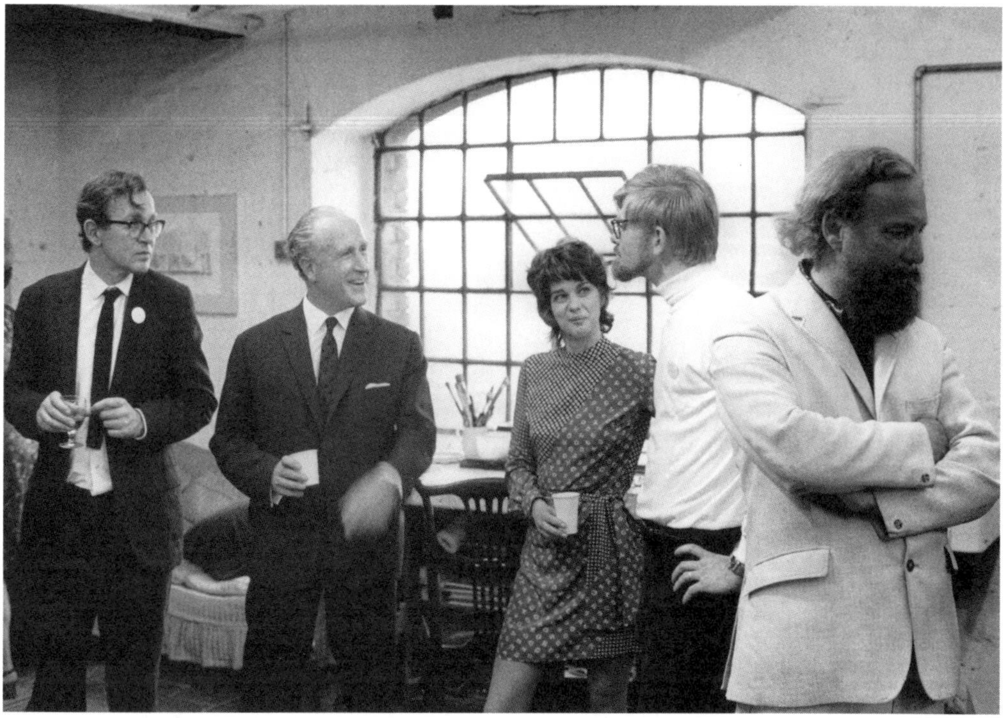

Bridget Riley and visitors at St Katharine Docks, c.1968-70.

St Katharine Docks with Graham Stevens' inflatable.→

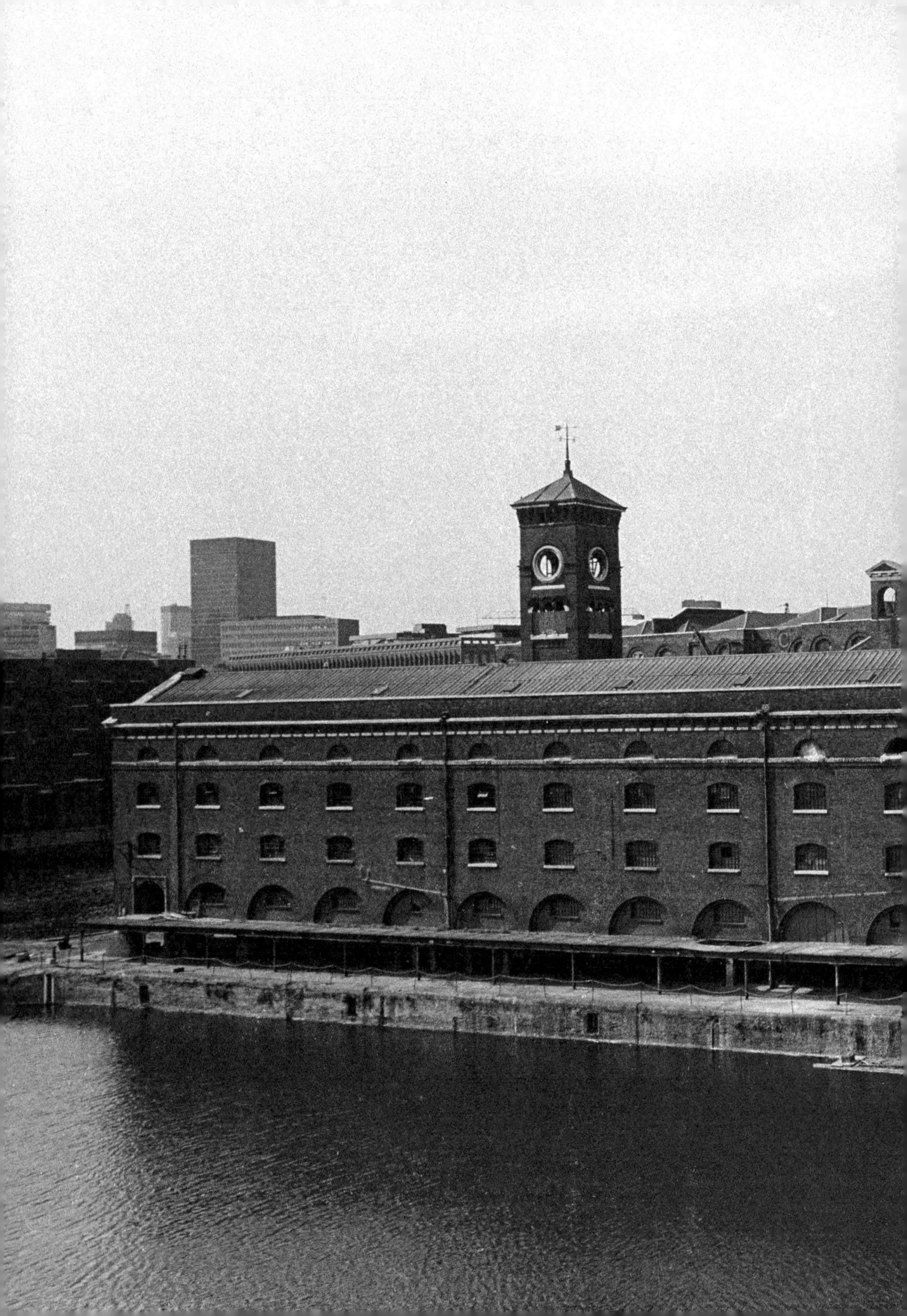

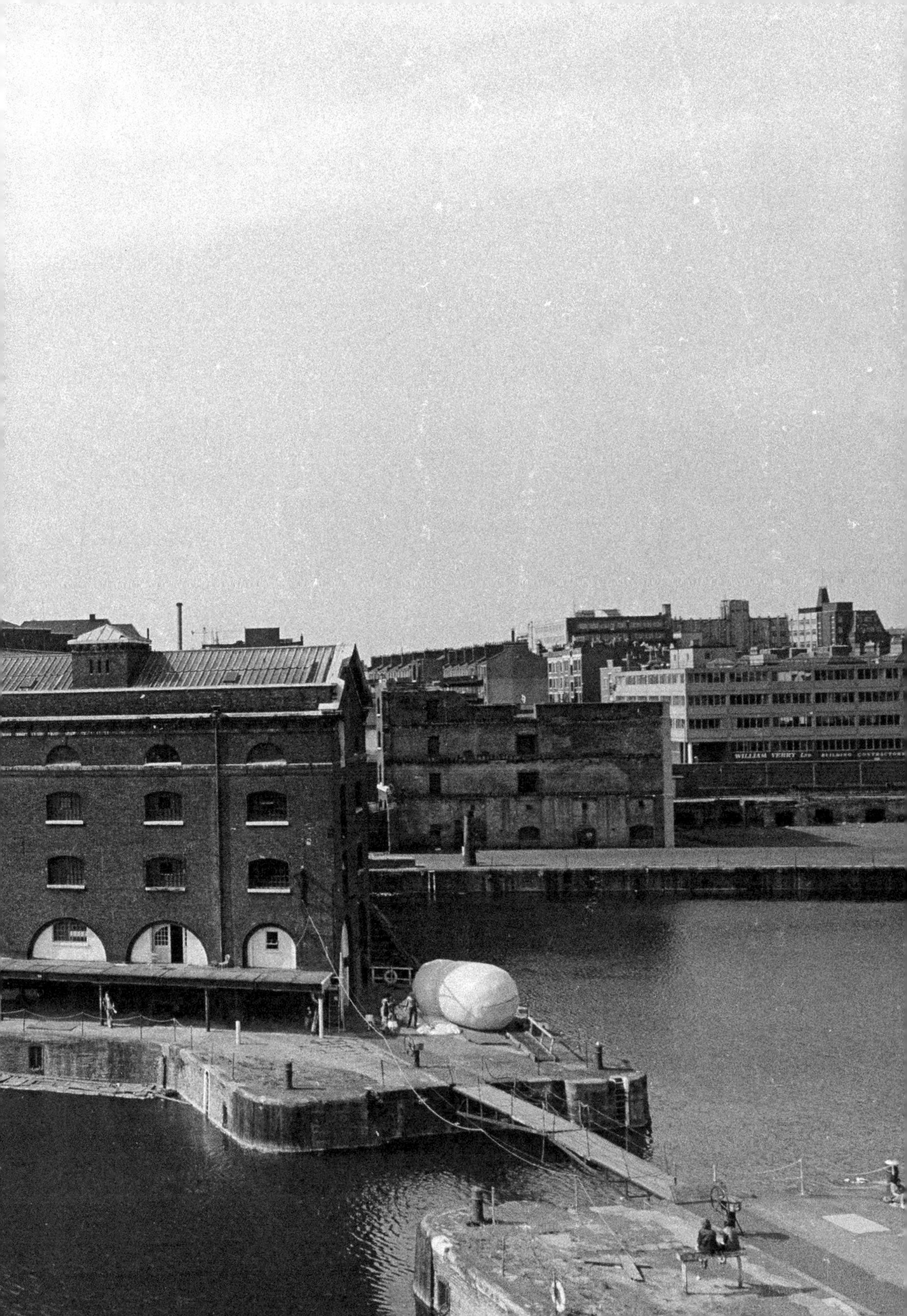
WILLIAM VERRY Ltd BUILDING

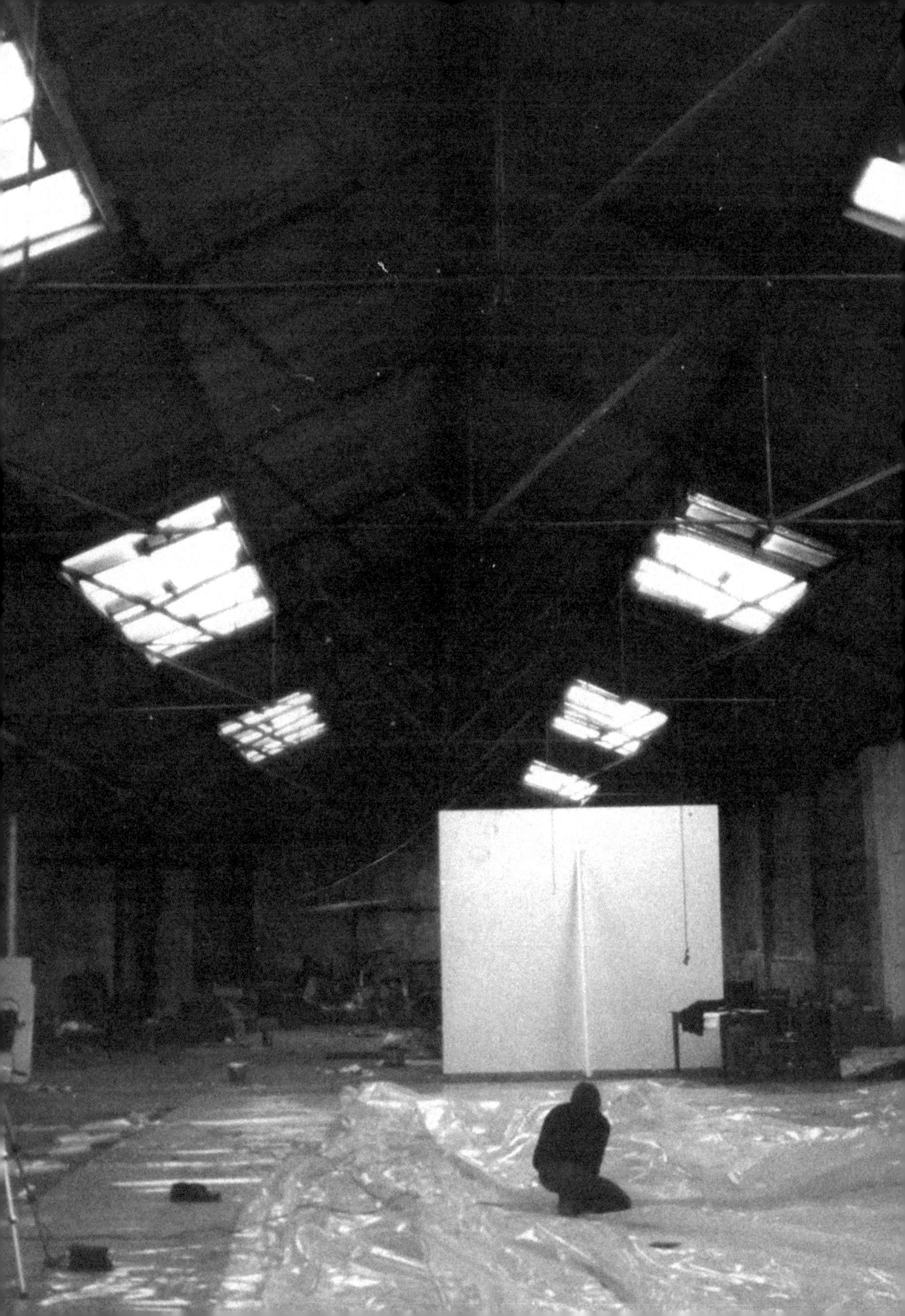

The founding of AIR and SPACE

Peter Sedgley

THE 1960s

It is generally agreed that the period famously known as the '60s effectively begins around the middle of the '50s, ending a prolonged post-war austerity period that demanded reparation and renewal. Actions had to be taken to free our community from reactionary tendencies seeking to revert to pre-war Britain, falsely believing that they represented the good old days.

A feeling of optimism was developing as the fear of nuclear annihilation waned. In the circumstances, people took the opportunity to occupy themselves with matters that they might have a chance of influencing, and this often took the direction of adopting a lifestyle modified with direct action.

A generation was inventing itself daily and creating an environment that it had the courage to occupy and defend against critics who rarely understood what was going on anyway. This attitude began to permeate our culture from the boutiques of Carnaby Street to the marble halls of the Tate. The increasing number of people adopting the arts as a profession sustained the impetus, but the artistic population was expanding more rapidly than the infrastructure could host an appreciative public.

A number of 'grassroots' organisations began to flourish in the mid '60s, mainly in response to this climate of growth but also to demonstrate the need for new attitudes and their implementation. A very practical, social tendency left over from this period was the 'do-it-yourself' culture.

← The match shed at St Katharine Dock, c. 1968-70

Artists at St Katharine Dock, c. 1968-70 →

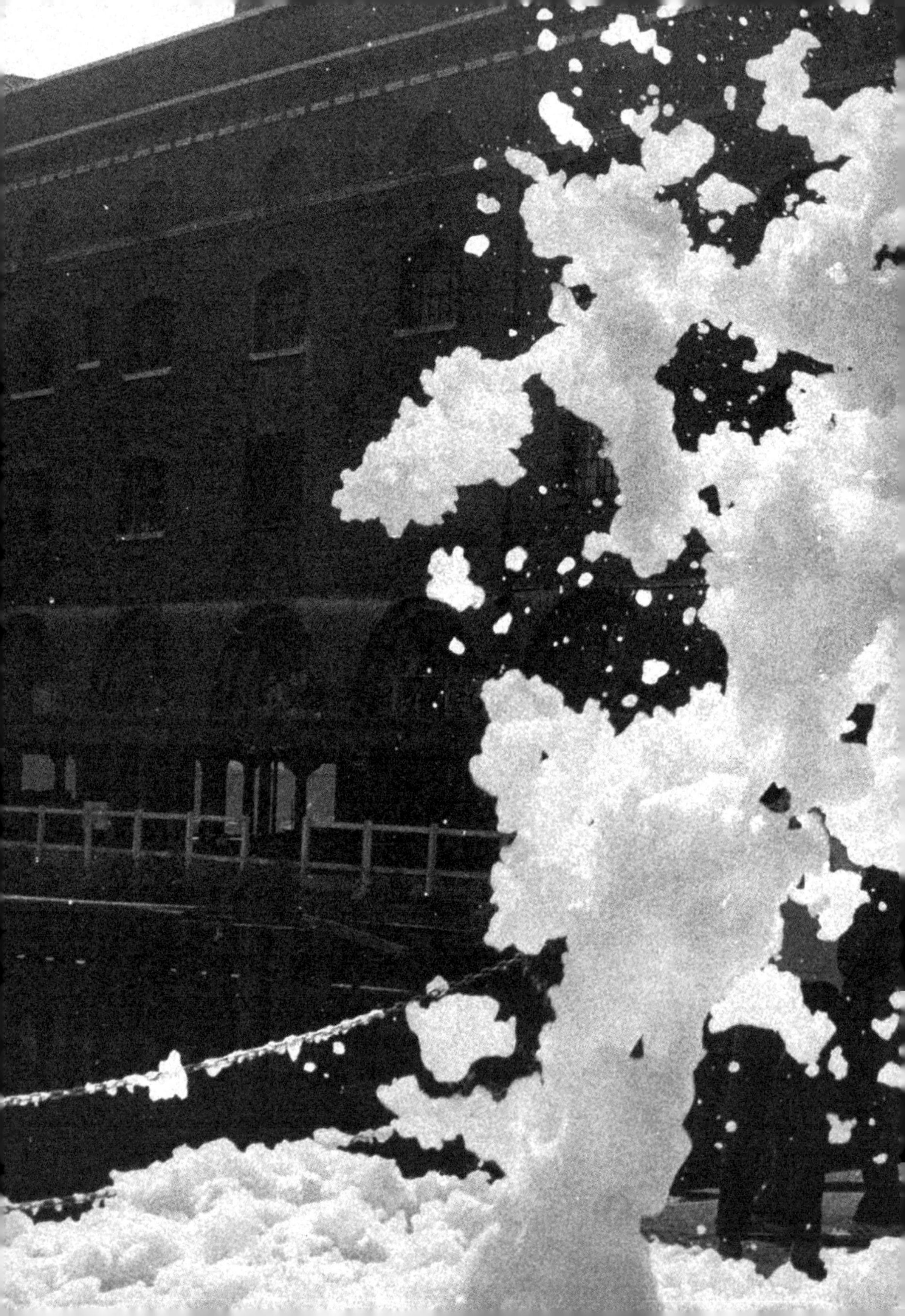

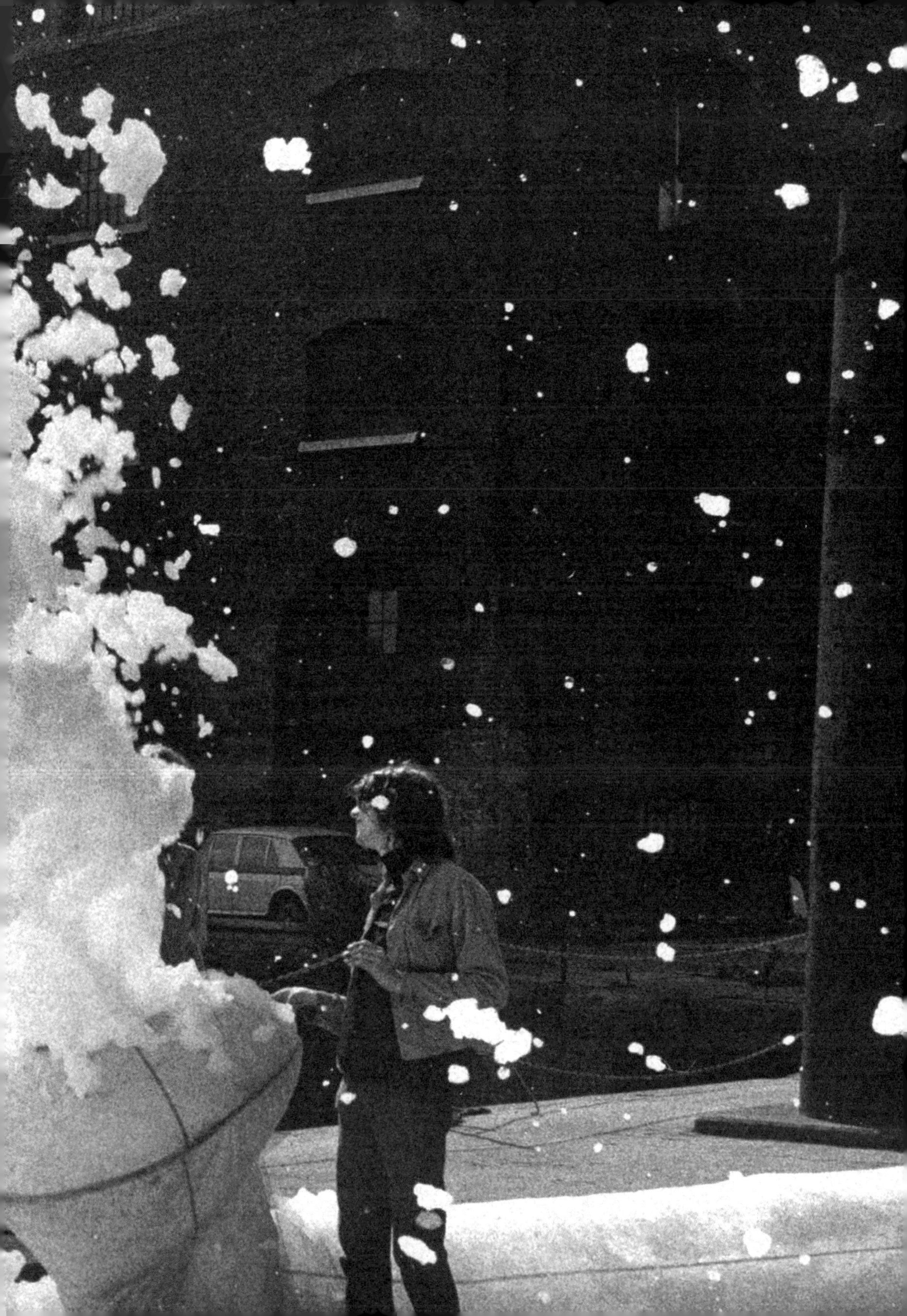

Pavilions in the Parks (PIP)

In 1960 as now, a big problem in the arts was finding suitable places to exhibit or perform work of an unestablished nature. Those towns that have art centres and theatres tend to book them months in advance, usually for art and performance of an 'established' nature. Premises to present new ideas were in very short supply.

A number of young artists, headed by sculptor Su Braden, tackled the problem. They made surveys of towns, noting open spaces that would be available for between one and six months during the summer – open spaces, such as parks, squares, even building sites awaiting development, literally any space that would accommodate two or three portable buildings that could house exhibitions and various art activities during the summer months.

Artists Placement Group (APG)

Another scheme, initiated by the sculptor John Latham and his wife Barbara Steveni, was targeted at industry and commerce. The basic idea was to compile a directory of artists who were prepared to work in or with a firm in some capacity where the artists' work might benefit or influence some aspects of the firm with some reciprocity. The organisation was called the Artist Placement Group (APG) and it was a relatively successful venture.

A common feature of both PIP and APG was their dependence on access to information related to user and producer.

Art Information Registry (AIR)

The organisation that I initiated in 1967, with the help of some artist colleagues was, in many ways, in harmony with the above schemes. Its practice depended on information about the arts on a broad and comprehensive scale, becoming a notional public relations agency for the arts.

Our premise was that art and artists had so proliferated since the end of World War II that the institutions customarily expected to disseminate the art were incapable of seriously representing much of the work that was being produced at that time.

The outlook was very bleak and so were the expectations of the 350 art graduates coming out of art colleges each year.

In the mid '60s, several important London galleries closed for a variety of reasons. During a conversation about this demise, somebody mentioned a chance remark made by John Kasmin, a young man on the 'art block' who had been gallery assistant to Victor Musgrave (the charismatic director of Gallery One, which was making a reputation for breaking the mould of the established conservative attitudes). John, or 'Kas' as he was called, had started to deal art from his apartment.

It was said that Kas had once remarked that a gallery was no longer necessary; what was required was for a dealer to know what artists were making and who they were and go out to find or inspire people to buy. In fact, he was soon to establish one of the smartest galleries in London, with a stable of the top international names.

What impressed me was the idea that information on art and artists might be a solution to the proliferation of artistic activity, providing that it was professionally administered. Could some kind of agency, documenting and collating information on art and artists, act as a catalyst to the further development and promotion to individuals and the public in general? Lengthy discussions took place about the pros and cons of such an organisation. I turned my bedsit into an office, and, with Jane Morris, artist, archivist and secretary, produced a questionnaire and posted it to some 100 artists to ascertain the support for such an agency.

This produced a 70 percent reply rate, about 80 percent of which were positive, with doubts being expressed about whether the proposed organisation would compete with established galleries. From this sampling, it was clear that any agency must be all-inclusive, i.e. non-selective (Van Gogh would be included), non-partisan or not in competition with other agencies (supplementing commercial artists with services not provided by their galleries). It would be passive after a fashion, yet militant in the manner of promoting its information to a widening interested public, a kind of Doomsday Book for the arts.

The name we decided on was Art Information Registry (AIR). The original signatories were Dick Ross, writer; John Spencer, businessman; John Hart, assistant; and myself. Jane Morris was secretary and coordinator. The nucleus of the agency was to be the Artist Index – the personal files, documents and images that

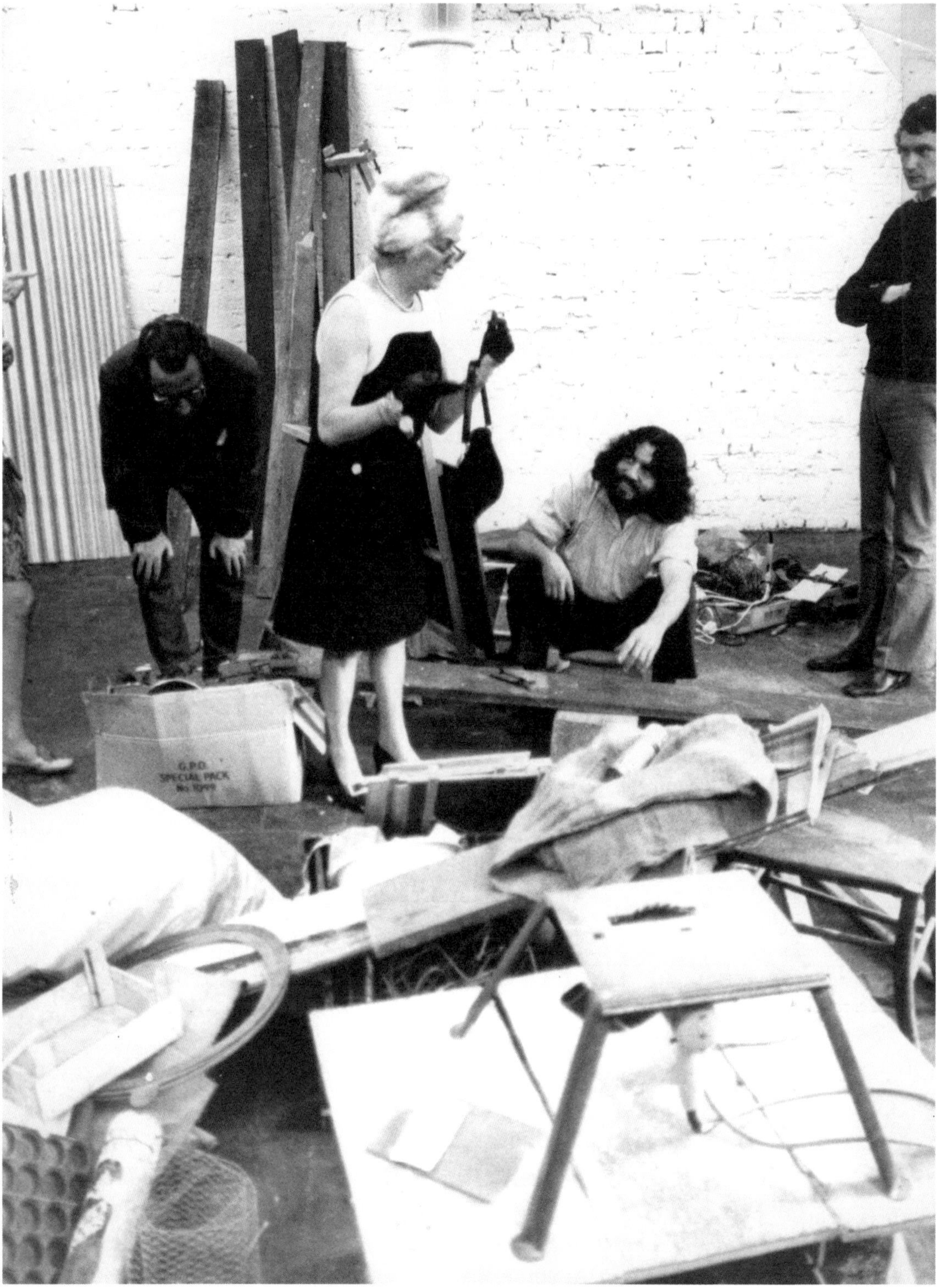

Visitor to St Katharine Docks studios, c. 1968-70

were the 'soul' of the programme. Without any formal registration, Jane Morris and I wrote to artists, to solicit their opinions and enlist their support by joining the registry. We set about accumulating information and collating it into specific folders. All data at this time was stored in metal filing cabinets; it was too early to take advantage of the cyber revolution.

The index housed accurate information on artists' work, with a carefully designed cross-referencing system for speedy retrieval of information. We understood that the success of the agency would depend on the willingness of artists to maintain updated information in the index, combined with the acumen of the administration in servicing the system and publicising the index to the widest possible public. It was presented in a professional manner, in a consulting studio for clients, e.g. collectors, critics, lecturers or students, in advance of an introduction to the artist or gallery to make independent arrangements.

Alongside the collating and registry work, Jane Morris organised four large exhibitions, one for the Nantenshi Gallery in Tokyo and the first Exhibition of Kinetic Art in Britain for the Harris Brush Festival in Birmingham, including, among the more established artists, Liliane Lijn, Stuart Brisley, Stephen Willats, Bill Culbert and myself. AIR organised countless other exhibitions, selected by independent curators from the AIR index between 1967 and 1975. Some examples include Bromsgrove Birmingham Festival (Kinetic Art); Greenwich Theatre Gallery (Kinetic Art); Onnasch Galerie, Berlin; Stadt Gelsenkirchen (British Movements); Midland Group Gallery (Mutation Phenomena Exhibition 2); Camden Arts Centre, London (Survey '69) and Hamburg Kunsthaus (Public Eye Exhibition). Exhibitions of selected SPACE artists were also organised under the auspices of AIR, with assistance given to the Greater London Arts Association in creating the Art Spectrum Exhibition in 1971.

AIR began making contact with other like-minded artist programmes. AIR published two periodicals, *AirMail* and *Catalyst*, containing information relevant to, and constituting a meeting point for, artists.

AIR coordinated action to thwart museum charges when a proposal to demand museum entrance fees to the public caused nationwide outcry. A postal strike prevented protest signatures being collected so AIR sprang into action and used the mailing list of the index to hand deliver pamphlets to several thousand individuals opposed to the museum charges. It was successful.

AIR also coordinated a conference convened by Friends of the Arts Council Operative (FACOP), an ad hoc lobby of artist groups, to discuss art patronage of the day. Other activities spawned at AIR included Grad 70, an archive of art graduates' work, collated through each art college, which was used for reference while encouraging students of the value of documenting their work for future presentation.

In 1968, the vacant Serpentine tearoom in Kensington Gardens was offered to the Royal College of Art, St Martin's School of Art and AIR to propose a function for its use. The first two declined. AIR's proposal was that, since the premises were in such a unique and prestigious position, it should have as its basis a current information service on the arts in general, coupled with a changing exhibition of young artists who had not had the opportunity to show in London. When the Arts Council of Great Britain (ACGB) saw our brief, they decided they would do something like that themselves but without the information service. This gave rise to the Serpentine Gallery.

In 1975, AIR and SPACE, which had been operating from a small basement beneath the Royal Academy, were obliged to vacate. When looking for a suitable replacement, large premises in Shaftesbury Avenue became vacant. This meant that not only could the offices be accommodated but also an exhibition space on the ground floor. Added to this was a second floor which would be suitable for three or four artists' studios. I became excited by this possibility and immediately tried to contact my fellow council members for advice. The only person who was available, since the others were away travelling, was Peter Townsend. We contacted Peter Bird of the ACGB and asked for his opinion as to whether they would be willing to consider supporting our move and taking on this extra burden. The answer was an unequivocal no. After long discussion, Peter and I bit the bullet and took on the lease. It was a difficult decision, but it proved to be a successful one. Robert McAlpine gave a grant to refurbish the premises, providing a substantial upgrade to our public services and giving the artist index adequate room to expand. The AIR Gallery was a welcome contribution to the art community. There was also accommodation for Henry Lydiate's Art Law Consultancy.

SPACE

During the 1950s, it was customary for artists to use a spare room or living room as a studio. Henry Moore showed concern that this had a detrimental effect on family life, especially as a new generation, generally from modest, working-class families, was adopting the arts as a profession. With the incentive of looking for studios beyond the domestic environment and following the exhibition of American abstract expressionist loft paintings at the Tate gallery, artists in London sought large loft spaces. Strict British tenure laws tended to restrict the possibility of artists using similar commercial premises, while high rents were also prohibitive, but the stimulus remained. Perhaps the most decisive motivation for seeking a different type of studio space was the changing physiognomy and scale of artworks. The boundaries between the customary disciplines of art began to dissolve, and the demand for space to produce and exhibit required reconsideration. Often, space was sought on a temporary basis, for experimental theatre, events and multi-media installations.

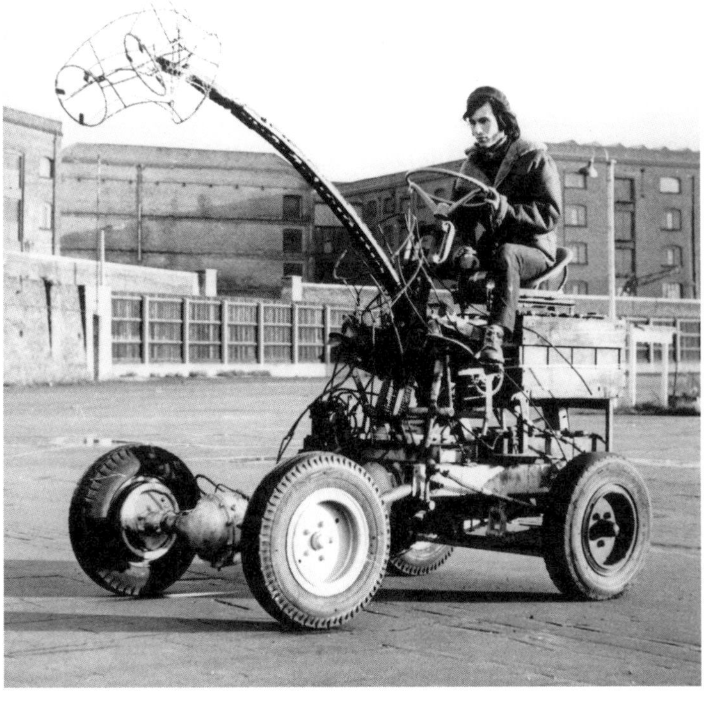

SPACE artist Robin Klassnik (Director, Matt's Gallery) at St Katharine Docks, c. 1968-70

Having developed my ideas from an architectural background and adopted a similar approach in the visual arts, namely constructivism, I became interested in developing my ideas in an environmental context, which involved some element of experimentation in both interior and exterior environments. I had a personal interest in the germination of an idea to use studio premises in community. I had lost my studio in London due to soaring rents, and AIR was in need of room to expand beyond my bedsit. AIR in fact pre-dates SPACE and was the administrative body behind it. It would become the ad hoc body for the formal foundation of SPACE as a corporate organisation in 1968.

In November 1967, I took part in a radio discussion, entitled 'The Dying Galleries', with Edwin Mullins (chair), art writer and critic; Andrew Forge, painter and professor of art; Leslie Waddington, West End gallerist and art collector; Michael Kaye, business entrepreneur and art sponsor; and myself, artist pioneer for the new artist organisation. The subject was the demise of a number of reputable art galleries in the West End. I put forward ideas about the future of the registry, and, as a result of this broadcast, we were offered premises to house the fledgling AIR, at a peppercorn rent, on the site of Marshalsea Debtors Prison by London Bridge. This enormous warehouse was too big for AIR alone, so the first use of the artist index came into play, to offer work space, at cost, to artists interested in occupying space in a large complex. We approached a cross section of artists then on the scene – including Joe Tilson, Tess Jaray, Marc Vaux, John Hoyland, Bert Irvin and Basil Beattie – and asked if they were interested in space at a nominal rent. The warehouse was in an appalling state of dereliction but about 20 artists set about clearing the place. Some weeks later, having made a start in negotiating a contract, the landlord withdrew his offer. After all the work we had done, it was a bitter disappointment to all involved. The enthusiasm had been so great for the idea that we had already decided to document the proceedings with a film. Douglas Smith, who had graduated from Portsmouth, was employed to capture any relevant events for the record in film and photo.

My own personal reasons for requiring a spacious working area were two-fold. As a development of my work using coloured light as a medium, I got the idea for making a total coloured environment whereby the observer was enclosed within a slowly changing environment of coloured light programmed to perform as a `Light Concert´. As a result of building a very large fibreglass cupola in the shape of an igloo, I was then to find a place to work on it, much bigger than a small studio in Chelsea. Subsequently, Harald Szeemann requested it for the forthcoming Documenta exhibition in Kassel.

Following the Marshalsea debacle, I was keen to find premises that might fulfil the potential that the previous building had offered. In London, this was a desperate endeavour. A close friend of mine, Bobby Brereton, had a sailing friend, Mr. Moanes Johnson, who was fitting his yacht out at St Katharine Docks in Wapping, so Bobby and I went along to see him there and have a beer. Arriving at the dock, I was astonished to see this large yacht dwarfed by a compound of empty buildings. Moanes told us he was the last tenant in the docks as the whole complex was to be sold.

When I later saw Bridget Riley, with whom I was then living, and told her of our exciting discovery, we made a visit to the dock to discuss the possibility of renting part of it. I was astonished at the enormous amount of space, totally abandoned, in what was the first dry dock to be built in London, adjacent to the Tower.

I had a wild notion that the docks could possibly meet our needs; there was space for the artists who had been let down at Marshalsea and space to house AIR. Enquiries were made, and it transpired that the Port of London Authority (PLA) was handing the premises over to the then Greater London Council (GLC). Bridget and I arranged to meet Lord Simon, Chairman of the PLA, who had once been the chairman of the ACGB. He lent a sympathetic ear, suggesting that we contact Desmond Plummer, Chairman of the GLC. Plummer was encouraging and advised that, if we formed ourselves into a corporate organisation, he would consider giving us a two-year lease until the area was required for reconstruction.

SPACE was formalised in November 1968 as a non-profit distributing company with a limited liability of one pound. The founding members and first Council of Management were Bridget Riley (artist), Peter Townsend (director of *Studio International*), Anthony West (professor of law), Irene Worth (actress) and Peter Sedgley (artist), elected as general secretary. I shared the payment of the pound with Bridget. Space Provision (Artistic Cultural and Educational), a name I devised, on account of its acronym, because the Company Registration Authority would not permit the use of Space as an organisation name), was an offspring of AIR. The GLC allowed us the use of the 'I' warehouse and the match shed, a spacious ancillary enclosure, for a peppercorn lease of £500 per year until 1970.

Occupying more than 100,000 ft^2, these massive premises posed an enormous challenge to those happy few who had undertaken to occupy them. 'I' warehouse, or 'I' site, had been a bonded warehouse with wines in the cellar, ivories on the top floor and rare spices and perfumes in between (the bouquet lingered still). Dead pigeons and guano were the prevailing contents of the open spaces that were to be our working space for the coming two years, so once again we cleared the place for action. The warehouse was on a peninsula surrounded by water – water that was soon used by some artists for their 'events'. Some finances for installations were gratefully received from Henry Moore and a grant from the ACGB, the first for such an initiative. Subsequently other donors were forthcoming.

When Bridget and I visited Docklands in 1968, we had no idea that it was to be the seeding of an activity that would grow, spread and influence other independent groups of artists helping to solve some of their professional problems. The varied nature of the work that artists produce now means there is no quick fix, but we were fortunate to have such wide-open space which it was possible to tailor to the requirements and means of individual artists. During this period, we were always grateful recipients of leftovers that could be used for practical purposes; a mass of dividing panels was donated from a dismantled exhibition at the Hayward Gallery.

I remember a visit by Jennie Lee, the first cabinet minister for the arts we had in Britain. Whilst we were trawling with her through the open spaces, which were being frantically arranged into studios, dear Jennie enquired whether the artists required any seats. She knew of some theatre seats available, baksheesh. I joked that, at the moment, no one had time to sit down. We did, however, have plans that SPACE might support the performing arts as part of its charter, but, in the circumstances of the dock area, this was not possible. When seeing the potential of SPACE, so many ideas came to mind.

The artists who took on studios became licensees without security of tenure, which was the only way the landlord would give us short-term occupation. Selection was made on a first-come basis, combined with a commitment to artistic intentions, irrespective of style, age or gender. There were a few exceptions, including a printing group, a fibreglass craftsman, who made himself available to artists requiring help in that technique, an electronics engineer and an inventor, who posed an interesting juxtaposition between the artist and inventor. Space was also allocated to rehearsal, performance art and the construction of theatre sets. Three London art colleges took space for selected students, and Pink Floyd and Soft Machine practised there at times. Peter Dockley created a sculpture/ballet entitled *Spaced*, to be performed at the Roundhouse in Camden. In addition, the British Council leased space for invited international artists.

We had discussed the possibility of a workshop for sculptors, and Ted Power, a benevolent art collector, offered to sponsor one, providing we could find a suitable manager. Our stay was too short to take up this offer, and there were other priorities, such as lighting, heating, water and the biggest problem, toilets! We did have a canteen, though, run by an Australian artist, Peter Upward, and the maverick Wapping pub, The China Ship, which appeared to stay open day and night, was a popular after-work venue.

It is helpful to envisage the atmosphere and social climate of the surrounding area. The Docklands begin East of the Tower of London – Wapping, Shadwell, Commercial Road and so on. When the shipping industry was thriving, the area attracted a significant criminal element, resulting in the formation of various rival gangs.

The most notorious of these gangs was led by the Kray brothers, whose brutal dominion over their 'manor' compelled the police and civic authorities to hunt them down and extricate them from the community for long terms. While the incarceration of the Kray brothers did not completely eliminate crime, it left their subordinates leaderless and less able to cause trouble. This happened at a time when the functioning of the docks was slowly degenerating and becoming deserted as the unloading of goods from container ships moved further downstream. This depletion of trade, combined with the bomb damage sustained by buildings, left the area desolate and macabre. The only signs of life were from some council dwellings and two public houses in the midst of this concrete and water desert.

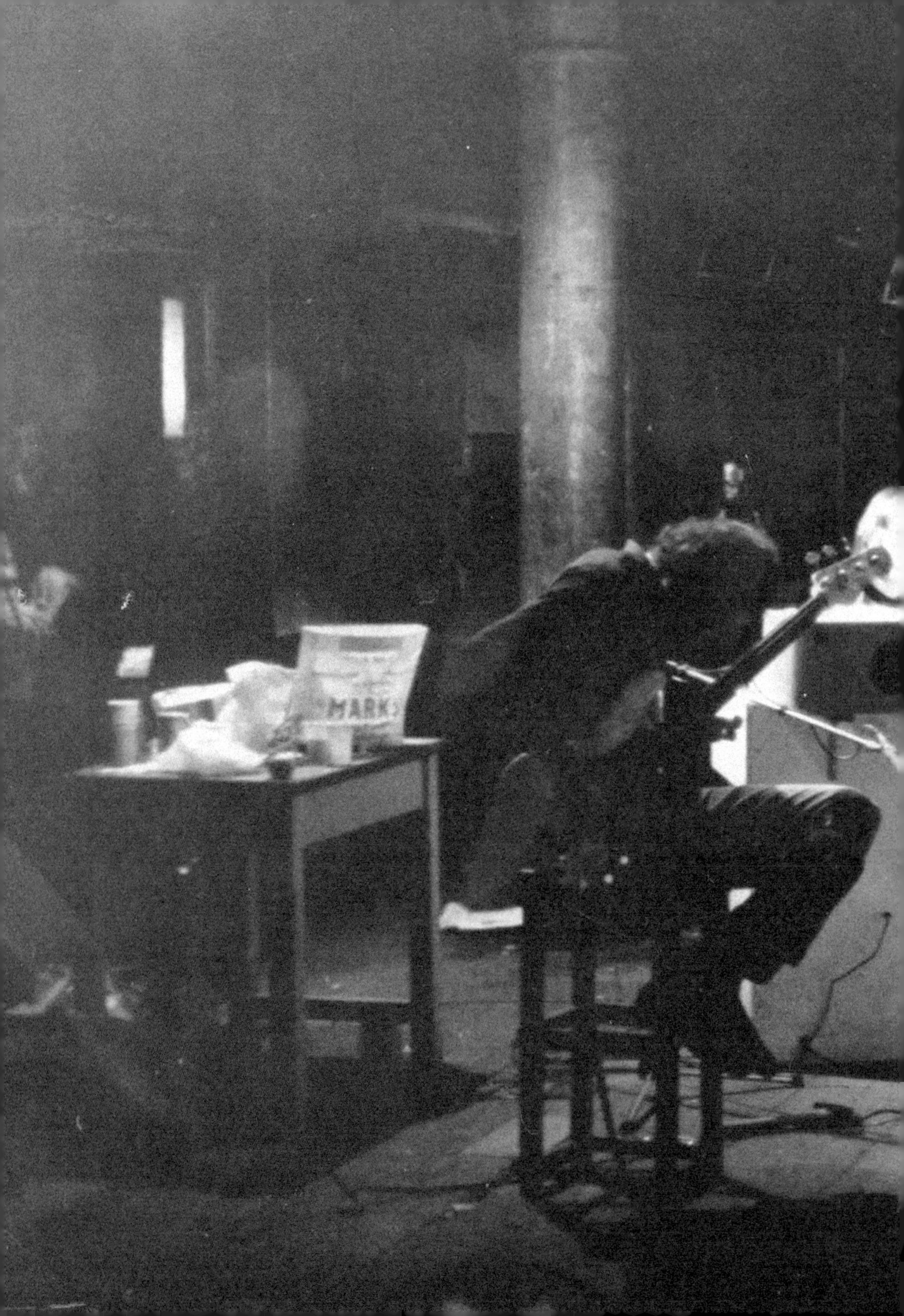
MARK

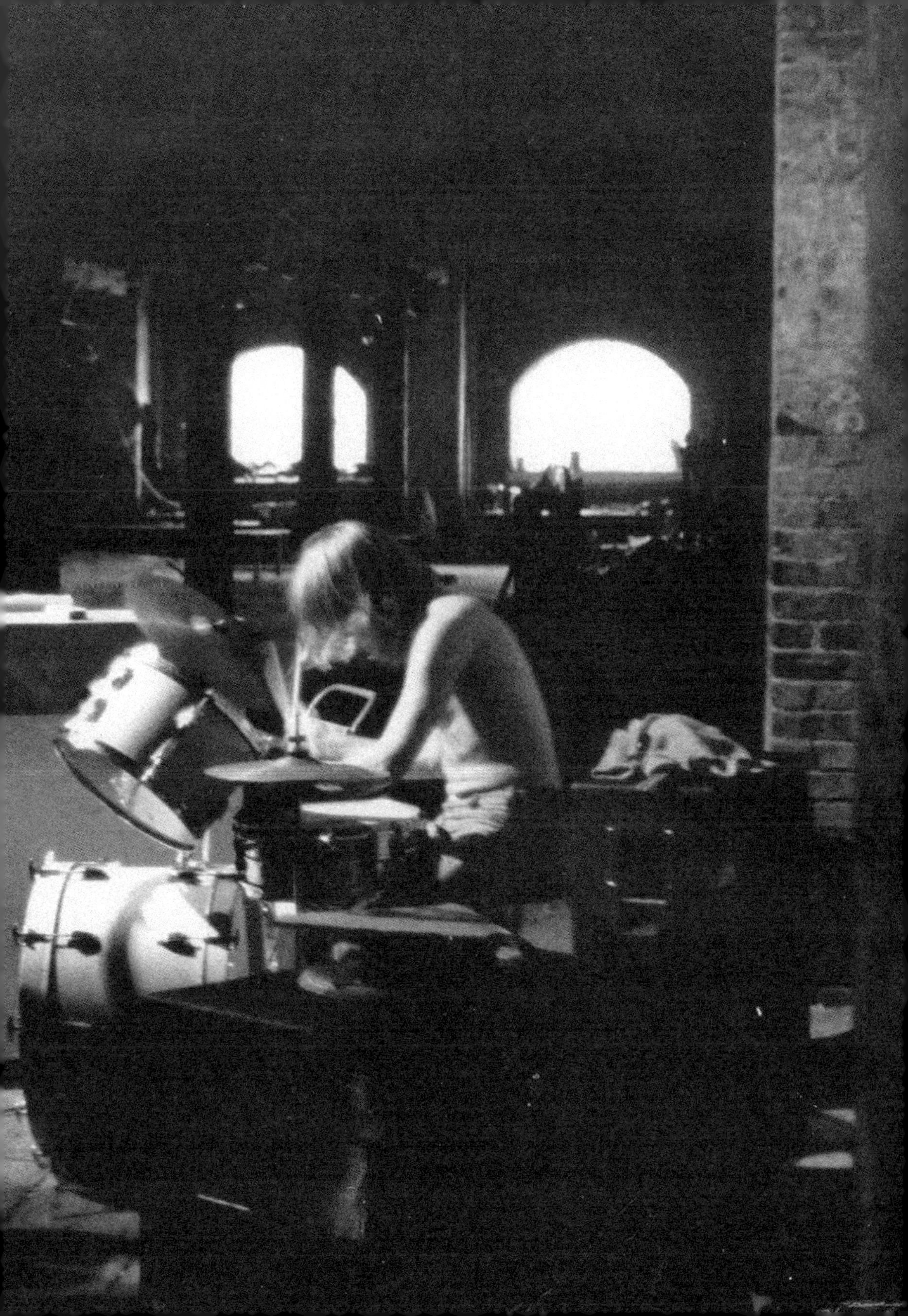

We had a few basic rules of tenure, which were made up as we gained experience: no pot, no living on the premises and no leaving the studio unused for extended periods. Demand for studios was enormous (with no publicity, there was a waiting list of over 200 artists), even though the rough and ready space could be uncomfortable and cold in winter.

Most of the SPACE studios have engendered a need to improvise, showing artists to be hardy and inventive people. A big problem for artists, then as now, was that the amount of time spent earning a living left little time to work in the studio.

When SPACE was finally established at St Katharine Docks, although it had been occupying a great deal of my time in its administration, I found it was perfect to facilitate my exploration into kinetic art. For my studio, I adapted an adjacent room to the match shed where the offices of SPACE were nearby in a small lodge at the entrance gate to the dock. The match shed, an enormous covered area isolated from the main complex, was ideal for artists needing open working space for assembly. It also provided the venue for a large celebration of SPACE's first year, which served to thank those who had helped by sponsoring the project and demonstrated the will to continue providing working space for artists. Coopted art students served refreshments. Dignitaries, including Lord Goodman and Desmond Plummer, came to speak and mix with the artists. Plummer arrived by helicopter just in time to hear the opening sounds of the Brandenburg Variations being played. On a stage decorated with mirrored foil, the VIPs held forth on the advantages of the project. It was a slightly incongruous but congenial occasion.

While students in Fine Art departments at Hornsey, Guildford and Brighton were holding 'sit-ins' and their counterparts in Germany, France and Italy were aping Che Guevara, SPACE was busy discovering ways of coaxing the establishment into permitting the use of derelict buildings as artists' studios, in another form of disguised protest. It was no simple matter to persuade property managers that the fine arts had a legitimate claim to be furnished with studio premises at reasonable cost.

Working space can be pivotal for communication between artists, providing an arena for discussing professional matters. During 1969, there was great criticism of the ACGB method of allocating grants to various artistic activities. A conference was

← Soft Machine playing at St Katharine Docks.

planned, with artists from all over the country invited to congregate at St Katharine Docks and discuss many facets of artists' professional problems in relation to the ACGB. The Need for an Artists' Council, organised by FACOP, took place on 8 June 1969 with various seminars throughout the day. This event critiqued current arts council structure and decision-making processes and proposed alternatives.

Toward the end of our two-year lease at St Katharine Docks, having proved that the programme worked satisfactorily, we knew we had to prepare to find subsequent accommodation and collate film material to demonstrate the efficacy of the idea. This required professional editing equipment and documentary expertise. With a small grant from the new film department of ACGB and our good fortune in meeting Peter Montagnon, who had recently completed the film *Civilisation*, a story board was created. The film was completed as we vacated St Katharine Docks and moved into our next two buildings.

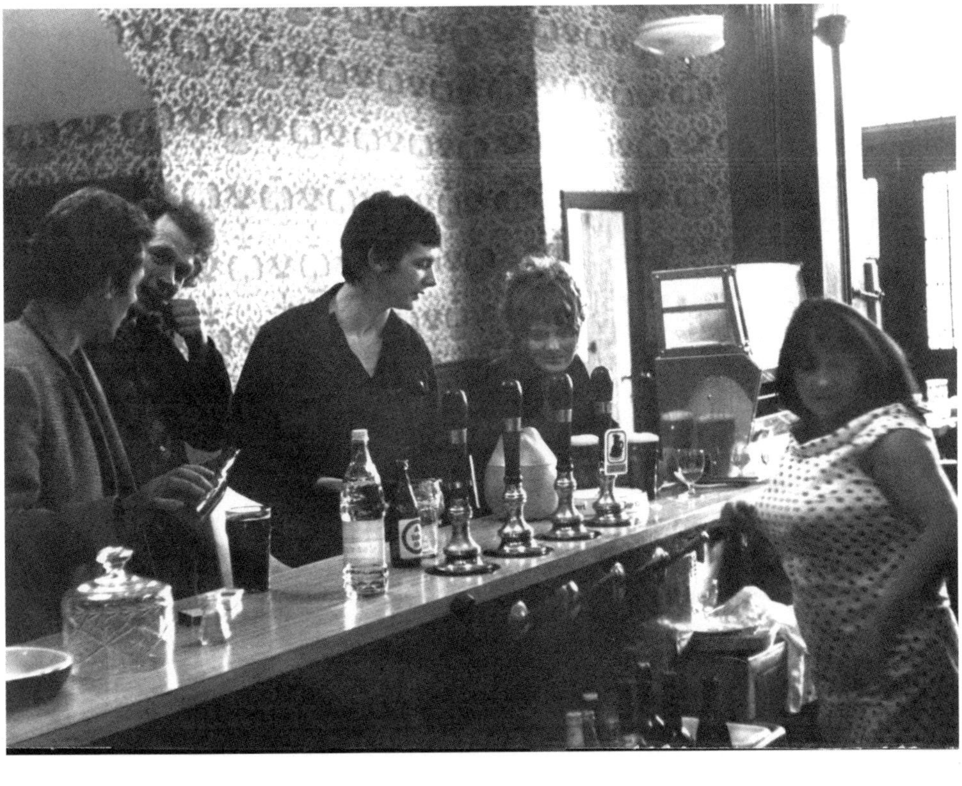

Inside the China Ship in Wapping, a popular after work venue for artists at St Katharine Docks.

Through the good offices of the borough of Stepney, the old Jewish Boys School in Stepney Green gave space for about 15 studios, and in Hackney a previous industrial complex on London Fields at Martello Street had room for another 15 or more studios. The playgrounds at the former premises were ideal for outdoor sculpture. In the expanding possibilities of the '60s, the concept of an arts laboratory made itself felt, and 'experimental art' became the forerunner of a great deal of the work that is being made today, while losing the epithet 'experimental'. The freedom to work unhindered by conventional studio space was one of the direct benefits of the kind of work areas that SPACE provided as cheaply as possible, work which could not easily be painted or constructed on a dining room table or in the corner of a room when the kids have gone to bed. As I write, SPACE is continuing to establish features involving experimentation in art and technology.

SPACE's International Influence

SPACE attracted a great deal of attention in the arts and from international visitors. Visiting was discouraged, as it disturbed the artists at work, but people who were helpful to the project were welcome. On one occasion, Werner Düttmann, an architect from Berlin, made a visit and was extremely impressed with the project, declaring it had given him an idea about a possible function for premises in Berlin. The building he had in mind was Bethanien Hospital in Kreuzberg, part of which would become Künstlerhaus Bethanien.

This project was well financed by the Berlin Senate, which renovated and converted the building into self-contained studios with permanent services, including drawing and painting accessories, plan chests, etc. The hospital chapel was ideal for use as exhibition space and even as a theatre for performance. Dr. Michael Heardter, then presiding as General Secretary of the Akademie der Künste was coopted as Director of Künstlerhaus Bethanien and I cooperated in its formulation. Over the following years, the scheme proliferated under Heardter's direction throughout Germany. Other studio programmes influenced by SPACE included SPACEX at Exeter, PS1 in New York and Acme Housing, each formulated to suit the specific local requirements.

SPACE IN BERLIN

While Heardter visited SPACE, he was in the process of preparing a cultural event called London Now in Berlin, which was to be staged from 26 March to 4 April 1971 and exemplify the notion of Swinging London. The constituents of this festival were pop music at the Deutschland Halle, theatre and visual arts at the Akademie der Künste and painting, sculpture and kinetic art at the Messehallen, a spacious exhibition hall beneath the radio tower in Charlottenburg.

Heardter invited me to organise the exhibition with him. As SPACE was widely covered in the news at the time, we decided to take artists working in the studios at St Katharine Docks as a nucleus, together with the other selected artists at the Messehallen, and to screen the newly produced SPACE film at the Akademie der Künste.

London Now in Berlin was a success in various ways; it cemented some private and communal relations and opened up possibilities for some UK artists. It also demonstrated to UK authorities the ability of SPACE and AIR to be reliable cultural ambassadors.

Conclusion

Soon after the evacuation of St Katharine Docks and while we were still in the process of settling into our new domain in Stepney Green, from where the preparations for the London Now exhibition were organised, Bridget Riley and I were invited to Germany as guests of the Berlin Artist Programme of DAAD. Our stipend was due to start in June 1971, following London Now in Berlin, which required me to arrange for my duties as manager of SPACE to be passed over to company secretary Richard Leachman.

Bridget Riley and I financed AIR from 1967 until 1970, after which the ACGB agreed to support it.

In 1977, the AIR index had to be dismantled owing to the withdrawal of modest funding by ACGB.

AIR survived only in the name of a gallery, an example of how resilient, tolerant and committed to the principle of free expression the AIR gallery was. The gallery continued with considerable help from Nancy Balfour, collector and art lover, exhibiting the work of young or unknown artists, giving them their first chances and encouragement for the future. Many of these artists were later to become established figures in the community, but when neither public nor private finances were forthcoming, the gallery had to close in 1989. When the funding for AIR Gallery was withdrawn, Nancy Balfour wrote 'we need important prestigious galleries like the Tate and the Hayward but we also need an AIR Gallery – several of them'.

SPACE continues to function for several hundred artists. To secure working space for artists under the conditions of fierce materialism promulgated by Thatcher is a formidable task. There is little support for such unglamorous activities as encouraging the work of artists if it has no popular or commercial appeal.

Behind this scene, artists continue to struggle for survival, grateful to the few benevolent sources that still provide for them. The Arts Council, run by civil servants acting as curators, only supports uncontroversial art for fear of retribution by its political paymasters. The story of the twin organisations AIR and SPACE is much larger than this short essay about a two-year experience allows, but, to those who became associated with them, they remain legendary.

Circuit 9, Friends of the Arts Council Operative (FACOP) publicising conference at St Katharine Docks on 8 June 1969 →

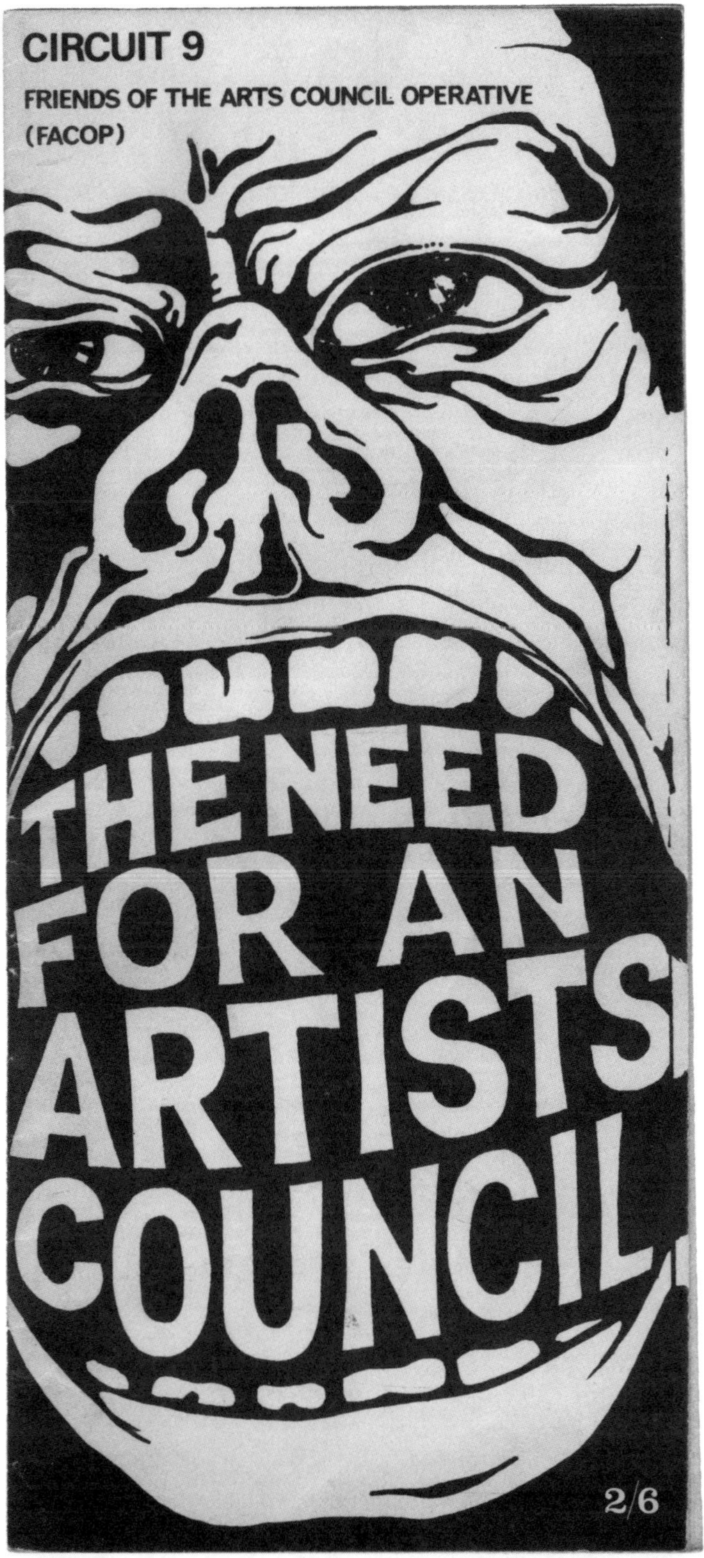
CIRCUIT 9
FRIENDS OF THE ARTS COUNCIL OPERATIVE
(FACOP)
THE NEED FOR AN ARTISTS COUNCIL
2/6

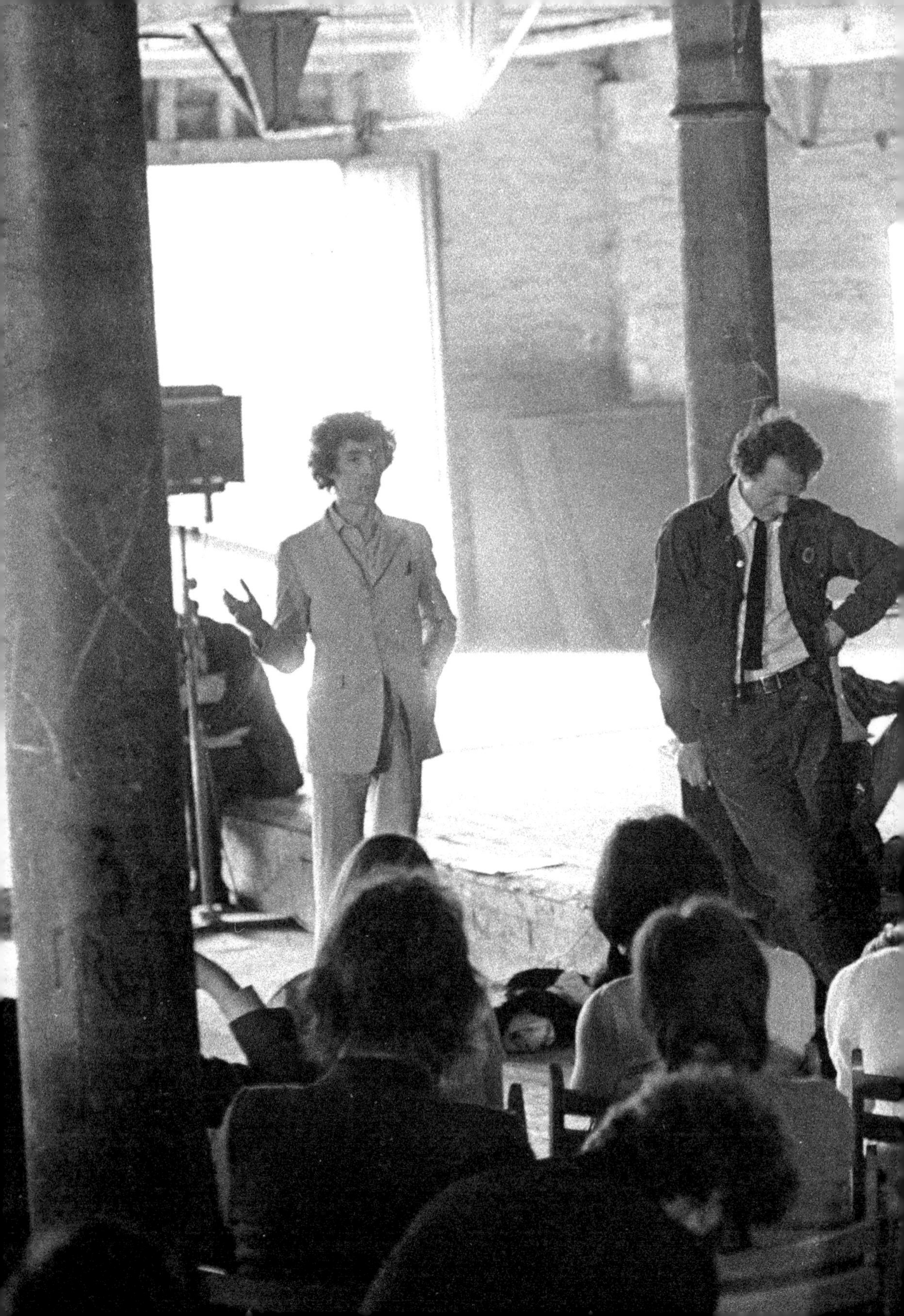

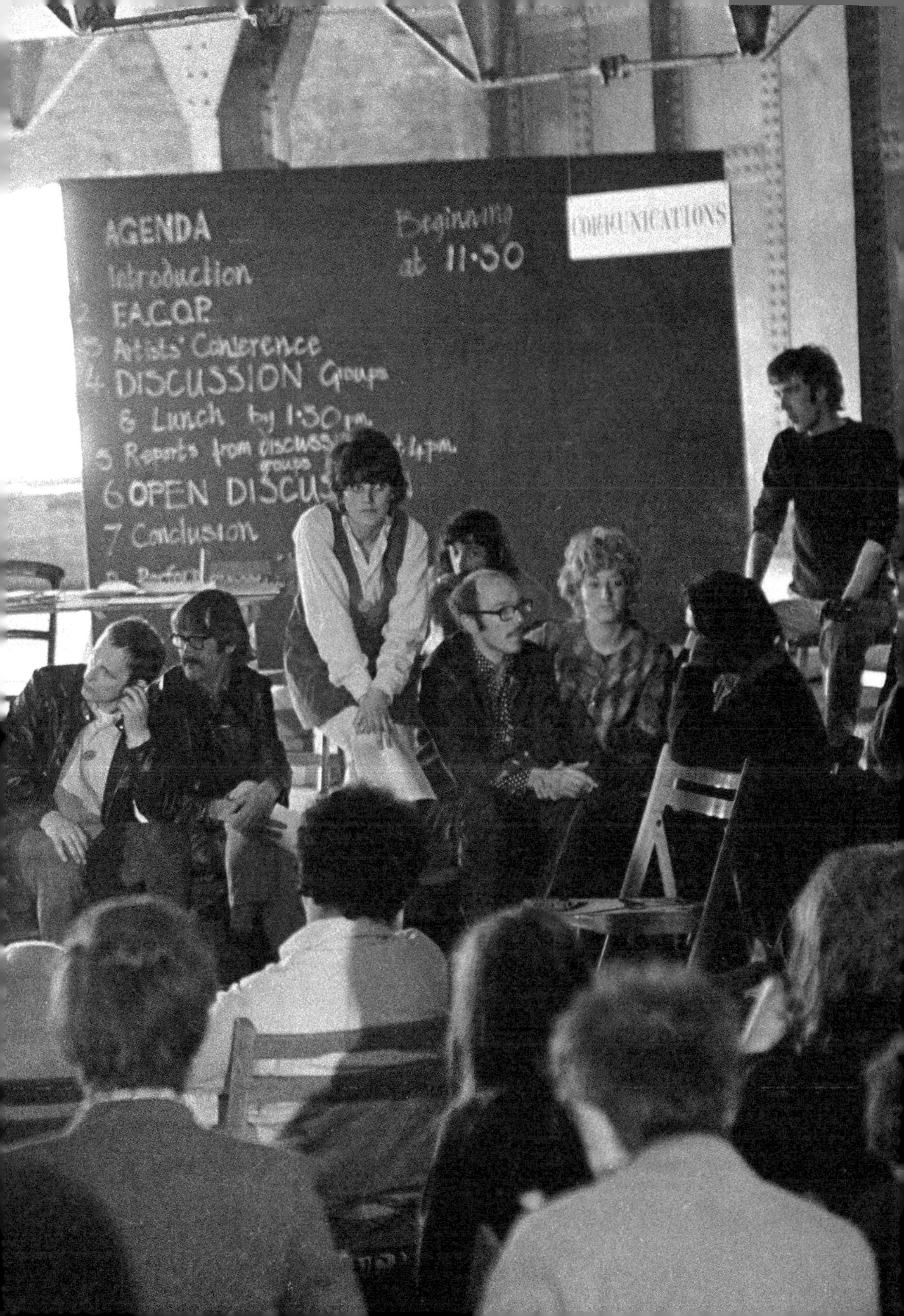
AGENDA
Beginning at 11·30
COMMUNICATIONS
Introduction
2 F.A.C.O.P.
Artists' Conference
4 DISCUSSION Groups
& Lunch by 1·30 pm
5 Reports from
6 OPEN
7 Conclusion

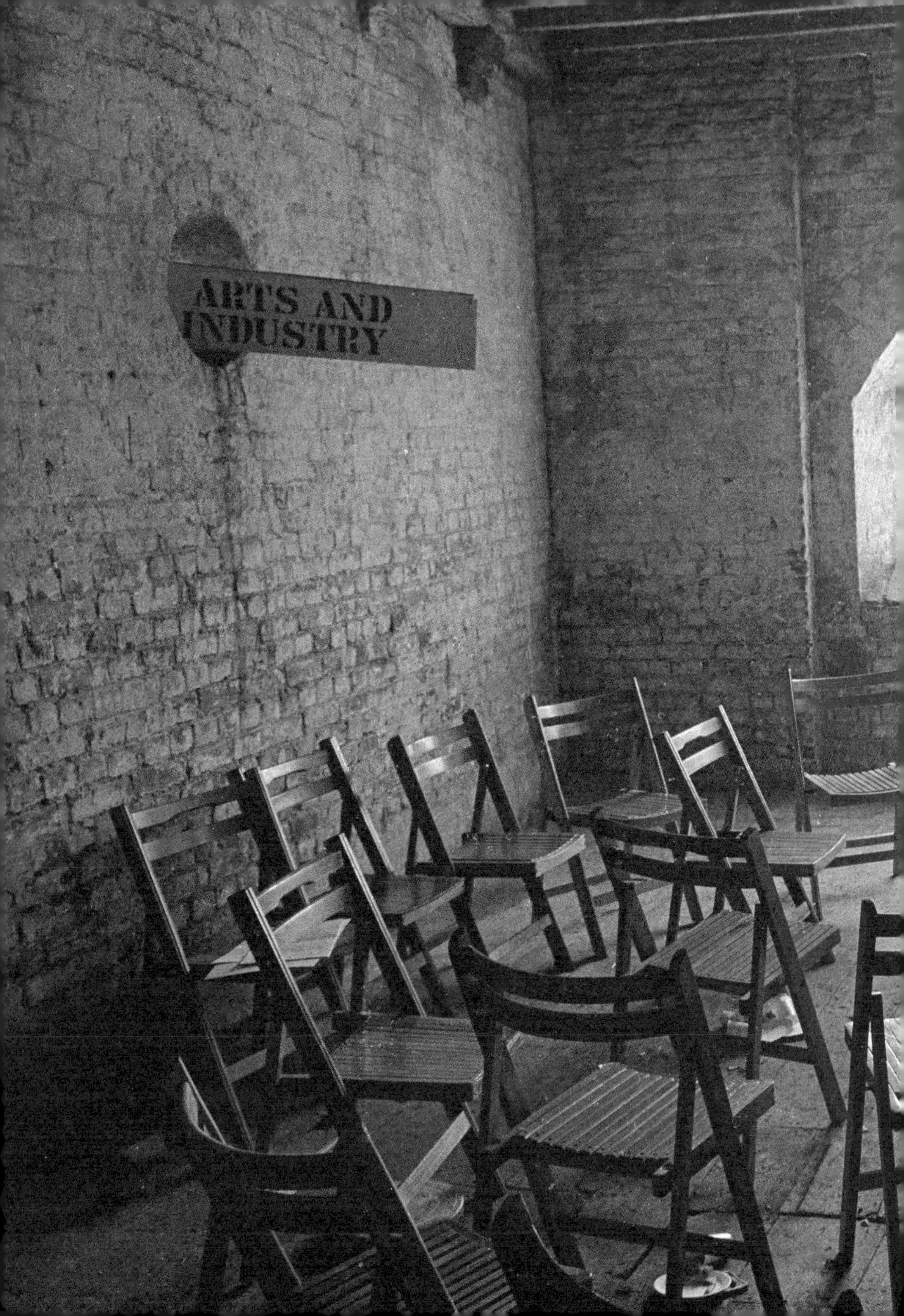
ARTS AND
INDUSTRY

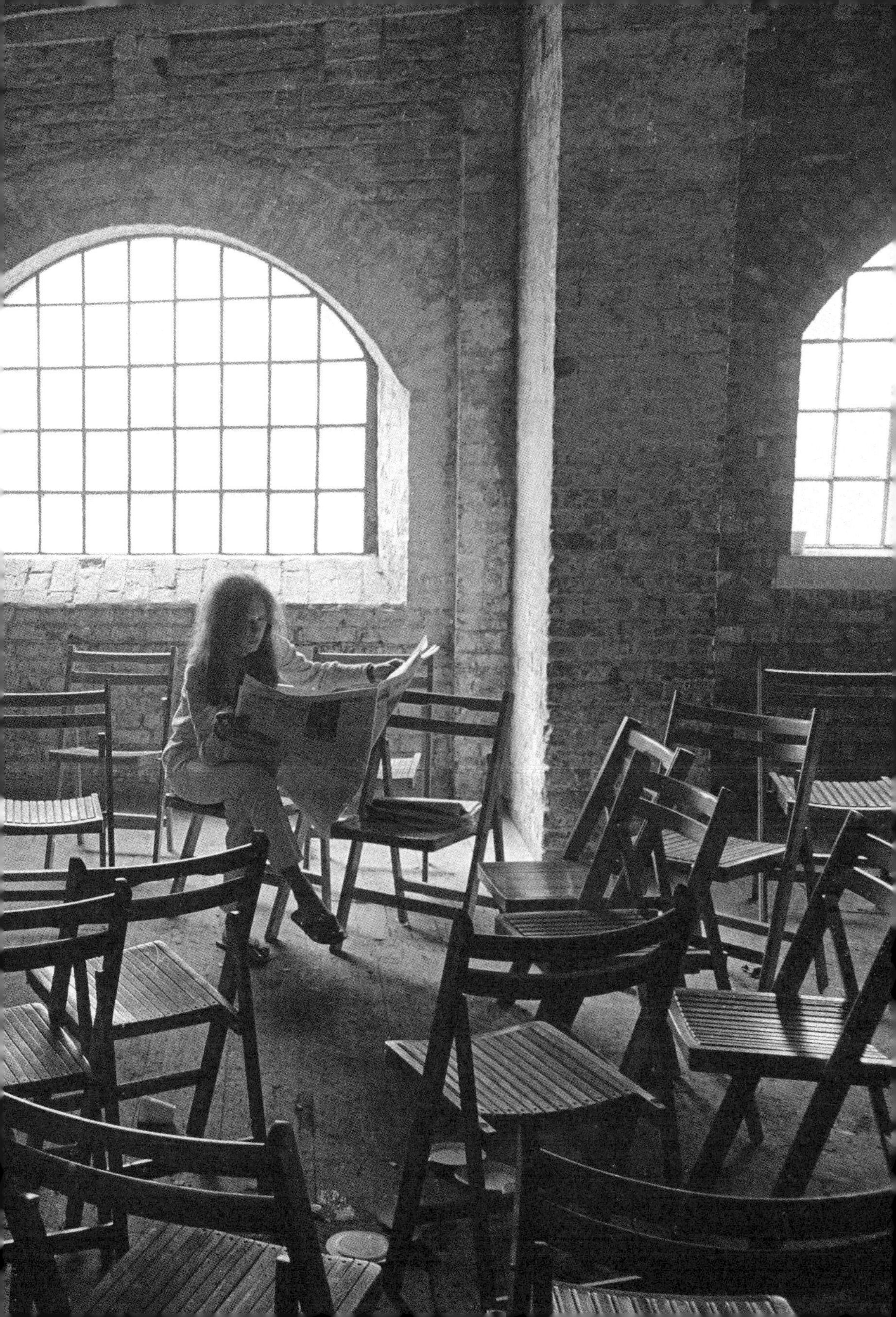

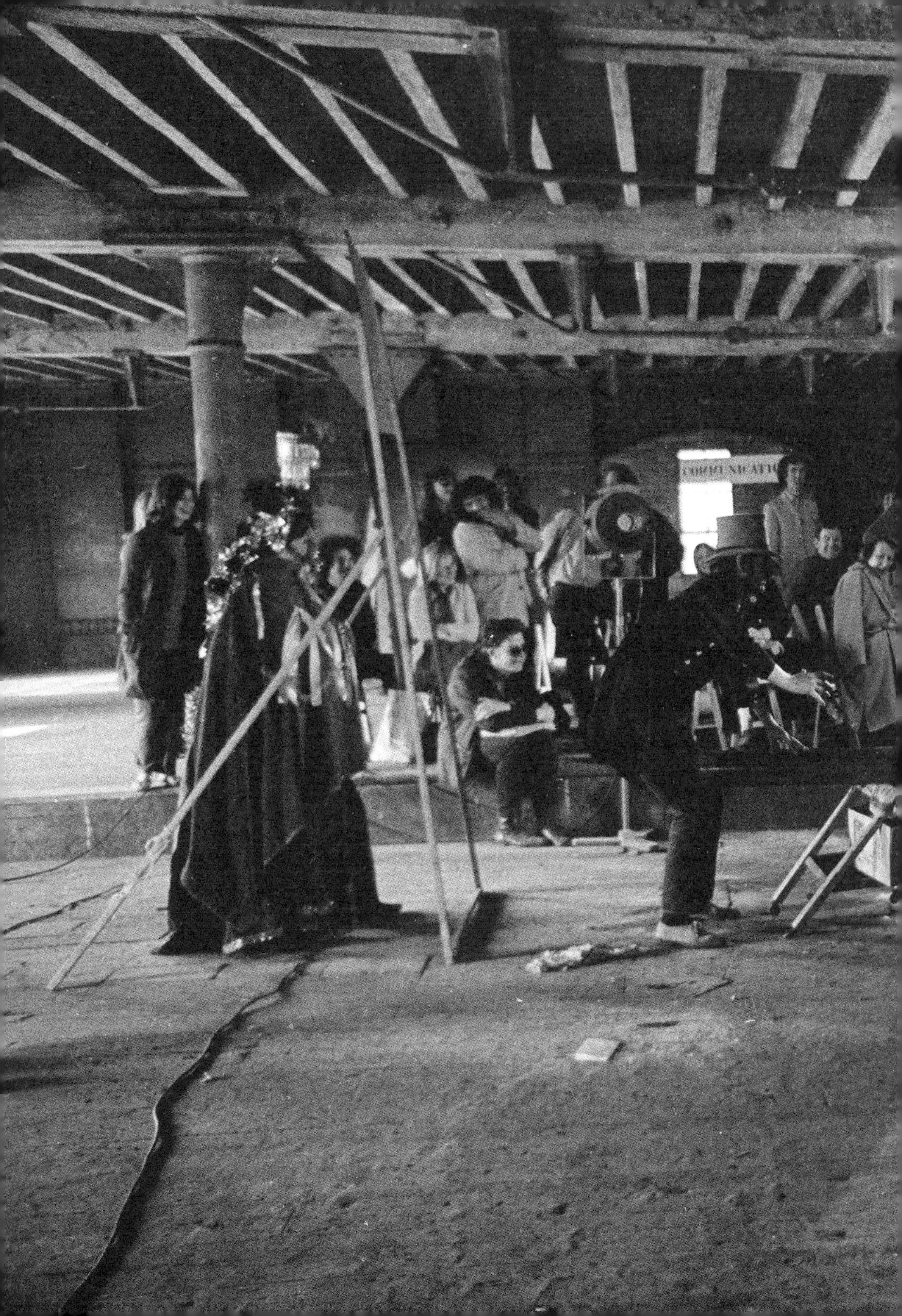

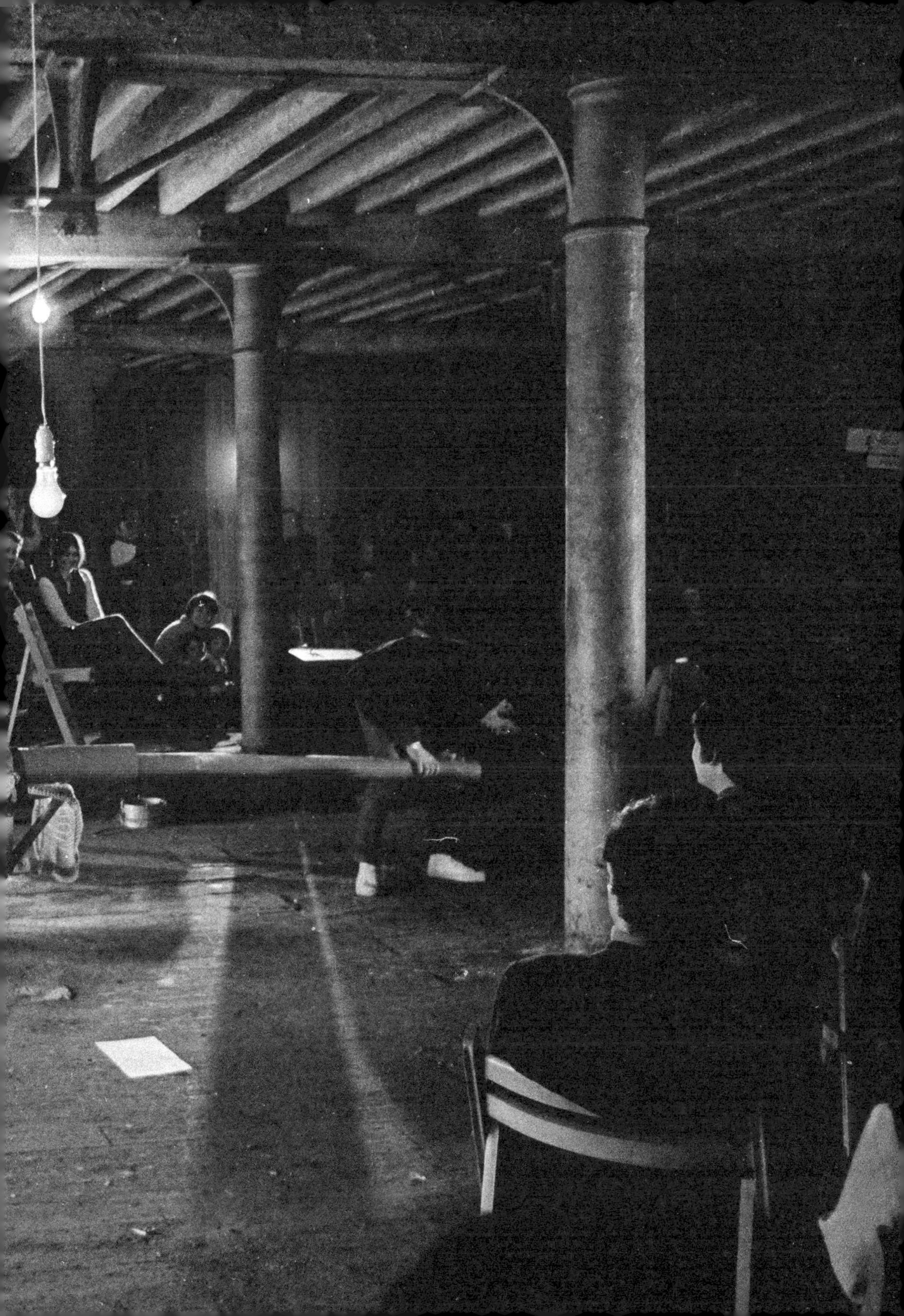

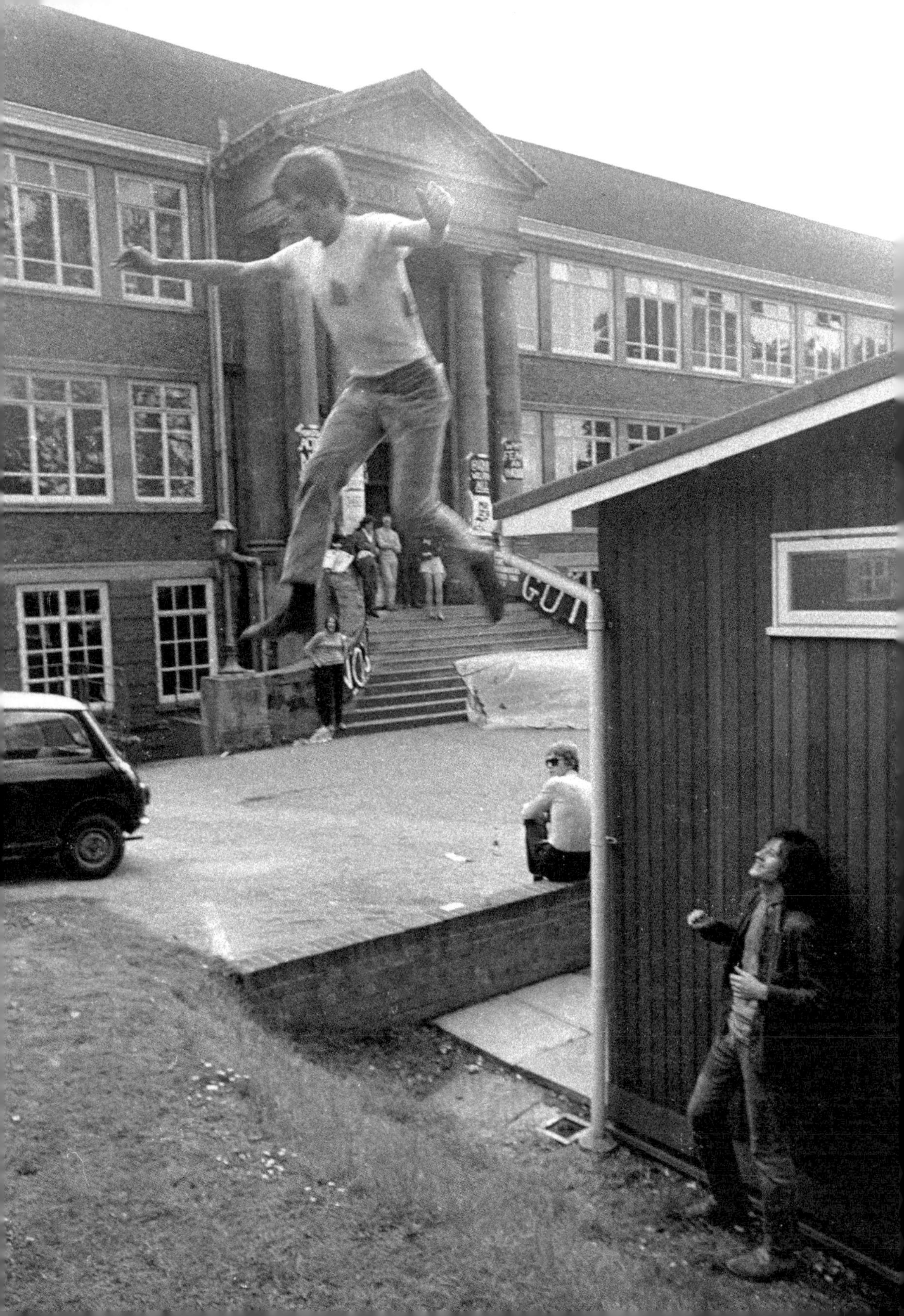

May '68 in London and the emergence of AIR and SPACE

Andrew Wilson

History hasn't ignored the fact that 1968 was the most explosive year in a decade of radical change. The international events of May 1968 marked a decisive cultural and political shift, entailing the breaking down of boundaries of all kinds and the attempt to forge a new grammar and language alongside new ways of living life. It is no coincidence that AIR and SPACE emerged during this moment, and it is instructive to consider here how they sat beside other examples of cultural change – most especially the Arts Labs movement, with which SPACE was allied, and the earlier Antiuniversity.

In Britain, the consequence of social, political and cultural change that the events of May 1968 marked has, broadly speaking, been typified as a conflict between those who followed ideals of personal liberation and those who pursued an organised political activism. Within these two streams, the countercultural underground never followed a single-issue politics, or even a single theoretical line. Instead, it espoused a bewildering but, in its own way, defining, mixture of issues. These included: black power and the campaign for racial equality; the personal explorations described by drug culture; the struggle for sexual liberation, typified by the rise of feminism and the gay liberation movement or the fight against censorship and obscenity laws; other liberation movements, for which Che Guevara had become an icon, which coalesced around protests against struggles in Vietnam, South Africa and Northern Ireland; alternative living, from communes to the squatting movement, from ecology to new age mysticism, vegetarianism, ley lines and the quest for Atlantis.

Preceding spreads FACOP conference at St Katharine Docks on 8 June, 1969.

← Student jumping off canteen roof in front of Guilford School of Art.

The wide-ranging artistic experimentation of the period similarly engaged with all of these issues. However, 1968 marked the moment at which a belief that social and political change might happen naturally was substituted for an understanding that such change had to be organised, willed and made to happen, that the achievement of 'power to the imagination' was indeed possible – and that this counted as much for the mainstream as it did for the counterculture.

Art colleges and universities were a breeding ground for the young post-war generation to test these ideas, as the occupations of the Sorbonne or Hornsey College of Art demonstrate. The aims and aspirations communicated through these and other occupations, as much as the ways in which they were defended, were, by necessity, the result of a particular organised form of collective action. Perhaps, for some, the new mood was also one of violence – exemplified by images of the barricades in Paris and the creation of 'the beach beneath the paving stones'. Mick Jagger's identification with both the March and October 1968 protests in London against the Vietnam War was underlined when he sent the lyrics of *Street Fightin' Man* to Tariq Ali so that they could be reproduced in his radical magazine *Black Dwarf*. Yet the essential nature of the October demonstration did not quite reflect the message of the Rolling Stones' song that had been released a couple of months earlier on 31 August 1968. This was a march accompanied by a weekend occupation of the London School of Economics (where, coincidentally, Jagger had been a student) – both as teach-in and sanctuary. The march provided a coming-together of different sensibilities and political outlooks under one banner (in much the same way that the Campaign for Nuclear Disarmament (CND) provided a position that was embraced by many political persuasions within the counterculture). However, a core tactic – almost the rationale of the demonstration, as revealed in a briefing note produced by the October 27 Ad Hoc Committee – centred not on a singular 'street fighting man' but on seizure of space, leading to 'street power' through collective action. The briefing note starts, 'We stick together – we go the whole route – we take the street – we want no arrests – we link arms – we keep arms linked – and then we link arms again!' It went on to explain that 'the unit of any demonstration can only be the self-disciplined group' and to describe how, with linked arms, 'even when standing still, we set the terms of our presence in the streets'.[1]

The capture of space to define 'the terms of our presence' provides a useful introduction to thinking about the creation, by Peter Sedgley of AIR and subsequently Sedgley and Bridget Riley of SPACE which led to the identification, in May 1968,[2] of two buildings on St Katharine Docks that were subsequently taken, on a two-year lease of £500 per year until December 1970, for artists' studios and services. SPACE brought together a large group of artists of different generations and practices. At the I Site (a deserted 60,000 ft^2 ivory warehouse, which was divided largely into studio space) and the match shed (another deserted warehouse within the 100,000 ft^2 complex that was used by artists, especially for those involved in large-scale projects).[3] In an article published in February 1970, critic Marina Vaizey described the growth of the community of 120 artists (made up of 90 individual licensees, alongside art students from Chelsea, Slade and Byam Shaw, who were experimentally using studio space, and a waiting list of over 200 artists):

> […] in all instances, the criteria for the selection by committee are based on the genuine need of the particular artists for the type of space provided by SPACE and his/her inability to find it elsewhere; and selection is naturally biased towards younger and as yet not particularly established artists working in idioms that require the unique working areas of St Katherine Docks [sic]; the result is a large number of younger artists with a core of older and more established artists who themselves require studios with the particular characteristics of the dock.[4]

An early promotional document for SPACE outlined the breadth of tendency and technique carried out in the studios: 'Printmaking, drawing, painting, photography, film-making, fibre-glass and plastic resin work, metal sculpture, kinetic work, environmental lighting, pneumatic sculpture, water sculpture, concept, process and minimal art are all flourishing within the complex, confirming the original intention of avoiding any aesthetic discrimination in relation to "style"'.[5]

In order to hold a lease for the St Katharine Docks complex, the Greater London Council (GLC) required SPACE to form itself as a company with directors.[6] Despite this necessity, its ideals were, in many ways, analogous to the spirit of other, more ad hoc, arts spaces. As the critic John Russell was careful to stress in an article in the *Sunday Times*, despite its institutional support (and the inference of becoming an institution itself), SPACE was, at its core, organised by and for artists. He wrote that

> What Space Ltd has in mind is… an artists' co-operative, an ideal republic made lawful by a benevolent GLC, and an alternative in embryo to the dealer galleries and the one-line nothings by critics taxed beyond the limits of rational condensation […] Space Ltd has the support of the Arts Council, and it operates on a site rented from the GLC, but fundamentally it is the artists' own idea, and it is being backed with their own money, with their own time, and with energies withdrawn for the purpose from their own work.[7]

The first Arts Lab, in Drury Lane, had been founded to similar principles by Jim Haynes and Jack Henry Moore and survived between 1967 and 1969 (before internal divisions and lack of funding forced its closure). In its demise, it perhaps had its greatest effect by being the model for Arts Labs to spring up across Britain and Europe, with a charitable trust to support their aims.

For Haynes, the Arts Lab was 'a non-institution… a Lab's boundaries should be limitless',[8] and Drury Lane's activities – between gallery, performance space, film space, café and living space – proved this. The breakaway New London Arts Lab, otherwise known as the Institute for Research in Art and Technology (IRAT), continued this permeable range of activities in a much larger building, a factory in Robert Street in Camden, from 1969 to 1971, mixing spaces of production with exhibition, screening and performance. The availability of the building in Robert Street was, like St Katharine Docks, made possible through a short-term lease in advance of impending redevelopment (and, like SPACE, IRAT was set up from the inside by practitioners and – again even if only notionally and of necessity – with directors, trustees, and individual supporters like Lords Harlech and Burgh). SPACE's identification with the Arts Lab movement was made explicit by its involvement with the National Arts Lab Conference in January 1969 – a gathering of groups which reflected the shift that 'art and social living should be more closely linked'.[9]

The terms of operation suggested by SPACE's acronym Space Provision (Artistic Cultural and Educational) reflects its ambitious ideals not just to provide space for artists in a new way, but also to break down boundaries – professionally, socially, culturally, politically, philosophically – between artist and audience as much as between artist and materials. SPACE was not only about studio provision but also about the belief that studios could go beyond being sites of individualistic expression. The ivory warehouse, and the acres of water around it, created an arena that was both metaphorical and actual. These particular opportunities that the environment of the docks afforded artists by being a space for making work as well as a space of meaning and display, provided a fertile ground for a number of artists who took studios there, such as Jeff Shaw and Graham Stevens. This is extremely well illustrated by Shaw and Stevens' 1969 *Inflatable Structures*.

The principles of SPACE were echoed by these sculptures – conceived as large-scale interactive structures – to present a site of physical freedoms – tools 'for decreasing social barriers and increasing social contact [...] not exclusive of race, class, age group, culture or section of society'.[10] These tools centred on collective participation which, for Stevens, included the notions that 'people are part of the structure making it whole; body energy activates the structure; the air structure is a tool, relating the body to the environment, and people to people; mental valency – connecting the structures with people's minds and lives; practicality – the experiences can be easily created and repeated; the structures respond to human scale'.[11] Stevens' list of pneumatic concepts well describes not only changes in perceptions of the relationship between art and life but also thinking at the heart of SPACE.

Overleaf Men inside Graham Stevens' inflatable. ⟶

pp. 58-59 Artist photographing Graham Stevens' inflatable at St Katharine Docks.

pp. 60-61 During the shoot of *Atmosfields* with Graham Stevens' inflatable and Stevens in a boat at St Katharine Docks with view of Tower Bridge.

pp. 62-63 Deserted St Katharine Docks with Graham Stevens' inflatable in the background.

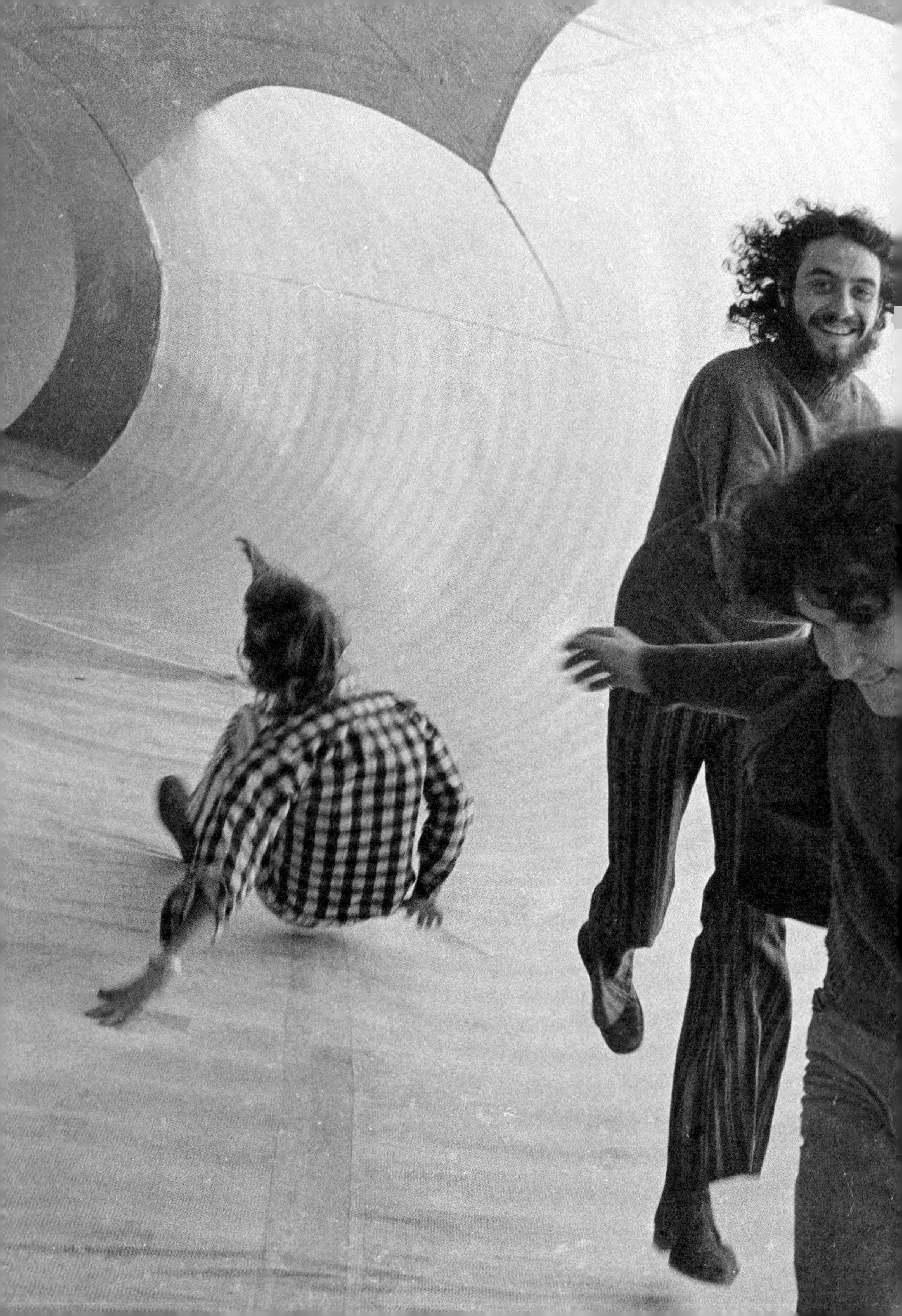

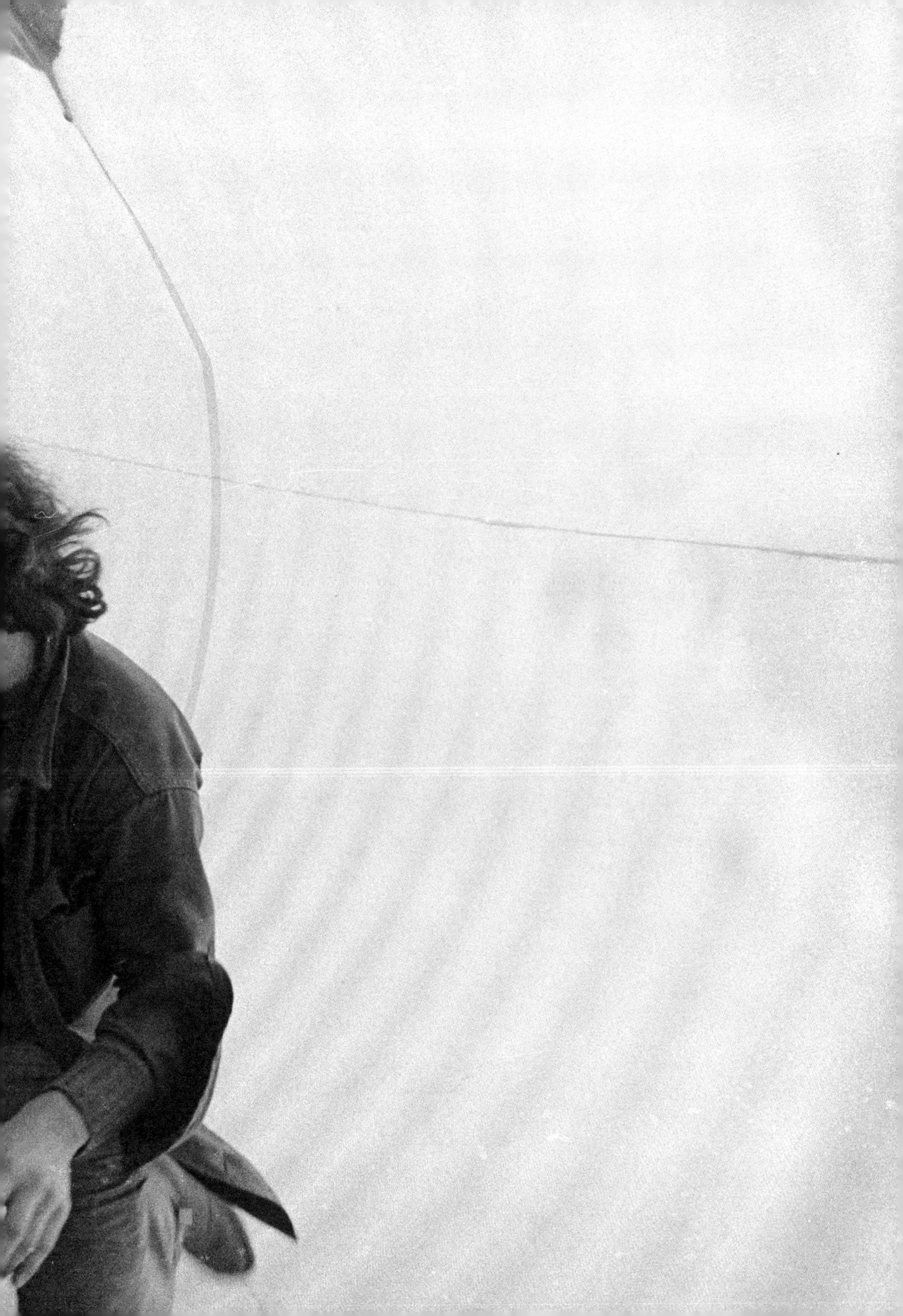

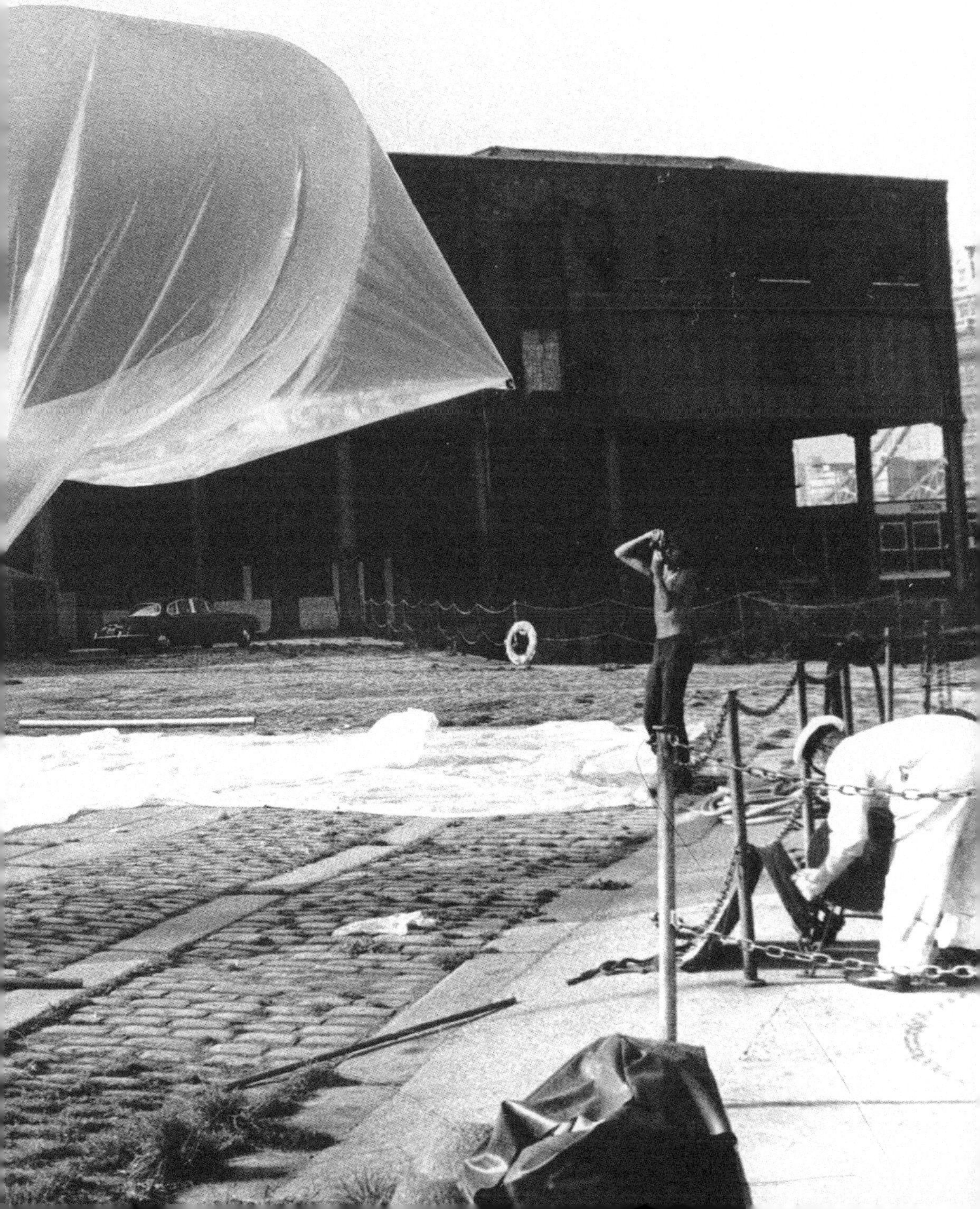

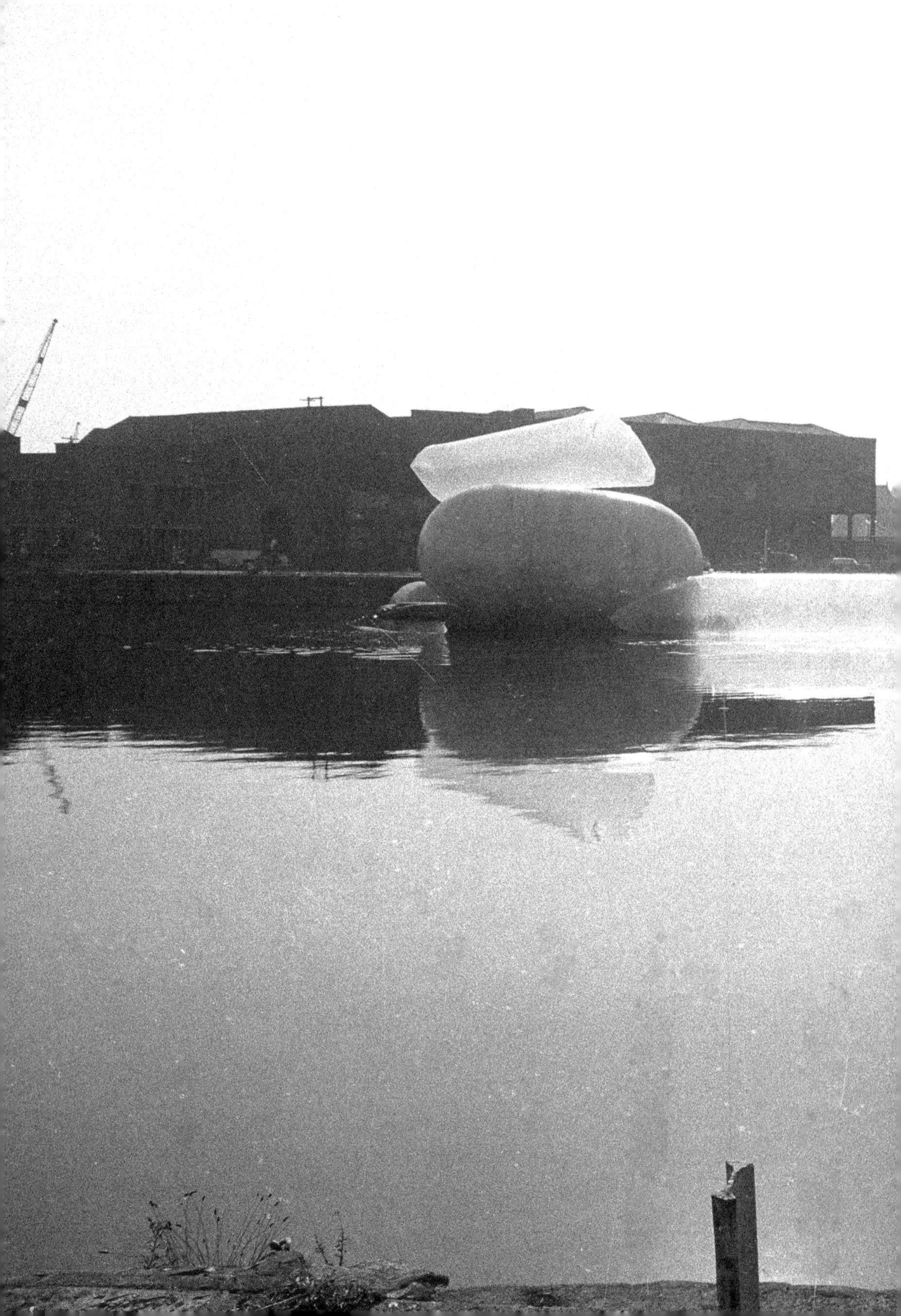

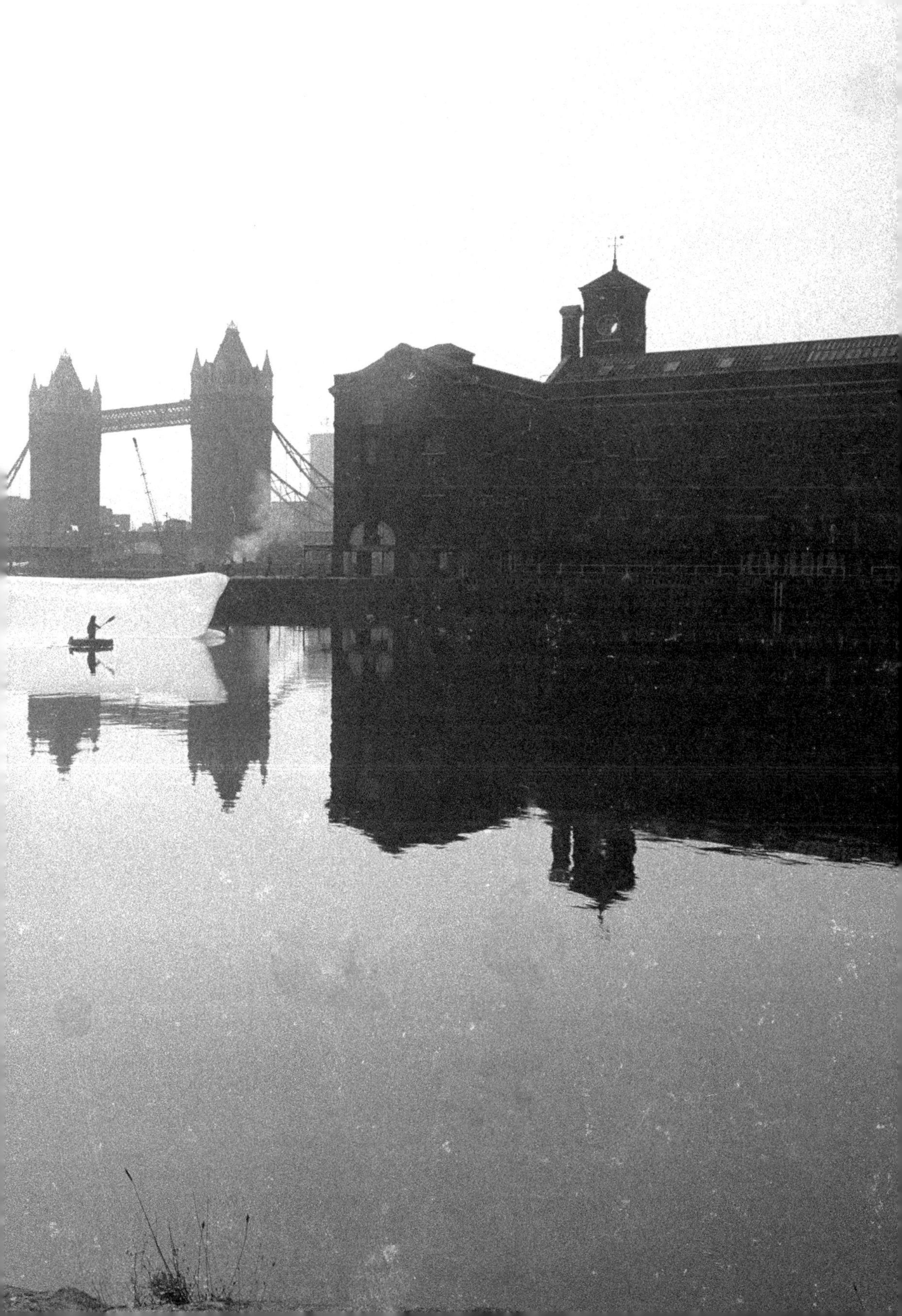

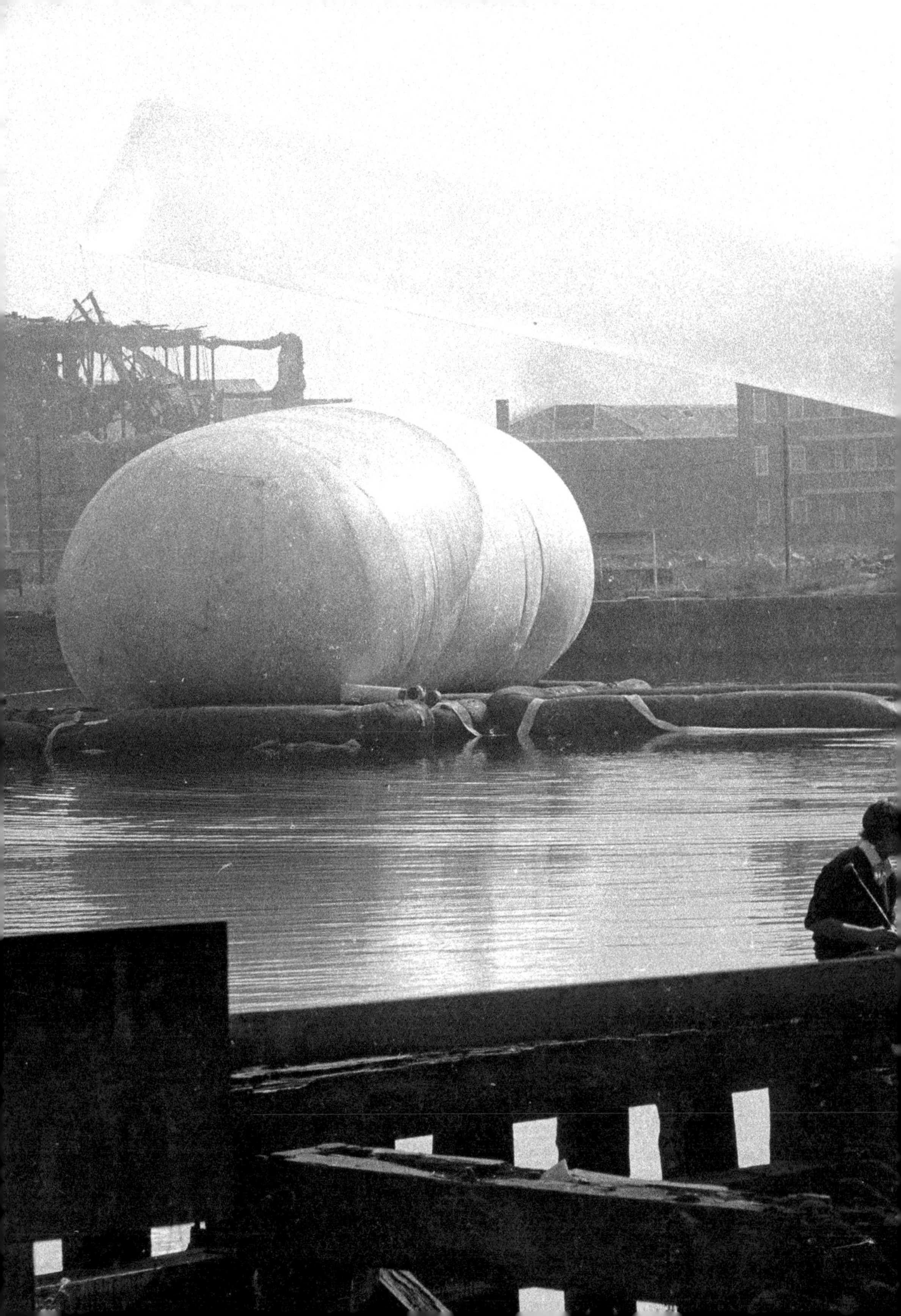

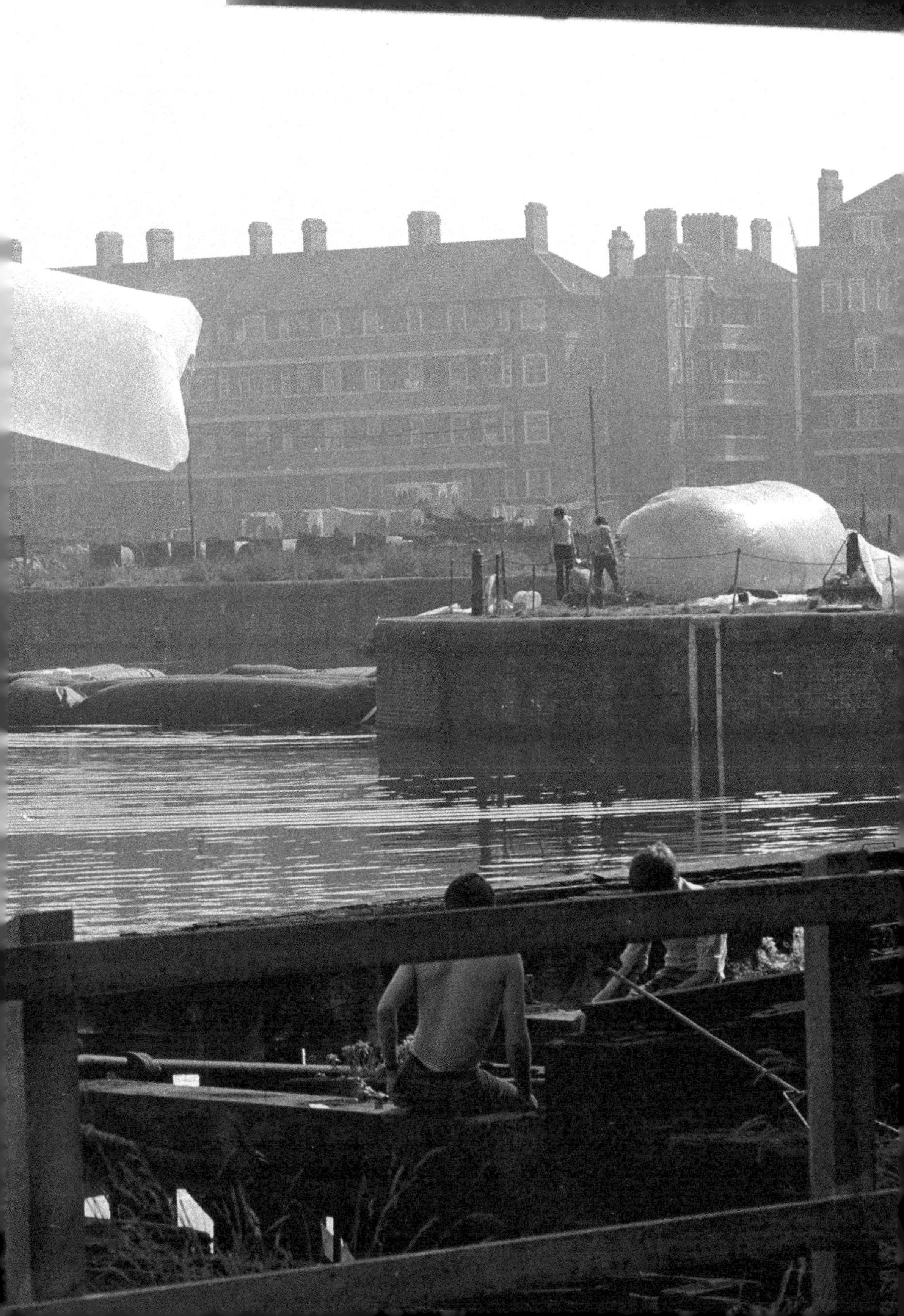

Stevens' work provides one model for understanding the set of principles communicated by SPACE at St Katharine Docks, as does the work of another artist who was also one of the original studio holders, Rasheed Araeen. His use of a lattice structure in his sculptures of 1966–67 had the effect of creating dynamism in minimal forms that were otherwise essentially static.

This was the essence of Araeen's sculpture, which reached its formative moment in 1968 with his conception of *Zero to Infinity* – a collection of 100 cubic structures arranged in a grid form that was disrupted not only through the optics of the lattice but also through the manual manipulation of cubes by viewers to create ever-changing, organic, situations. While at SPACE, Araeen used the environment of the dock to create new participatory sculptures – *Chakras* – which involved floating discs being thrown into the water. The situation that was set up by Araeen used the passage of the discs within the particular dockland context as an example and metaphor for interaction and participation of a different kind to *Zero to Infinity*. Here an event is initiated and left to unfold for the participants who contemplate the flow and movement of the discs on water that perhaps disrupt their rational form.

The Antiuniversity was, by contrast to the organic growth of the Arts Lab movement, a short-lived experiment set up under the banner of 'Music Art Poetry Black Power Madness Revolution' by an ad hoc committee mostly made up of psychiatrists associated with the Philadelphia Foundation's Institute of Phenomenological Studies – Joseph Berke, David Cooper, Allan Krebs and Leon Redler, as well as Juliet Mitchell and figures such as the poet publisher Asa Benveniste. It had direct links to the earlier Free University of New York, with which Berke had been involved. When it opened in February 1968 in Rivington Street in Shoreditch, it embraced the non-hierarchical structure practised by anti-psychiatry and its breaking down of difference in questioning the nature of schizophrenia. The Antiuniversity sought to 'unify disparate perspectives. [...] We must do away with artificial splits and divisions between disciplines and art forms and between theory and action',[12] aims that were reflected in SPACE as much as the Arts Lab movement. If the poster advertising the opening of the Antiuniversity stressed that there were 'No Formal Requirements', this was aimed as much at its teaching faculty staff as at the students. The lack of formal requirements underlined the fact that, although it presented 'a meeting ground for discussion, discovery, rediscovery and revelation ...an on-going-experiment in the development of consciousness',[13] the structure of the Anti-university as an institution was not only up for discussion but likely also being dismantled.

Soon after the opening, Robert Tasher, writing in *International Times* (*IT*) declared 'Don't enrol as a student, only as a teacher', before succinctly adding that 'A real system of alternative education does not solely depend upon breaking down the teacher-pupil relationship. It requires too [...] the total rejection of the old goals of education as practised now. For the "alternatively educated" person will not only think differently; he will also act differently'.[14] By the start of the Antiuniversity's second quarterly session in May, there was optimism about its survival and possible growth. A general meeting was called to discuss the possibility of 'an end to the distinctions between "student", "teacher", "administration", and all that implies socially and financially', which suggested the need for an 'anti-Anti-University'.[15] The result of this meeting was the commencement of Counter University Sessions, which would find their echo in the contemporary demands being made in Paris and those being prepared at Hornsey.[16] Despite this optimism, by July, the premises in Rivington Street had to be given up for lack of money. Some courses continued to take place at members' homes, pubs and Arts Labs, but by September it was all over.

What the examples of the Arts Lab and the Antiuniversity reveal is not only the significance of self-organisation but also that this is a social act. The boundaries being broken down were as much artistic as they were cultural and educational, and, in this way, the politics of space and the need for space – workspace as well as sites of social exchange – was the determining factor for SPACE itself. One aspect of this exchange was centred on information. The 1969 Arts Lab conference was structured largely around an examination of organisation and sustainability, with workshops on administration and information exchange and an additional focused discussion about administration. SPACE was represented at the conference as an aspect of AIR and described itself as having the aim of being 'ultimately self-supporting' with AIR acting as its 'administrative body'.[17] Furthermore, like the growth of the Arts Lab movement, it was understood that, 'once a precedent has been established, there will be few problems in extending the idea to incorporate large numbers of like premises'.[18] AIR was seen as crucial to the realisation of this ambition.

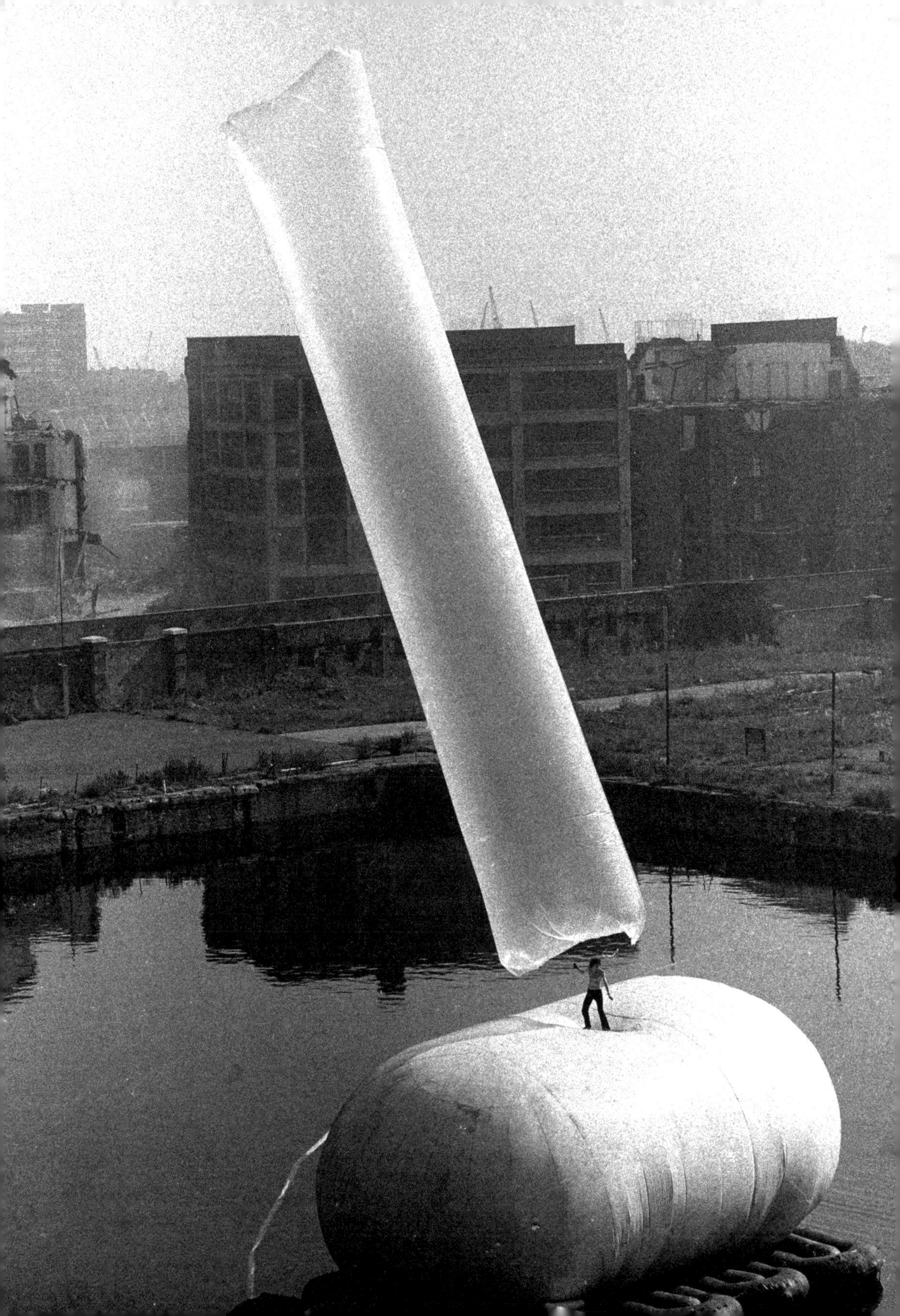

Just as Sedgley was imagining AIR, John 'Hoppy' Hopkins, one of the co-founders of *IT*, was conceiving BIT in London and Stewart Brand was starting to publish his *Whole Earth Catalog* in California under the motto 'Access to Tools'. AIR's clear purpose was simply expressed by Vaizey as 'a clearing house of information for the arts, not only for the artist, but for the promotion of the arts in general'.[19] AIR comprised an index of artists with visual and textual information, an information register of working techniques and materials and documentation about arts organisations and individuals working in the arts. To these indices was added a newsletter and calendar of events as well as a directory of people active in the creative arts. The directory had the title *Catalyst*, and, in a sense, the ideal of space provision was similarly catalytic.

The provision and sharing of information, as much as the creation of publicly accessible networks, were common strategies followed by the international counterculture.[20] And in a similar way, just as AIR and SPACE were so bound together, the connection of information with action closely reflects BIT's birth in May 1968 as an offshoot of *IT*. BIT was first publicly announced on the front cover of *IT* no. 32 for 31 May 1968, the issue which carried news of the events in Paris: 'It has become apparent that *IT* is really a machine for processing, collecting and publishing information, we are consciously turning the first two parts of the machine into an information bank and an information processing plant. [...] *IT* will then become one of the media making use of BIT'.[21]

BIT's remit was wide and sprawling, yet for just over a decade it succeeded in its aim of providing information to the underground community, in print, over the telephone and in person. Similarly, as SPACE artist Gerry Hunt made clear in an article responding to criticism of the Art Spectrum exhibitions staged across Britain through 1971 by Regional Arts Associations, AIR's provision of information to a range of exhibitions and other activities, its role as a generator of data flows, had the capacity to change fundamentally the character of the art world: 'SPACE provides a context to work in and AIR could, if it was developed, help to break the West End, Arts Council and Museum paternalistic grip'.[22]

A short-circuiting of the art world's structures aimed to offer support and opportunities to the widest range of artists in ways that traditional structures had failed because they had not taken account

Stunt man Eddie Bowery on Graham Stevens' inflatable at St Katharine Docks during the shoot of *Atmosfields*. Photo: Andrew C. Tweedie, 1968-70. © GASACT of recent changes to art and society. As Sedgley stated within his 1970 manifesto-like letter on AIR: 'Artistic endeavor has moved beyond the salon; the artistic revolution – large-scale paintings, earthworks, light projections, etc. – demands a reassessment of the situation. The present platforms for the creative arts – galleries, museums, theatres – inherited as they are from the elitist society of the nineteenth centuries, are totally inadequate for the presentation of the scope and talents of the creative arts today'.[23] If AIR aimed to counter such a situation through the dissemination of information, SPACE continues to set the terms of its presence through the capture and use of space by artists.

Notes

1 October 27 Ad Hoc Committee, 'Briefing to all demonstrators: "Street Power"', printed sheet, 1968.

2 Anthony Everitt, 'An artists' haven in a disused dockland warehouse', *The Birmingham Post*, 6 September 1969; reprinted as 'SPACE 1969' in David Mellor, *The Sixties Art Scene in London*, exhibition catalogue, Barbican Art Gallery, 1993, p. 202.

3 The match shed was also known as Centre H, and the notice 'St Katherine Docks' [sic], *Studio International*, July–August 1969, p. 7, states that it 'will be used for theatre, music, light and environmental art. It is hoped to build an experimental theatre/performance space shortly in this building, and to use one of the floors as permanent exhibition space for the artists in St Katherine Docks [sic].'

4 Marina Vaizey, 'S.P.A.C.E. Ltd.', *Canvas*, vol. 4, no. 10, February 1970, p. 9.

5 *A Proposal to Provide Studio Workshops for Artists* (an expanded and rewritten version of an article in *Studio International*, vol. 177, no. 908, February 1969, pp. 65–67, both written by SPACE Director and *Studio International* editor Peter Townsend, unpaginated, bound into *SPACE* (Cambridge: Joshua Taylor Gallery, 1970). This aspect was in contrast to Stockwell Depot, set up in 1967 by a group of sculptors associated with St Martin's School of Art who created studios in a disused brewery building in south London specifically for sculptors. The Joshua Taylor exhibition catalogue provides a graphic representation of this mixed aspect of SPACE's makeup through the grid reproduction of photographs of 49 of the artists with studios there. This exhibition, like other SPACE exhibitions of the period, were equally eclectic: London Now in Berlin, Akademie der Künste, Berlin 1971; Midland Group Gallery, Nottingham 1971; Geffrye Museum, London 1971; Space – paintings and sculpture from St Katharine Docks, Marble Hill House, London 1971; and Arts Council of Northern Ireland, Belfast 1971.

6 SPACE was incorporated as a non-profit company, limited by guarantee in November 1968. Its first directors were Riley and Sedgley, Professor West of Reading University's faculty of urban and regional studies, the actress Irene Worth and the editor of *Studio International* Peter Townsend. It received crucial early support from Henry Moore who donated his Erasmus Prize money, as well as the Calouste Gulbenkian Foundation and the Arts Council of Great Britain (ACGB) which contributed a modest refurbishment grant; financial support was also gained from collectors and other individuals such as Tom Bendham, Sidney Lewis, EJ Power and Lord Sainsbury.

7 John Russell, 'A space to watch', *Sunday Times*, 2 February 1969.

8 'The Arts Lab Movement', *International Times*, no. 66, 10 October 1969, p. 16.

9 *Report on National Arts Lab Conference, Cambridge 25 – 26 January 1969,* (organised by New London Arts Lab and Cambridge Arts Lab), duplicated sheets, unpaginated.

10 Graham Stevens, 'Blow-Up', *Art and Artists*, May 1972, p. 44.

11 Ibid, p. 45.

12 *The Antiuniversity of London*, self-published course catalogue, Spring/Summer 1968. Courses that were offered included, amongst others: Stephen Abrams on 'anti-social psychology'; Roy Battersby and Leon Redler on 'Time and Timelessness'; Joseph Berke's 'Anti-institution Research Project'; Barry Flanagan on 'Space'; Jim Haynes' 'Dialogues about relevant and irrelevant matters'; John Keys on 'Everything'; Allen Krebs' 'Life in a Television Set'; John Latham on 'Antiknow'; Gustav Metzger's 'Theory of Auto-destructive Art'; Barry Miles' 'Underground Communication Theory'; Jeff Nuttall's 'Day Long Mind Merger'; and Yoko Ono on 'The Connection'.

13 *The Antiuniversity of London*, course catalogue (London: Trigram Press, February 1968).

14 Harold Norse, Alexander Trocchi, Robert Tasher, 'Three views on the Anti-University', *International Times*, no. 26, 16–29 February 1968, p. 6.

15 Mimeographed flyer for the general meeting, 11 May 1968, 'You and the Anti-U'.

16 This discussion was programmed to be carried out at a series of weekend events: at Regents Park on 6–7 July; a 'Kip-In' at the Antiuniversity 12–14 July; and an 'Anti-U Course Creation Rally' on 21 July at Speakers Corner. The breaking down of hierarchy within a pedagogical structure was key to the Antiuniversity (and its demise) as it was also to the sorts of questioning of education that was at the root of much of the events of May 1968 exemplified in London by the occupation of Hornsey College of Art (see Various, *The Hornsey Affair*, Harmondsworth 1969 and Lisa Tickner *Hornsey 1968: The Art School Revolution*, 2008). Such principles also informed the founding of AIR and SPACE.

17 *Report on National Arts Lab Conference, Cambridge 25–26 January 1969*, op. cit.

18 Ibid.

19 Marina Vaizey, 1970, op. cit., p. 10.

20 See Andrew Wilson, 'Project Sigma: An Interpersonal Log-Book', in Jo Applin, Catherine Spencer and Amy Tobin (eds.), *London Art World: Mobile, Contingent, and Ephemeral Networks, 1960–1980* (Pennsylvania: Pennsylvania State University Press, forthcoming), for a discussion of how the public sharing of addresses was at the heart of a the constitution of the London counter-culture of the early 1960s as registered in Alexander Trocchi's Project Sigma and Jeff Nuttall's *My Own Mag*.

21 'BIT', *International Times*, no. 32, 31 May –13 June 1968, unpaginated [front cover]. The title of BIT announced itself as being a part of *IT*, as much as FIT did – the Free bank that was announced in BIT's first information service bulletin for 8 August 1968. The title also made a direct reference to cybernetics – Binary Information Transfer – 'the smallest unit of information handled by a computer', ibid. This aspect was expanded on in its second information service bulletin also for 8 August 1968 that announced that BIT was being advised by a cybernetician in its storage and deployment of data. By the early 1970s, BIT became an integral part of the commune and squatting movement.

22 Gerry Hunt, 'After Spectrum', *Art & Artists*, November 1971, p. 14. Hunt also discusses other bodies besides AIR and SPACE that challenged the orthodoxies of the Arts Council or the commercial art market – ranging from the exhibitions sponsored through Pavilions in the Park to the activities of the Artist Placement Group.

23 Peter Sedgley, 'Art Information Registry', *Studio International*, vol. 180, no. 924, July–August 1970, p. v.

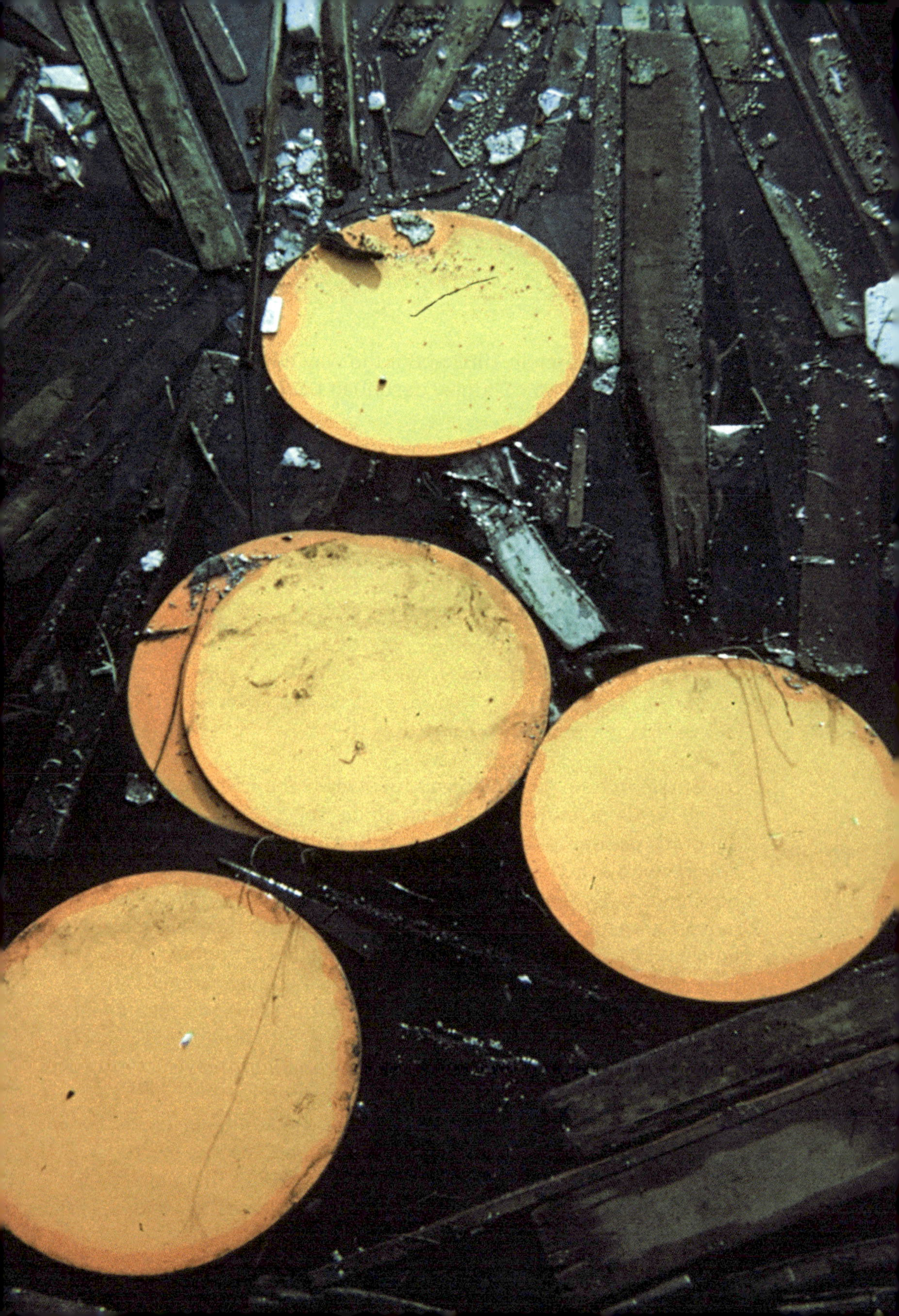

The studio and the city: SPACE Ltd. and Rasheed Araeen's 'Chakras'

Courtney J Martin

Speaking from Berlin in 1982 about the way he incorporated film into his practice, Peter Sedgley described London as a studio space:

> I produced in 1971, a cinema film in which I tried to convey to West Berlin audiences my reactions to the ambience of London by presenting its contrasting ambiguities and the pace and sometimes boredom of those who live and work there. It is a film collage recording a seemingly endless trip along a motorway, with repeated sequences and superimposed images of the docks of East London, where the SPACE studios are located. The film may have been made as a reaction to my rejection of figurative subject matter in my paintings and sculptures.[1]

The studio that he mentions was most likely the I Site studio, one of the buildings in the SPACE Ltd. studio scheme. The 'ambience', London's post-empire dereliction, would have been jarring to anyone who assumed that the city had regained its pre-war prominence. By the end of World War II, the East End docks, once a major transport hub (with similarly far-reaching names like East India and Cyprus) became spaces of vacancy and vagrancy with little commerce moving through them. As Sedgley suggests, to describe London to Berliners (or anyone) would require a mention of the docks, which stood in as a metaphor for the decline of London's grandeur and power. The docks were a locational and visual record of what the city had once been and what it had become.

The metaphor of London as a derelict, post-imperial, post-colonial, post-industrial dock was fitting, given that Sedgley had steered a group that pushed the British government to reuse these spaces as artists' studios. But this metaphor was double-faced. If London's fall

Rasheed Araeen, *Chakras* (waterdiscs), installation shots of performance, St Katharine Docks, 1969-70. Photo: © Rasheed Araeen reduced it to disuse, the city was a massive studio of remnants and refuse – one that artists like Sedgley drew from conteptually (as was the case with his film), formally and materially.

SPACE Ltd.

SPACE Ltd. grew out of artists Bridget Riley and Peter Sedgley's idea that post-war London produced a population of artists, among others, who were not able to find reasonably priced working space.[2] In their white paper on the subject, they described the situation for artists lacking studios thus:

> […] the rise in land values and rentals in every urban centre; the development for high-rental residential purposes of those districts traditionally provided with facilities for artists (one thinks, for example, of Chelsea, Hampstead, Kensington, where studios are converted into 'desirable' flats and there is no replacement of working studios); the greater scale on which painters and sculptors are working.[3]

All three factors – rising costs, development and new forms of art-making – contributed to a squeeze on space in London. These factors also defined the ways that industry had altered in Britain in the post-war period. Workers, now employed in different sectors than before the war, looked for homes within the city but were being pushed to its suburban margins or enticed to live in the high-rise complexes completed in the mid 1960s.[4] In calling for what might traditionally have been a part of Britain's (or most European governments') social contract with artists, SPACE's proposal aligned them with industry. Artists were workers whose workplaces needed to be provided and regulated by their employer, the city. As they noted:

> Not to have adequate space can be near-crippling because capacity and performance alike may be diminished when the available space is too small for work or for showing off work to good advantage, and the resultant tensions in domestic or professional life can retard an artist's development.[5]

Indeed, SPACE's founders fit this new model. Riley was a large-scale painter, and Sedgley had moved from traditional painting and sculpture into installation and film. Their practices mirrored those of other London artists who needed larger and more flexible workspace. Riley and Sedgley caught a glimpse of a solution in Manhattan, which they visited for the exhibition The Responsive Eye at the Museum of Modern Art in 1965. There, they were inspired by the repurposing of industrial and commercial space for artists in downtown Manhattan.[6]

Upon their return to London, they began to organise SPACE Ltd. (Space Provision, Artistic, Cultural and Educational), which was launched in the autumn of 1968 as an incorporated non-profit, with a board of directors that included WA West, Irene Worth, Peter Townsend and Maurice de Sausmarez. The directors represented the wider field of the arts. Worth was a noted expatriate stage actress; Townsend was the editor of *Studio International*, the most circulated contemporary arts magazine of the time; and de Sausmarez, an artist, was the principal of the Byam Shaw School of Art. Along with de Sausmarez, West, a professor at the University of Reading, gave the group institutional clout.[7] SPACE functioned as a cooperative to obtain short-term leases from the Greater London Council (GLC) on vacant buildings, some set to be demolished for commercial expansion, others simply derelict.[8] With minimal accommodation (the provision of electricity, running water and heat), these buildings were converted into work-only studio spaces for artists. At the end of the lease (or licence, as it was called), SPACE and the artists vacated the property and moved on to another vacancy.

One of the first SPACE endeavours was at St Katharine Docks, a suite of warehouses just east of the Tower of London and Tower Bridge in an inlet on the north bank of the Thames. An active port in the 19th century, St Katharine had been severely damaged during the blitz. SPACE arranged a two-year lease from the GLC for the facility, which comprised 'three large water basins of 10 acres surrounded by warehouse buildings covering some 100,000 sq. ft. and rising four and six storeys in height'.[9] The main artists' studios and office area were located in a warehouse dubbed I Site or I Warehouse.

While the original mandate for SPACE outlined affordable studio space for artists, particularly young artists and art students, there was also a clause for studio workshops for 'artists of all nationalities working in the visual arts'.[10] The latter reflected the utopian component of the undertaking; Riley and Sedgley envisioned the studio programme as a communal forum for work wherein socialist values would be combined with internationalism. This clause also recognised the post-imperial reality of London. After World War II, many residents of former British colonies had relocated to the United Kingdom, many settling in its largest city, London, whose docks had been the major outlet to the country's colonial posts. By 1968, London was a city whose past had returned to it in the form of new citizens.[11] Though Britain did not experience social upheaval like continental Europe in 1968, great social changes resulted from the influx of immigrants.[12] More progressive than the government, which viewed nearly all immigrants as manual labourers, SPACE recognised that some of these new citizens were artists who might share in their ideals about art-making.

Chakras in the Thames

Rasheed Araeen was one of these new arrivals, having reached London in 1964 from Karachi, by way of Paris. Previously a draftsman for British Petroleum, Araeen had moved continents, sacrificed material comfort and radically altered his career path with the intention of becoming an artist.[13] His work, stemming from his knowledge of engineering and building structures, was interstitial; he was neither a painter nor strictly a sculptor. In the mood of the times, he was exploring what would come to be known as installation through a variety of means. From the outset of his residency, he produced minimalist forms that he called structures.[14] These were gridded, geometric works, often painted, that required a great expanse of space to construct (as well as workshops for wood joinery and welded steel) and to exhibit and store.

Thus, following in the manner of the new forms of sculpture being produced at the time, Araeen required a large multifunctional space in which to conceive and craft his work. As one of the earliest occupants, he found at I Site a place to develop his work and enjoyed a freedom that Lynn Schafran also noticed during her visit in 1969: 'Some areas are partitioned for additional wall space, others function as large, unbroken expanses where groups or neighbours work freely'.[15]

The sheltered water surrounding the I Site studio was also available for residents' use.[16] Enclosed by commercial buildings to the north, east and west and a lock that led out to the Thames to the south, St Katharine Docks was an urban island. The water was relatively calm, though as Araeen noted, it was littered with the detritus of the city:

It became my obsession there to look at the water and observe the floating pieces of wood and plastics which were drifting from one place to another owing to the action of the movement of water and wind. Every day it was a completely different experience by finding the pieces of wood and plastic etc. in different relationship to each other and at a different place on the water.[17]

Like Sedgley's allusion to the dock's captivating contrasts, Araeen's description of the floating objects serves as a metaphor for the city's evolution. London was being altered daily by new arrivals, whose languages, customs, sounds and movements rearranged its previous patterns. The once Eastern European and Jewish immigrant enclaves in East London, for example, were being replaced by Bangladeshi and Pakistani migrants. South London saw large influxes of African and Caribbean populations, while the North of the city housed groups of Turkish and Greek Cypriots.[18]

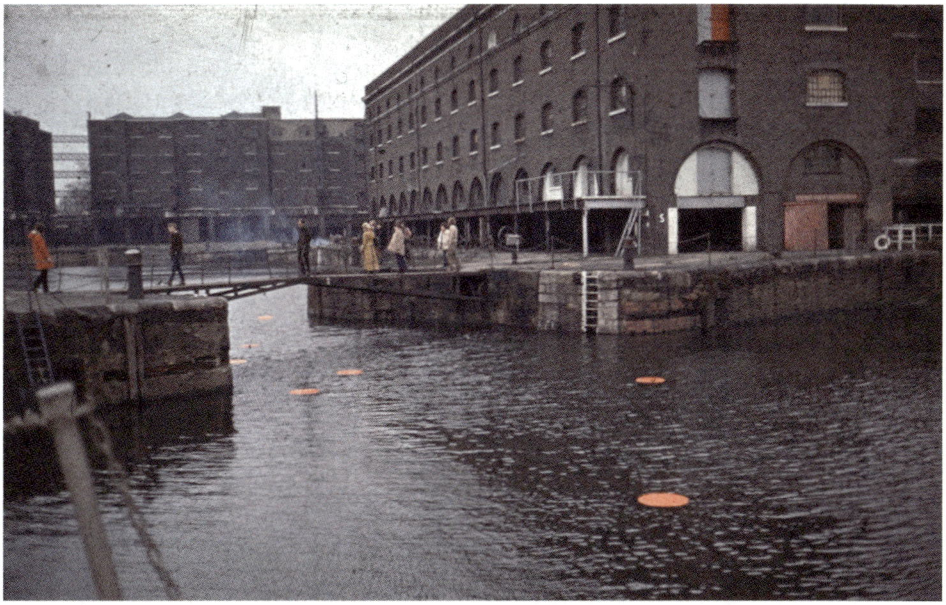

Rasheed Araeen, *Chakras* (waterdiscs), installation shots of performance, St Katharine Docks, 1969–70. Photo: © Rasheed Araeen

The movement that Araeen noticed in the water was thus replicated on the streets. During this time, he also became involved in community and participatory art events, many of which expressed a commitment to combating the stigmatising and harassment of immigrants in Britain.[19]

Begun in 1969 and initiated in February of 1970, *Chakras* was Araeen's first environmental and participatory project at I Site. Araeen invited friends, some other SPACE artists and passersby to throw discs into the water. In total, 16 red fluorescent plastic discs, each two feet in diameter, were floated in the water. Like the debris that Araeen had seen there, their movement was contingent upon the variable conditions of the water and the wind. Unlike the debris, however, they were consistent in size, colour, shape, weight and buoyancy; eliminating such variations, which Araeen termed 'relations', meant that either all of the discs would float or all would sink. In this case, they all floated.[20]

Araeen's later social justice and political art actions position *Chakras* as a comment on the ways in which difference (be it class, race, ethnicity or gender) was an uneasy fit in Britain in the late 1960s. On one level, *Chakras* is a commentary on London's adaptation to its new citizens.

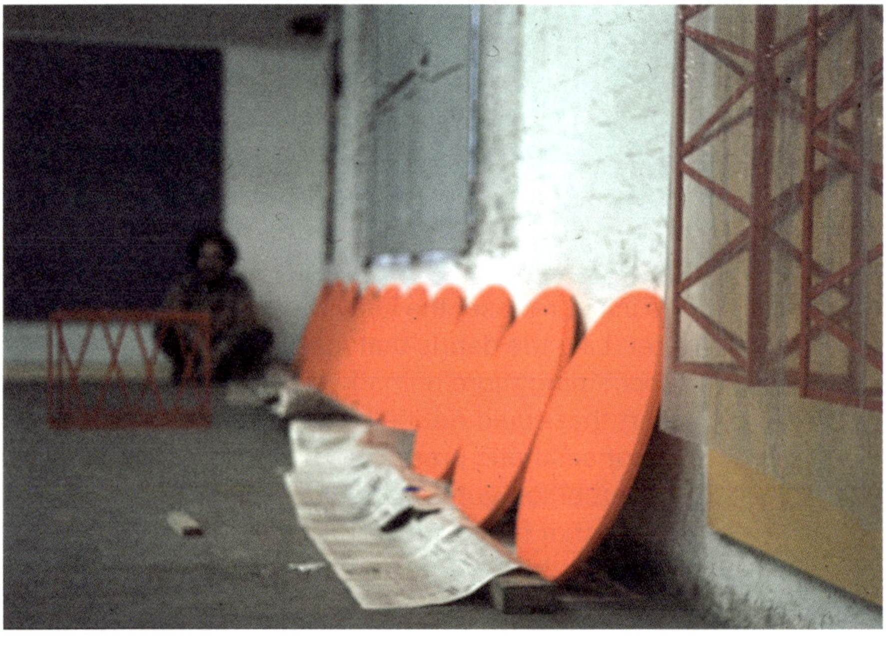

Rasheed Araeen in his studio at St Katharine Docks creating *Chakras* (waterdiscs), 1969-70.
Photo: © Rasheed Araeen

The sink-or-swim uncertainty is not without humour, if not also irony. Floating a symbolic object with bodily connotations drawn from Eastern spiritual traditions (chakras occur in both Hinduism and Buddhism) in water that leads to the open sea, is a performance of reclaiming, of liberation from imperialism, and with it, slavery, colonialism and all it implies.

But was this performance satirical? For this to be done by an immigrant working in a communal art programme with utopian overtones, that opinion has to be considered. On a formal level, the action sought to resolve a tension Araeen felt between a secure understanding of minimalist form (here shown through uniform, geometric objects) and a more expansive art practice that depended on the participation of others and the coordination of uncontrollable elements: wind, water and the ever-present possibility of rain in London. Each of these aspects drew attention to the manifest condition of late 1960s London as it confronted urban deterioration amid population regeneration. It was a city falling down and expanding simultaneously.

For Araeen, there was also another component – making art that had little or no commercial potential. He described the aims of *Chakras* thus: 'If we want that art should become [an] essential part of our life or that all the people should have access to it, it is essential that first the monopoly of one particular class to own and appreciate the work of arts must be destroyed'.[21] *Chakras* realised this destruction of the 'monopoly' by being almost completely intangible. The discs were allowed to float on the water under the terms of 'release', a historically weighted synonym for manumission. Like most actions, *Chakras* was a one-off performance that circulated through a few photographs, which Araeen did not edition or sell.[22] (At the time, London had almost no viable art market, particularly for experimental art.) After the initial release, the individual discs were not retrieved from the water. Like the debris that inspired them, they went with the current, becoming more unmarked remnants of the city.

Making art that could not be sold was itself a release from a certain type of aesthetic pressure. This is not to suggest that Araeen lacked ambition with regard to his work or his career. In the same year that he began work on *Chakras*, he was awarded the second prize at the seventh John Moores Liverpool Exhibition at the Walker Gallery in Liverpool. Araeen's entry, *Boo* (1969), completed at his I Site studio, was one of only a few purchased by the Walker.[23] London, by way of the SPACE programme, allowed Araeen and other artists to maintain a conventional studio practice while also inventing and experimenting with new forms.[24]

St Katharine Docks had a metonymic relationship to the city, just as SPACE did to the government from which it funnelled resources to artists in the hope of establishing art and artists as significant features of municipal, if not national, culture. *Chakras* was only one example of the innovations fostered by these interactions. As a new arrival, Araeen's presence in London, and in St Katharine Docks in particular, challenged the city and the programme to live up to its ideals. Within the confines of the SPACE studio programme, he was able to harness the potential of the 'sheltered water' outside its door, and thus of the surrounding city.

Notes

1 Peter Sedgley and Heinz Ohff, 'My Kinetic Artworks and Paintings (1971–1982)', *Leonardo* 15, no. 3, Summer 1982, p. 184.

2 Despite the ongoing relationship between Bridget Riley and Peter Sedgley, early press releases cite Sedgley as being charged with 'most of the organisational work' for SPACE. John H Holloway, 'International Science-Art News (Art et Science: Nouvelles de L'Etranger)', *Leonardo* 2, no. 4, October 1969, p. 450.

3 'A Proposal to Provide Studio Workshops for Artists', *Studio International* 177, no. 908, February 1969, p. 66. This is a shorter version of Space Provision Ltd., 'A Proposal to Provide, on an Ultimately Self-supporting Financial Basis, Studio Workshops for Artists, Together with Such Additional Facilities as Areas for Light Projection Work, Workshops for Light Metals etc., and Exhibitions Spaces' (1969). A slightly longer version of 'A Proposal to Provide Studio Workshops for Artists' was circulated in the same year; see publicity leaflet issued by Space Provision Ltd., Tate Library and Archive.

4 For a longer discussion of architecture in London after World War II, see Peter Murray and Stephen Trombley (eds.), *Modern British Architecture since 1945* (London: F Miller/ RIBA Magazines, 1984).

5 'A Proposal to Provide Studio Workshops for Artists', op. cit., p. 66.

6 Jonathan Jones, 'Interview with Bridget Riley', *Guardian*, 5 July 2008. Riley incited a great deal of media attention while in New York because her work was taken to be emblematic of the commercial potential in so-called Op art, spawning fashion styles and decoration. See John Canaday, 'The Responsive Eye: Three Cheers and High Hopes', *New York Times*, 28 February 1965. Despite Riley's discomfort with the way that her work was received, it is likely that her fame lent weight to the SPACE project.

7 In 1969, SPACE's sponsors were Henry Moore, David Benson (Minister of Parliament) Niall McDermott, Desmond Plummer (Leader of the Greater London Council) and Norman Reid (director of the Tate Gallery).

8 In addition to the GLC, SPACE received public support from the Arts Council of Great Britain and private support from individuals.

9 Space Provision Ltd., 'A Proposal to Provide, on an Ultimately Self-supporting Financial Basis...', op. cit., K2. Other press material lists the square footage as 60,000.

10 Ibid.

11 As Dominic Sandbrook demonstrates in *White Heat: A History of Britain in the Swinging Sixties* (London: Little, Brown, 2006), immigration was one of Britain's key issues throughout the decade.

12 One of Britain's major conflicts in 1968 occurred around art school education. In a battle between education administrators and students, along with some tutors, students sought to have more input into their education. The most important of these battles took place in May at the Hornsey College of Art in north London. Students there staged a sit-in that led to some curriculum changes for the nation. Riley taught at Hornsey from 1960 to 1961. During the exhibition, Hornsey Strikes Again, at the Institute of Contemporary Arts in July, which was a corollary to the sit-in, she was invited to speak in support of changes to art education. Her involvement with Hornsey was simultaneous with setting up SPACE and may account for the attention paid to students in the SPACE proposal. For a longer discussion of the Hornsey College of Art revolt, see Lisa Tickner, *Hornsey 1968: The Art School Revolution* (London: Frances Lincoln, 2008).

13 Interview by the author with Rasheed Araeen, 1 November 2006. In addition to his art practice, Araeen (b. 1935) founded the journal *Black Phoenix* (1978–79), which continued as Third Text (1989). In 1989 he curated the first major museum exhibition of Asian and black artists in Britain, The Other Story: Afro-Asian Artists in Post-War Britain, at the Hayward Gallery.

14 For a longer discussion of Araeen's structures, see Rasheed Araeen, *Making Myself Visible* (London: Kala Press, 1984) and *Minimalism and Beyond: Rasheed Araeen at Tate Britain* (Third Text/Tate Britain, 2007).

15 Lynn Schafran, ''I' Site and Westbeth: Two Solutions to One Problem', *Members Newsletter* (The Museum of Modern Art, New York) no. 7, Winter 1969–1970, p. 5.

16 Guy Brett, 'Introduction', in Rasheed Araeen, *Making Myself Visible*, op. cit., p. 8.

17 Rasheed Araeen, 'Karachi, April 11, 1974', in ibid, p. 64.

18 For a longer discussion of post-war immigration in Britain, see VG Kiernan, 'Britons Old and New', in C Holmes (ed.), *Immigrants and Minorities in British Society* (London, Allen and Unwin, 1978).

19 Araeen's most prominent social justice connection was with the British branch of the Black Panther Party, which he officially joined in 1973. Interview by the author with Rasheed Araeen, 1 November, 2006.

20 Rasheed Araeen, 'Karachi...', in *Making Myself Visible*, op. cit., p. 65.

21 Ibid.

22 Interview by the author with Rasheed Araeen, 1 November 2006.

23 Memorandum from Hugh Scrutton, CBE, to the Arts and Recreation Committee of the Walker Art Gallery, undated. John Moores Exhibition archive, Walker Art Gallery. See also Gail PD Engert, 'Acquisitions of Modern Art by Museums', *Burlington Magazine* 113, no. 815, February 1971, p. 118.

24 In 1971, the year after SPACE vacated St Katharine Docks, Araeen exhibited in *Space: Paintings and Sculpture* from St Katharine Docks, at Marble Hill House in Twickenham. It was the sixth exhibition organised for SPACE artists by Sedgley and the Art Information Registry (AIR), an off-shoot of SPACE. I am thankful to Alicia Miller for sharing her knowledge of the SPACE Archive, particularly the history of AIR. For more on experimental art in Britain after 1968, see David Curtis, *A History of Artists' Film and Video in Britain* (London: BFI, 2007); Neil Mulholland, *The Cultural Devolution: Art in Britain in the Late Twentieth Century* (London: Ashgate, 2003); and John A Walker, *Left Shift: Radical Art in 1970s Britain* (London: IB Tauris, 2002).

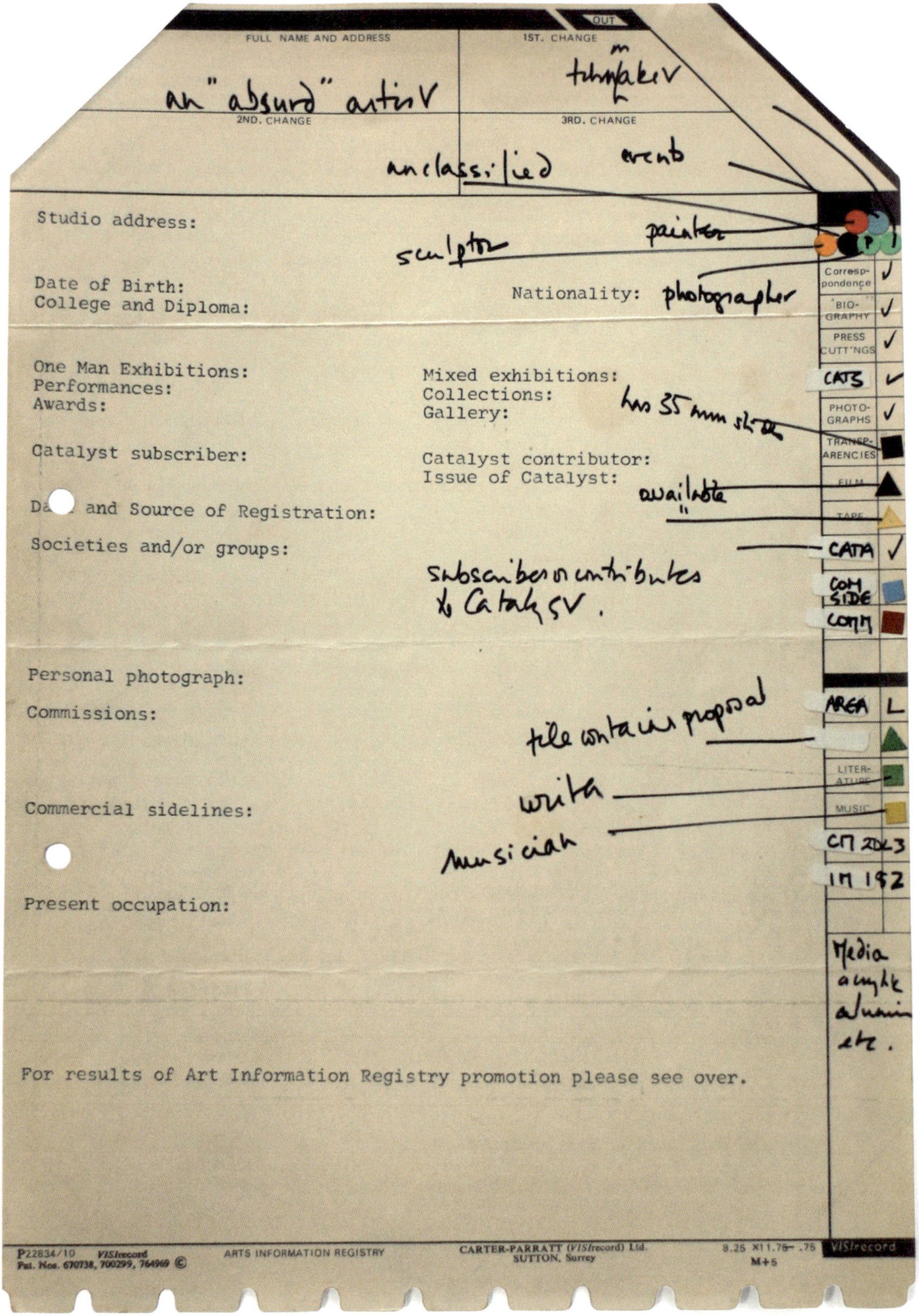

OUT

FULL NAME AND ADDRESS — an "absurd" artist

1ST. CHANGE — filmmaker

2ND. CHANGE — unclassified

3RD. CHANGE — events

painter

sculptor

Studio address:

Date of Birth:
College and Diploma:

Nationality: photographer

One Man Exhibitions:
Performances:
Awards:

Mixed exhibitions:
Collections:
Gallery:

has 35 mm slides

Catalyst subscriber:

Catalyst contributor:
Issue of Catalyst:

available

"

Date and Source of Registration:

Societies and/or groups:

subscribes or contributes to Catalyst.

Personal photograph:

Commissions:

file contains proposal

Commercial sidelines:

writer

musician

Present occupation:

For results of Art Information Registry promotion please see over.

Correspondence ✓

BIOGRAPHY ✓

PRESS CUTT'NGS ✓

CATS ✓

PHOTOGRAPHS ✓

TRANSPARENCIES

FILM

TAPE

CATA ✓

COM SIDE

COMM

AREA L

LITERATURE

MUSIC

CM 2043

IM 192

Media acrylic aluminium etc.

P22834/10 VISIrecord
Pat. Nos. 670738, 700299, 764969 ©

ARTS INFORMATION REGISTRY

CARTER-PARRATT (VISIrecord) Ltd.
SUTTON, Surrey

8.25 X11.75 .75
M+5

VISIrecord

An 'absurd' artist in the AIR Index

Naomi Pearce

This VISIrecord was created by Letty Mooring (previously Woods) around 1970; the exact date of its origin is unknown. It is A4, single-ply, slightly thicker than a polling card, beige in colour with signs of discoloration; its surface is foxed in places. Three horizontal folds score its surface, one created with decisive pressure, the others scored with less conviction. It smells like almonds. This annotated VISIrecord was used as reference by administrators working within the AIR Index. It was the key to the registry.

Printed by Carter-Parratt in Surrey, the VISIrecord's bespoke professional design challenges expectations of a lo-fi artist-led aesthetic. A vertical panel along the right-hand edge of the card is divided into 41 rectangles, each containing a combination of printed and handwritten text as well as coloured sticker symbols. These boxes refer to different sections of the AIR Index including biography, press cuttings, commissions, transparencies and so on.

The bottom edge of the VISIrecord is scalloped with a plurality of notches intended to embrace (now phantom) supporting rods. The body portion of the filing cabinet in which these rods were positioned was almost certainly made of fire-proof board or metal. According to Robin Klassnik, a studio holder at St Katharine Docks at the time, it may have been silver.[1] The location of the filing cabinet in which it would have fitted is unknown.

Other mysteries which cannot be solved include: Were the cards arranged vertically or horizontally? Were they organised alphabetically by name or grouped by discipline, separated from one another by dividers or sub-groups? How many artists were filed under 'unclassified'? Where are the contents of the more than 700 artist files which were contained in the AIR Index when it closed in 1977?

Reference VISIrecord, AIR Index, 1969-77.
Courtesy Letty Mooring

The facts of this VISIrecord are that it is a fiction. This sample is extraneous, as are the actual records and the index they formed. Each record takes an artist's data and translates it into an alternative representation. It analyses their practice and allocates an appropriate label. Activity is divided by context: Is it public or private, solo or group?

The VISIrecord tries to make things easy. It provides a useful means of cross-referencing information. Identifying material sits next to an assessment of commercial viability, details of the groups an artist belongs to and an indication of the kind of work they make. All this information is summarised in one quick-to-reference piece of card.

The VISIrecord is true to its name; it is visual. Letty devised the cross-referencing sticker categories. She told me she thought artists would appreciate this pictorial system as they wouldn't have wanted words describing their work.[2] Letty named the subject of this sample VISIrecord 'an "absurd" artist'. Was this because of a lack of detail or too much? The 'absurd' artist is a high achiever who paints, sculpts and makes films, a careerist hustler with catalogues, commissions and newspaper clippings. This doesn't sound so absurd when thinking about the ways in which artists are required to operate today. Perhaps I should read Letty's intervention differently – as a practice of pleasure, of writing, 'somewhere between personal expression and social system,[3] not dissimilar to dirty drawings hidden within the gold leaf of illuminated manuscripts. Or perhaps the absurdity was being levied elsewhere, at Letty's administration of the index itself.

The practice of administration is often considered absurd. Think of pencil pushers. Administrative tasks are described as Sisyphean in the sense that, like the myth's relentless rolling rock, they never end. Albert Camus defined Sisyphus as an absurdist hero; having defied the gods in life, Sisyphus' body was assigned to the underworld, his whole being orientated towards accomplishing nothing. The absurd hero relates to life as a constant struggle without hope and yet, despite this, continues anyway. Camus acknowledges an internal bind: 'The world in itself is not reasonable, that is all that can be said. But what is absurd is the confrontation of the irrational and the wild longing for clarity whose call echoes in the human heart'.[4] The index was a physical manifestation of this bind; in its attempts to categorise artistic practice, it tried to order the disorderly.

The index dissected first the artist community, then an individual's practice. It zoomed in and out to capture information at different levels of magnification. This procedure was undertaken systematically, with boxes to be ticked or filled with brightly coloured stickers. The index now looks archaic, but its desire to log, share and connect feels contemporary: a computer before computers.

The index connected. Each record acted as a mediator, an avatar circulating whilst the artist continued their work behind closed doors. Collector, curator and the general public were temporarily sutured together through this shared portal.

The index captured. Its visibility distributed 'life chances',[5] opportunities for exhibitions, commissions, media representations. As with other systems that store information, the ease with which life chances were distributed depended on how well things fitted in a box. An AIR brochure dated 1974 describes a system of 35mm transparencies stored within classified slide magazines divided into the following categories:

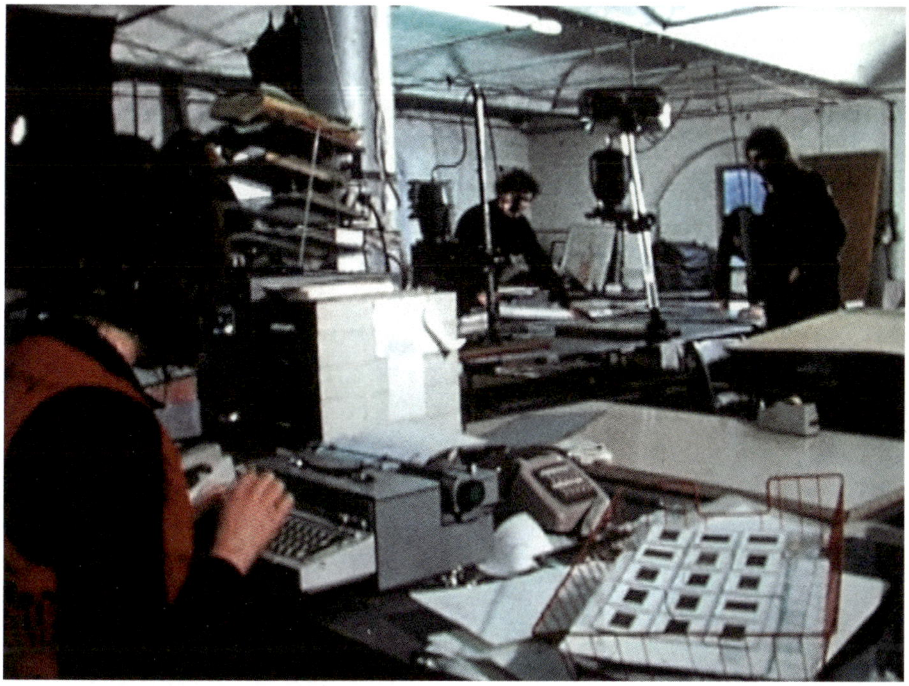

AIR's offices at St Katharine Docks, still from SPACE Film, 1970 ©SPACE

> 2D paintings small (under three inches), 2D paintings large (over three inches), Graphics, Drawing, 3D wall pieces, 3D free standing small (under three inches), 3D free standing large (over three inches), 3D moving, Multiples, Suspended, Open Air, Environments, Events, Theatre and Music.[6]

If categories can be seen to invent, what new ways of being did the index construct? For all those who didn't fit into a particular box, there was a black circle meaning 'Unclassified'. This symbol demonstrates the power of absence; a black hole has no ends, its expansive quality captures anything. What possibilities did this ambiguity provide? Notable categorical absences are gender and ethnicity; either the index liberated through what it chose not to label or the absence of these categories demonstrates the male and pale homogeneity of the art world at the time.

A classification system, argue sociologists Susan Leigh Star and Geoffrey C. Bowker, is a 'set of boxes (metaphorical or literal) into which things can be put to then do work'.[7] In which bureaucratic systems did the index participate? What new knowledge did it help to generate? In one sense, the index's capturing logic coincides with Benjamin Buchloh's observations regarding Conceptual Art's 'aesthetic of administration'.[8] Buchloh argues that the development of this aesthetic was connected to the rise of a post-war middle class, an identity structured around 'merely administering labour and production [...] and the distribution of commodities'.[9] With this in mind, the index might be understood to have been working at cross-purposes. On the one hand, it was a non-profit organisation providing an egalitarian service – a public platform that allowed artists to circumnavigate the gallery system. On the other hand, the index's reliance on categorisation arguably perpetuated, rather than re-invented, the terms on which artists operated. Its files still asked for press cuttings, commissions, commercial sidelines, whether an artist had a gallery or not. In which ways, then, did the index work to assimilate artists within existing conditions more efficiently?

VISIrecords cannot simply be looked at; they must be used. I can't use them properly because no one knows where the files are. In the case of the absurd artist's VISIrecord, I don't even have one side of the story; the art practice which it references never existed. Instead, I have the key to the story – all the components, but no actual plot. This sample record is unable to surrender the index's logic; without the artists' files, there is no material to study, nothing to be cross-referenced. The index only really exists as intended, in relation to its moving contents, when fingers are fumbling through its records and eyes are scanning their surfaces.

In writing about the index, I am always writing about absence. Materially, the VISIrecord can't help but recall the architecture of its container; its indentations trace the shape of what is missing. The index embodies the trace. Reflecting on artistic practice in the 1970s, Rosalind Krauss indentified an indexical sensibility to work produced in this period. She wrote that an indexical logic involves 'the reduction of the conventional sign to a trace, which then produces the need for a supplemental discourse'.[10] Even if Letty's 'manual monster' were still here, its 700 files intact, the AIR Index would persist in existing as a trace: of artworks, of activity, of time spent looking and making.

Notes

1 Robin Klassnik, interview with the author, London, 29 June 2017.

2 Letty Mooring, interview with the author, London, 13 December 2016.

3 Johanna Drucker, *Figuring the Word: Essays on Books, Writing and Visual Poetics* (New York: Granary Books, 1998), p. 57.

4 Albert Camus, *The Myth of Sisyphus* (London: Penguin Modern Classics, 2013), p. 17.

5 Dean Spade, *Administrative Violence, Critical Trans Politics and the Limits of Law* (New York: Duke Press, 2015), p. 44.

6 AIR information booklet 1974, p. 3, Letty Mooring's personal papers, London.

7 Susan Leigh Star and Geoffrey Bowker, *Sorting things out: Classification and its Consequences* (Massachusetts: The MIT Press, 1999), p. 10.

8 Benjamin Buchloh, p. 105 'Conceptual Art 1962–1969: From the Aesthetic of Administration to the Critique of Institutions', *October*, vol. 55, 1990, pp. 105–143.

9 Ibid, p. 128.

10 Rosalind Krauss, p. 59, 'Notes on the Index: Seventies Art in America', *October,* vol. 3, 1977, pp. 68–81.

A meeting in the AIR office at St Katharine Docks, c.1968-70 →

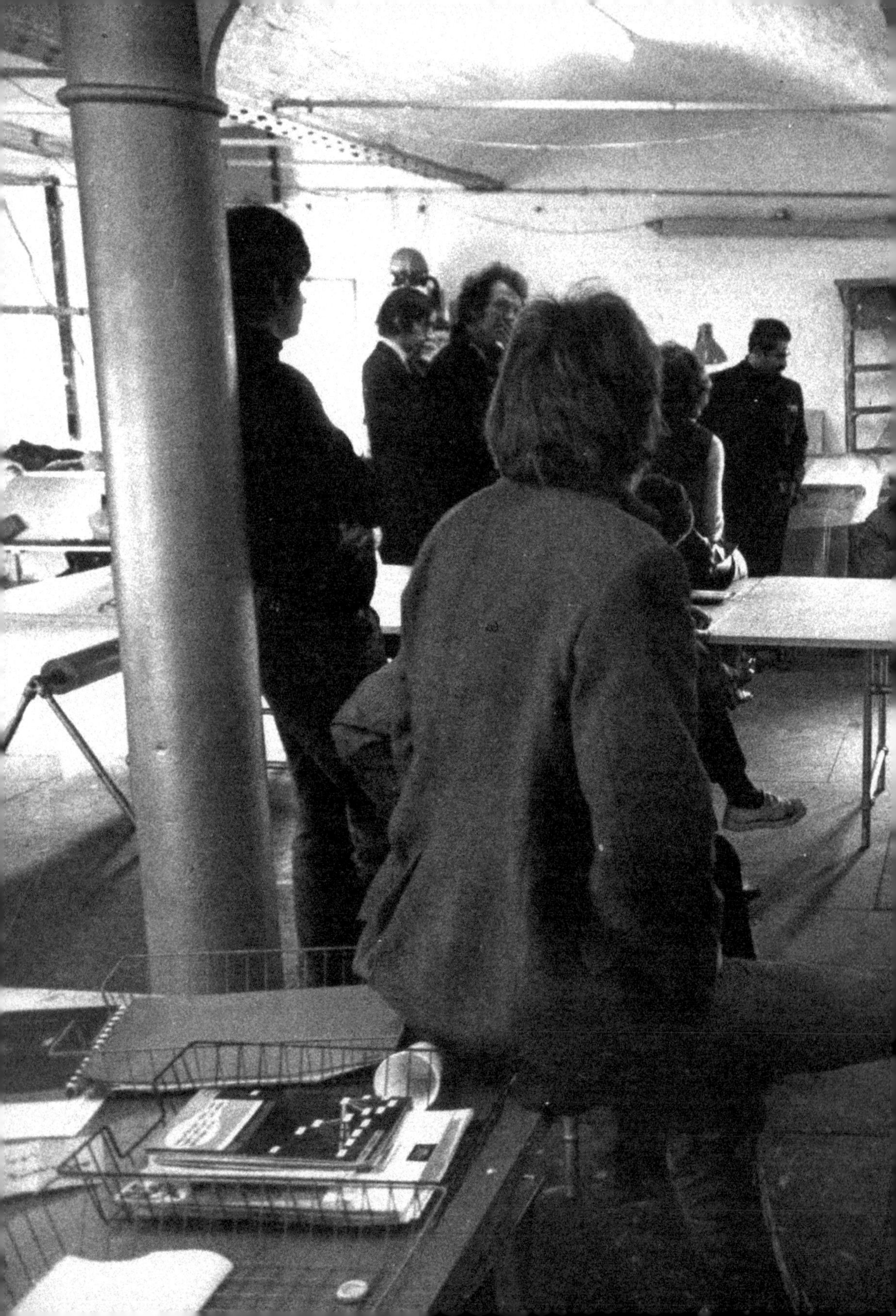

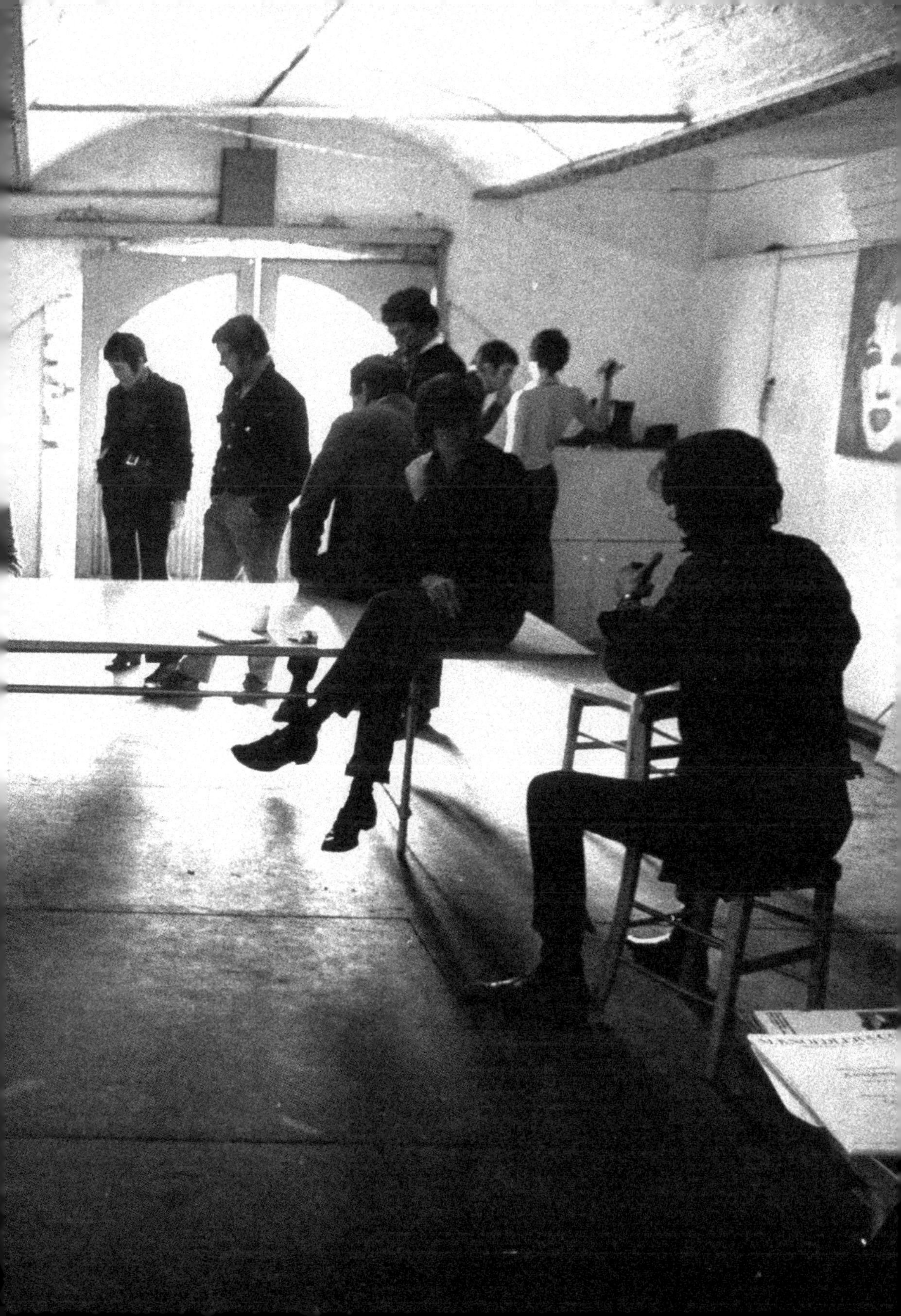

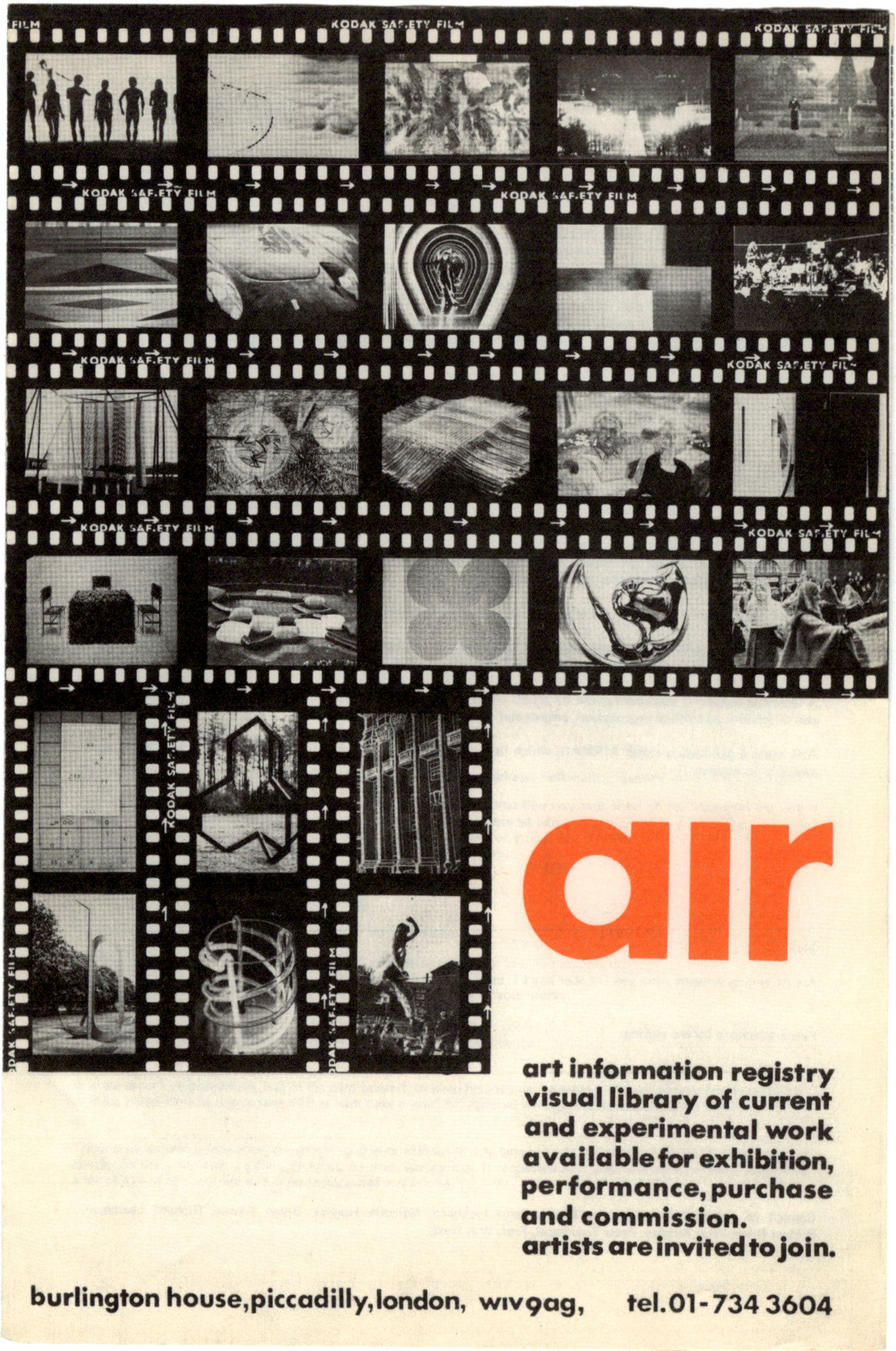
air
art information registry
visual library of current
and experimental work
available for exhibition,
performance, purchase
and commission.
artists are invited to join.
burlington house, piccadilly, london, w1v 9ag, tel. 01-734 3604

Give this work an AIRing

Naomi Pearce

Letty tells her husband that I'm there to 'sort things out'.

She wants me to draw a timeline, to get everything in order, a who did what and when. Instead I ask her: What did St Katharine Docks smell like? She laughs, humours me sweetly, slightly confused.

I'm sitting in her study in Twickenham. On the small desk are two mismatched ring binders, one a standard black lever-arch, the other white plastic with the words 'Sound Sorba Acoustic Panels' printed in blue along its spine. Next to these, a creased manila folder, a handful of typewritten pamphlets and a small stack of publications. This collection of material is Letty Mooring's archive of the Art Information Registry (AIR).

Letty was its administrator from 1969 to 1972 and again, after a brief period working at a picture framers, from late 1975 to the summer of 1976. She continued to collect material relating to AIR and SPACE even after she left the organisation to go and work at *Art Monthly*. Her archive contains papers – minutes, internal correspondence, publicity booklets. Letty isn't sure exactly why she's kept what she has, why certain documents are still here and others have been lost. In 2008, she started working on her own history of AIR and SPACE in collaboration with another PhD researcher. The project was never completed: 'she lost steam, I lost steam, you know,' Letty sighs. Is this a gentle warning? A premonition? Looking down at the folders, I pray for stamina.

Letty's going through the material, explaining her system and what everything is. 'I did try and document it', she tells me, flicking through hole-punched plastic folders and loose pieces of paper. She's worried everything's a bit 'muddled'. Letty's not a trained archivist, and no one employed her as custodian. Despite this, everything's labelled and arranged in chronological order. The care she has taken over the years demonstrates the extent to which she feels responsible for AIR and how it's remembered. I ask how it is she has so many of her own letters in the archive. Did she take copies? 'I must have done,' she tells me. Picking up a loose piece of paper printed with artists' headshots, Letty scans the faces:

Front cover of AIR information leaflet, 1974, SPACE Archive

'Not alive, not alive, not alive, mmm maybe still alive. We don't know, he's disappeared. Well she's in her 80s, as is Peter.'

Peter is the artist Peter Sedgley. The drive to establish studios arose because of the registry's growth and the need for alternative accommodation. In this sense, the demand for administrative representation came before that for physical space; artists sought to exist on paper before they occupied buildings in the city.

The climate which enabled AIR to materialise saw a convergence of increased artistic activity, 'intellectual and political disturbances'[1] and a lack of available contexts.

During a 1967 BBC Radio 3 programme called 'The Dying Galleries', aired in response to the recent closure of five reputable London galleries, Peter argued that conditions were changing: 'Art is no longer a purchasable object. It is becoming an abstract experience, an event'.[2] Dematerialisation was beginning to challenge the status of artworks, whilst formal possibilities were expanding with the aid of technological advances: 'these days the borders [between disciplines] are very woolly and sometimes intangible'.[3]

There was a proliferation of artists also; educational reforms, such as those instigated by the 1960 Coldstream report, saw more students enrolling on new National Diploma of Art and Design (Dip AD) courses with numbers increasing from just over 1,400 in 1963 to more than 7,300 a decade later.[4]

The existing system wasn't coping with these shifts; AIR would provide an alternative structure. Originally conceived as a non-profit national public relations agency for the arts, the organisation was dedicated to documenting and collating information on art and artists, to 'act as a catalyst for further development and promotion to individuals and the public in general'.[5]

From its inception, AIR intended to function as a two-way service, a mediator between artists, exhibitions and event organisers, dealers and collectors. It did this by organising exhibitions for its members, periodicals, first *Catalyst* and later *AirMail*, a directory for jobbing artists and, as Peter described it, 'the "soul" of the programme',[6] the artist index.

Letty uses her body to try and recall the filing cabinet's size. She stretches her arms out and gestures at the large table in front of us. 'It was a manual monster', she says. Despite its commitment to representing artists exploring the atmospheric, which was reflected in the acronym of its name, the index was a very material thing; it took up space. Artists submitted biographical material, catalogues, newspaper clippings and other promotional information alongside 35mm slides, film documentation and audio records of their work.

The index was a non-profit venture, funded by the Arts Council of Great Britain (ACGB) from 1969. Initially it was free of charge for artists to join, with an annual subscription fee introduced at some point. A 1974 AIR brochure lists this as £2 (£22.20 at today's prices). Significantly, it was unselective, the only requirement being that artists were 'professional'. I ask Letty how this was determined; she remembers they had to have gone to art school but also, 'I guess by whether they had a studio or not'. By 1976, an average of twelve new members were joining each week, and, when the index closed in 1977, – due to the Arts Council withdrawing their funding – it held the records of more than 700 artists.

None of these files exist now, or at least I haven't been able to find them. Letty tells me the slides, catalogues, press clippings and other contents were returned to the artists. With this dismantling, the infrastructure of the index disappeared; its artist files aren't in the official archive at Mare Street, and Letty doesn't have any either. She's not sure where they are. 'Maybe they got lost?' Some material seems to have been disposed of; minutes from 12th January 1978 advise administrator Liz Richardson 'not to make special arrangements for the return of very old (pre 1974 and unrevised) AIR material'.[7] Although the index officially ceased operations on 31 March 1977, all remaining files and their contents were still in the organisation's possession more than a year later; 'a number of artists are somewhat impatient at the situation'.[8]

This was held up by the pending findings of a research study funded by the Gulbenkian Foundation which faced considerable delay. Conducted by Jasia Reichardt, this project was intended to consider the 'usefulness and practicability of setting up a national artists index, on a non-fee-paying basis, to be open to all professional British artists, and to be available for consultation without payment'.[9] The proposals laid out in this study were not taken up by the Council of Management, with some members being 'disappointed by certain aspects of the report, in particular the very large cost'.[10]

In archival terms, the registry appears as a 'defiant object'; it remains awkward and hard to define. When it does appear fragmentally, in minutes or correspondence, it is always a point of contention.

In his emails, Peter uses the words 'accurate', 'speedy' and 'carefully designed'.[11] The index was always intended to be a professional entity with a clear purpose. And yet, one story Letty's archive tells us is that it was this passivity, and the registry's unselective policy, which led to its eventual demise.

From comments in internal reports – 'there are [...] a large number of artists in the Index whose work is of extremely poor quality.'[12] – to a lengthy article in the magazine *Artscribe* – 'it lacks direction in terms of having a specific policy and fulfilling a specific role'[13] – the Index was dogged by criticism. When ACGB's grant committee withdrew its funding (£3,000 in 1977, £42,650 today), it's chair Peter Bird explained: '[we are] not convinced that a non-selective registry could really carry the material which would make it worth consulting'.[14]

It is clear that, even at the time, Letty was aware of AIR's difficulties. As early as 1971, she wrote to Peter outlining her concerns. Peter left London that year to take up a DAAD scholarship in Berlin. He was still on the Council of Management but was not so hands-on anymore. Letty was the cord keeping him tethered to AIR's activities in London; she was his eyes and ears.

In a letter, typed on paper so browned with age it appears burnt, Letty writes that AIR needed an advocate, someone upfront, a 'defined sales person'.[15] She wasn't the right person for the job, preferring to be behind the scenes. The index was too 'easily bypassed' she explained; it needed to 'define its limits and policies'.[16] Reading this, I wonder whether Letty is being self-reflexive or just lacking in confidence.

Despite her awareness of its limitations, Letty was (and continues to be) an advocate of AIR. We talk about the registry as something visionary, its utopian 'open to all' policy a direct challenge to the gatekeeping elitism of the art world. My favourite document in the archive is a letter she wrote to the editors of *Artscribe*, in response to its critical article 'Air Cuts', published in April 1977. Although Letty had left the registry more than a year before, her anger is palpable: 'Please check your facts before your magazine knocks something up'.[17] The article itself, written by Terence Maloon and Peter Rippon, is annotated extensively by Letty's hand. Whole sentences are highlighted, either with a wavy inquisitive line or a harsher double line, the pressure of her pencil apparent in its tone and indentation. Words like 'NOT SO' or 'inaccurate' appear in the margins. In her letter, she counters the article's claims about the registry's lack of publicity drives, and she clarifies details concerning the organisation's origin. Towards the end of the letter, she reminds the editors of the registry's pre-eminence and its adoption as a model by 'most Regional Arts Associations, the Crafts Advisory Council and similar schemes',[18] which, she argues, should be considered 'some measure of its success'.[19]

Letty's argument was vindicated in an ironic twist; within two years of the ACGB withdrawing its registry funding, it had set up its own registry. In contrast to AIR, the ACGB Index was for those artists already included within its collection and, according to Peter, was 'well financed, with a staff of superannuated employees'.[20] Although imitation might be considered the sincerest form of flattery, this derivation was limited to content and did not extend to supporting or offering services to artists. The ACGB venture failed and, to Peter's knowledge, closed within a year: 'So much for State Patronage'.[21]

It's difficult not to fixate on what's been lost. I ask Letty if there was ever an awareness of the future, of the index as a potential archive. She doesn't think so. The registry was firmly in the present, an urgent project always meant to be in use. Writing now, from a digital context in which even our most innocuous activities are automatically archived, this lack of posterity feels unimaginable, unfortunate but also radical.

Notes

1 Peter Townsend quoted in Lynn MacRitchie, 'AIR & SPACE', *Art Monthly*, Issue 156, May 1992, pp. 6–7.

2 Peter Sedgley, 'The Dying Galleries' in *The Lively Arts*, BBC Radio 3, 8 November 1967.

3 Ibid.

4 Nick Green, *From Factories to Fine Art: The origins and evolution of East London's artists' agglomeration, 1968–98* (London: Southern Universities Press, 2012), p. 38.

5 Peter Sedgley, email correspondence with the author, 18 July 2016.

6 Ibid.

7 January 1978, SPACE Archive.

8 Minutes, Council of Management Meeting of Art Services Grants Limited, 14 September 1978, SPACE Archive.

9 Annual Report, Annual General Meeting Art Services Grants Limited, 19 April 1977, SPACE Archive.

10 Minutes, Council of Management Meeting of Art Services Grants Limited, 14 September 1978, SPACE Archive.

11 Ibid.

12 Jennifer Warren, 'Gallery Report', 6 December 1977, SPACE Archive.

13 Terence Maloon and Peter Rippon, 'AIR CUTS', *Artscribe*, no. 6, 1977, pp. 11–16.

14 Peter Bird, letter to Peter Townsend, 23 December 1976.

15 Letty Mooring, letter to Peter Sedgley, 13 December 1971.

16 Ibid.

17 Letty Mooring, letter to James Faure-Walker, 20 May 1977.

18 Ibid.

19 Ibid.

20 Peter Sedgley, email correspondence with the author, 18 July 2016.

21 Ibid.

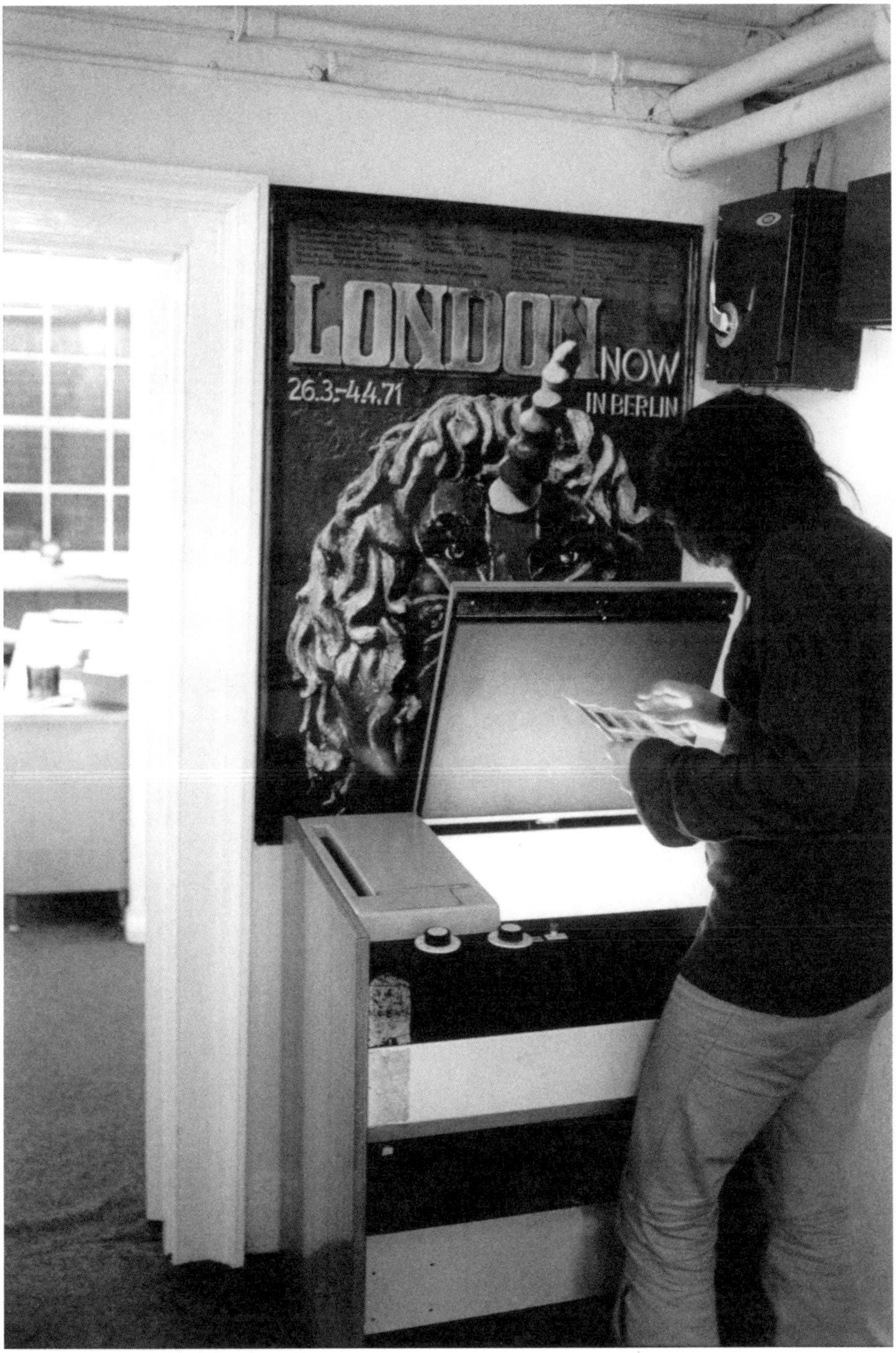

Hugh Gilbert in the AIR office at St Katharine Docks.
Photo © Ingeborg Lommatzsch, 1972

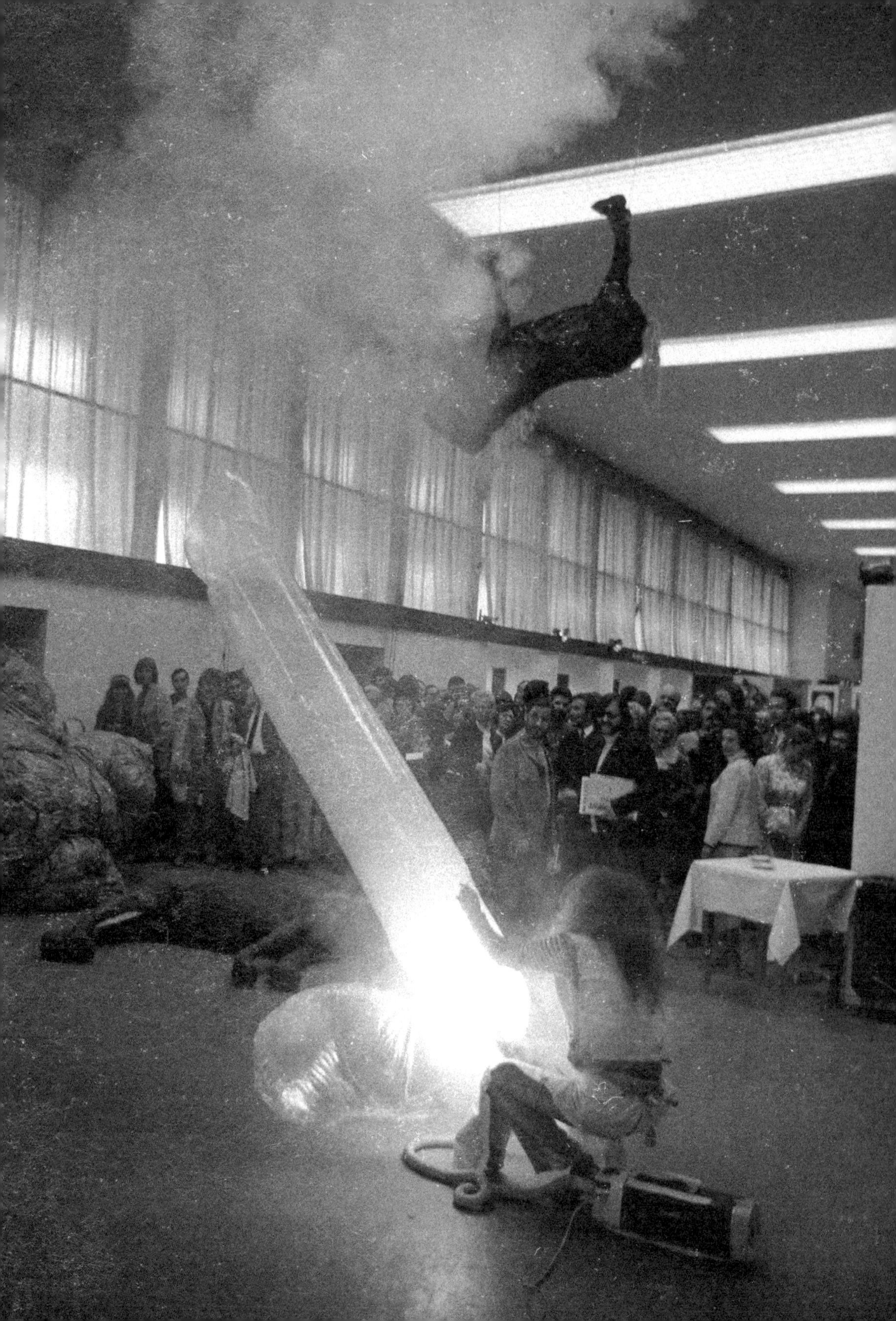

Art in London today: a way out of the dilemma

Robert Kudielka

First published in the exhibition catalogue London Now in Berlin, *Akademie der Kűnste Berlin 1971.*

The liveliest art scene in London today is to be found less and less in the London galleries. It is true that the moguls of Mayfair continue to show contemporary painting and sculpture, but their taste for the glories of the past detaches them from the living art of the present. The galleries are reluctant to commit themselves, to take risks, particularly since the already precarious situation in the English art business (which is finding it increasingly difficult to attract a private clientele) has been damaged by the prevailing economic crisis.

The number of galleries which have been forced to close is alarming. In 1967, McRoberts and Tunnard, who specialised in English Op art, gave up; a year later, the Hamilton Galleries, who had backed Hard Edge, and Robert Fraser, the leading promoter of Pop, packed in, followed by Signals and Indica, both Kinetic galleries; and finally, in 1970, the Axiom Gallery, home of the Constructivists, disappeared from the scene.

Not that the difficulties of the London Art trade are all economic – if the most promising art is to be found outside the galleries, this is due as much as anything to the new independence shown by the artists themselves. Indeed English painters and sculptors have always been in a position to treat their dealers rather cavalierly, since their habit of holding down small but well-paid teaching posts in the numerous art schools makes them less reliant on sales. In the past two years, however, the gap between artists and dealers has widened to an almost complete separation, because the latest developments in contemporary art make it impossible for most galleries to discharge even their primary function of providing exhibition space.

British artists creating a happening during the opening of London Now
at the Akademie der Künste, Berlin, 1971, with Scotty SWIZ setting an inflatable prick on fire.

There are many young sculptors for whom the small rooms of a gallery are simply unsuitable, while, on the other hand, the second generation of Action painters and especially the Conceptual artists are naturally unwelcome in smart galleries whose whole basis is the material value of works of art. So it is hardly surprising that more and more artists prefer to show their work to interested visitors in their studios. But how many independent artists can find or afford a well-proportioned, well-lit studio? It is as difficult to find as a committed, properly spacious and financially sound gallery.

The credit for being the first to discover a way out of the dilemma must go, without doubt, to a group of former students of St Martin's School of Art, who, in 1967, leased an empty warehouse – the Stockwell Depot in South-East London – and turned it into studios and exhibition spaces.

But the idea of artists' self-help was finally realised by SPACE Ltd. This is a collective association which has the purpose of providing artists with studio space, formed by the painter Peter Sedgley, who was himself looking for a studio. In 1968, Sedgley discovered St Katharine Docks, a group of buildings in a long-abandoned part of dockland near Tower Bridge. He saw at once that here, at reasonable cost, there was room for a large number of artists to work.

He succeeded, with Bridget Riley and several other friends, in renting these warehouses, and, with the help of private and public contributions, made possible the necessary interior alterations so that, early in 1969, 90 painters and sculptors were able to move in.

However, the need for studios and the crisis in the art trade were not the only reasons for founding SPACE. Artists, and especially English artists, are usually too individualistic to show much interest in group activity for its own sake; if they move in that direction it is because they are driven by real distress. It was also the lack of contact and exchange, those indispensable ingredients of any creative life, that added to the timely momentum of SPACE.

A German visitor may easily misunderstand the situation in England; he may assume that once a lively and attractive centre like London exists, quite naturally important cultural activities will exist and thrive in this propitious atmosphere. But the appalling isolation and the sense of frustration felt by the artists in London during the late '60s is striking evidence to the contrary.

When several of the most important contemporary English artists – among them Robyn Denny, Richard Smith, John Hoyland and Phillip King – turn their backs on the 'Swinging City' and retire to the country, this is clear indication. Even the painter Peter Blake, who, more than any other artist, had drawn on the folklore of the metropolis, has buried himself in the solitary, if idyllic, refuge of a disused railway halt.

SPACE attempts to remedy this situation; it acts as a kind of catalyst, in the sense that artists who work under the same roof will be brought into contact with one another without pressure. The importance of this sort of casual contact has been well demonstrated by earlier developments in English art. One can hardly think of English Pop without those discussions on the theme of 'Continuum fine art – pop art' which the critic Lawrence Alloway arranged in the Institute of Contemporary Arts at the beginning of the '50s. Both Richard Hamilton and Eduardo Paolozzi developed on the basis of these discussions. And one may date the emergence of Hard Edge to the Situation exhibition of 1960.

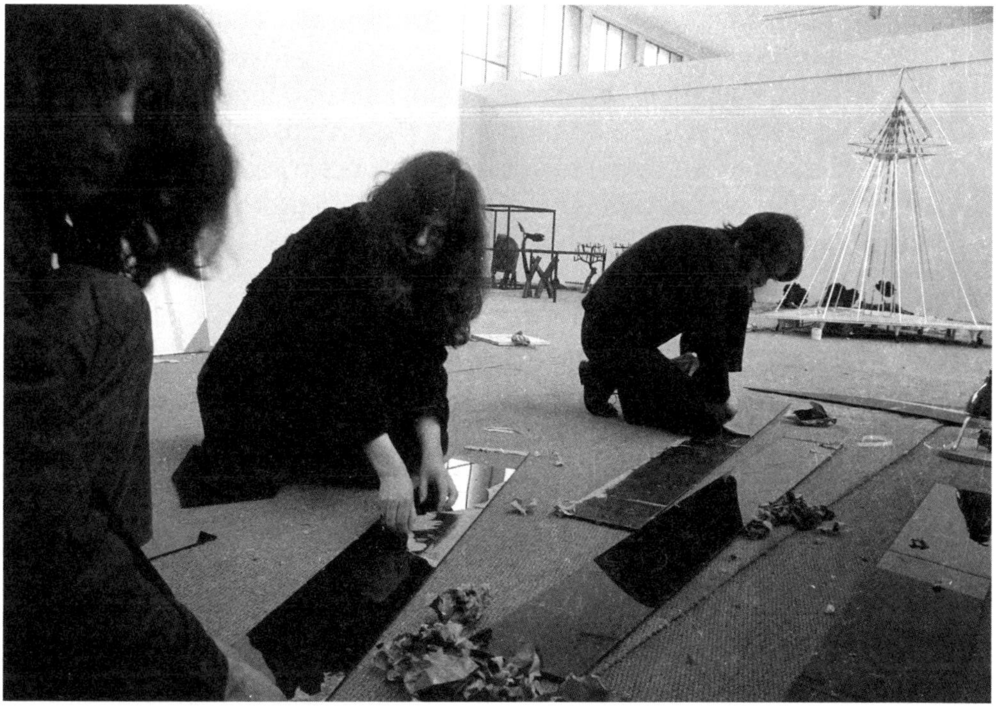

Artists applying finishing touches to the exhibition London Now in Berlin at the Akademie der Künste in Berlin, 1971.

It was again Alloway who pushed certain artists living in the neighbourhood of Camden Square (Turnbull, the brothers Cohen, Peter Coviello, Denny and others), on the basis of endless discussions in their studios, into that common endeavour.

The new English sculpture, London's most recent contribution to modern art, certainly began with Anthony Caro's voluntary evening classes at St Martin's School of Art, in which the participants encouraged each other to embark on some daring sculptural experiments. In short, it was the spark of a common departure that made artists jump the barrier of insular provincialism.

One may measure what is new in SPACE, as compared with what the earlier group activities attempted, by observing the change which has taken place in the relationship between artists and society over the last twenty years. The London version of Pop art started with the ambitious aim of creating a direct link between art and the rapidly growing mass culture, the American-type consumerism and entertainment industry of the post-war period. In this context, Hamilton set out to forge the epic of a technological civilisation.

Later, at the end of the '50s, the artists adopted a new attitude to society, diametrically opposed to those earlier attitudes: Hard Edge claimed to hold up against the contemporary world's moral indifference a strict counter-image. William Turnbull's rigorous standpoint – the picture as an ethical statement – still holds good today.

With Anthony Caro's attempt at St Martin's to boost more radical thinking about sculpture, a new reconciliation between art and society appeared on the horizon, even if on a very elitist level. But this possibility was crushed by the global cultural upheaval of 1968 that affected English art schools in common with so many other educational establishments all over the world.

At the end of the '60s, artists in London were overcome with a new sense of frustration; everyday iconography had been proven commercially corrupted; moral sentiments seemed overstrung and hollow; art schools, as well as the art trade, had lost their reputation. Add to that the distressing problem of studio space – in summa, no encouraging situation for independent artists in any regard.

At this point, Peter Sedgley came up with his idea and put it into action: an artists' association which would organise itself of its own accord. The practical needs of artists in society were so pressing that they eclipsed questions of style and conceptual dissent. The important thing was to make sure that artists could

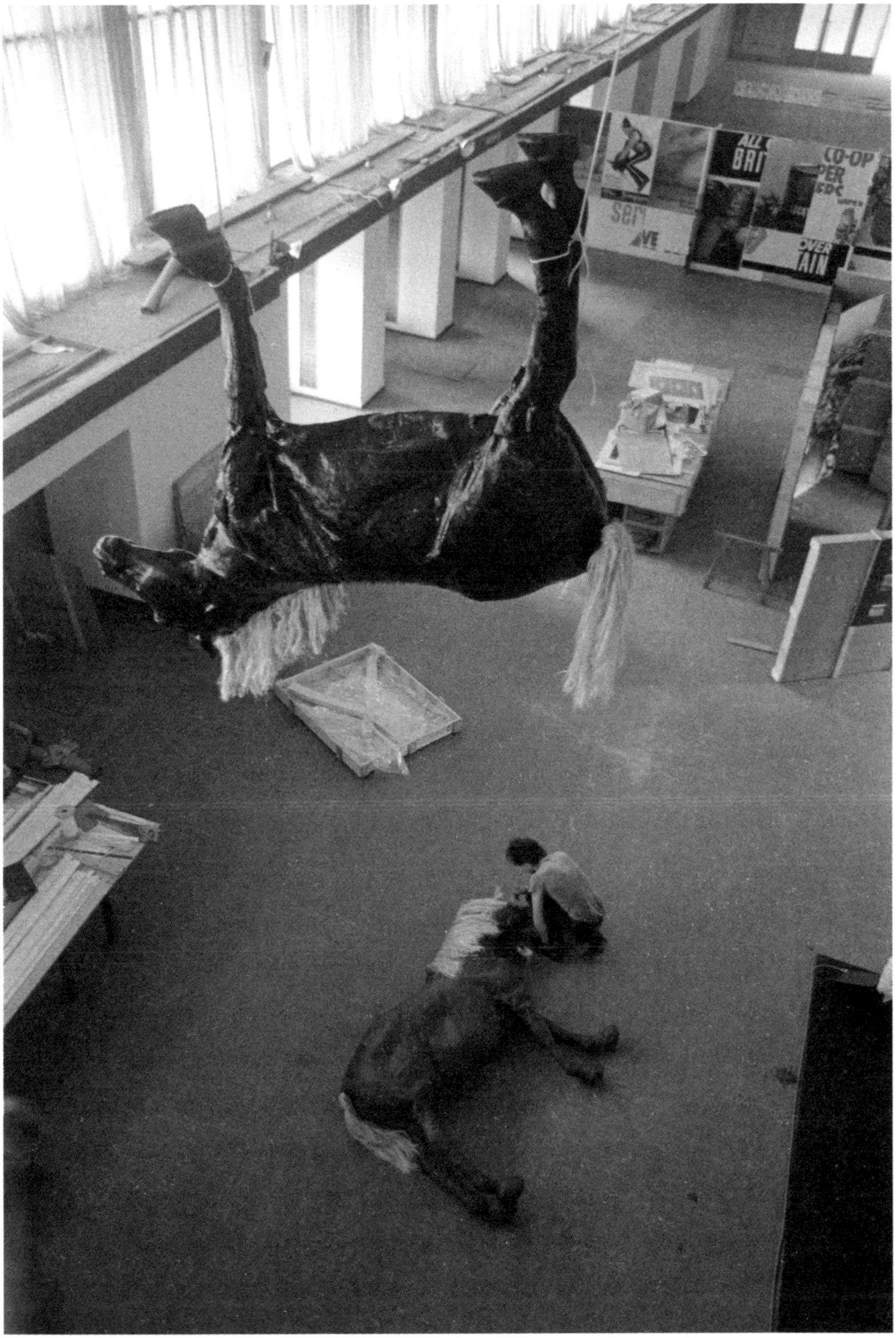

Artists applying finishing touches to the exhibition London Now in Berlin
at the Akademie der Künste in Berlin, 1971.

keep working. SPACE did not proclaim that art should move in any new direction; it simply counted on artists' solidarity in the basic matter of professional existence. Of course it was hoped that, out of such a working community, some artistic development might grow. The Stockwell depot had already established itself as a centre of Conceptual art in England. But SPACE made it a fundamental principle to avoid regimenting the work of the artists involved.

The organisation concerns itself only with practical administrative details: committees deal with applications and the apportioning of working space; an information section records the list of works and the curriculum vitae of each artist; and Peter Tunnard, who had been a director of McRoberts and Tunnard, was invited to negotiate sales to the growing number of clients. Even so, this relatively loose form of coordination was enough to turn SPACE into an important factor in the art world. Even the Arts Council of Great Britain cannot ignore a body which takes care of more than three hundred individual studios all over London.

The idea of an artists' work community, as it has been put into practice in St Katharine Docks, is now respected, beyond the little circle of the art world, by the general public. When, towards the end of last year, it became likely that the dock buildings would soon be demolished, the Greater London Council promptly offered the Old Jewish Boys School in Stepney as an alternative.

In political terms, there is a principal difference between this London venture and the Californian artists' communes which turn their backs on civilisation or other seemingly related projects. Because it is only concerned with the basic practical interests of the individual artist, SPACE Ltd does also not share the socio-political views which prompted the Westbeth Corporation in New York to convert the Bell Telephone Company's abandoned laboratories into a comprehensive art centre.

Aside from the obvious differences that distinguish the collective efforts of artists at the beginning of the '70s, there is one common tendency which deserves attention: it seems as though artists will take up the challenge of society's indifference to the basic prerequisites of art and will increasingly present themselves as a group.

It is ironic that, of all places, it should be in a dark corner of English history, near the Tower of London, in buildings made for the coarse traffic of imperialism, that an idea was born which one hopes, paraphrasing Nietzsche, may lead 'on pigeons' feet' into the future.

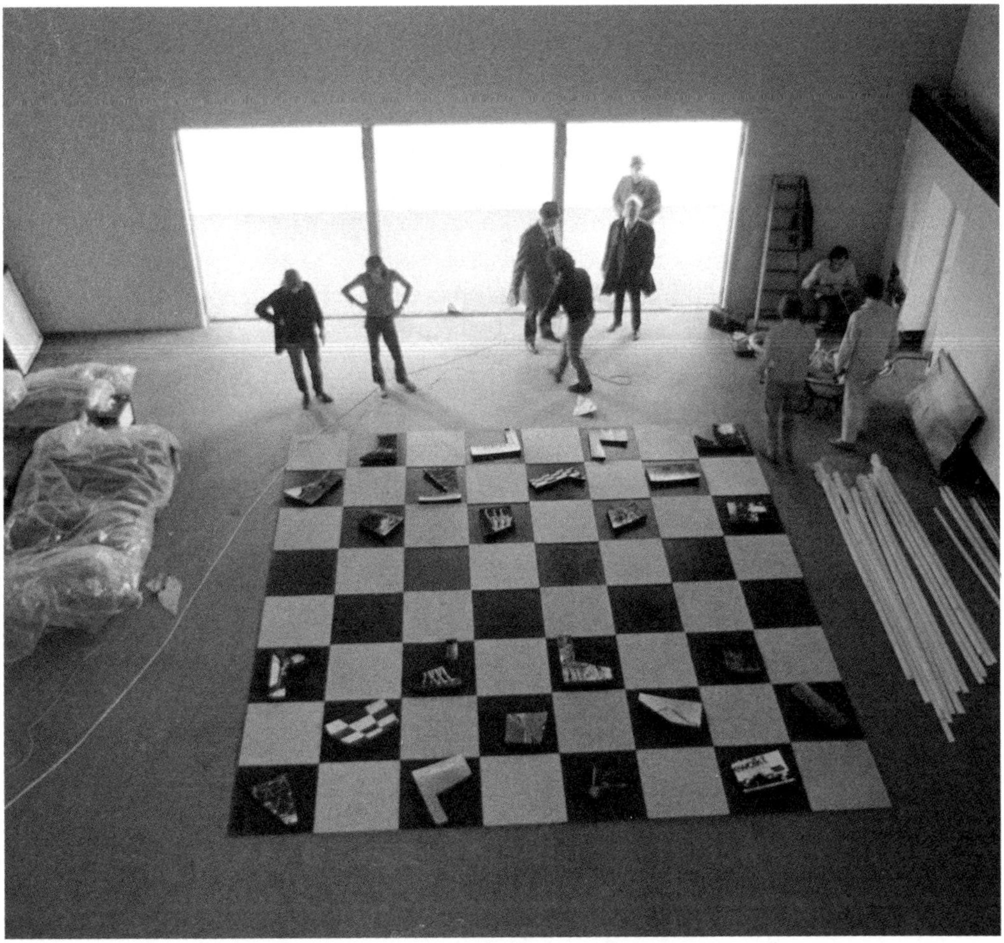

Aerial view of artists finishing the installation of AIR's exhibition London Now in Berlin at the Akademie der Künste, Berlin, 1971.

70s
Artists & Studios

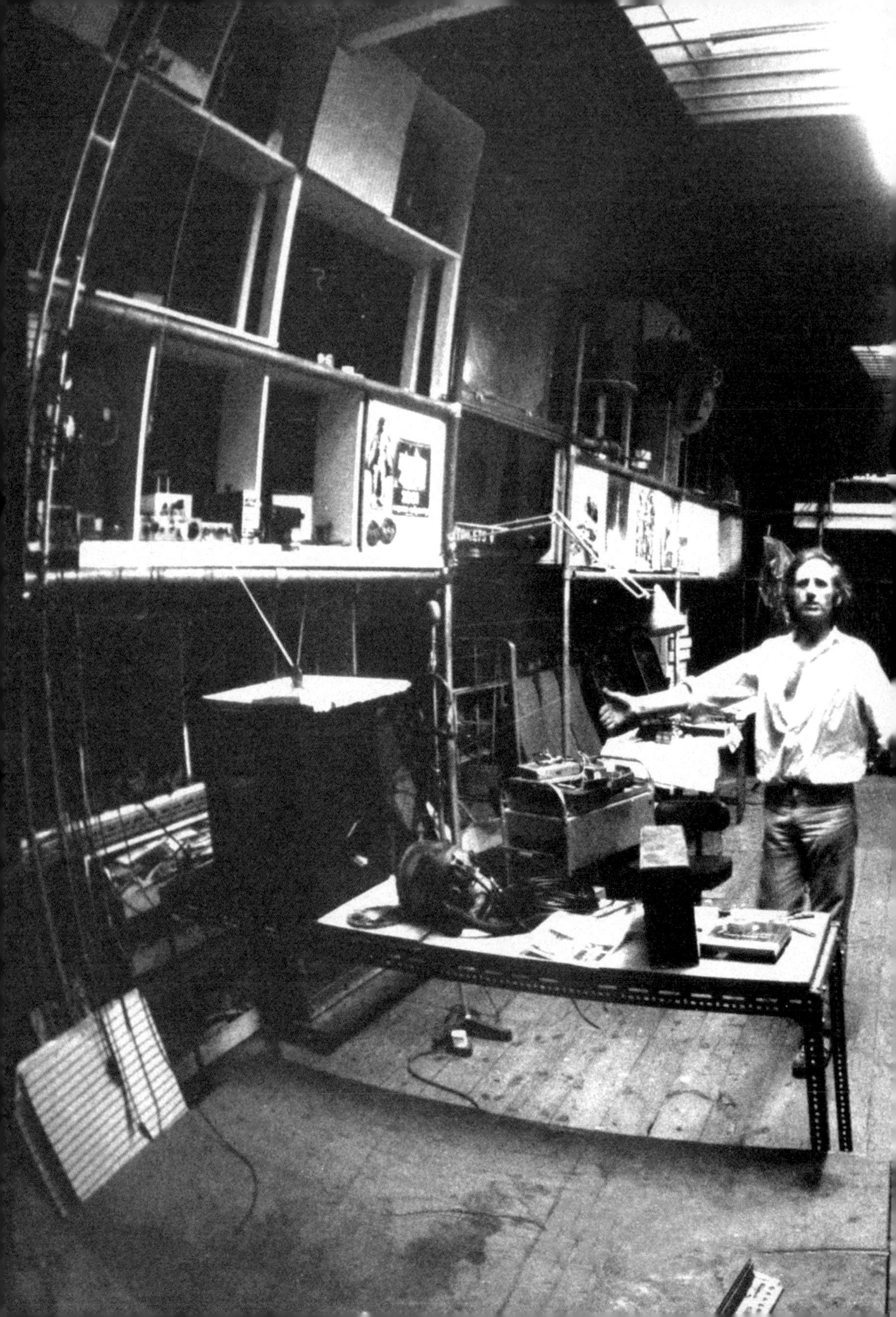

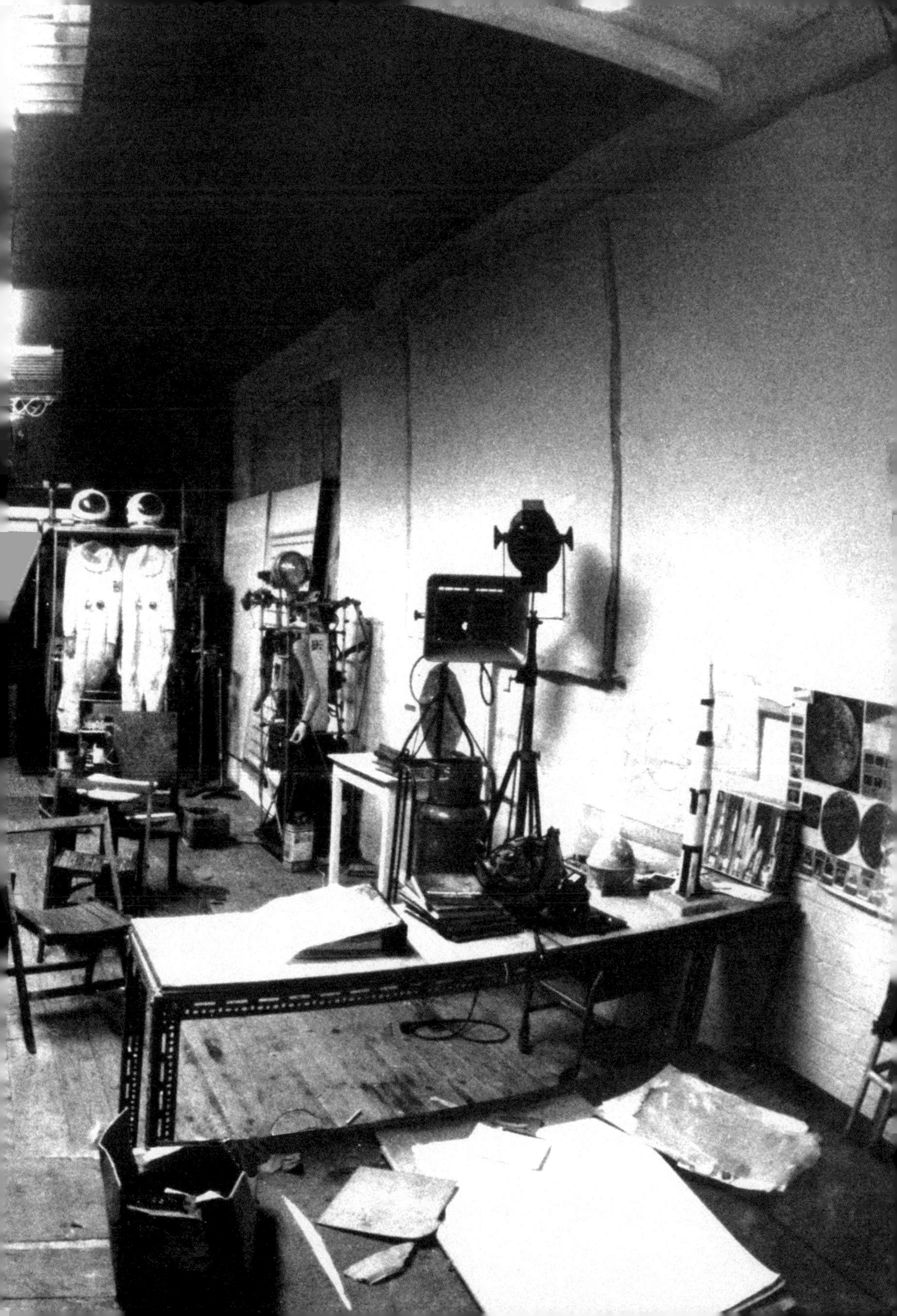

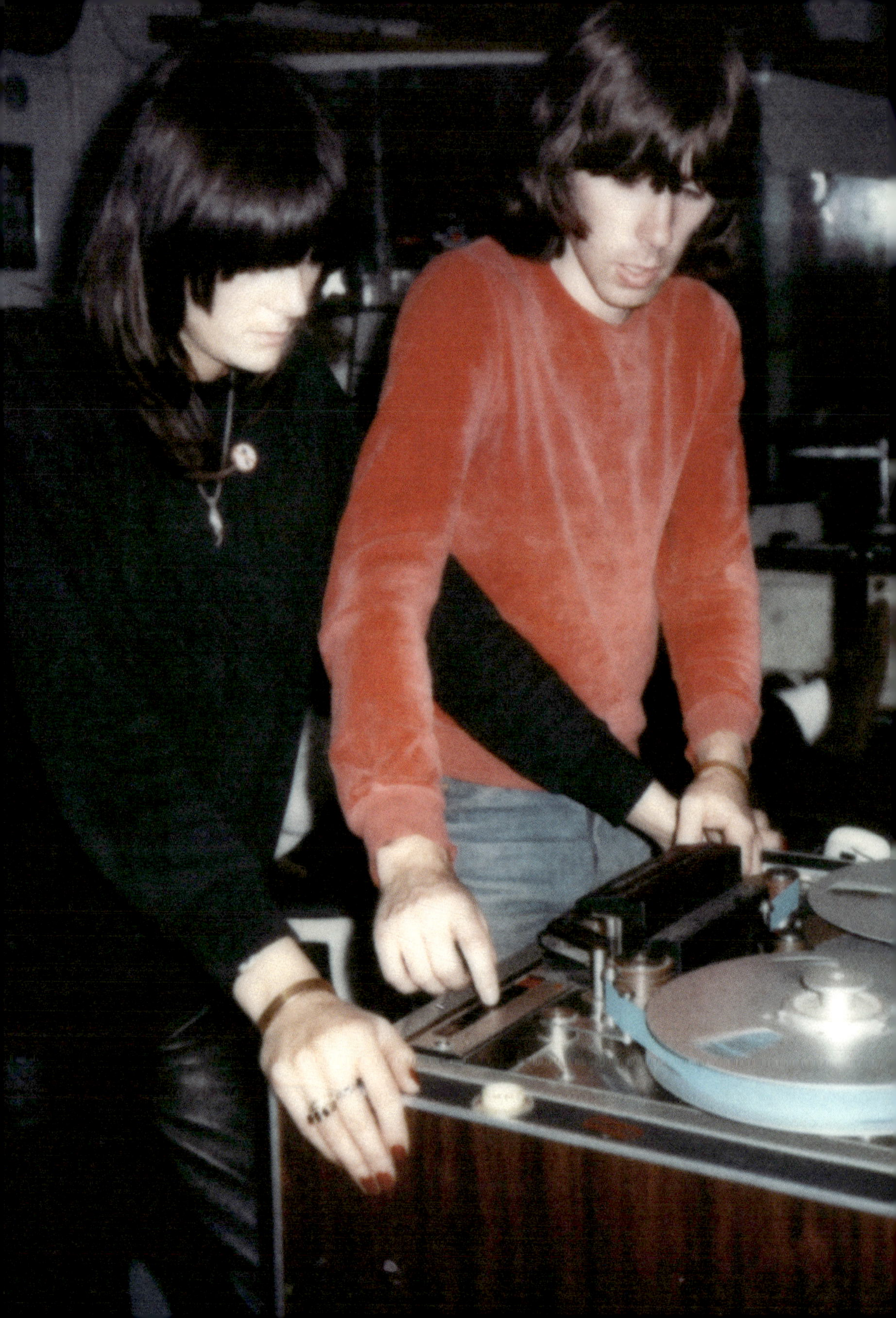

Industrial Ritual Performance SPACE

William Fowler

> The development of the conceptual and performance genres changed the rules of art till it became virtually unrecognisable to those who had thought it was theirs. The art activity flowed into darkness beyond traditional boundaries and explored areas that were previously as unmapped and mysterious as the other side of the moon. In recent years a tendency has been underway to close the book on this investigation, to contract again around the commodifiable aesthetic object, and to forget the sometimes frightening visions of the other side. Yet if one opens the book - and it will not go away - the strange record is still there, like the fragmentary journals of explorers in new lands, filled with apparently unanswerable questions.[1]

The SPACE studio building at 10 Martello Street, Hackney, London, feels dark and labyrinthine. Previously a trouser factory, it contains numerous rooms, passageways and tunnels which turn in unexpected directions. The basement curls around a corner before suddenly stopping, and damp persists on the walls and make-shift roof of the basement walkway. There is also a more solid looking cottage in the open and ample courtyard. Recent developments include new roofs, windows, partitions and extensive decoration. The complex has provided studios to artists for some 45 years.

It was perhaps because of its unusual structure and ambience that, in 1970, artists working in experimental filmmaking and installation were attracted to the building. Art soon began to take over 10 Martello Street and to bleed out into the neighbouring London Fields and into the Caribbean-themed All Nations nightclub where regular SPACE visitor John Lacey, amongst others, presented lightshows.

Preceding spread Bruce Lacey in his studio at Martello Street, early '70s.
Photo: © Ingeborg Sedgley

Chris Carter & Cosey Fanni Tutti working a rented multirack at Industrial Records studio, Martello Street, Hackney, in 1979. Polaroid photo: Sleazy (Peter Christopherson)

In cultural terms, the area became best known as the stomping ground for pioneering 'industrial' band Throbbing Gristle, and several of their record covers featured photographs of the grey roads and byways near Martello Street, where members Cosey Fanni Tutti and Genesis P-Orridge shared a basement studio. Transgressive titles and suggestive photos collided in collage fashion with an image of a canal, an industrial space and a local Tesco on records *Something Came Over Me*, *United* and *D.o.A: The Third and Final Annual Report* respectively – all of which they released themselves.[2] Band pictures were also shot close by.

Throbbing Gristle, which formally began in late 1976, had evolved out of the art performance collective COUM Transmissions whilst also drawing in Chris Carter and Peter 'Sleazy' Christopherson. Each member introduced a unique element and their music collided abrasive, DIY electronic technologies; free improvisation; and spoken or shouted vocals. Imagery was urban, aggressive, disturbed and alienating. Their controversial tendencies extended to renaming Martello Street Studios the 'death factory', referencing both the Nazi death camps and the victims of the black death that they said were buried beneath London Fields. It all felt shockingly new as the four-piece accumulated a considerable following, but, by way of COUM Transmissions and SPACE, it sat within a larger, localised art experimentation context.

Cosey Fanni Tutti and Genesis P-Orridge arrived at Martello Street from Hull in 1974. 'We were close to a number of people including our studio neighbours Bill Meyer, Robin Klassnik and SPACE caretaker extraordinaire Bruce Lacey,' Cosey Fanni Tutti recalled, but the building 'was so large that we didn't meet some of the artists at all'.[3] First visiting in 1972, she had been shown around by Lacey and observed 'his amazing workshop full of sculptures and robots, an Aladdin's cave of disparate parts awaiting assembly alongside experimental electronic machines, synthesizers, effects units and circuit boards'.[4]

Bruce Lacey was a powerful presence, but the decision to informally invite him[5] to join as caretaker was a curious one given his long-standing reputation as a member of the absurdist comedy circuit, working with the Goons, before then re-establishing himself as an artist in the mid to late '60s (largely pulling on art school contacts from the 1950s). The robot contraptions and automata that he exhibited turned up in feature films such as *Smashing Time* (1967), and he was often on TV. To many, he appeared to be from a distinctly different generation to the younger artists at Martello Street. For one, he had served in the Navy during World War Two (his references to war were more oblique than Throbbing Gristle's), and he was in his 40s. Lacey's then wife, Jill Bruce (now Smith, and hereafter referred to as such), thought some artists resented that they'd been given the free live-in caretaker's cottage. But, with three children in tow, they were struggling, indicating what it meant on the ground to be an artist at that time, even a moderately well-known one.[6]

Lacey had arrived at SPACE as a kind of industrial engineer artist before blossoming into other areas, as did Jill Smith, finding new contacts and new ways of making work and critiquing authority. Their children wandered the studios, turning the building into a playground of sorts whilst infecting it with a kind of non-nuclear-family domesticity that would become an important part of their parents' art. Kevin, who lived there between the ages of ten and 17, remembered:

> […] there were some really interesting people that were working there. You'd know, they were maybe in their studio and you'd knock on their door and go in and maybe hang out with them for half a day. I spent quite a lot of time with a guy called Jules Baker, and he used to do these sort of blow-up things that were like inflatables, and he also made some *Doctor Who* monsters [the Axons, made with creative partner Rosie Antrobus]. In the days before it was very easy to make an inflatable, you'd have made things out of canvas and then latex and seal it all. At one point, he did these huge great sumo wrestlers that you'd wear on your back, all inflatable, that might have been thirty-feet tall. He did all sorts of really interesting things that you'd bounce and jump on.[7]

Speaking in 2017, Kevin also recalled Peter Dockley:

He used to do castings, and he'd cast his body in wax in sections and make life-sized figures of himself. One of them, he embedded seeds and nuts in the wax, and he had them seated in chairs in a cage about the size of a room, and then left them and let loads of rats in there. So, the rats slowly ate away at the wax to get at the seeds. There was another piece he did where he had maybe ten or fifteen wax figures of himself standing and sitting in various positions in a big room and he did a time lapse film where he very slowly, with a blow-torch, melted them.[8] His studio was amazing. He had these huge glass jars with objects inside that he'd use for casting. For my twelfth birthday, as a present, he made me a figure of a crucifix about two-foot high of Jesus made of wax but the head was replaced with an elephant's head - a Ganesh.[9]

Artists rejecting the commercial gallery system instead explored the gaps between technology and art, objects and performance, passivity and participation. Options exploded and traditional notions of how a fine artist might support themselves – i.e. through sales or patronage – changed radically.

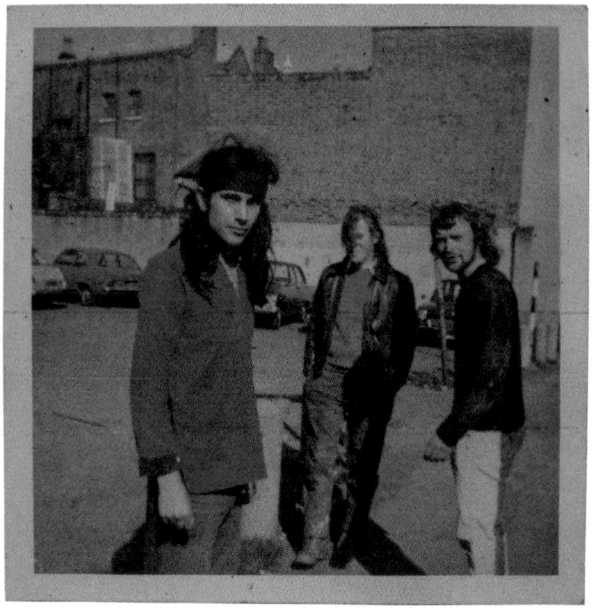

Robin Klassnik with friends in front of Martello Street studio.
Polaroid photo: © Kathryn Klassnik, 1972

This openness regarding what constituted art extended, in Robin Klassnik's case, into a practice that encompassed 8mm film, photography, mail-art and performance, plus a distinct blurring between artist, curator and exhibitor. Moving from St Katharine Docks to Martello Street in 1971, he opened his personal studio in 1979 as Matt's Gallery and invited artists to create site-specific pieces. (He had been heavily involved in SPACE's 1975 Open Studios, an important, London-wide event.) The new venture opened with David Troostwyk's *Our Famous Culture: An audio cassette/object work*,[10] and important exhibitions by Rose Finn-Kelcey, Willie Doherty, Susan Hiller and Richard Wilson, amongst others, followed. Matt's moved from Martello Street in the 1990s and still exerts considerable influence. Speaking to Anna Harding, SPACE Chief Executive, in 2017, Klassnik described SPACE as his 'formative education'.[11]

In the 1970s, in the absence of a traditional fine art model, including its finance, who would support this new type of art and happenings culture, and how?

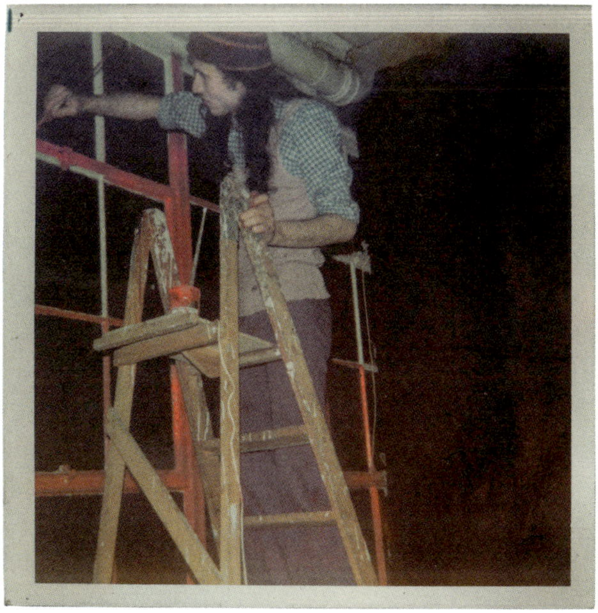

Robin Klassnik painting the crittall windows in his Martello Street studio either red or white. Polaroid photo: © Kathryn Klassnik, 1972

The Arts Council of Great Britain (ACGB) stepped up and established its New Activities Committee in 1969, which transformed into the Experimental Projects Committee, operational from 1970 to 1973. The latter recognised the movement's 'apparent opposition to established art forms and methods of presentation'.[12] Artists were required to outline their activities and expenditure for the year ahead, including all operational, administrative costs and promotion, and, if successful, received an annual stipend. Performance activity was supported by way of the ACGB brochure magazine, *Groupvine*; artists sent in an A4 page describing their projects, and the sheets were circulated to recognised regional arts venues. It also enabled international connections.[13] A demand for clarity reduced the spontaneity and variety that much of this art had actively courted in preceding years; the professionalisation process arguably pushing down the movement's appealing, rough edges by way of the introduction of categories.[14] But in the words of Smith: 'it enabled us to do all the work we did – we couldn't have done it otherwise'. Smith and Lacey received funding for several years, beginning in 1974 with 'Stella Superstar and Her Amazing Galactic Adventures', an apocalyptic sci-fi touring project that incorporated performance, music, sculptural structures and expanded cinema.[15] (The structures were built in the inner courtyard at Martello Street – a large space that encouraged numerous artists to increase the scale of their activities.)

By identifying themselves as 'performance artists' for the purposes of funding, COUM Transmissions received their first grant in 1971 and a bursary in 1974,[16] following their move to London. They had reacted with Fluxus-style pranksterism to government attempts to measure, support and arguably contain art and labour in 1972, however, by forming The Ministry of Anti-Social Security. They distributed official-looking forms that used the language of social security whilst evoking the practice of the art strike, later associated with Gustav Metzger: 'I declare that, for each day, for which the register opposite bears my signature or is marked '"NO ART" I did no art'.[17] In her autobiography, *Art Sex Music*, Cosey Fanni Tutti described how this 'represented our opposition to defining people and art, and was an ironic, cynical statement in the form of a playful twist on the bureaucracy of government form-filling, filing systems and qualification criteria that we knew so well from applying for our Arts Council grant and our time signing on'.[18] Throbbing Gristle's resistant stance could also be found in COUM. Proposed performance 'Tree of Life' used chance strategies, à la John Cage, to determine where each performance should take place, thus avoiding the official Arts Council venue tour circuit. Their application was rejected. COUM's use of props, projections, films, tapes and flashing lights included 1972's *The Alien Brain*, which, billed as 'A Journey Through Inner Space to Another Dimension', evoked and yet preceded the Laceys' *Journey Through a Black Hole to a Coloured Planet*. The two groups had yet to meet properly, but it indicated a shared thinking about the transformative potential of otherworldly play.[19] *COUMing of Age* from 1974 benefited from full ACGB support as the group moved towards sexualised, extreme, bodily actions.

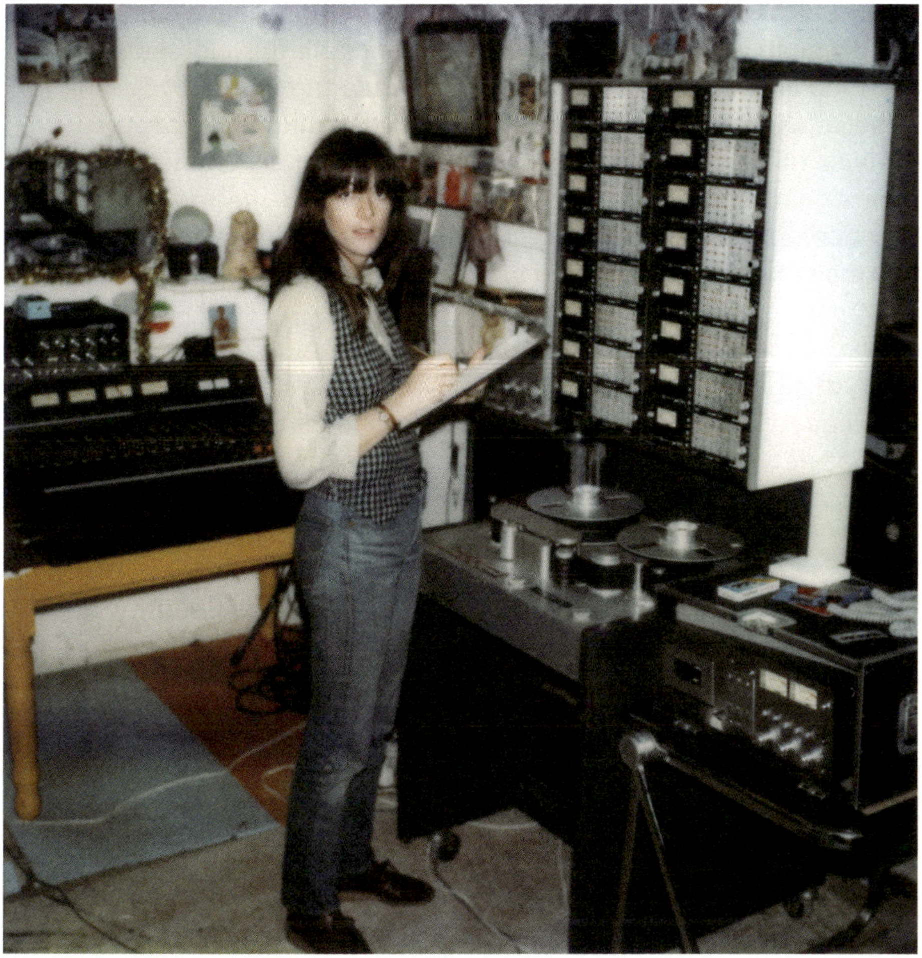

Cosey Fanni Tutti at the Industrial Records studio, Martello Street, Hackney, 1979.
Photo: © Industrial Records

In many respects, COUM resisted the arts funding system that fed them and by transforming into Throbbing Gristle (having also shed old members for new) they finally, and fully, turned their backs on these models. Curiously, the first Throbbing Gristle album still mimicked the language of officialdom, however. *The Second Annual Report* was intended as 'a specialist government report, or thesis. It's just information on how far sound researches have got after a year' P-Orridge told artist Paul Buck.[20] It was as though previous attempts to describe and control them had created an opposing, contrary force, arguably contributing to their very identity. SPACE continued to support them, regardless.

Whilst the art object, with all its attendant aura, had been firmly rejected by many in the wake of the 1960s happenings, the same could not be said of technology, particularly in its cheaper, more kit-like forms, which combined a DIY professionalism with affordable consumer prices – important for sound enthusiasts who could not contemplate the formidable cost of a Moog synthesiser. In the case of the newly-formed Throbbing Gristle, this allowed whole new audio worlds to be unlocked via equipment built – and regularly tweaked – by Chris Carter, 'an avid electronics magazine buyer and builder of circuits'.[21]

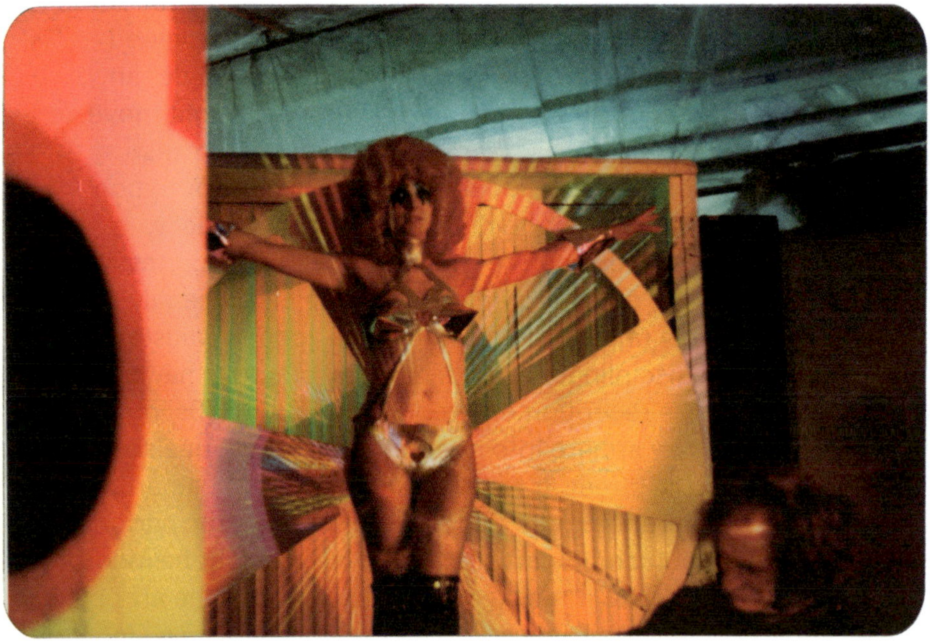

On the set of the film *The Lacey Rituals* (1972).
Photo: © Jill Smith and Tiffany Lacey-Edwards

The sourcing, construction and creative potential of new electronics materials provided a common currency between artists otherwise separated by studio walls and the pressures of making work. They also provided a conduit for Carter to be brought into Throbbing Gristle through John Lacey, Bruce Lacey's son from his first marriage, with whom Carter had stayed in Muswell Hill. Another electronics enthusiast, John Lacey became technical director of COUM in its later stages (going under the name John Gunni Busck) and has regularly collaborated with Carter and Fanni Tutti.[22] Listed in *Groupvine*, John's 1970s group, Vacuum Multimedia Theatre Troupe, went beyond official confines and moved between lightshows, slides, 8mm semi-narrative filmmaking, dance/performance – including an action in which Lacey stole a tripod from a camera crew and danced with it – and experimental electronic music, seemingly in any iteration, often foregrounding technological equipment and John Lacey's relationship to it.

Like Carter, Lacey was proactively engaged in electronic kit construction; he read *Practical Electronics* magazine and regularly visited Crescent Radio in Wood Green, obtaining equipment and circuit boards, thus expanding the psychogeographical map of Martello Street. John Lacey did not have a studio at SPACE, but he used the open, internal courtyard to build, document and practise with his set-up. Like Bruce Lacey's other son, Kevin, he slipped between different studios. Performance in his eyes became 'an increasingly defined area, but in the 1970s an artist might move fluidly between different types of activity'[23] and, for him, also different groups. John was an influential figure in the formation of Throbbing Gristle, assisting technically and conceptually, also performing with them before they solidified as a quartet. He assumed a similar, or even greater role in the Lacey Family. It's difficult to concretely unpick, but his influence appears substantial.

Art as a multi-disciplinary, even theatrical, practice may be familiar today, but its reception differed in the early 1970s, moving away from the gallery sphere into not just art centres but also houses, pubs and the street. It became an abstracted, cathartic activity, often foregrounding the audience as much as the performers. Film was newly embraced by artists, and, while it might be incorporated into larger projects, it resisted the uniqueness of the art object by way of its capacity for duplication. As the 2003 Norwich Gallery show On General Release: Artists and Films in Britain 1968–1972 asserted, artists could simultaneously present the same single work in multiple iterations, in multiple venues (though, in practice, usually only one or two prints were ever actually made). Several 16mm films were shot, edited or conceptualised at Martello Street, sometimes using new cameras and film stocks introduced at the end of the 1960s. Technology was increasingly becoming a key part of art, or art as it was reimagined.

The Lacey Rituals (1972) captured the ritualised minutiae (and at times mania) of Lacey and Smith's daily family life as performed at Martello Street. Mistakes/mis-takes, clapper boards and re-takes were all wilfully included and the results screened in both cinemas and galleries. *After Cease to Exist* (1977) by Throbbing Gristle featured, by way of contrast, black film leader, footage of the group performing in Southampton, and a vigorous fake castration, all rendered in grainy black and white. Throbbing Gristle's abrasive music provided the soundtrack, but, in keeping with their reworking of the relationship between art and music/commerce, the finished article was defiantly more faux snuff and experimental film than proto-pop video. Both works, just two examples from a whole new wave of artist activity, took film in unexpected, off-the-map directions.

From the perspective of traditional fine art, films and records engaged new audiences in distinctly new ways. A small crowd was invited to Martello Street in early 1980 for the recording of Throbbing Gristle's album, *Heathen Earth*, and the event was recorded on video, whilst even more participatory forms of art activity and happenings were rolled out though Lacey Family touring projects *The Incredible Whatsit Machine* (1971), *Journey Through a Black Hole to a Coloured Planet* (1973) and *The Magic Fun Factory* (1974). By this point, Bruce Lacey had given up on 'de-programming' adults, thus signalling a further move away from the gallery, and, with his family, set-up experiences for the young, variously supplying music, microphones, costumes, climbing frames and inflatable structures. ACGB documentary *Outside In* (1973) includes footage of children romping wildly through *Journey Through a Black Hole*, with John Lacey operating tape loops. In due course, Throbbing Gristle also toured the country, but they engaged their audiences in ways more head-on and cathartically punishing (though a boy screaming into a mic looks like a proto-industrialist in a Super 8 film of *The Magic Fun Factory*.)

These new modes of public engagement brought a wider awareness of artist activity, even as artists tried to blur the boundaries between different creative zones, and Martello Street found its way onto the cultural map. In 1971, perhaps aware of his tendency towards showmanship and direct address, the BBC filmed Bruce Lacey getting off a train at London Fields and walking to Martello Street, all the while in a gravity-test space suit. The sequence opened the programme *Art and Technology*, and thereafter experimental works by sculptors David Hall and Garth Evans were discussed in considerably more sober terms.[24]

The Central Office of Information, the UK Government's marketing and communications agency, also sent a camera crew for *This Week in Britain: Space for Artists*. Sadly, the film no longer appears to exist.

Despite a flowering of more experimental modes of practice and increasing public renown, the ACGB began to reduce its support as the decade progressed. Funding in this area had never been great in comparative terms – £15,000 of the £95,500 spent across the visual arts as a whole[25] – but economic recession, following the 1973 oil crisis, and policies introduced by the new Conservative Government saw ACGB's grant-in-aid decline relative to inflation.

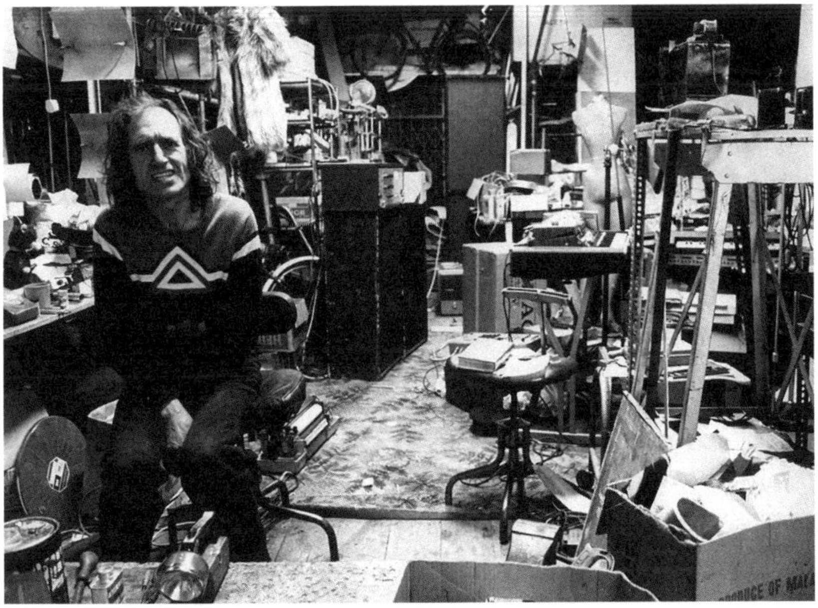

Bruce Lacey in his studio at Martello Street, early '70s.
Photographer unknown.

The ACGB's 1975–76 annual report, *The Arts in Hard Times*, appeared to unwittingly refer to both financial and cultural difficulties as the House of Lords complained about art's moral function and a new retrogressive attitude emerged.[26] Unfortunately, by now, some art groups had got so used to ACGB support that their very existence became threatened without it.

COUM and Throbbing Gristle had consciously extricated themselves from this increasingly difficult, if not outright Faustian relationship. Smith and Lacey received regular money until 1982 and thereafter ceased working together, triggering other changes in their lives. Like Throbbing Gristle, they had already moved away from performance art circles and begun attending alternative fayres in Norfolk, where they now lived, having left Martello Street in 1979. Changes in emphasis and an increasingly reactionary press and government signalled larger changes still, with no immediate signs of abating. Throbbing Gristle famously hit the front pages with their 1976 Prostitution show at the Institute of Contemporary Arts, when and where Fanni Tutti's pornographic magazine poses were exhibited amongst other objects and images, including decorated tampons.[27] Even the apparently 'family friendly' Laceys were treated to outraged column inches when misconstrued reports came in of Smith stripping for art students and Lacey, in the same session, demonstrating how to go to the toilet – both reviving ideas from *The Lacey Rituals* film (and poking-fun at the concept of 'Performance Art'). The press' full wrath was reserved, however, for the Laceys' exhibition of goat droppings (alongside a large serpentine structure, costumes, writing and other details) in the 1981 Serpentine Gallery group show Continuous Creation. In a sense, whatever the ACGB did or did not do, art remained capable of pressing buttons.

Martello Street was not unique in the development of art making through the 1970s, but it was a locus for new ideas about art forms, audiences and exhibition contexts. Much more happened in these studios than has been accounted for here, and the story of 1970s British art has been far from told – there were numerous other performance, community and expanded theatre groups – but the Laceys and Throbbing Gristle together illustrate how diverse, dynamic, exploratory and interconnected art could and can be; notable when these particular groups have historically been received very differently. SPACE was able to provide space and studios for the two modern, extended, post-nuclear families,[28] and many other artists too.

Returning to Martello Street today, still an active SPACE studio building, one looks for the imprints of history, the noise in the walls, and the marks of films and experimental sculptures made over 40 years ago, but layers of stratification have since piled up many times over, and aura – the very thing artists rejected in the 1970s – remains pleasingly absent, a reminder that it's just a building, a space to work. Martello Street's external appearance has altered relatively little, but wander the surrounding area – with its coffee shops and new roads, communities and ambience – and it's impossible to ignore the changes. About finishing the first Throbbing Gristle album back in 1977, P-Orridge noted: 'I remember going outside Martello Street as a train passed on the railway line, and there was a transistor radio blaring round the corner, and a sawmill cutting up wood, and a dog barking, and I just said, "We haven't invented anything. We've just put down what's here all the time, without knowing it"'.[29] Throbbing Gristle's abrasive, atmospheric sounds seemed to belong to both the era, and the locale.[30]

Locations resonate and SPACE Martello Street certainly occupies an important place in the history of British art. It provided a context and a site for mutually supportive dialogue, and its notable that while Smith and Fanni Tutti have felt that their groups and efforts were not then considered 'real art' by other artists – being either too 'silly' or too 'shocking' – both continue to practice. Smith makes art on the Isle of Lewis and had works made with Bruce Lacey included in the 2012 Camden Arts Centre exhibition The Bruce Lacey Experience, and on a BFI DVD.[31] And Fanni Tutti is represented by art dealer Cabinet and increasingly profiled in both commercial and public-sector galleries. SPACE and Matt's Gallery, with the help of Arts Council England, also continue to support developing artists. Elements of the 'art in the dark' – to refer back to the Thomas McEvilley quotation that opened this piece – have been brought into the light, and the audience is substantial.

With thanks to Cosey Fanni Tutti, Anna Harding, Christine Jakobson, John Lacey, Kevin Lacey, Mark Pilkington and Jill Smith.

Notes

1 Thomas McEvilley, 'Art in the Dark', *Artforum*, Summer 1983. p. 62.

2 On 'Industrial Records', thus giving the name to the genre.

3 Cosey Fanni Tutti, interview with the author, 2017.

4 Cosey Fanni Tutti, *Art Sex Music* (London: Faber and Faber, 2017), p. 112.

5 As remembered by Jill Smith, interview with the author, 2017.

6 Ibid.

7 Cosey Fanni Tutti, 'Jules made Gen[esis P-Orridge] a shoulder bag in the shape of a large alien-like vagina, with latex labia teeth and long tentacles all around it'.

8 According to Jill Smith, on at least one occasion, Dockley accidentally set the building on fire.

9 Kevin Lacey, interview with the author, 2017.

10 Richard Grayson, *Present Tense* (2008) at tinyurl.com/y9x2te89

11 Klassnik in conversation with Harding, 2017, unpublished.

12 Robert Hewison, *Too Much: Art and Society in the Sixties 1960–1975* (London: Methuen, 1986), p. 199.

13 COUM Transmissions met European artists through international tours.

14 For example: music, dance, theatre, performance art and mime. The 'Performance Art' category was a later introduction – previously such practices were identified as 'Theatre'.

15 Typically, when performing as a duo, Smith and Lacey were billed as 'Galactic Theatre', whilst films and exhibitions were credited to Bruce Lacey and Jill Bruce. 'The Laceys' was used for larger, family, community art projects.

16 Simon Ford, Wreckers of Civilisation: The Story of COUM Transmissions and Throbbing Gristle (London: Black Dog Publishing, 1999), p. 4.11.

17 Simon Ford, *Wreckers of Civilisation: The Story of COUM Transmissions and Throbbing* Gristle (London: Black Dog Publishing, 1999), p. 2.13.

18 Cosey Fanni Tutti, *Art Sex Music*, op. cit., p. 123.

19 Jill Smith recalls that the Lacey name was thought up by their daughter, Tiffany. Bruce Lacey's 1968 participatory structure 'Journey Through the Human Body', and Throbbing Gristle's 1982 album 'Journey Through a Body', also used similar language.

20 Simon Ford, op. cit., p. 7.20.

21 Cosey Fanni Tutti, interview with the author, op. cit.

22 With friend Chris Cobb, also part of Vacuum, John Lacey built a set of 200 watt quadraphonic speakers that were used by COUM and then Throbbing Gristle, as well as mixing desks, a customised tape deck and more.

23 John Lacey, interview with the author, 2017.

24 Hall presented his new film *Vertical* (1970) and Evans his inflatables.

25 John A. Walker, *Left Shift: Radical Art in 1970s Britain* (London: IB Tauris, 2002), p. 23.

26 Robert Hewison, *Too Much: Art and Society in the Sixties 1960 – 1975* (London: Methuen, 1986), p. 192.

27 The exhibition signalled the move from COUM to TG.

28 With John Lacey moving between the two.

29 Simon Ford, op. cit., 1999: p. 7.23.

30 Also, if TG's music and record sleeves were, however obliquely and unlikely, partially about the day-to-day, then again there was link to the Laceys and their interest in domesticity.

31 *The Lacey Rituals: Films by Bruce Lacey and Friends*, BFI DVD 2012. A number of Jill Smith and Bruce Lacey's films have also been preserved and blown-up to 35mm by the BFI National Archive.

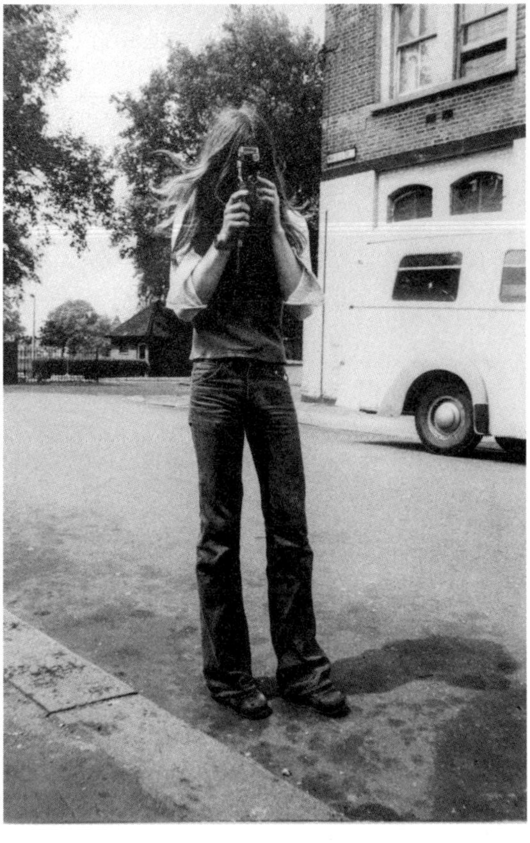

Chris Carter outside Martello Street, c.1970

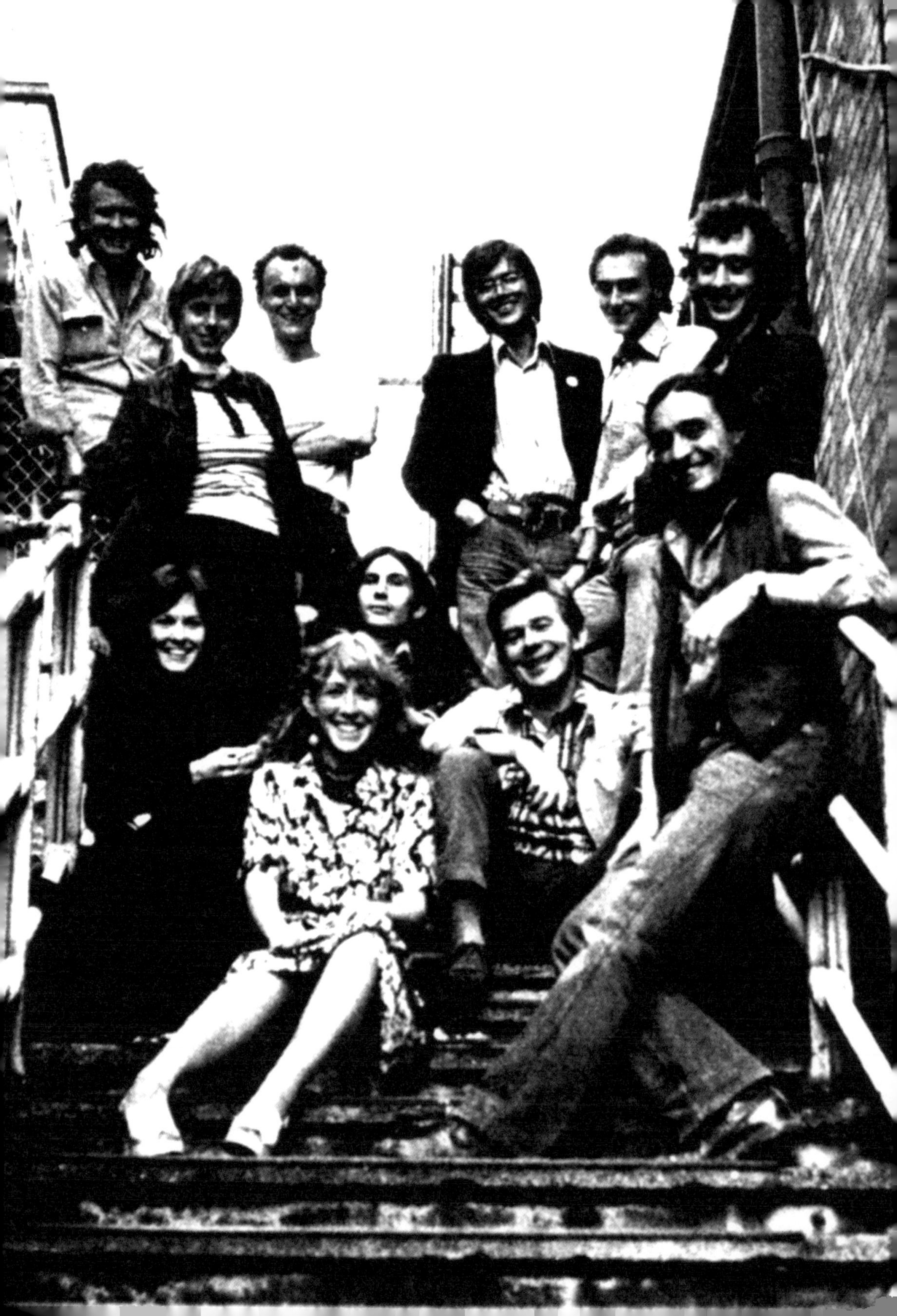

The Dairy and the 1975 Open Studios

Shirley Read

I moved into the Dairy in July 1972 and became studio rep almost by default, because of being caretaker I think. When Helen Dickson left SPACE Martin Argles asked me to apply for the job of Studio Manager because he knew me from the Dairy. I dealt with the artists, studio allocation, rents, the waiting list, enquiries and any general business as it came up. However, as a team of only two people and with fairly broad job descriptions we discussed everything and worked closely together so I would, for instance, go and look at new buildings and my role became very hands-on. Martin claims that I oversaw all the plasterboard deliveries at Wapping and I do remember being very involved with that building when SPACE first acquired it.

Martin and I were very involved with Space Open Studios and found a desk for Robin Klassnik and Alexis Hunter, the main organisers of the event, in the SPACE office. He drove me round all the buildings so I could photograph them for the catalogue and I photographed the reps meetings and the reps because I was in the habit of photographing events.

I also handled the negotiations with Bob Dallow of Camden Council over re-housing the Dairy. My memory is that Camden were unsure about offering us another building because they had previously had an unsuccessful foray into creating live/work space in the borough and were concerned about being drawn into a permanent commitment. I put together a portfolio about the building and took Bob Dallow round the Dairy to show him that serious work was being made. He was open to helping us and found Fitzroy Road. I then hired a van and organized the move.

I am not sure when SPACE moved into the Diary, 1970 at a guess. I think Graham Stevens was the only person there from St Katharine Docks but may be wrong. It was unlike other SPACE

The Steering Committee of SPACE Open Studios 1975
Standing left to right: Jeff Instone, Philippa Beale, John Imhasley, Martin Argles, Peter Rippon, John Crossley, Mike Rhodes. Seated left to right: Alexis Hunter, Shirley Read, Robin Klassnik, Ben Jones. GLAA Newsletter 1975.

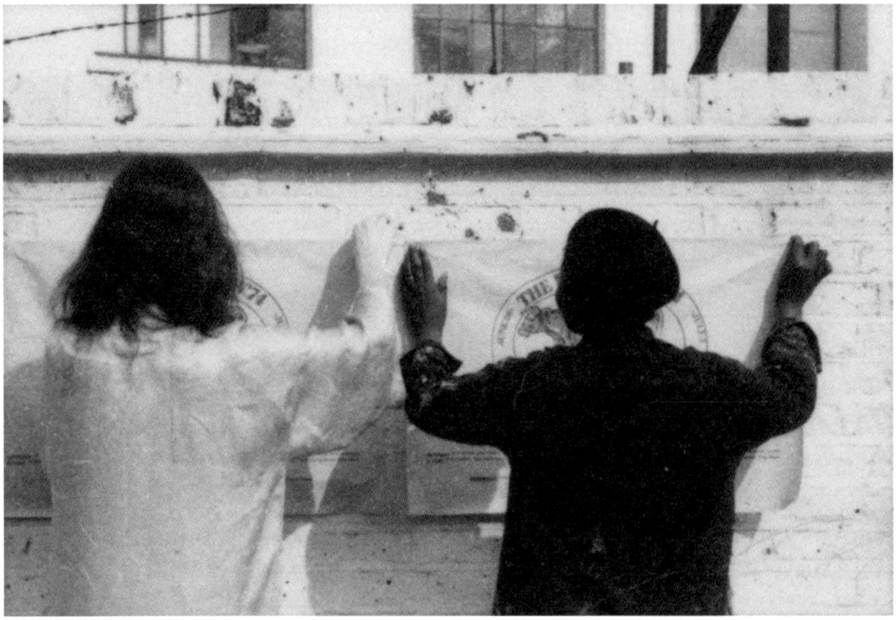

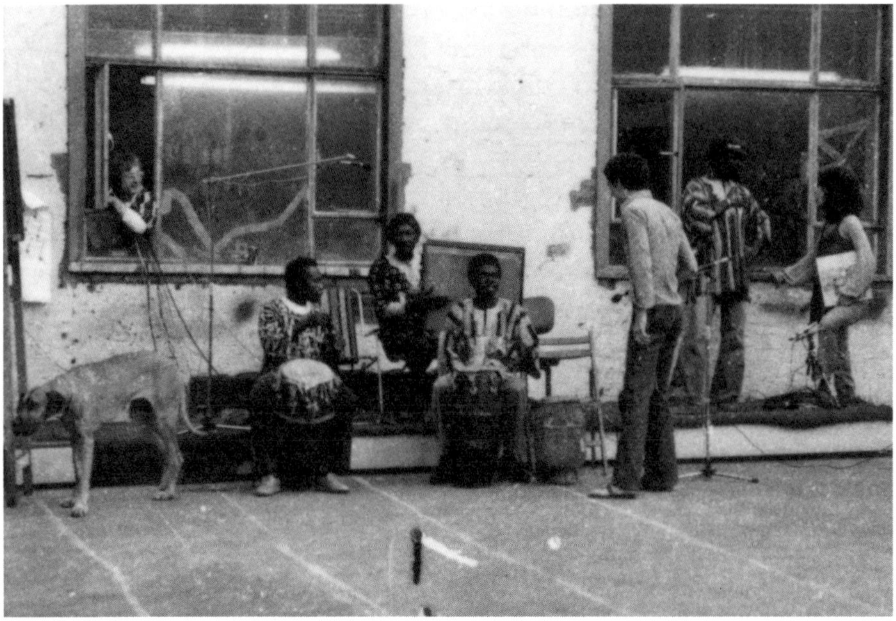

The Dairy Festival, 1974, putting up posters and Awake performing.

buildings in that it had a much wider range of art practice. I think the reason for this was that the building had been initially taken over by the Arts Lab not SPACE. The Arts Lab movement was founded by an American, Jim Haynes, in the 1960s in Covent Garden and then moved to just off the Hampstead Road then to the Dairy. Jim Haynes had moved to Paris by then so the Arts Lab movement had more or less come to an end. I can't remember which organisations/people came from the Arts Lab except for the London Film-makers Co-op and the Photo Co-op. Awake, the African drummers, were Arts Lab members I think. CATS video makers which included John 'Hoppy' Hopkins lived across the road (I think they were also IRAT and had an office in the Dairy but I'm not certain) – I'm not sure if they had been part of the Arts Lab but they were rehoused from the Dairy with our help. The Arts Lab was based in performance rather than the traditional fine arts which SPACE dealt with. It was sort of hippy and ground breaking. I don't quite know how SPACE took on the Dairy but I think the Arts Lab approached SPACE because the building was too big for them and they didn't want to run it themselves. SPACE also had charity status which helped keep rents down.

As the name suggests the building itself had been a dairy. It had a large yard which was used for parking, making things, vehicle repair, and performances. For a time film-maker David Larcher parked his two trucks there (his son was born in one of them) and Adam Brown (?) lived in his converted double decker bus there – and drove several of us to Knebworth festival in it. The river Fleet ran through the basement – the dairy had had pumps to keep the water out but turned them off when they left so the basement gradually filled up with water and every now and then someone would walk down in the dark and get soaked. Most people had large studios because they were very cheap. At that time the Arts Council paid for calor gas heaters (which are now illegal). The roof was flat and someone set up a hydroponic green-house there.

The Dairy was on one side of Prince of Wales Crescent, right in the middle of a community of squatters and students as well as two local community-based arts organisations – Interaction and Action Space. One was in Harmood Street, which backed onto the Dairy, and the other was just by West Kentish Town overground and run by an American, Ed Berman, who was quite famous for his work at that time. Student Community Housing (SCH) was based in the area where housing as well as light industrial buildings were being taken down. It was a sociable building and we spent time together and worked together, friends visited a lot, there was a grand piano in the caretakers' flat and people would drop in for jam sessions. The LFMC had regular film shows which drew people to the building (they had no seats so the audience lay on mattresses on the floor). There were sub groups within the building and a number of the studios were used by groups who were friends of whoever had the studio. Bob Janz, for example, was an American who was lecturing at Hornsey and loaned his studio to all sorts of music and performance events. We were also part of a bigger community, there was always something going on in Prince of Wales Crescent, including music events, a community café and health food shop. All this gave me an interest in performance, interactive art and working with the community which I think was shared by many of the artists in the Dairy.

I can't remember how the idea for the Dairy Festival came up. It was organized by Gil Gililian, Mike Goldwater and me with a small grant from GLAA.

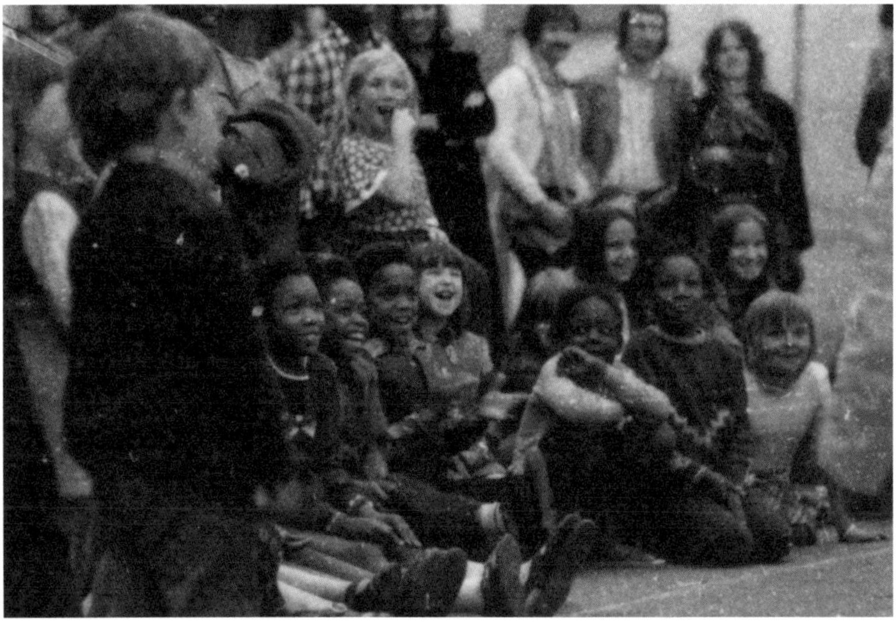

Children watching a performance at The Dairy Festival, 1974.

It may well have been Gil's idea – he was involved with community events and festivals – I remember taking his inflatable to Trafalgar Square with him one day and being absolutely terrified when some children tried to roll it into a fountain with me in it. Mike and I also went to a Gog-Magog festival in Plymouth with Gil. The festival was both an open studio and a performance event – the LFMC showed film in the yard, David Larcher had some sort of flight simulator so 35mm films could be moved around the space, Malcolm Le Grice set up an interactive piece in which he played football with the screen until local boys pinched his football and played with it themselves. I think Kate and Mike Westbrook played, the drummers did, John Imhasly did a performance but I can't remember who else performed.

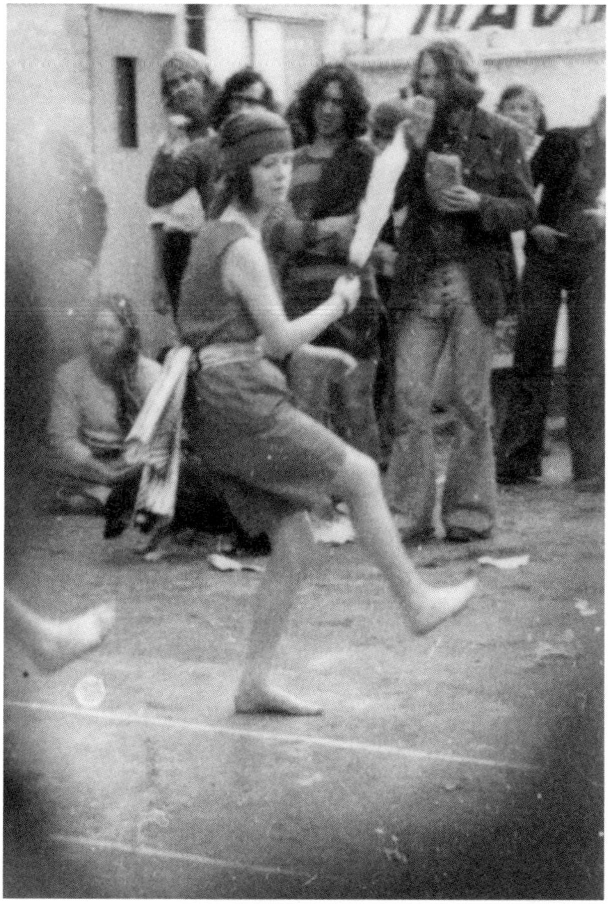

Performance from The Dairy Festival, 1974.

Exhibition in Tom Evans' studio as part of the Dairy Festival,1974 →

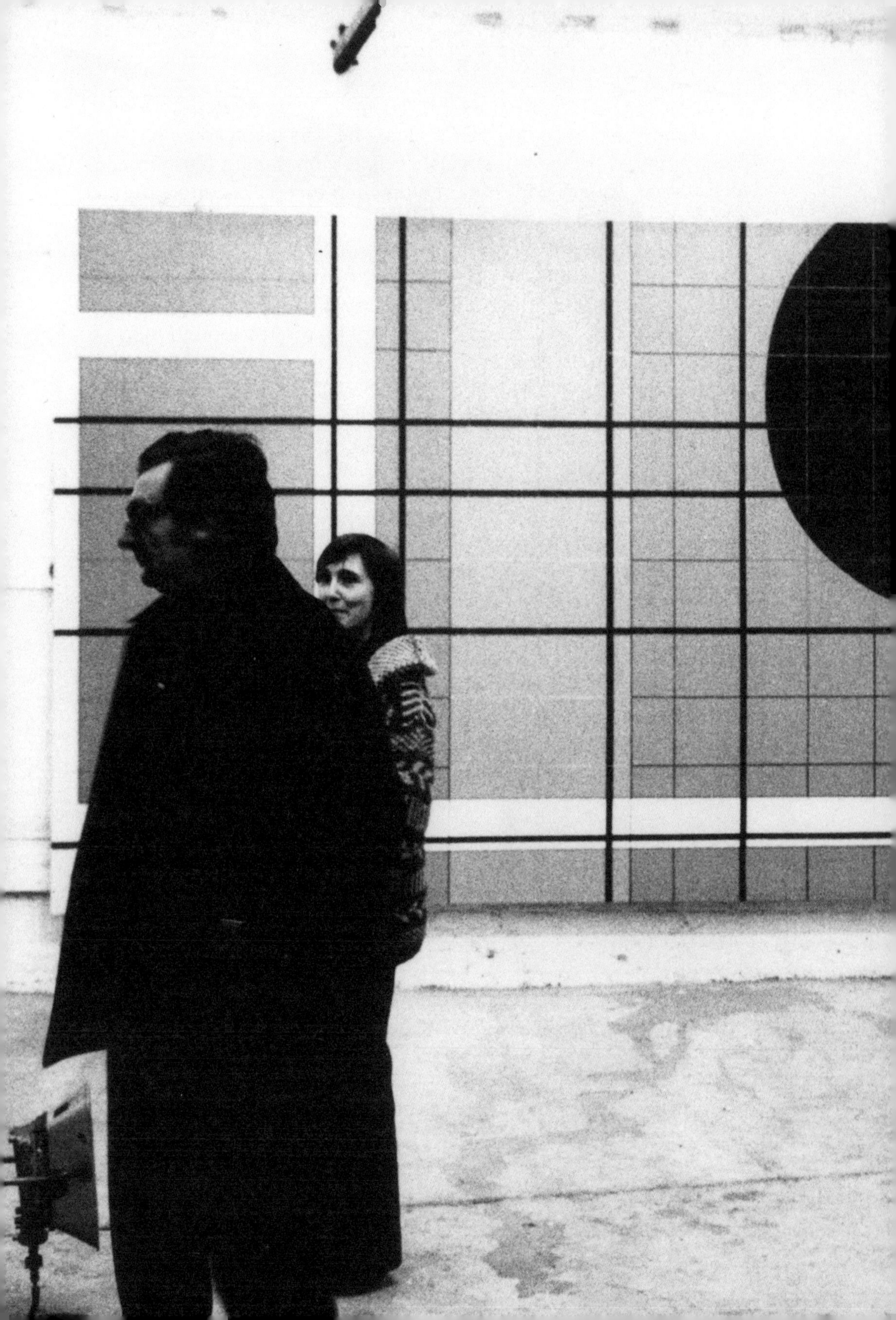

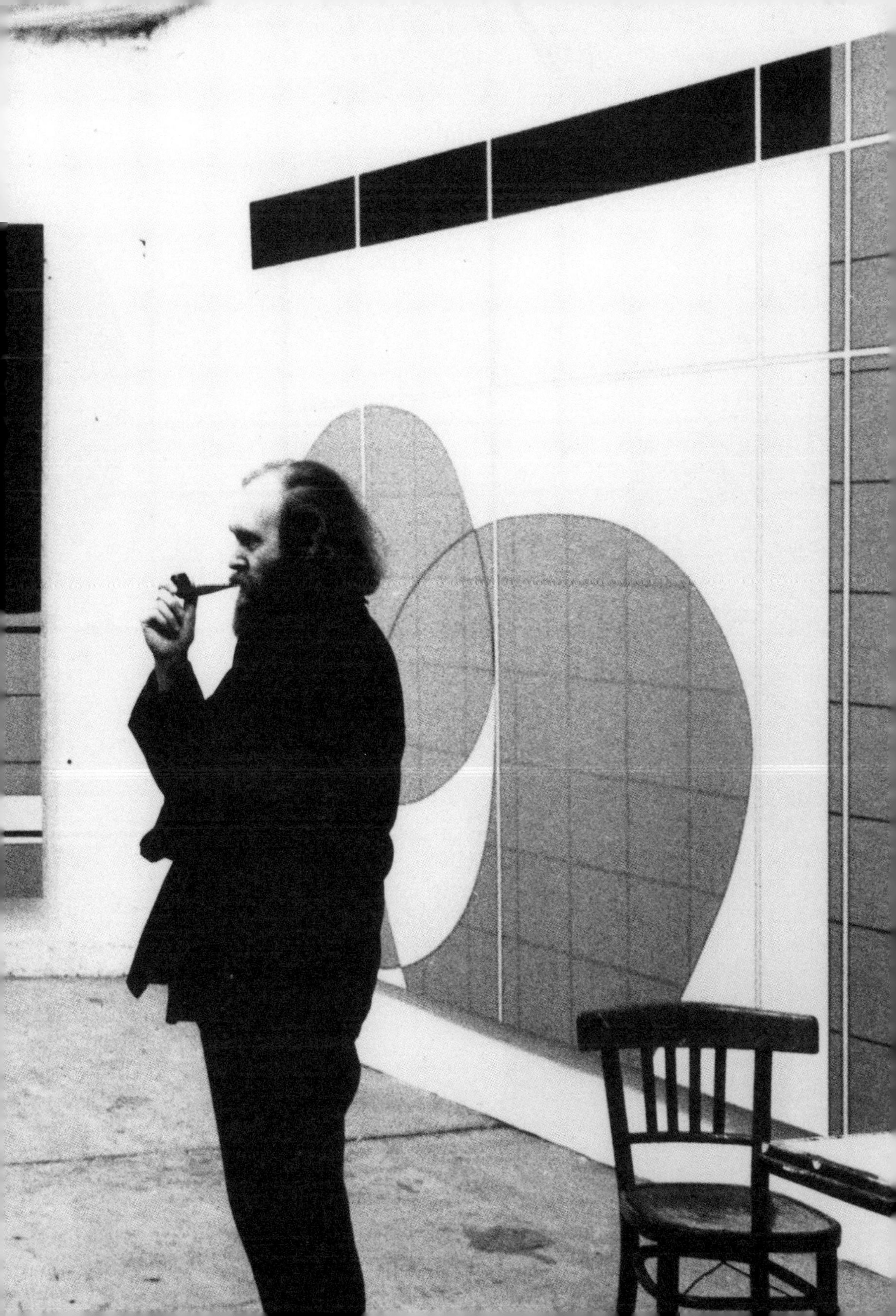

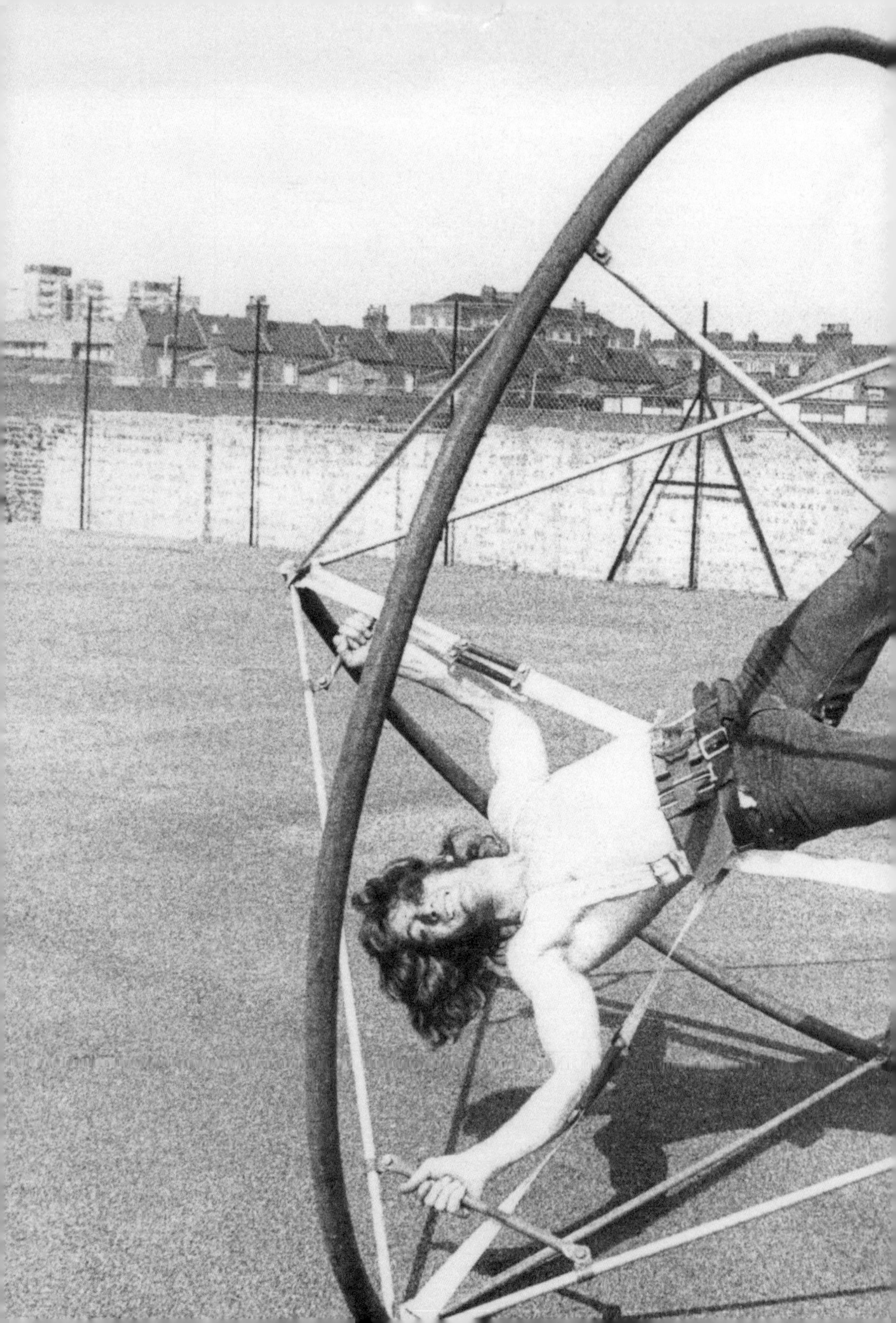

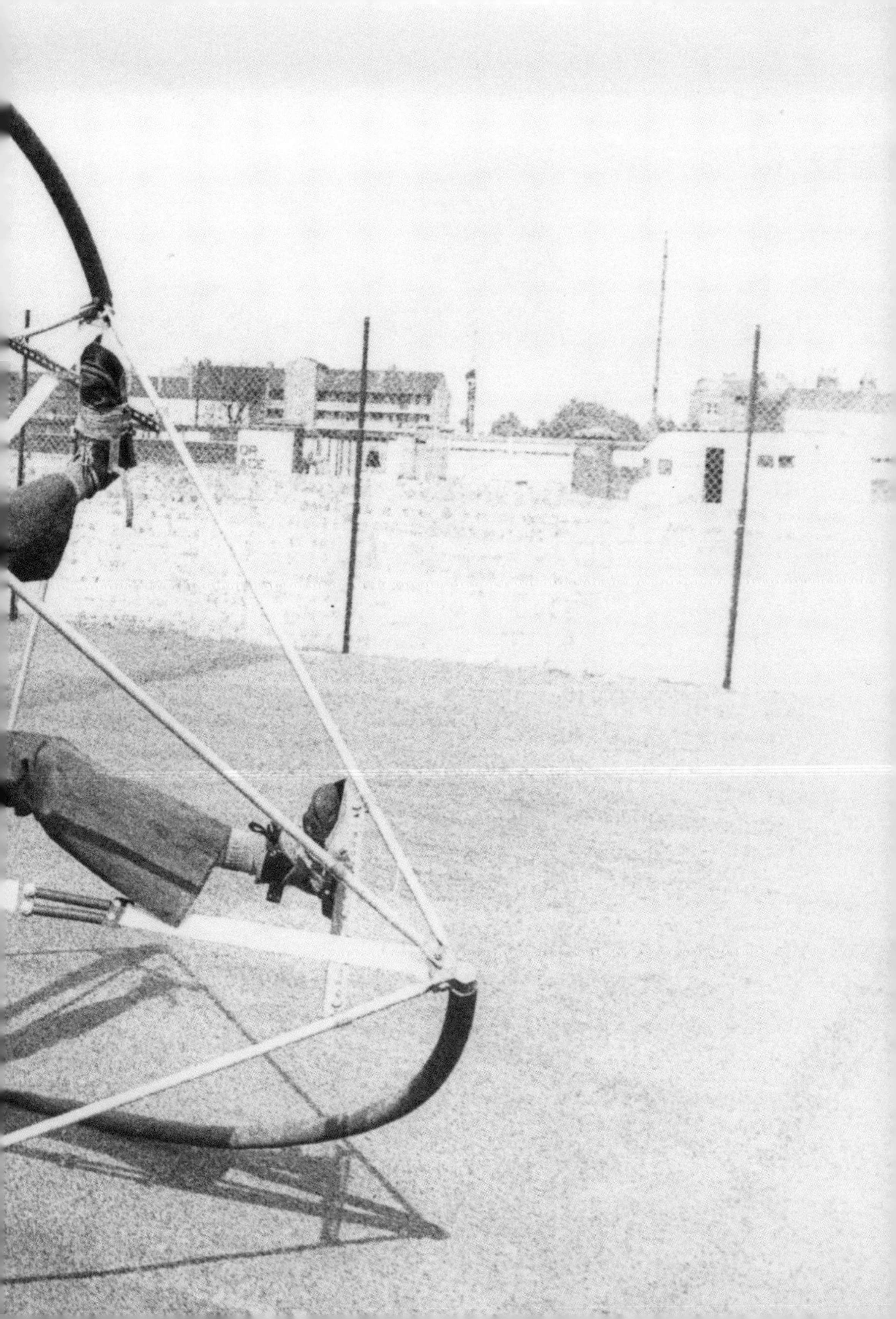

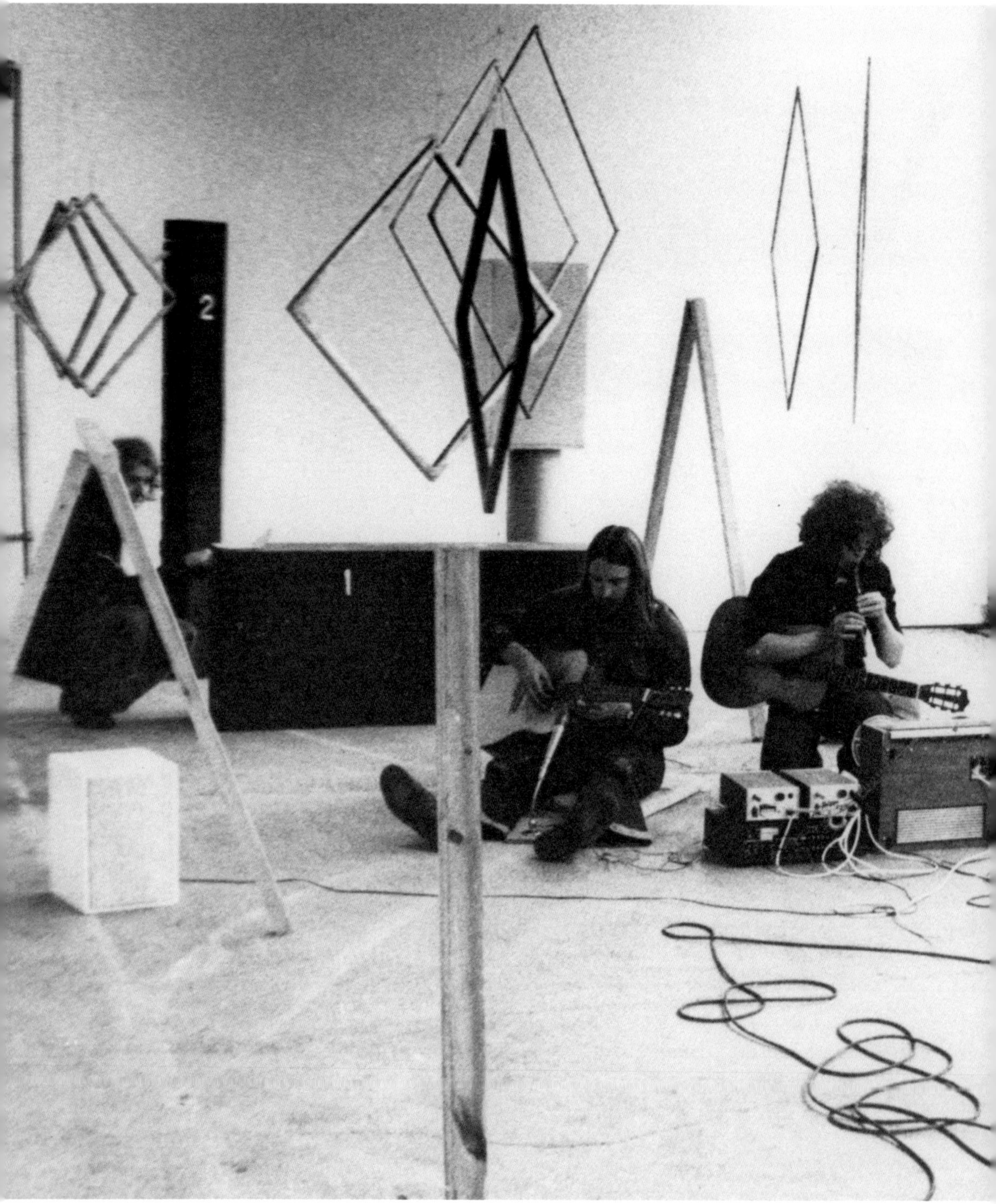

↑ Performances by the Ting as part of the Dairy Festival, 1974.

← Tony Hill, *Orbal*, early 70s. Photographer unknown.

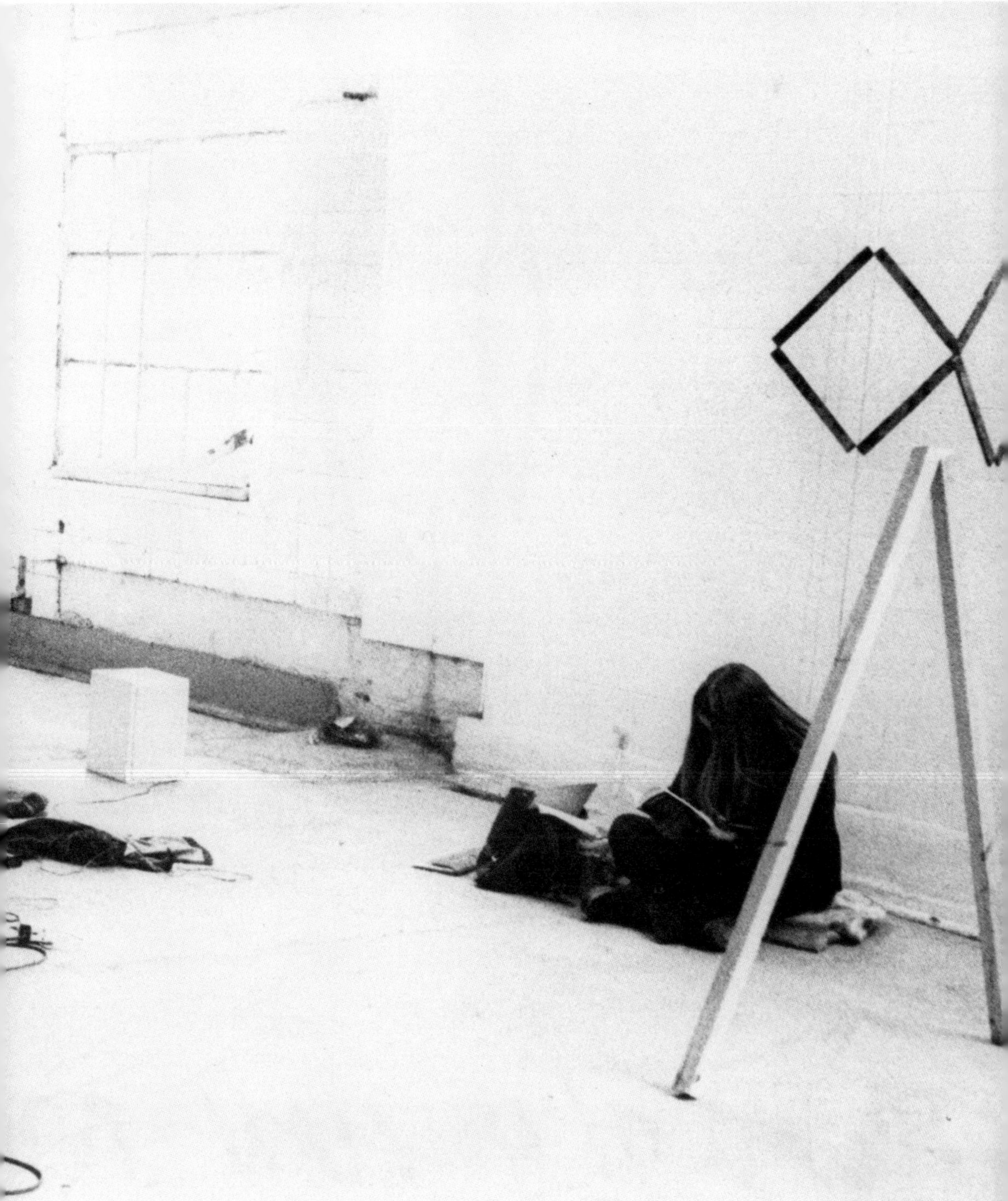

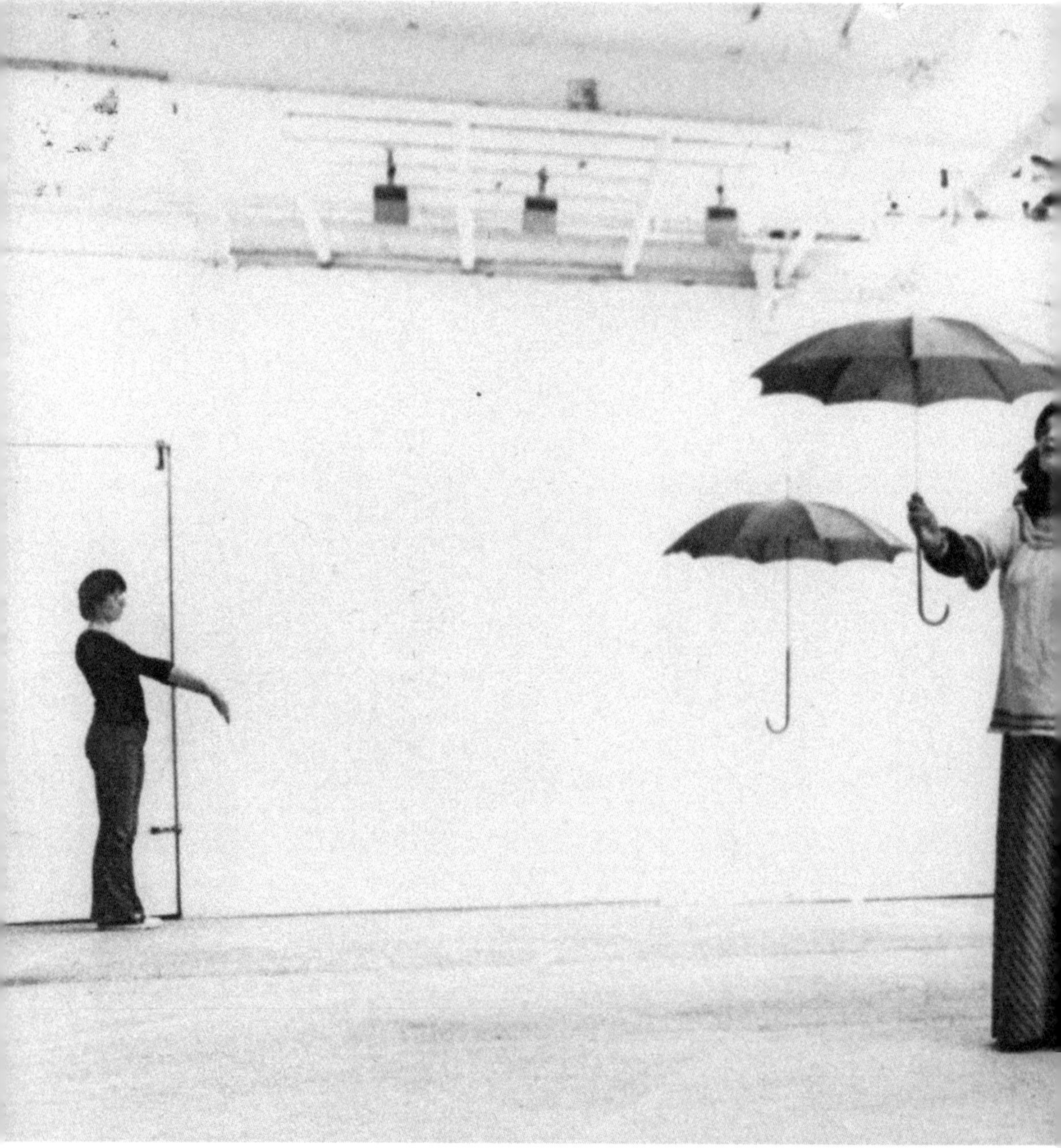

Performances in Bob Janz studio as part of the Dairy Festival, 1974.

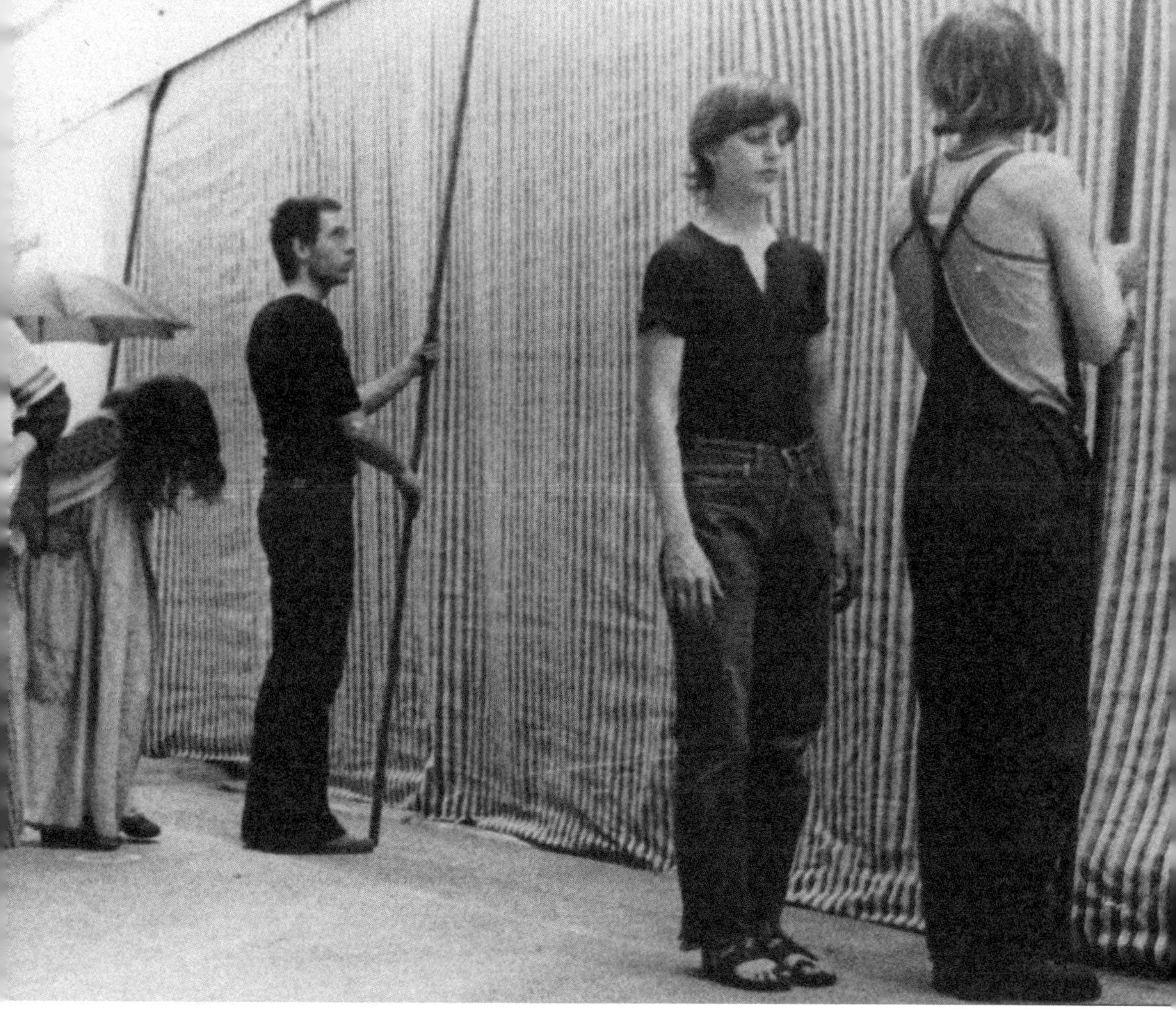

A.U. NEWSLETTER

October 1976

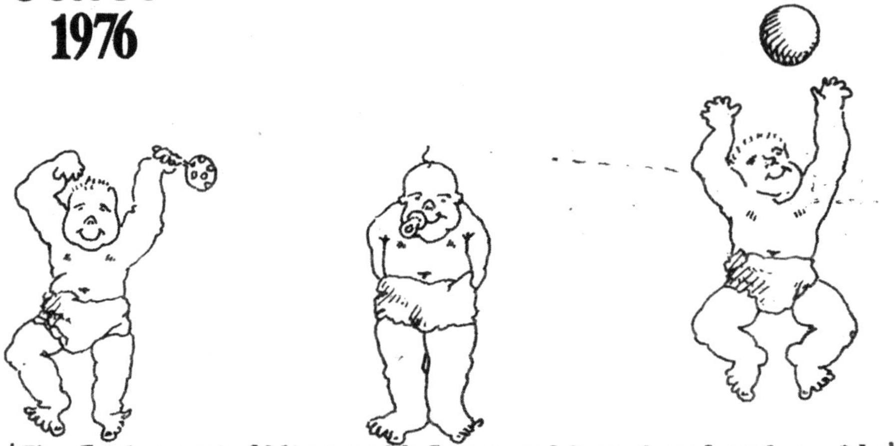

'The Employment Office said I was self employed and couldn't get dole'-'I couldn't support my family'-'The gallery lost my work'-'My college wouldn't let me keep the work I needed' 'My gallery threatened to destroy unsold work'-'We began working as a group and started to get out into the community 'He asked me why I was an artist if I didn't make a profit' 'They just ignored women students at our college as far as any ability in art was concerned'-'We've always got by,one way or another'

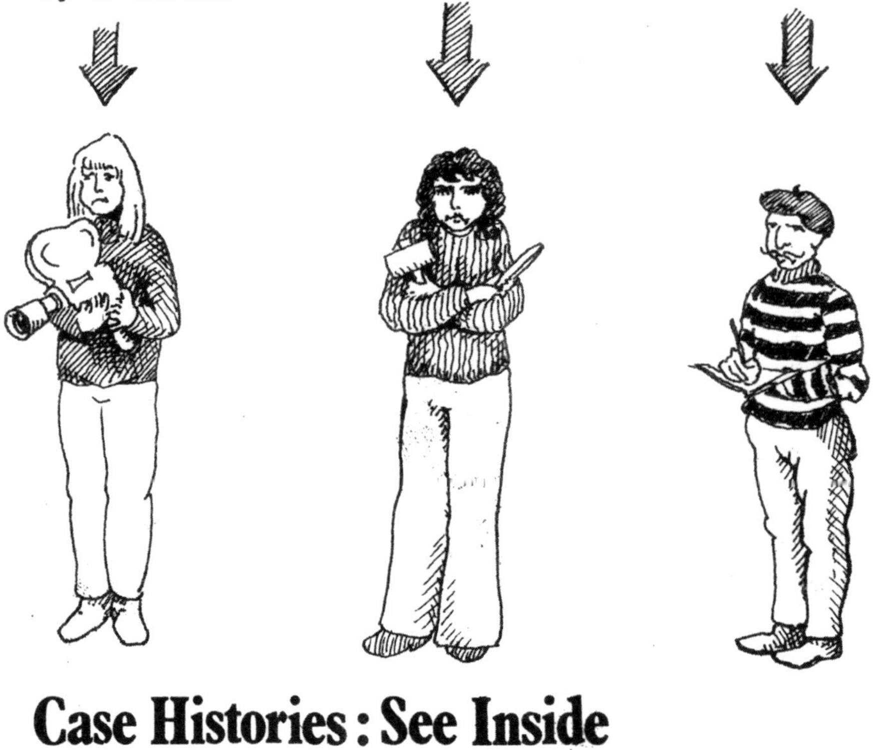

Case Histories : See Inside

Joining a struggle, not a mailing list

Ana Torok

The 1970s, as an art historical period, remain significant for the extent to which artists engaged meaningfully with the social, political and economic issues of their day. In the midst of explosive cultural change, intense political debate and heightened trade union power, certain artists were turning their attention to the representation of workers and their labour-organising efforts. In 1972, for instance, Conrad Atkinson produced *Strike at Brannans*, an artwork documenting a year-long industrial dispute spearheaded by female workers at the Brannans Thermometer factory in the artist's home town of Cleator Moor. Around the same time, Mary Kelly was taking part in the production of the documentary *Nightcleaners* (1975), about a London-based campaign by the Women's Liberation Movement to unionise the women working for office cleaning companies. Kelly also collaborated with Margaret Harrison and Kay Fido Hunt to produce *Women And Work: A Document on the Division of Labour in Industry* (1973–75), which centred on a metal box factory in Bermondsey where management was skirting the 1970 Equal Pay Act to avoid paying female workers a fair wage. Similarly, Stuart Brisley's 1970 *Hille Fellowship,* which enabled the artist to work at a furniture factory at Haverhill in Suffolk and create a massive sculpture out of 212 stacked chairs, also included an inquiry into the dynamics between management and those on the shop floor. While raising awareness of workers' rights through their art practice, these same artists, alongside many others, began identifying as workers themselves and ultimately undertook efforts to mitigate what they came to see as their own economic exploitation. One such endeavour, begun in London in the early 1970s, was directed toward the establishment of a trade union for artists. Considering the strength of trade union power in the 1970s, the existence of the Artists Union (AU) from 1972 to 1983 is easily situated historically. Recently, however, at a time when trade union membership has declined

Artists Union Newsletter Cover, October 1976.
Courtesy MayDay Rooms

sharply since its peak in 1979,[1] artists are once again looking to unionise. On May Day in 2014, a group of 10 artists launched Artists' Union England (AUE). With it, they sparked a critical reconsideration of the cultural value of artistic practice and the power of labour organisation in the face of an inequitable art world system.

In November 2016, artist Katriona Beales, one of the founding members of AUE, was invited to speak at a roundtable discussion entitled *Infrastructures of Making*, organised by Theatrum Mundi at SPACE. It was part of a series, prompted by London Mayor Sadiq Khan's projected Cultural Infrastructure 2030 plan, which sought to understand 'if and how we can design the conditions for culture'.[2] Beales' talk, 'Cultural Capital Won't Pay My Rent: On the Importance of Redefining Artistic Labour as Work', served as a powerful provocation. Clarifying at the outset that she was not speaking as a mouthpiece for AUE, her presentation effectively put a face to the challenges confronting artists in London, following, as she herself said, the poignant feminist tradition of making the personal political. It outlined a series of systemic obstacles, from the debt incurred through art education to the unsustainable cost of rent, and explicitly aligned her living and working conditions with those of other low-paid workers in the United Kingdom. Drawing on recent data, she cited a 2010 study commissioned by the Design and Artists Copyright Society (DACS), which found that the median annual income for the fine artists surveyed was £10,000,[3] as well as a 2014 report produced by a-n, which found that 71 percent of artists exhibiting in publicly-funded institutions received no fee for their work.[4] To provide a concrete example of the difficulties met by artists, Beales told the story of an early AUE member who secured a solo exhibition at a prestigious contemporary art gallery in Wales. The artist agreed to the terms, including a fee of £5,000, which seemed modest considering that preparations for the show were expected to involve a year's worth of labour. Halfway through the production period, after purchasing materials and beginning to execute the work, the gallery explained that, due to local authority budget cuts, the artist's fee would be rescinded. According to Beales, this situation is not unique. When arts budgets shrink, artists' fees are seen as soft targets, the assumption being that exposure alone should provide enough of an incentive.

Beales essentially argued that, as economic conditions become increasingly unsustainable, artists should refuse to accept cultural capital in lieu of financial capital. Anticipating a well-worn argument against the professionalisation of the artist, she suggested that this objection was often 'perpetrated by better-established artists who went to art school when they didn't have massive debts accrued, who were given grants... who lived in squats... and then could also afford to purchase a three-storey Georgian house in Hackney when they were cheap', before retorting incisively that emerging artists today 'can't afford to be unprofessional.'[5] Comparing her situation to that of artists in the 1960s and 1970s, Beales – who readily admitted she would relish those same circumstances were they still available today – pointed an accusatory finger at voracious property development and the underlying logic of neoliberalism.

The persistent debate around the professionalisation of art is inextricable from wider unease around the conflation of artistic practice and labour. In *Art Workers: Radical Practice in the Vietnam War Era*, Julia Bryan-Wilson explains that what makes this equivalence 'challenging – and even oxymoronic – is that under capitalism art also functions as the "outside," or other, to labor: a nonutilitarian, nonproductive activity against which mundane work is defined, a leisure-time pursuit of self-expression, or a utopian alternative to the deadening effects of capitalism'.[6] The endurance of this notion across decades, despite the escalating profitability of the art market, means that an artists' union continues to face the same objections today as it did in the 1970s. Sceptics outline perceived flaws, such as the lack of a common employer or workplace and the competition supposedly inherent to the profession. While initially seeming a contradiction, however, the fact that artists are not automatically remunerated for their labour makes the existence of a solidarity-building project like a trade union all the more necessary. As artists navigate an art world system which discourages them from demanding fair payment for their work, it becomes especially beneficial to shift the onus onto the collective through the leverage that attends institutional support.

Faced with many of the same obstacles and criticisms, the artists organising in the 1970s were quick to point out that most other cultural workers in the UK were already unionised. If others with similar employment conditions – including musicians, actors and journalists – had succeeded in organising, the argument went, artists should be able to follow suit. During the upheaval of the period, marked by spectacular anti-authoritarian action, many artists adopted administrative strategies in their campaign for change.

In London, artist-led endeavours were founded in a bid to correct what was seen as a dysfunctional art world system. SPACE, for instance, was formed to provide low-cost studios, while AIR sought to sidestep gallerists by introducing artists and interested collectors through its slide registry and by creating a communication network for artists via its newsletter. During this moment of seemingly boundless possibilities, two separate groups of artists had begun to consider the idea of an artists' union. One of these groups involved Stuart Brisley, who, at that time, was part of a collective which included Gustav Metzger, Ed Herring and Barry Barker, among others. Brisley suggests that it was 'not surprising that they were thinking in those terms', considering the many artist-led efforts which marked the period.[7] According to Brisley, in around 1970, the collective undertook two years of research and meetings with trade unions, including the National Union of Journalists, The Association of Scientific, Technical and Managerial Staffs and the Trades Union Congress (TUC), with the ultimately unsuccessful aim of affiliating with an established labour organisation.

Simultaneously, in August of 1971, a London-based exhibition entitled Art Spectrum, supported by the Arts Council of Great Britain (ACGB) and the Greater London Arts Association, gathered together over 100 artists. According to Conrad Atkinson, those involved in the show 'started comparing notes'.[8] He added, 'Because we were working all night at Alexandra Palace, we began to collect for supper and drinks and talk about art'.[9] Margaret Harrison also suggested that the exhibition provided an outlet from the isolation she had previously felt: 'Artists would be in studios, like at SPACE, but you didn't really meet anybody... you would hear a radio tinkling in the background and you'd think, 'Oh, I wonder who that is,' but there wasn't a sort of meeting place'.[10] The discussions that arose among the exhibiting artists articulated a shared set of grievances that Atkinson eventually addressed in a paper entitled 'Some Aims for an Art Workers Union', which he presented during a meeting at the ICA that same year and which proposed ameliorative solutions for artists, such as resale rights. His paper also raised fundamental questions about the role of artists and, like Beales' provocation, compared their situation to that of the wider working class:

> But who or what is an artist? The gallery 'super-star' system would have us believe we are something special, members of an elite… It sounds good, but is it true? […] Give it careful thought and you realise that we are, in fact, about as privileged as old age pensioners, and our situation is rather similar to theirs. Like them, we are without money, without employment, without strength, without control, and worst of all without group identity.[11]

After the meeting, artist Carol Kenna approached Atkinson and offered to help realise the proposal. A second group was then formed, which, along with Sarah Kent and Atkinson's partner Margaret Harrison, began meeting in the couple's Notting Hill Gate flat. Brisley, who described the two groups as rivalrous, contended that their ideological differences derived from the second group's more traditional alignment with the Labour Party, while his collective was 'more broadly culturally-based'.[12] In his account, Atkinson recalled that his group planned to call themselves the Art Workers Union because they 'objected to the word "artist" as a loaded and a slightly upper class term' which might deter the established trade unions from taking them on.[13] The collective to which Brisley belonged organised a public meeting in 1972, which the second group attended, and, together, they agreed to form a union, voting in Mary Kelly as their first Chairperson. According to Kelly, two male candidates split the male vote, handing her the win.[14] Despite the ideological differences of the two groups, they collectively ratified a constitution outlining their various aims. As John A. Walker wrote in *Left Shift: Radical Art in 1970s Britain* (2002), the AU's central objectives were:

> […] to promote and protect the economic and cultural interests of members and artists in general; to regulate relations between members and patrons; to campaign for democratic reform of national bodies concerned with art patronage and for greatly increased national expenditure on art; to promote participation by artists in local government and regional bodies; to campaign for legislation for the benefit of artists; to seek affiliation to the Trades Union Congress (TUC) and to support the Labour Movement in general.[15]

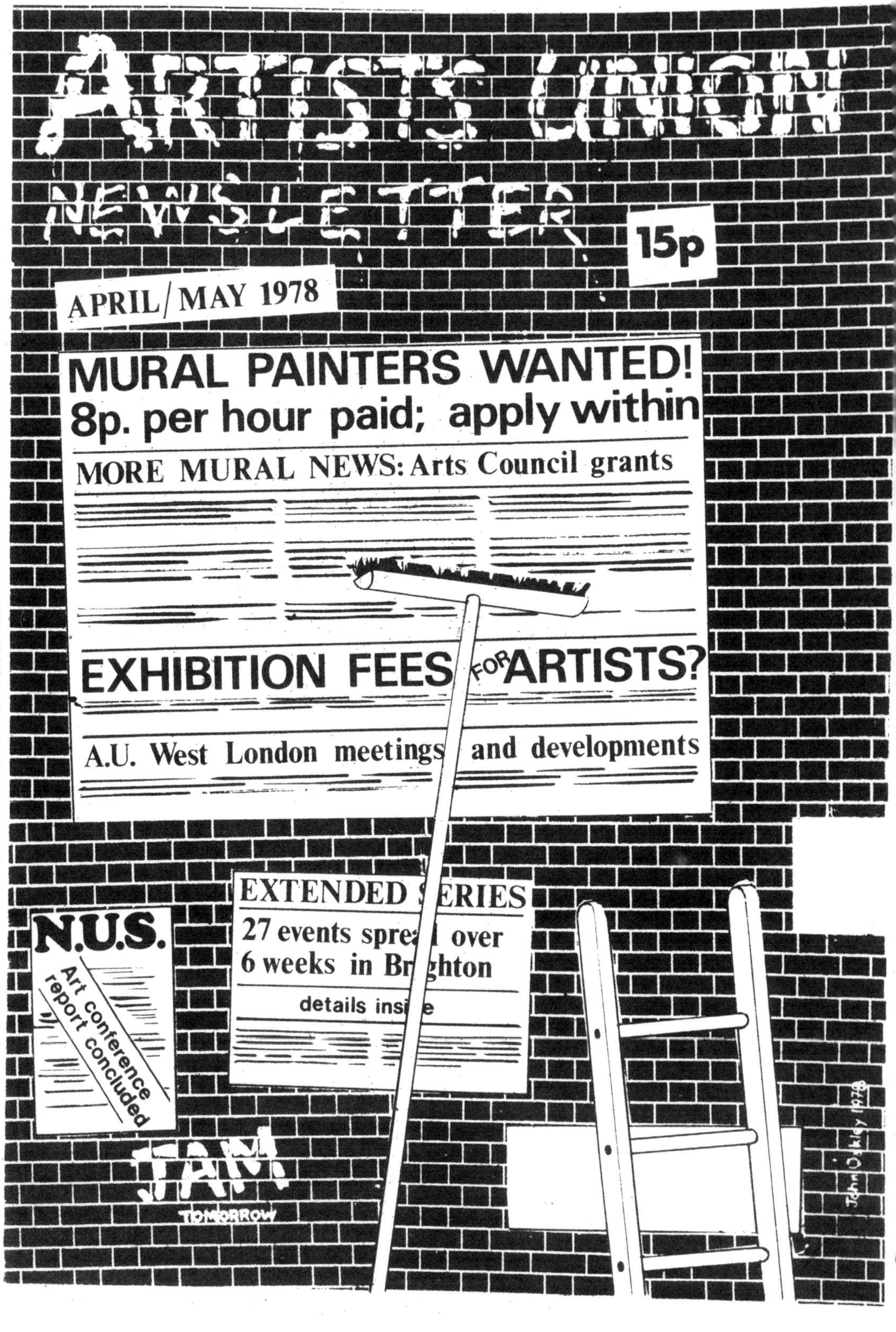

A.U. APRIL-MAY NEWSLETTER

Fundamentally, the AU focused on those aspects of the art world system that had the potential to generate a profit for artists, including exhibition fees and resale rights as well as those procedures which would benefit from increased transparency, such as decisions made by the powerful ACGB. In her 2010 essay 'Artists and the Labour Movement', Kirsten Forkert explained that, '[a]s the art market was generally weak in the 1970s, the ACGB was the most significant source of support. However, ACGB support for experimental art practices was limited. Major institutional clients such as national theatre and opera companies remained the primary recipients'.[16] Visual artists were left competing for the limited budget that remained. As AU Chairperson Charles Gosford outlined in a 1977 AU publication entitled *Why Do Artists Need a Union?*, 'The Arts Council budget this year is £42 million. 5% goes to the visual arts. 1.7% will go to the artists themselves'.[17] Recognising this disparity, the AU focused on increasing the funds allocated to living artists while holding organisations such as ACGB accountable.

When artists came together in 2014 to launch Artists' Union England, they looked to the AU as a historical precedent, inviting Metzger, Atkinson and Harrison to speak at their 2016 Certification Launch in the House of Commons, because, according to Beales, 'some of the questions they were asking [in the 1970s] are still incredibly pertinent'.[18] Mirroring the initial motivations of the AU, three of AUE's founder artists – Beales, Angela Kennedy and Sally Sheinman – had noted the absence of an independent, collective voice for artists capable of intervening into decisions being made in the cultural sector. After growing to include 10 members in May 2014, AUE was officially launched from Beales' living room. As none of the participating artists had experience forming a union, they relied on advice from trade union representatives, including Beth Farhat, Northern Regional Secretary for the TUC, who suggested that they introduce themselves to other organisations to clarify exactly whom they sought to represent.[19] The resulting conversations, with the Scottish Artists Union (SAU), Musicians' Union, Equity, Bectu and Unite, proved helpful and encouraging, with the SAU lending their Rule Book for use as a template. While Kennedy described the initial process as 'all DIY, a bit rough-and-ready',[20] AUE has since grown to include approximately 300 members, due in large part to its active social media presence

Artists Union Newsletter Cover, April / May 1978.
Courtesy MayDay Rooms

and its simple and inclusive online membership registration. The speed with which AUE gained its Certificate of Independence – within just two years of forming, in June 2016 – bodes well as an indication of its potential long-term success. Necessary as proof that the union is not controlled or influenced by an employer or employers' association and required before affiliating to another union, certification had evaded the original AU, which never held a successful vote on the matter despite propounding its importance often during its decade of activity.

As the artists involved in the original union could not rely on traditional union tactics such as collective bargaining or strike action, they instead focused on administrative strategies in their pursuit of economic justice. The AU's 1977 *Wages for Artists* report articulated the power of standardised contracts and collectively sanctioned documentation, explaining that 'artists need standard contracts which can cover the various transactions they have to make, so that the present confused, irregular situation whereby so many artists are cheated or frustrated can be avoided'.[21] Among other efforts, the AU circulated a Reserved Rights Transfer and Sale Agreement in 1974,[22] attended meetings of the British Copyright Council before becoming a full member in 1979,[23] proposed quota agreements intended to benefit local artists and even suggested dictating a minimum price guide for artworks.[24]

Equally aware of the benefit of collectively sanctioned documentation, AUE consulted the work of other cultural trade unions to produce its official Rates of Pay document in 2015. While the AUE website acknowledges that 'in real terms what [they] are proposing remain modest figures that still represent low level artist's incomes', the document is meant to provide artists with a suitable base rate to which they can refer during pay negotiations relating to various activities, from performances to residencies.[25] Thanks to the development of these standards, as Kennedy explained, '99.9 percent of the time, the people who have set up the contract verbally then get paid… because [the institutions] know that it's not about that person as an individual, but that they're actually undermining a whole body of cultural work, a whole industry'.[26] In other words, the value of the documentation lies in its function as a concrete stand-in for the strength of the collective.

The AU also sought to cultivate a sense of group identity and reinforce its solidarity through its establishment of a series of workshops – a key feature since its inception in 1972. Serving as forums for discussion, the list of topic-specific workshops included: The Artist's Role in Society; Policy within the Trade Union Movement; Artists in Education; Media; Women's Workshop; Art, Science, Technology and Industry; Art Patronage, Marketing, Money; Government Policy for the Arts, and the Exhibition Workshop. The wide range of topics signalled an ambition to dissect and correct multiple systemic issues through research and deliberation. Crucially, the dedication of a workshop to the artist's role in society reinforced the logic that at the core of a successful labour struggle was the justification of the artist's societal function and value.

Following in the vital tradition of study groups within the Women's Movement, the formation of a Women's Workshop served to highlight another significant concern among members. Appearing in a 1974 issue of the feminist magazine *Spare Rib,* the workshop founders declared: 'We share similar, if not identical problems of isolation; both from other women artists and the general isolation of artists in a society which is alien to collective creative activity'.[27] Women in the AU saw their struggle in alignment with fellow artists and workers, while maintaining that they faced additional discrimination on account of their gender. In *Framing Feminism,* Rozsika Parker and Griselda Pollock write that the workshop members 'discussed each other's work and general issues relating to the situation of women artists of the past, familiarized themselves with contemporary feminist work in other parts of the world, notably the USA, and organized day schools at universities and art colleges'.[28] They also focused on redressing the relatively small number of women teachers in art schools and what they saw as its detrimental effect on female students' likelihood to identify as artists.[29] Serving as a corrective to the flawed system of art education, the workshop members presented slides of their artwork for feedback and discussion during meetings. Harrison recalled the Women's Workshop as a place 'where people learned to speak' and emphasised the sense of self-confidence which their all-women public exhibitions helped to foster.[30] A 1973 newsletter, however, hints not only at discord within the union concerning women's issues but also at a more general breakdown of solidarity among members. Following the proposal of a rota for the staffing of crèche facilities, some members 'pointed out that they had been to considerable lengths to avoid having children and did not intend to start now looking after other people's'.[31] In response, the author of the newsletter asked 'On one hand, are we going to uphold the principles of the state and nuclear family (each look after their own), or share the responsibility that the government has refused (in its lack of free nurseries) in order to enable parents to attend meetings and be people (instead of parents) for a while?'[32] While AUE's agenda is not as explicit regarding gender discrimination, women comprise approximately 70 percent of its membership. In fact, union membership among women is higher than it is among men, despite an overall decline since the late 1970s.[33]

Alongside an emphasis on workshop activity, the AU's archival material suggests a central preoccupation with the production of union literature, explaining '[the newsletter] represents our principal channel of communication, member to member [...] but more importantly it is the medium through which members can air their views, make suggestions, express opinions and criticisms upon a whole range of issues'.[34] It warns that 'Without it [...] there exists the danger that the only real views in circulation between Annual Conferences are those of the Executive and NEC [National Executive Committee], filtering downwards from the top. Such a tendency must be resisted!'[35] Several examples of meeting notes reveal that the newsletter often ran into production setbacks because of a lack of copy from members and low funds. Due to a reliance on printers and the postal system for the production and dissemination of union material, the AU required unsustainably high costs to survive and had little resources; a Treasurer's Report from 1975 calculated the union's budget at just £8.[36] Aside from the financial and structural issues that these difficulties illuminate, they also indicate a lack of involvement on the part of union members. Tellingly, a poster competition advertised in the December 1977 newsletter was postponed due to disappointingly low member response,[37] while a 1979 Editor's Report complained about not receiving enough newsletter illustrations, adding 'this is an artists' union after all'.[38]

While AUE produces a newsletter for its members, the voice of the union seems best expressed through its Twitter account. A look at its feed reveals an active communication platform from which the efforts of fellow unions are often retweeted and artists pose and answer questions, including, for instance, how to price their artwork. Furthermore, as Kennedy explained, if an exploitative employment opportunity is advertised online – such as an artist's residency with an application cost and no fee – union members will often tweet at AUE. Not only does this quickly bring matters to the attention of the union for potential action but it also serves to publicly highlight – and shame – the offending institution. The benefit of using an online platform is that, unlike the AU newsletter of the 1970s, the dialogue between union leaders and members is continuous and transparent. The public nature of this dialogue functions not only as an advertisement to prospective members – showing the union 'in action', as it were – but it also allows for the sort of generative artist-to-artist communication that the original union members sought.

As the strength of AUE depends on the size of its membership and its authority as a voice for artists, the measure of influence afforded by its highly visible online presence helps to bridge the gap between a growing, volunteer-run endeavour and a sustainably large and well-funded union supported by a paid Executive Committee. While the commitment of volunteers involved in the early development of AUE represents a notable sacrifice of the individual to the greater good, in what is often characterised as a deeply competitive profession, the artists contributing unpaid labour risk perpetuating the same unfair working practices that they fundamentally condemn. Very much attuned to this contradiction, Beales explained, 'We don't want to be running off the backs of volunteerism, but at the same time, if we want the union to be established and exist, it wasn't going to happen without some of us sacrificing time and energy to get it started'.[39] The AU faced a similar situation. Described as a 'battle of priorities' by the AU's Newsletter editor, Gordon Ramsden, in a January 1980 report,[40] accounts of personal conflicts between the administrative work of the union and each volunteer's artistic practice abound throughout the archival material, especially nearing its final years. Foreseeing the ruinous consequences of a disinterested membership in an article entitled 'Union Life' in the 1980 Emergency Edition of the Newsletter, National Secretary Richard Mann wrote:

> I don't understand why the majority of the work done within the AU devolves onto the shoulders of a handful of people, but it seems to be a fact of life [...] a proportion of the membership believe the amount of work done to be enormous and the pressure unbearable,

> the rest tend never to hear about it […] the only real remedy is to share in the work […] Union life is after all supposed to be about joining a struggle, not a mailing list.[41]

As Forkert explained, the AU 'came to an end in 1983, within a wider climate of trade union defeat. All agreed that Thatcher made it difficult for all trade unions, let alone an organisation as small as the AU'.[42] Echoing this assessment, Kelly suggested that the failed early vote to affiliate with a larger trade union marked, for her, 'the beginning of the end',[43] as the AU remained too small to survive autonomously. She emphasised, however, that the long-term existence of the AU may have been beside the point; its real success was consciousness raising among artists and the mutual support it encouraged among workers across other industries. Crucially, artists' labour organising efforts, both in the 1970s and today, represent more than just a campaign for economic justice. By sacrificing individual time and effort on behalf of the collective, artists have taken the first steps in radically transforming an inequitable art world system. Considering the rise of the gig economy and growing job precarity overall, their efforts serve as a useful reminder of the concrete benefits of solidarity – for all workers.

Notes

1 Department for Business, Innovation and Skills, 'Trade Union Membership 2015', May 2016: tinyurl.com/ydxg3vtb

2 Theatrum Mundi, Can We Design the Conditions for Culture? tinyurl.com/yakghnhx

My sincere thanks to Elisabetta Pietrostefani at Theatrum Mundi, Jacob Bard-Rosenberg at MayDay Rooms and Oliver Jelf for helping to source faraway materials.

3 Martin Kretschmer, Sukhpreet Singh, Lionel Bently and Elena Cooper, 'Copyright Contracts and Earnings of Visual Creators: A survey of 5,800 British designers, fine artists, illustrators and photographers', 2011: tinyurl.com/yab3sytl

4 'Paying Artists': payingartists.org.uk

5 Katriona Beales, 'Cultural Capital Won't Pay My Rent: On the Importance of Redefining Artistic Labour as Work', as part of Infrastructures of Making, *Theatrum Mundi*, 10 November 2016.

6 Julia Bryan-Wilson, *Art Workers: Radical Practice in the Vietnam War Era* (Berkeley: University of California Press, 2009), p. 27.

7 Stuart Brisley, interview with the author, 22 July 2017.

8 Conrad Atkinson, interview with the author, 16 July 2017.

9 Ibid.

10 Margaret Harrison, interview with the author, 16 July 2017.

11 Conrad Atkinson, 'Some Aims for an Art Workers Union', c. 1970–71, Tate Archive, TGA 201020/11/21.

12 Brisley, op. cit.

13 Atkinson, op. cit.

14 Mary Kelly, interview with the author, 18 August 2017.

15 John A Walker, *Left Shift: Radical Art in 1970s Britain* (London: IB Tauris and Co. Ltd., 2002), p. 85.

16 Kirsten Forkert, 'Artists and the Labour Movement', in Laurel Forster and Sue Harper (eds.), *British Culture and Society in the 1970s: The Lost Decade* (Newcastle upon Tyne: Cambridge Scholars Publishing, 2010), p. 56.

17 Artists Union, 'Why do Artists need A Union?: An account of a meeting of Artists held in Manchester 9 May 1977 with a view to setting up an organissation in the North West,' June 1977, p. 3, MayDay Rooms, AU/ADS/1/8/1-8.

18 Katriona Beales, interview with the author, 25 June 2017.

19 Angela Kennedy, interview with the author, 23 July 2017.

20 Ibid.

21 Artists Union, 'Wages for Artists? And Other Suggestions for Improving the Artist's Situation', November 1977, MayDay Rooms, AU/ADS/1/8/1-8.

22 *Artists Union Newsletter*, January 1978.

23 Roland Miller, 'Artists Union – Representative's Report: Report to Annual Conference on the British Copyright Council', c. 1980, Tate Archive, TGA 200116/2/4/22.

24 Artists Union, 'Wages for Artists?', op. cit.

25 Artists' Union England, 'Artists' Rates of Pay', 2015: tinyurl.com/y8acnwqo

26 Kennedy, op. cit.

27 Rozsika Parker, 'Exhibition at the Arts Meeting Place', *Spare Rib*, no. 29, 1974, p. 37.

28 Rozsika Parker and Griselda Pollock, *Framing Feminism: Art and the Women's Movement 1970–1985* (London: Pandora Press, 1987), p. 7.

29 Artists Union, 'The Artists Union', August 1972, p. 4, Tate Archive, TGA 709/5.

30 Harrison, op. cit.

31 *Artists Union Newsletter*, c. November 1973, MayDay Rooms, AU/ADS/1/1/1-13.

32 Ibid.

33 Department for Business, Innovation and Skills, 'Trade Union Membership 2016: Statistical Bulletin', 31 May 2017: www.gov.uk/government/uploads/system/uploads/attachment_data/file/616966/trade-union-membership-statistical-bulletin-2016-rev.pdf

34 Peter Dunn, Charles Gosford and Richard Mann, 'At the Cross Roads', *Artists Union Journal*, August 1980, p. 3, MayDay Rooms, AU/ADS/1/5/1-3.

35 Ibid.

36 *Artists Union Newsletter*, March 1975, p. 3, MayDay Rooms, AU/ADS/1/1/1-13.

37 *Artists Union Newsletter*, December 1977, MayDay Rooms, AU/ADS/1/8/1-8.

38 Ian Phillips, 'Editor's Report', August 1979, Tate Archive, TGA 200116/2/4/14.

39 Beales, op. cit.

40 Artists Union, 'Editor's Report', 8 January 1980, Tate Archive, TGA 200116/2/3/15.

41 Richard Mann, 'Union Life', *Artists Union Journal*, August 1980, p. 12, MayDay Rooms, AU/ADS/1/5/1-3.

42 Forkert, op. cit., p. 60.

43 Kelly, op. cit.

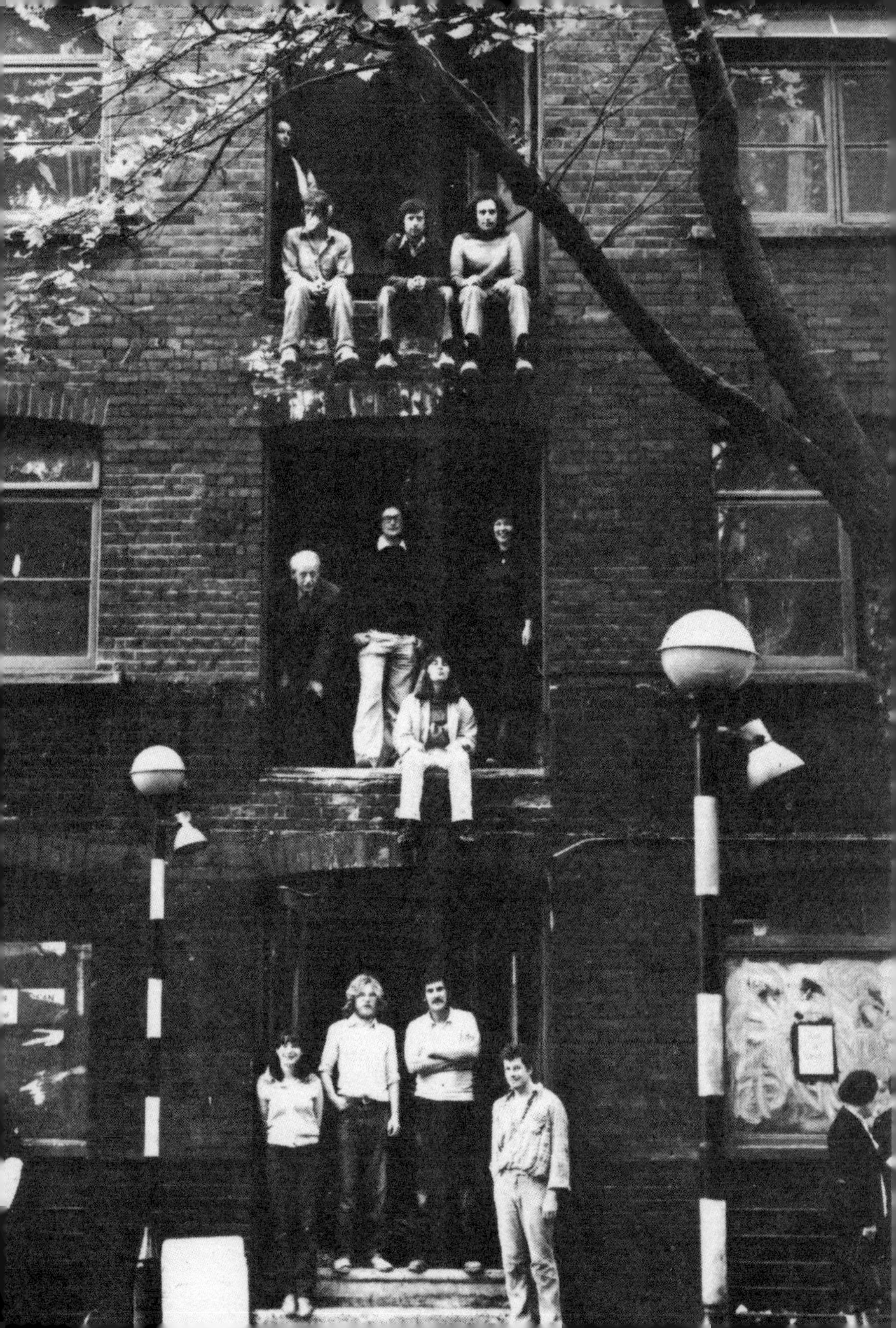

Artist-led initiative to arts charity

Alicia Miller

As the socio-economic landscape of the global city has changed, artists have been increasingly challenged in their pursuit of studio space. A critical component of artists' practice, the studio space has multiple functions, both public and private. While remaining a workspace for artists, it is also a 'resource', 'set and setting', 'stage'[1] and many other things, being manifested as far more than the dominant conception of a 'solitary lair shut off from the world'.[2] The studio is immanently involved with the public sphere even as it nurtures, protects and covets the artists' creative practice. As a space, it emblematises the duality of the artist and the artwork. The studio is necessary to artists, not just for creative production but also for the professionalism it confers upon them and the threshold it offers between them and a wider public. As such, artists have long been engaged in finding affordable workspace that allows them to continue making their artwork and offers a non-domestic space in which to contextualise and validate their practice.

SPACE's story illuminates the pressures on, and concerns of, artists in finding workspace and the value and necessity of space to their work. In 1974, SPACE and AIR gained charitable status under the umbrella of Art Services Grants Limited (ASG).[3] This was testament to the ingenuity of the founding artists to create a structure that not only facilitated the production of their work but also functioned as an interface between public bodies, such as local authorities, the Arts Council of Great Britain (ACGB), landlords and developers. According to co-founder Peter Sedgley, ASG was set up, on the advice of Arts Council Chairman Lord Arnold Goodman, with a deliberately wide-ranging constitution, giving it a remit similar to ACGB.

The incorporation of ASG implied a shift from an artist-led initiative to a charity, with the artists as beneficiaries rather than instigators, whereby SPACE became explicitly responsible for the day-to-day management of ASG's portfolio of buildings and its expansion.

AIR Gallery & SPACE Office at Rosebery Avenue.

Artist-led initiatives are arguably vulnerable constitutionally, as administrative responsibilities inevitably impinge on artistic practice in the longer term. Having been the driving forces behind the establishment of SPACE and AIR from their inception, Sedgley and Bridget Riley withdrew slowly, to attend to their own practice. Sedgley moved permanently to Berlin in 1972, after receiving a DAAD fellowship. His decade-long relationship with Riley had ended, and the close working relationship they enjoyed during the founding of SPACE had shifted. A small number of artists retained a role on ASG's Council of Management (COM) (at the time of incorporation, these were Sedgley, Riley, Bryan Kneale and John Hubbard), with a small staff relieving them of much hands-on involvement in the running of the organisation. Martin Argles and then John McEwan became the first coordinators. Neither were artists at the time,[4] so they were unencumbered by the struggle to maintain an artistic practice.

The transition from artist-led initiative to arts charity prompted significant issues around SPACE's direction. Questions of governance impacted the organisation for decades, with disagreements, debates and even mutinies around its priorities and aims. While SPACE, under ASG, took responsibility for leasing buildings – providing and maintaining studios – the artist constituency became distanced from the COM. This was a departure from the situation at St Katharine Docks, where Sedgley and Riley both had studios and where Sedgley, in particular, was an active presence. Artist Bert Irvin commented that, 'Peter, for all his Marxist ideals, was a sympathetic despot; he ran SPACE and there was no doubt about it', adding that, if he wanted to talk to Peter, he could 'go in the pub… and tell Peter exactly what he thought to his face'.[5]

This separation between governance and members was a significant change to the organisational model. Artists became beneficiaries of the organisation, rather than its agents, leaving them space (literally) to pursue their work. With Riley withdrawing to look after her mother and Sedgley moving to Berlin, the key drivers of SPACE and AIR withdrew from the project. Without the 'sweat equity' of the founding artists (both of whom had put their time and money into SPACE and AIR), a more formal structure of compensation was required if the organisation was to continue to grow. That SPACE and AIR had always been perceived as Sedgley and Riley's project might have precluded other artists involving themselves at this level.

This change in constitution raised other issues around the input of the artist constituency into the actions and aims of the organisation. The most notable of these manifested itself in autumn 1975. Referred to at the time as 'The Revolution',[6] it culminated in staff members Argles and Shirley Read calling for the removal of the COM and subsequently being sacked. The impetus for the original dispute was the dismissal by the COM of Norma Binney, who was running AIR, for reasons that the staff felt to be unfair, combined with plans to restructure the organisation. Artists became concerned about the organisational disruption of staff being dismissed en masse, which gave way to wider existential concerns about SPACE ceasing to have artistic representation. Argles commented that:

> There was a general sense that the Council of Management didn't think that the management of AIR and SPACE - particularly AIR I'm afraid - were doing very well… Anyway, it all boiled up, and there was essentially a walk-out by the staff… I think that Richard Leachman [one of the original administrators of SPACE in 1968] felt that the organisation had become… too remote from the artists themselves and that, essentially, it had a moral purpose, which was to ensure that artists weren't trampled on by the gallery system but took control of their own affairs and ran things the way that they would prefer to run them… But, when it actually came down to it, I think artists essentially just wanted a studio space… they didn't want day-to-day hands-on involvement in how it was run. So, the rebellion, if that's what it was, failed.

After the sacking of Binney, Argles and Read, a motion was forwarded to the COM by a group of studio holders to 'discuss the democratisation of the structures of AIR, SPACE and ASG'.[7] At this 1975 meeting, artist Avis Saltzmann stated that 'the artists felt that there was no contact between themselves and the COM and that the artist had no say in arrangements made by the COM in the running of the companies'.[8] The artists were drawn into the conflict between staff and the COM because they wanted to protect themselves from any disruption to their practice.

ROLE AND RESPONSIBILITIES OF ARTIST ADVISORS

ACCOUNTABILITY:

ARTIST AS TRUSTEE

↓

(SPACE ARTISTS)
A.S.G.

ARTIST AS ADVISOR

↓

SPACE ARTISTS

FORMALLY

↓

LOST RESPONSIBILITY/
ACCOUNTABILITY
TO A.S.G.

BOTH ? OR ONE ?

ACTUALLY

RESPONSIBILITY WITHOUT
ACCOUNTABILITY

(STEERING COMMITTEE,
STAFFING SUB-COMMITTEE,
ETC.)

Undated document reflecting on the role of artist advisors, SPACE Archive

The issue of artists' input into SPACE and AIR has arisen repeatedly through the organisation's history. For most of its existence and despite the ongoing sense of disconnection between them, SPACE studio holders occupied up to half the seats on the COM. In 2003, a new constitution was drawn up by the trustees. While artists continue to have a place in the governance as voting members, those who hold studios no longer stand as trustees. Having studio holders on the governing body was seen to be a potential conflict of interest – for example, when budgets with rent increases had to be agreed. There were wider constitutional issues as well – the organisation, set up as an arts and educational charity, needed to deliver on wider objectives than that of simply providing artists' studios. Out of this developed the public engagement programme, which broadly serves as a form of advocacy for the role of the artist in the city by making their presence and work visible and socially active. Open studios, participatory work with schools and community, training and exhibitions all became part of SPACE's public facing activities and were necessary to SPACE expanding and developing its ability to negotiate and secure studio space for artists.

Help Yourself to Studio Space

The establishment of SPACE was written about extensively by both the art and mainstream press,[9] providing a visible and widely publicised model for studio provision. Most artists still worked at home at this time;[10] studio buildings were rare and never, previously, on the scale of those at St Katharine Docks. The publicity garnered by SPACE, undeniably helped by Riley's notoriety, gave currency to the idea of using disused industrial buildings as studio space. SPACE played a significant role in influencing others to use the same model, supporting them with expertise. In this way, St Katharine Docks directly and indirectly influenced the founding of many organisations including SPACEX in Exeter and PS1 in Long Island City, New York.

Alanna Heiss, founding director of PS1, had been an intern at St Katharine Docks, where her then husband, Jene Highstein, had a SPACE studio. On her return to the US, Heiss became the

SPACE BY-ELECTION

Did you know that there is an ELECTION going on NOW, for one of your Space Representatives to the SPACE/AIR/ASG MANAGEMENT COUNCIL

Have you VOTED yet

Your BALLOT PAPER if you have not got it yet will be in the MAIL BOX - possibly in an envelope entitled 'Space Licence Holders'or something similar.

GET YOUR BALLOT PAPER

VOTE NOW - IT MUST BE IN TO THE SPACE OFFICE IN SHAFTSBURY AVENUE BY THIS MONDAY(22 NOV) AT NOON

DONT FORGET TO SIGN THE BACK OF THE ENVELOPE THAT YOU TAKE OR SEND IN.

Please VOTE, if you want your voice to be heard in the management council. We must support by our own personal efforts the forwarding of our candidates by our democratic votes.

VOTE NOW

1975 SPACE by-election document, SPACE Archive

key arbiter of the 'alternative space movement' which sought disused, derelict and 'alternative' buildings and outdoor spaces in which to stage site-specific projects and exhibitions. What began as the Institute for Art and Urban Resources would finally lead to the founding of PS1 in a redundant school.

Heiss has made reference to her time at St Katharine Docks, saying 'I was kind of an artist liaison assistant. I used to give tours of the giant studio complex'.[11] The mix of artists' studios, AIR and other organisations and periodic exhibitions and events that were staged on the site provided a resonant example of an 'alternative space' for artists. In a 2004 interview, she described how 'When I came back to New York... I decided that, instead of struggling with the museum, I could do shows in factories and in industrial areas that would be much more appropriate for the work that was being done. It looked better there'.[12]

The development of SPACEX in Exeter resulted much more directly from SPACE. Artist John Butler, one of the founder members of SPACEX, had been aware of SPACE and AIR, and the model they provided for studio space and the promotion of artist practice, when he was living in London and teaching at Croydon School of Art. In 1974, Butler became a research fellow at the Exeter College of Art and Design. The College had no studio provision for staff, so Butler became part of a cooperative that secured a 19th century quayside warehouse space with the aim of providing affordable studio space to artists. Butler wrote to SPACE and met with staff in March of 1975, receiving general advice on the set-up of studio spaces and the wider format that SPACEX wanted to pursue (which would include an artist-led gallery as well as studios). The original articles of association for SPACEX were taken, with little modification, from SPACE. SPACEX was the first artists' studio organisation, outside of London, to set up in England. Butler has recently established a new artist-led gallery space in Exeter – PS45 on Preston Street, where the original studio spaces were located.

Nick Green has carefully mapped instances of SPACE support and its impact. Discussing the establishment of studios at New Crane Wharf in 1974, Green observes that:

> [...] the New Crane Wharf group benefited from knowledge originally acquired by SPACE. [...] This is intriguing simply because it is another example of the way in which the transfer of information contributed to the survival not only of individual artists and a single group of artists, but also to the growth of the East End arts community as a whole. If we think of this community as a system [...] then we can argue that the system is learning through information transfer, and becoming stronger as a consequence.[13]

ASG was constituted with a third role – the distribution of grants. SPACE began working with ACGB to disburse small studio conversion grants to artists. ACGB had originally contributed to the conversion of studios at St Katharine Docks and, since then, had every year set aside money for studio conversions as part of its provision for housing the arts. SPACE notably provided a grant to ACME for conversion of the latter's first seven houses for artists.[14] In its grant-distributing capacity, SPACE helped to instigate the efflorescence of artists' studios.

A few years later, the dissemination of ideas around studio provision led SPACE, in collaboration with Acme, to publish *Help Yourself to Studio Space*. The pamphlet detailed the activities of SPACE and AIR and provided an accessible outline of how an artist might find cheap and affordable studio space, not only in London but also in other cities throughout the UK. It advised 'If you are finding it difficult to obtain adequate and cheap space, please contact us'.[15] On the final page was a diagram detailing the process of securing studio space, which included such steps as considering 'What are your needs?'. The advice to 'Find empty buildings' was complemented by the questions 'Is it really suitable?', 'How many people are involved?' and 'What assistance is available?'.[16]

'Meanwhile Use'

In SPACE's early years, leases were most frequently on short-life buildings, generally for two or three years while buildings awaited demolition or redevelopment. After vacating St Katharine Docks, SPACE rolled out this model producing a brochure in 1973 that outlined its role:

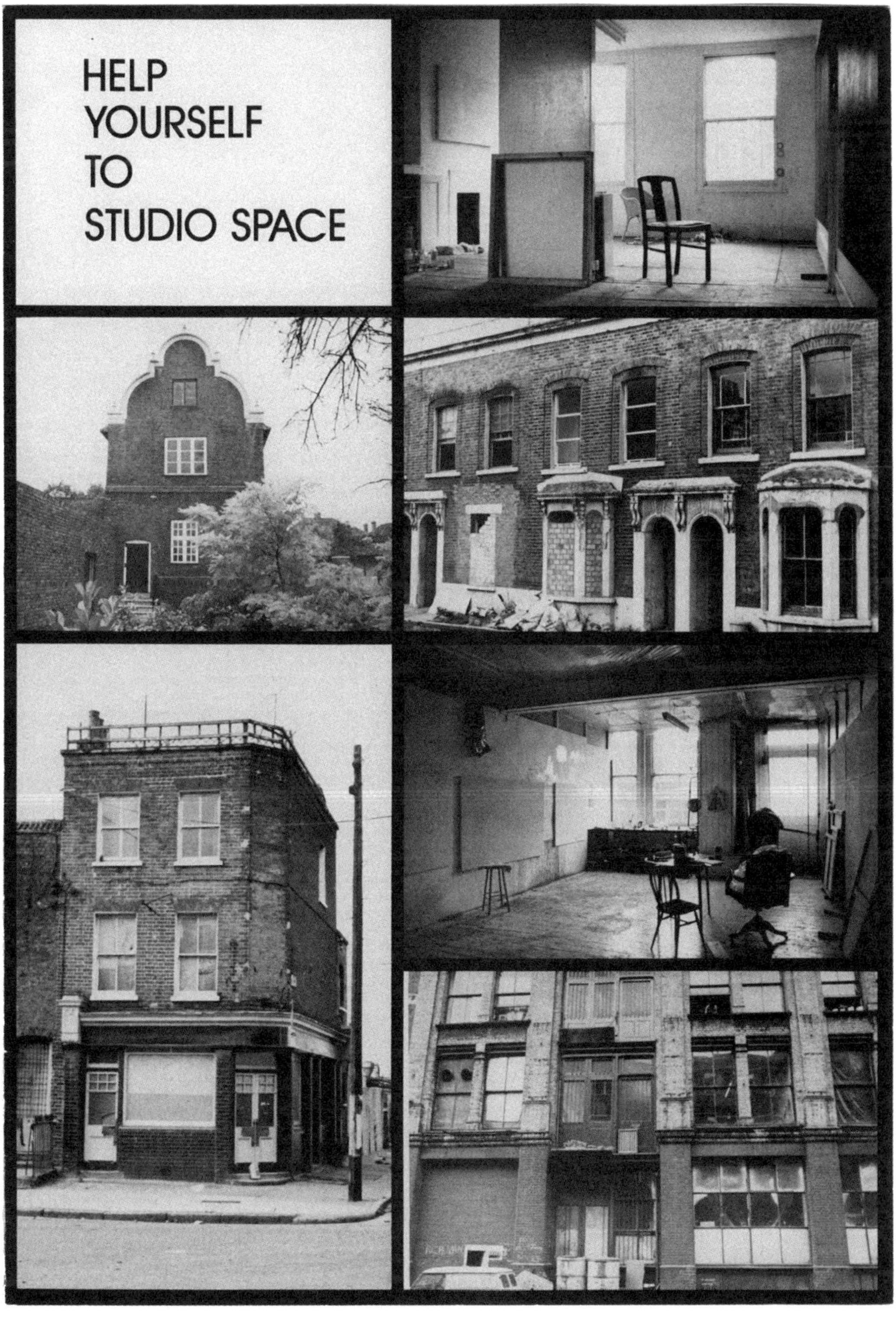

Acme and SPACE. *Help Yourself to Studio Space*.
London: Arts Council of Great Britain, 1975.

This diagram shows the likely steps involved in getting studio space. If you have problems at any stage we should be pleased to help.

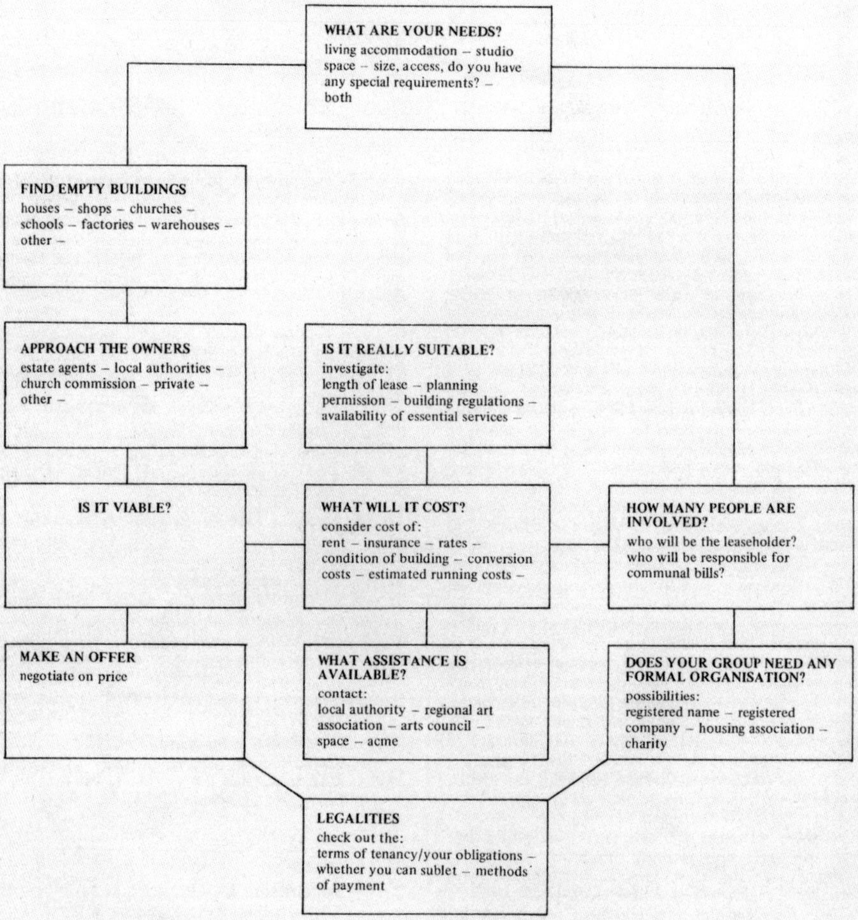

THE ARTS COUNCIL

The Arts Council began to grant-aid the conversion costs of artists' studios in 1968 when St. Katharine Dock was first occupied by SPACE. Since then a specific sum has been set aside each year to give some help to groups of artists who were engaged in converting premises into studios. This year the scheme has been extended to consider applications from individual artists. Schemes are assessed on the viability of the scheme in question (including the overall cost) and also on the seriousness and commitment of the artists involved.

The Arts Council of Great Britain

Acme and SPACE. *Help Yourself to Studio Space*.
London: Arts Council of Great Britain, 1975.

> SPACE's policy now is to negotiate, on behalf of professional artists in need of working space, for buildings that tend to be commercially unusable (due to scheduled redevelopment or demolition) and which are rented by artists for a moderate cost and usually on a short-term licence basis. The experience and practical assistance that SPACE also offers on leasing agreements, rates, conversion grants, planning permission, means of escape, fire regulations, insurance and the general administration of studio projects is invaluable to artists organising their own studios, and very many such independent projects have been successfully established. [...] This service is given free to all artists and where practicable to projects in any part of the British Isles.[17]

The presence of artists in disused buildings is valuable to the building's owners; it inhibits misuse of vacant buildings by providing 'caretakers' – people with rights to, and personal investment in, the space. The 'meanwhile use' of unused real estate can also help increase its value when it is subsequently redeveloped. What began as an exploitation of the opportunity of 'meanwhile' spaces led to a quest to secure space in the longer term. Jim Madge, director of SPACE from 1982 to 1991, outlined the limitations of his role:

> I had no experience at all. But at the salary, they were never going to get anybody who was going to be good at it. I mean, for my job, you needed to be a brilliant man manager, you needed to have profound knowledge of property law, architecture, be really interested in the arts and be a good accountant. £5,000 a year? Thank you! It was fairly amateur in the old sense of enthusiastic amateurs.[18]

Madge identified poorly negotiated leases as one of the biggest challenges facing SPACE during his tenure. Lease negotiations were undertaken on a pro-bono basis by a long-time ASG board member and solicitor with no expertise in property law.

While no blame is to be assigned, this situation points to organisational vulnerabilities. Aside from dilapidations (liabilities for any deterioration of the building), rent reviews required skill to achieve a beneficial agreement. Poor negotiation skills could result either in the loss of a lease or in an onerous rent increase with the potential to push studio fees beyond the means of many studio holders. Along with expensive dilapidations demands, SPACE suffered from poorly negotiated leases throughout the 1980s.

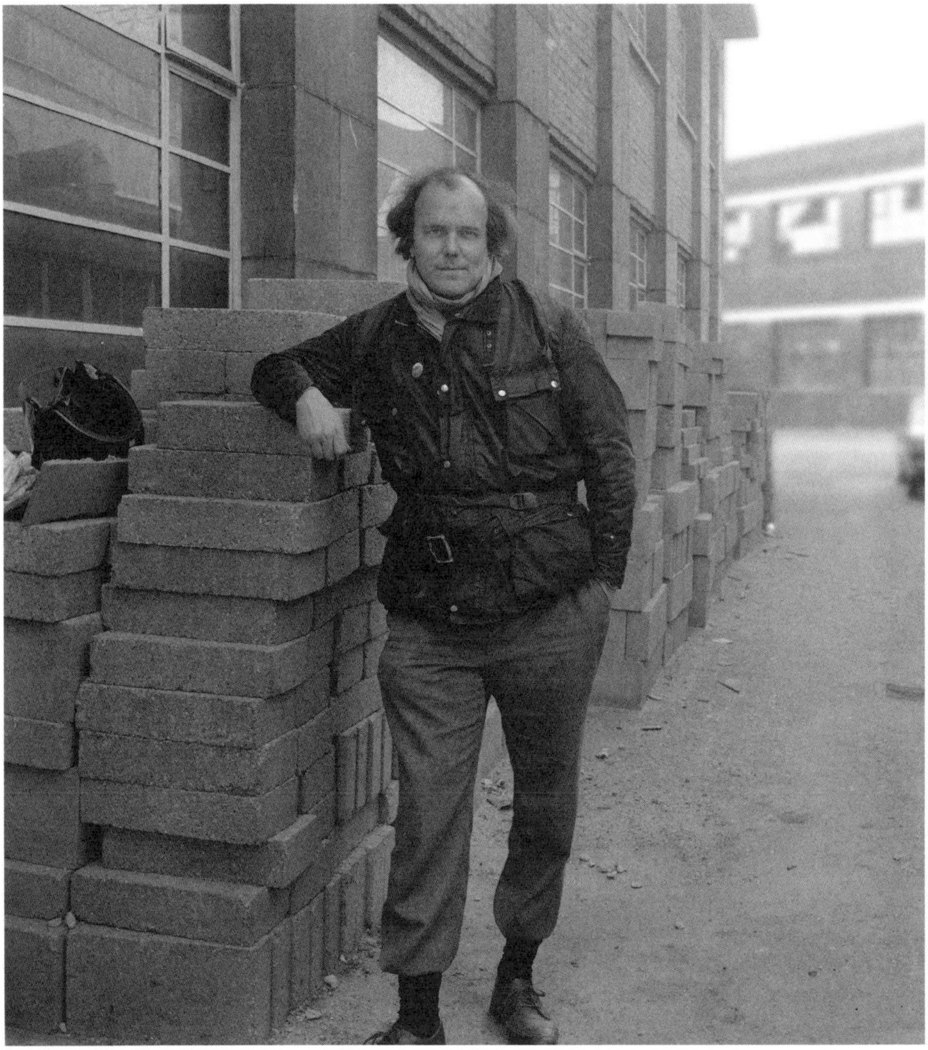

Jim Madge, director of SPACE from 1982 to 1991.

The End of 'Meanwhile Use'

Even before the dodgy leases had a financial impact on SPACE, securing buildings with long-term leases or on a freehold basis became an explicit aim of the organisation. In the Annual Report of 1982, the desires and difficulties of sustainability were laid out:

> In the present economic climate landlords seek a realistic return on their property, and the particular circumstances of the Seventies, which enabled us to secure many of our buildings on low rents, are now over. [...] One of the most positive developments this year has been in the area of longer leases. SPACE has secured Milborne Street, Belsham Street, Richmond Road and Columbia Road on 20 year leases. [...] Our efforts to secure a freehold property during the year were unsuccessful. SPACE made bids for two ILEA owned schools and one privately owned premises. The main difficulty is a financial one. And the fact that many of the premises are also very attractive to developers with whom we cannot compete.

Ownership of a building would be a goal for nearly 30 years, until 2010, when SPACE purchased its first building. The organisation has since bought and fitted out two more.

Part of the push towards a more sustainable organisational model, based on long-term leaseholds and ownership, was motivated by shifts in public funding priorities. In the mid 1980s, ACGB was restructured to implement its 'Glory of the Garden' strategy, with funding for SPACE devolved to the Greater London Arts Association (GLAA). In the ACGB restructure, the 'Housing the arts' programme was ended along with the 100 percent studio conversion grants, from which SPACE had greatly benefitted during its first 15 years. SPACE was warned that it 'should become administratively self-sufficient within four years'.[19] This warning blindsided the organisation, and Madge noted that the threatened cut to their core funding 'would mean that the monthly licence fees paid by the artists would have to be loaded with the administrative costs – resulting in a prohibitive increase of 25%'.[20] ACGB agreed that SPACE should aim to purchase a freehold to improve its sustainability, but the funding body offered no financial support in realising this aim.

AIR Gallery was also facing withdrawal of its £40,000 ACGB subsidy and trying to address how it might survive. This exacerbated the schism in the COM. The arguments that arose from this new threat demarcated competing organisational aims – that of supporting artists' practice through studio provision and that of facilitating access to, and engagement with, artists' practice for audiences via the gallery.

Civic Duties?

As an arts and educational charity, SPACE had dual aims. Its core objective had always been to 'aid, assist and educate necessitous artists',[21] primarily through the provision of affordable studio space. However, the charity aimed to deliver benefit to a wider public beyond its studio holders, as stated in the charity's objectives 'to foster, promote, advance, maintain and improve public education and to promote interest and appreciation of all forms of art'.[22] With the push towards self-sufficiency, the COM was forced to consider its priorities. This process illuminated fundamental tensions between the needs of artists, served by SPACE, and the wider remit of delivering public benefit through AIR. It also illuminated the interdependent nature of these aims, which served each other in practical ways.

News of ACGB's desire that SPACE (and also Acme) move towards self-sufficiency spread from the COM to studio holders. In light of the parallel threat to the studios' affordability, concerns about keeping AIR Gallery open began to be raised. Artist and COM member John Dugger acted as instigator of, and conduit for, a studio holders' protest. The COM Executive Committee meeting minutes of 11 July 1984 note that:

> […] the question of capital funding for AIR and SPACE seemed to have been put aside in favour of finding money to keep AIR going. […] Alan Haydon (GLAA) said that he did, to an extent, share John Dugger's view that all efforts appeared to be directed towards keeping the Gallery open and that this could be to the detriment of SPACE. […]

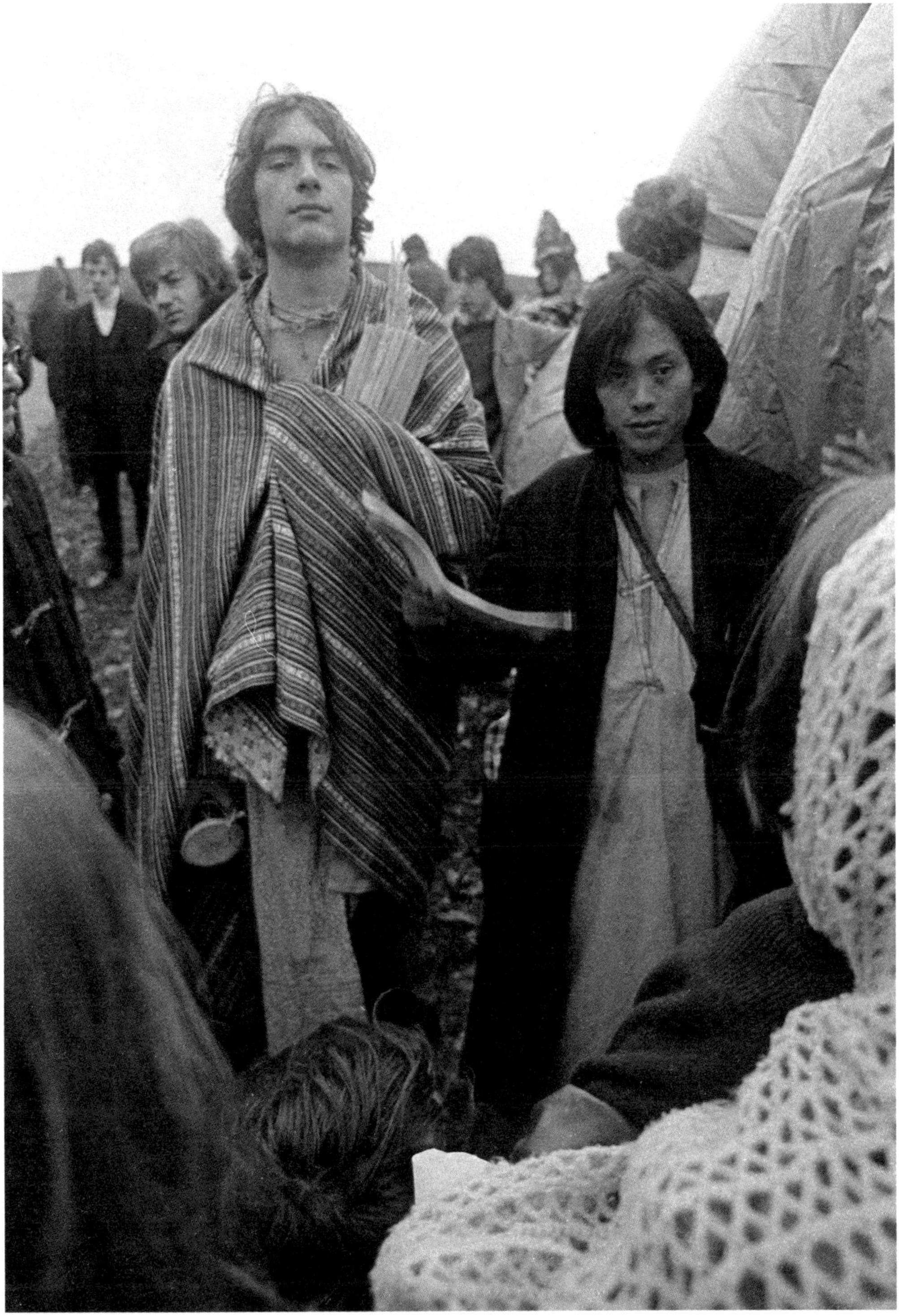

John Dugger and David Medalla at a happening on Parliament Hill Fields standing next to Graham Stevens' inflatable.

> Ian Jenkin said that he had always felt that SPACE was the most important part of ASG. [...] Jim Madge said that whatever the Art Panel decided, it was necessary to aim to be more self-sufficient and this was only possible by buying buildings, it was vital that ASG continued to accumulate a capital fund. [...] Laurie Lowenthal [a trustee] felt that there was a clash of interests... when the last thing the organisation should be doing was pulling in different directions.

The counter argument was provided by the Chair of Trustees, Nancy Balfour, who was so committed to keeping AIR open that she loaned her own money to help facilitate it. A report produced on 6 September 1984 by a Working Party of the COM to resolve the schism in priorities stated that:

> [...] the [AIR] gallery is, in the view of those involved in fund-raising, an essential part of such an effort, acting as a shop window for everything that ASG does: offering occasions for news stories and public relations exercises [and] providing a venue for money-raising events which benefit the whole organisation. It also provides a service which is essential to many artists and a basis for educational programmes which appeal to financial sponsors.

This position argues for the need to engage a broader public, not simply to deliver 'public benefit' as a charity but also because it provides profile and visibility for the organisation as a whole. The delivery of public benefit is an essential element in ensuring the continued access to affordable studio space.

Notes

1 Mary Jane Jacob and Michelle Grabner, *The Studio Reader / On the Space of Artists* (Chicago: University of Chicago Press, 2009) v – viii.

2 Ibid, p. 2.

3 Company registered 21 December 1973, charity registered January 1974.

4 Argles subsequently became an esteemed photojournalist who worked for *The Guardian* for many years; at the time he took the job at SPACE, he had been studying architecture and had been working for a community-based organisation working to preserve Covent Garden as it faced the destruction of its eponymous market (Martin Argles, iInterview with the author, 12 May 2010).

5 Bert Irvin, interview with the author, 21 January 2011.

6 Martin Argles, op. cit.; Letty Mooring, interview with the author, 10 December 2010; Shirley Read, interview with the author, 2 September 2010..

7 17 November 1975, Minutes of the Meeting of the COM, 1973–2004, and the Elected Artists Deputation. SPACE Archive.

8 Ibid.

9 In 1969, the SPACE Manifesto appeared in *Studio International*, and SPACE was featured in *The Guardian*, *Times Educational Supplement*, *Sunday Times*, *New York Times* and *Birmingham Post*.

10 C. Nick Green, *From Factories to Fine Art: The origins and evolution of East London's artists' agglomeration, 1968–1998*. Thesis (PhD), University College London, 2001, p. 60.

11 'Alanna Heiss in Conversation', *The Brooklyn Rail*, 18 December 2014, tinyurl.com/ybz3sbxw

12 Rachel Small, 'Alanna Heiss, on the Horizon', *Interview*, 2014, tinyurl.com/ybjjosu4

13 C. Nick Green, op. cit., p. 21.

14 Arts Council of Great Britain, Letter to Helen Dickson, Company Secretary, 1973, SPACE. SPACE Archive.

15 Acme and SPACE, *Help Yourself to Studio Space.* (London: Arts Council of Great Britain, 1975). Available through: tinyurl.com/y7robxw2

16 Ibid.

17 SPACE publicity brochure, 1973, SPACE Archive

18 Jim Madge, interview with the author, 11 August 2011.

19 27 April 27, 1984, executive committee meeting minutes, SPACE Archive.

20 7 and 27 April 1984, Minutes of the Meeting of the COM, op. cit.

21 Art Services Grants Limited, Annual Report 2010, SPACE Archive.

22 Ibid.

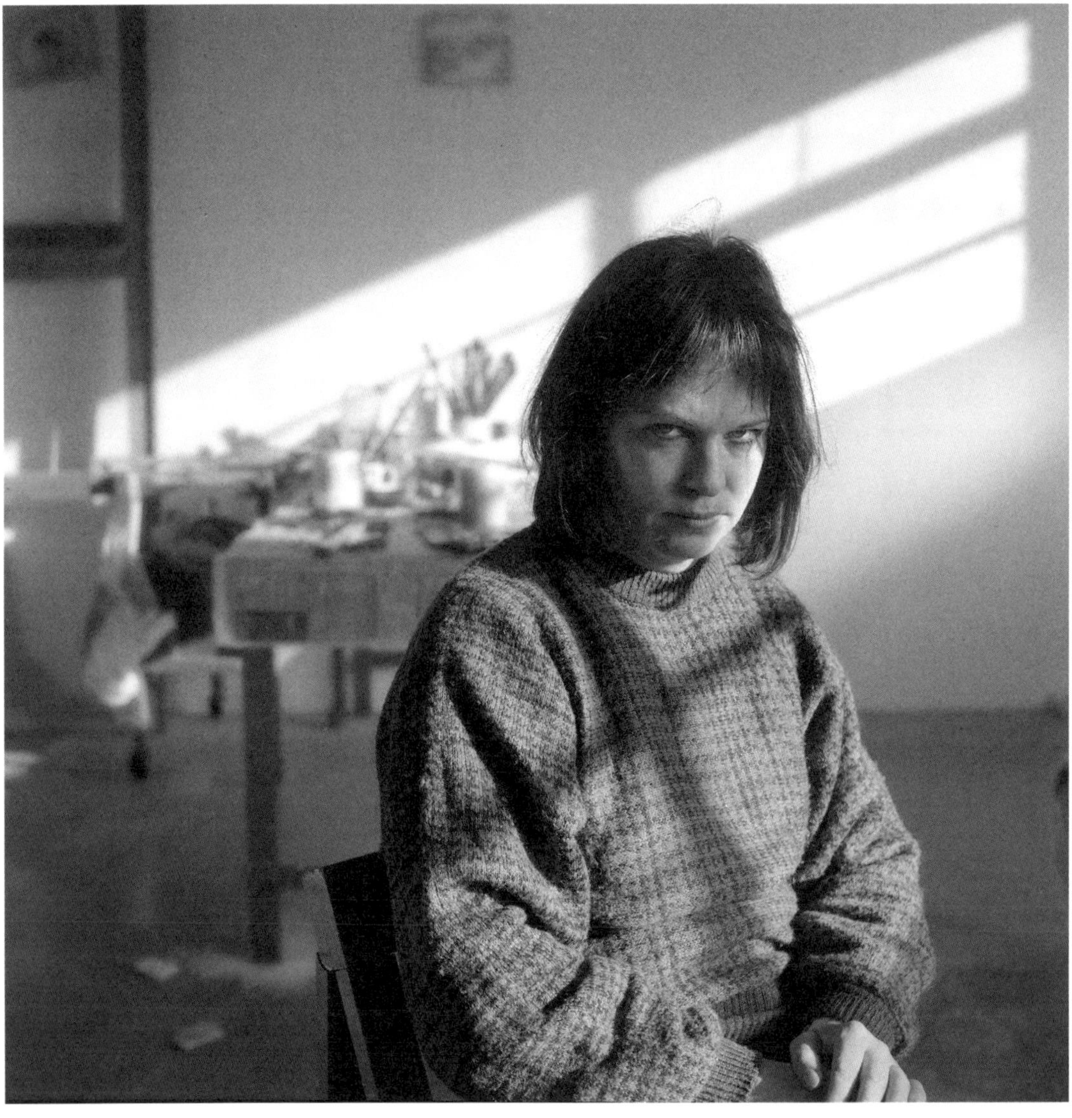

Artist Alexis Hunter in her studio in 1986.

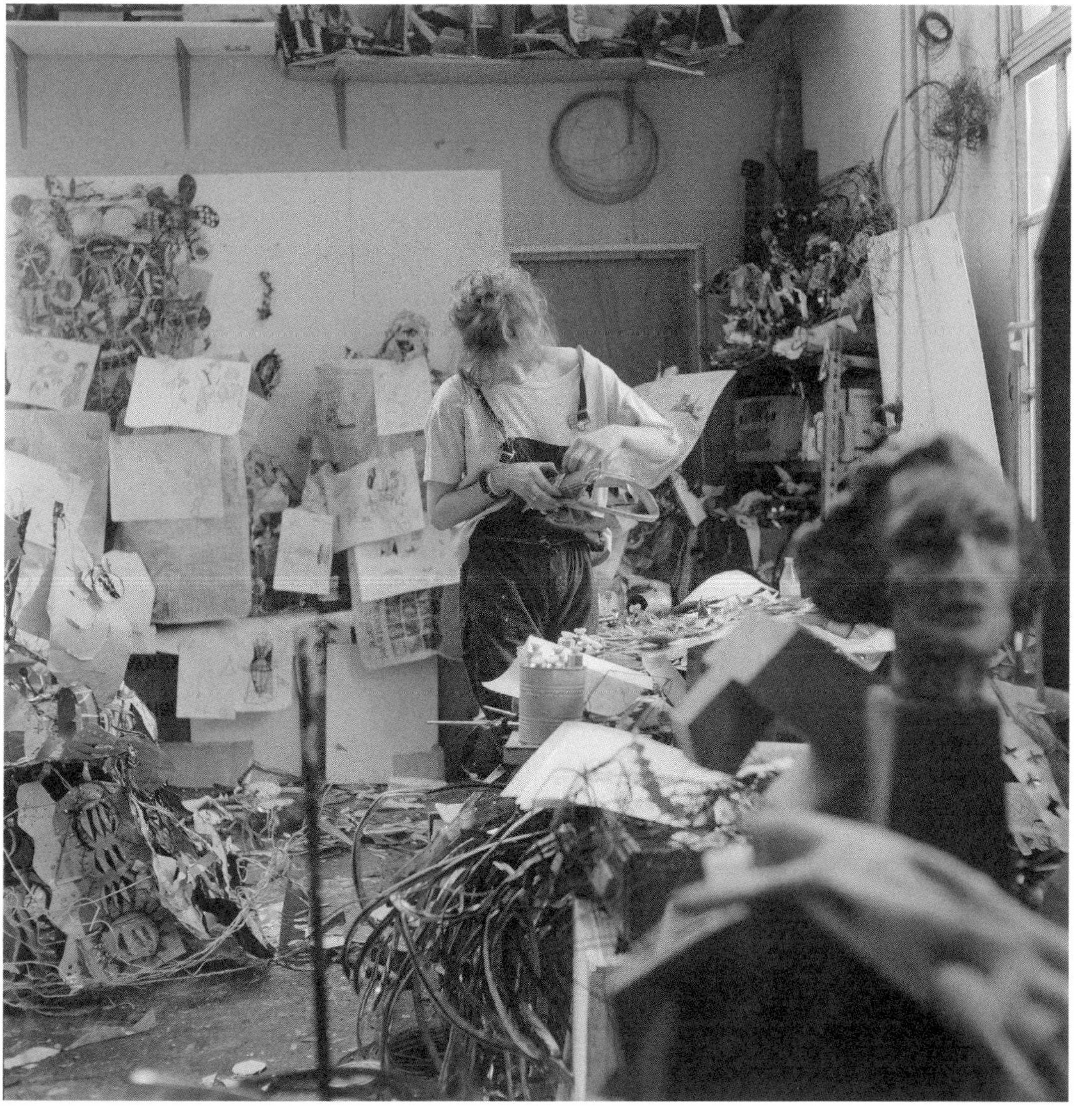

Artist Amanda Benson in her studio in 1987.

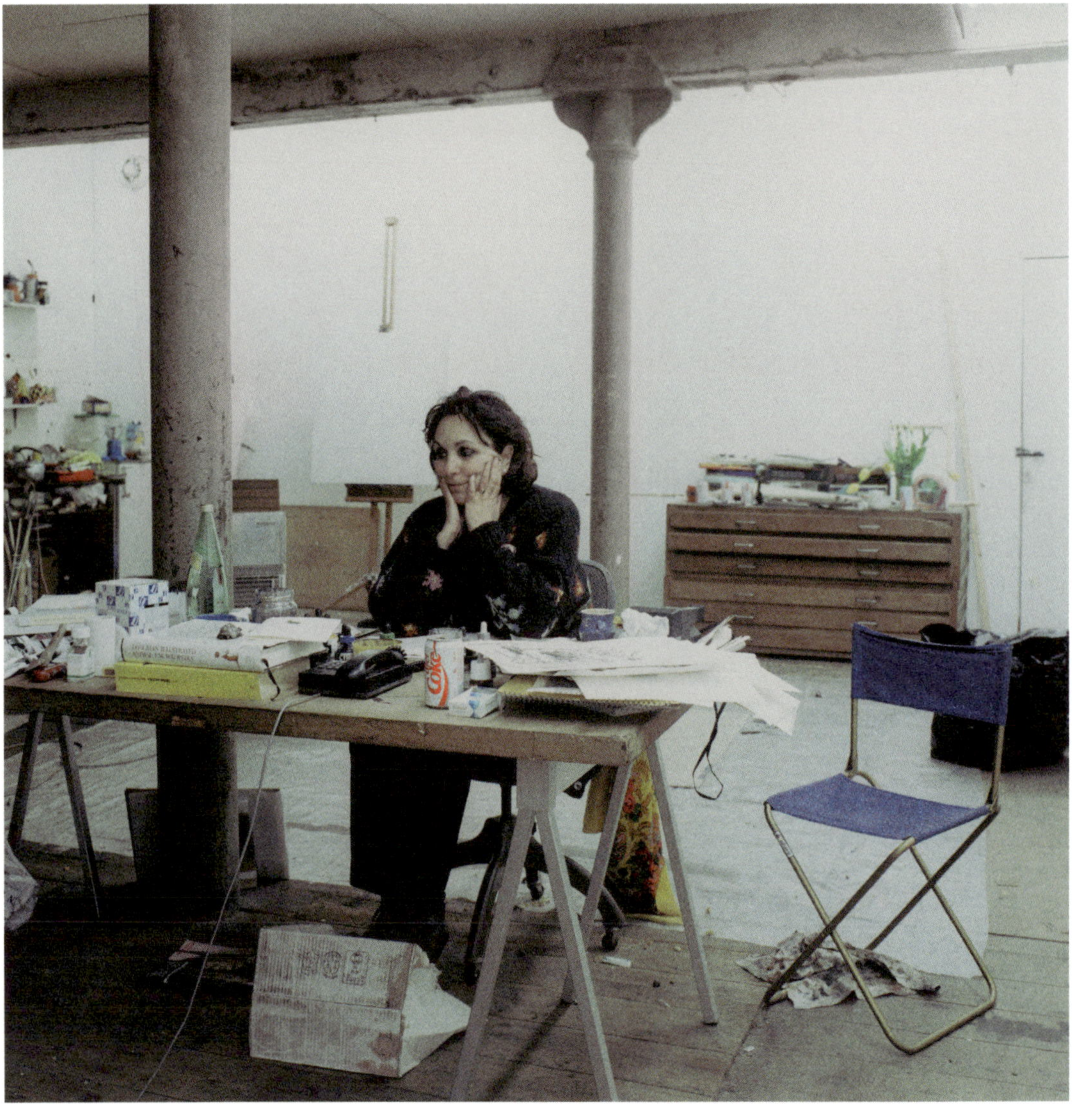

Artist Paula Rego in her studio in 1989.

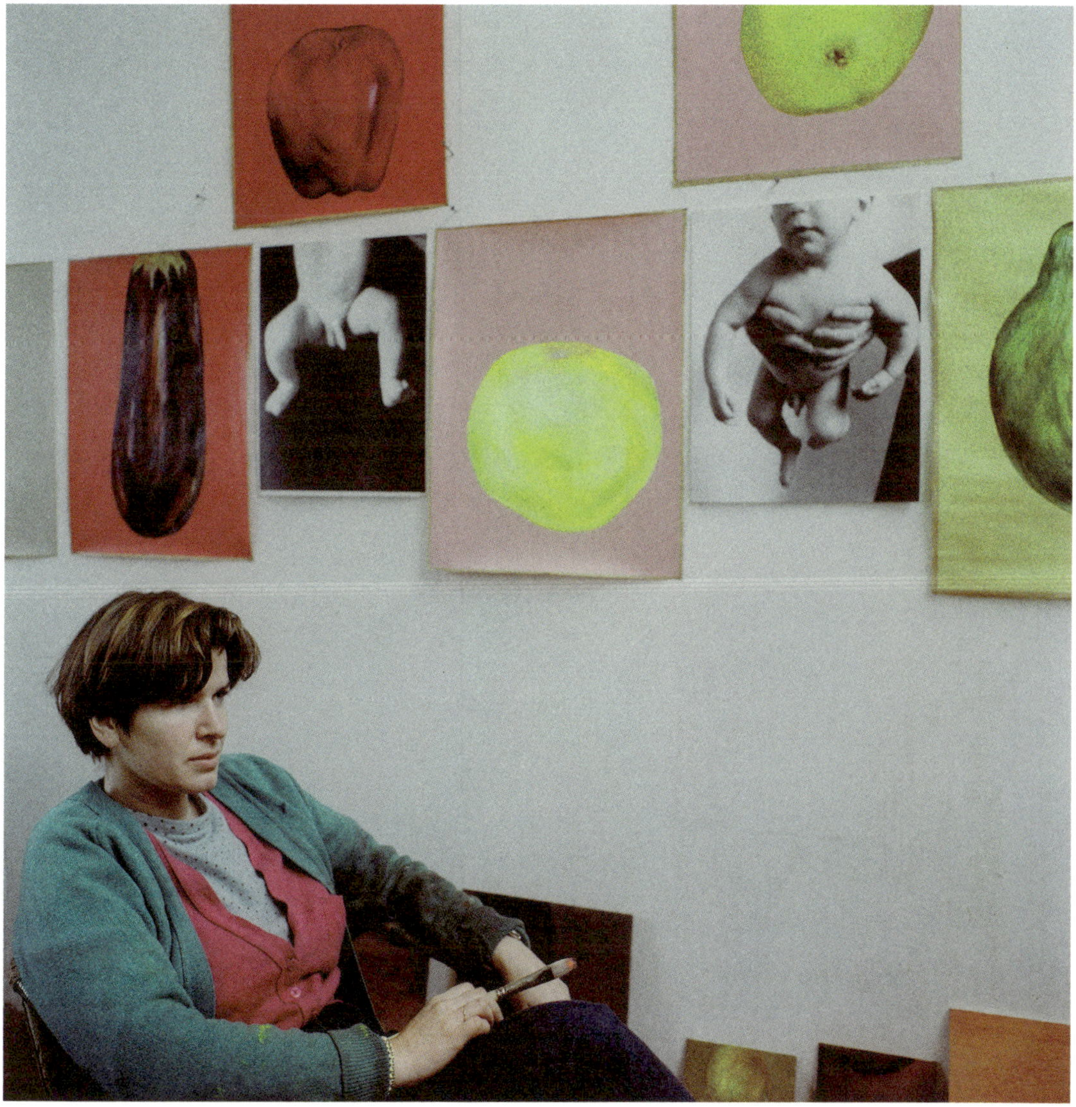

Artist Felicity (Flick) Allen in her studio in 1989.

Change

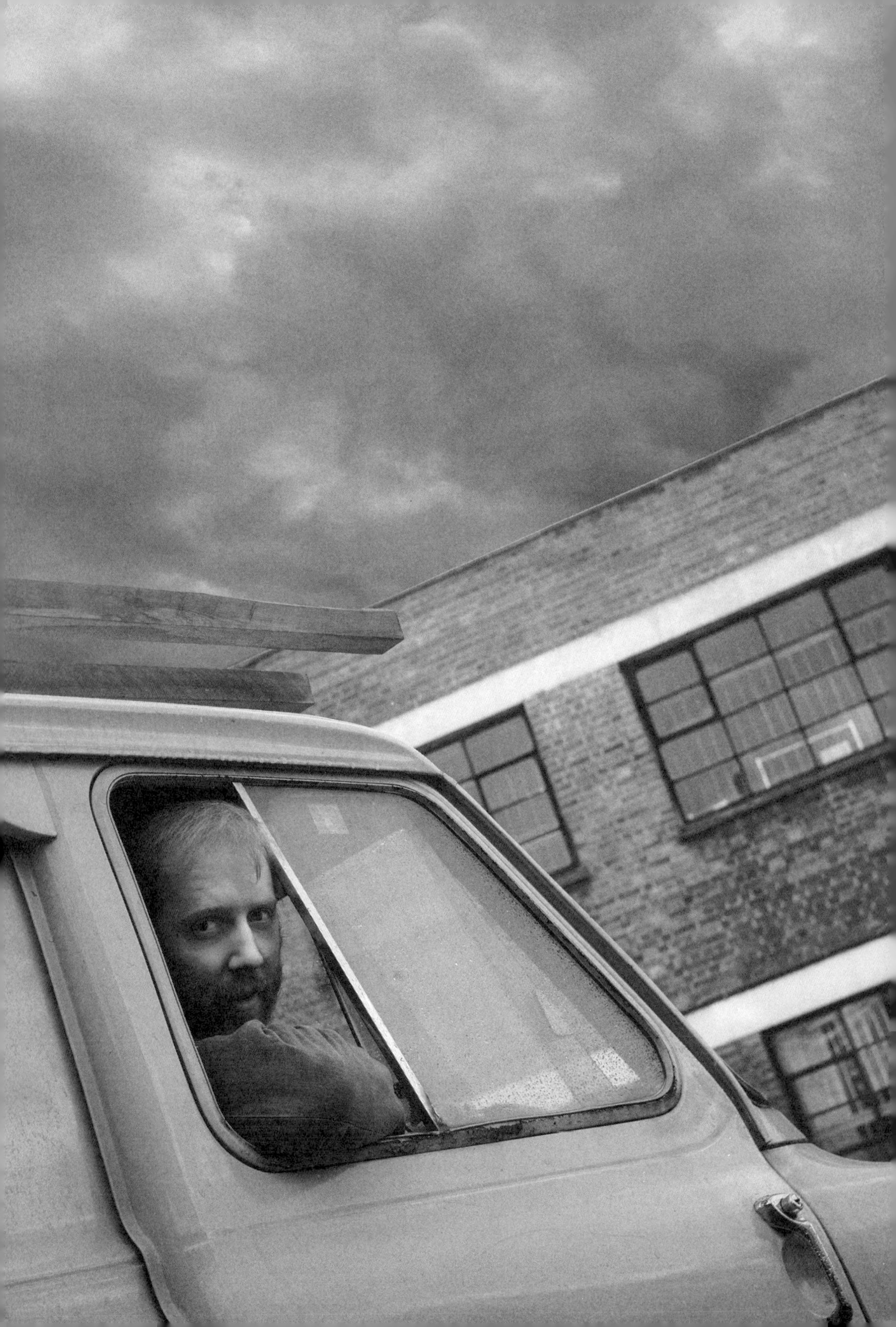

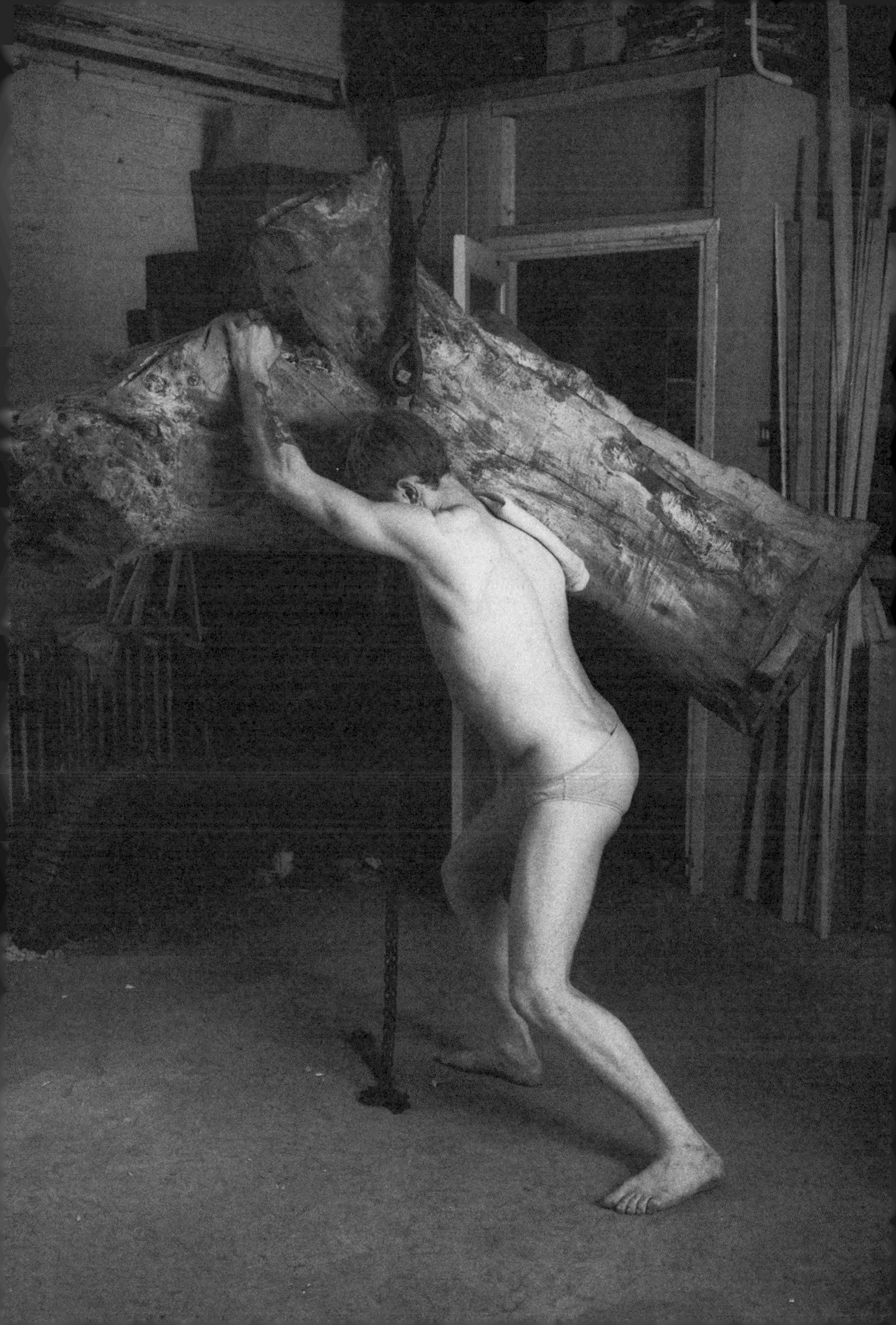

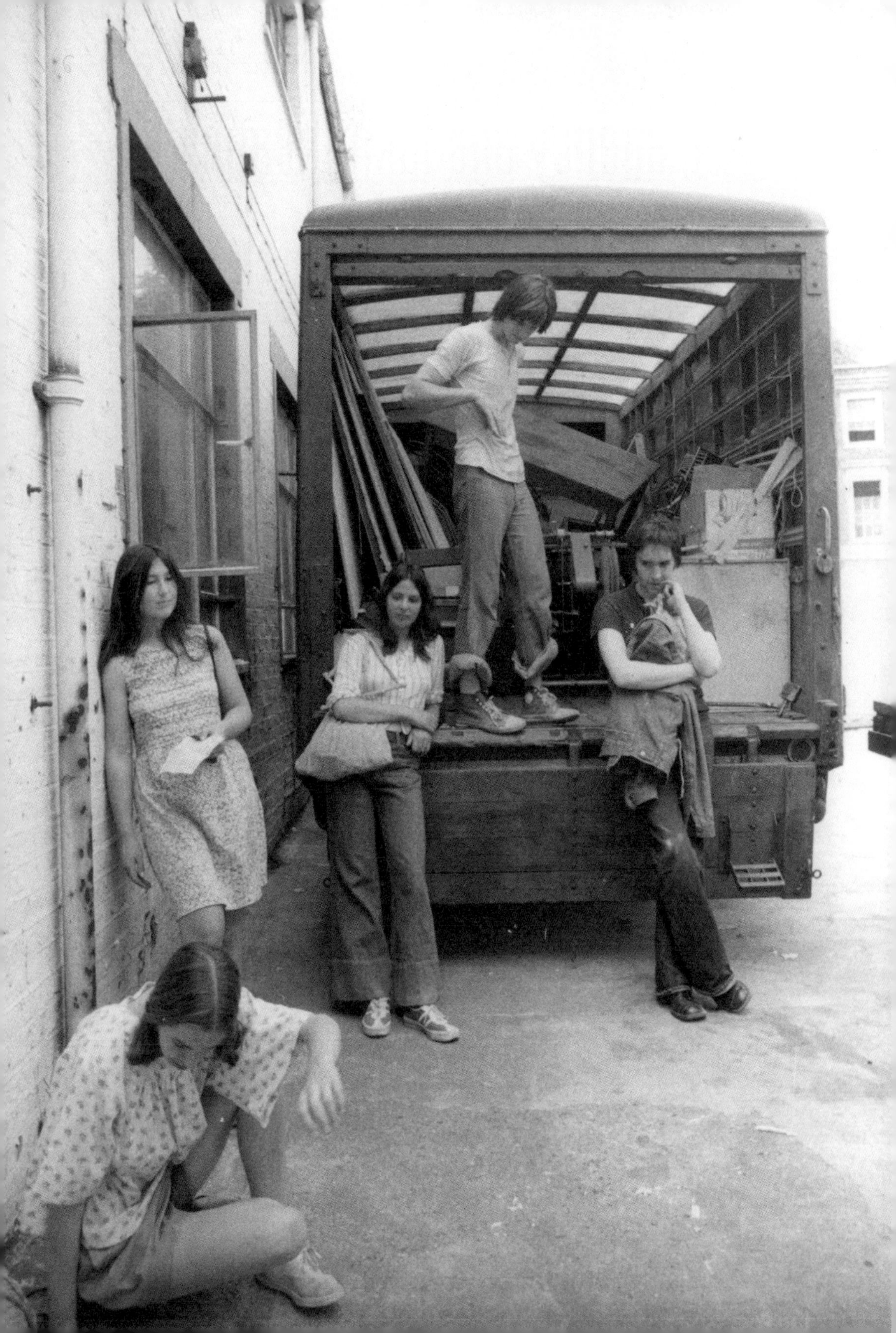

Art, agency and identification

Larne Abse Gogarty

In their 1984 article 'The Fine Art of Gentrification', Rosalyn Deutsche and Cara Gendel Ryan argued that the art world had played a 'crucial role' in the drastic transformation of Soho and the Lower East Side in New York.[1] In analysing gentrification as a form of neo-colonialism, Deutsche and Gendel Ryan emphasised the racialised dimension of 'reclaiming' primarily working-class, black and Latino neighbourhoods as 'frontiers' of urban renewal in New York City. Since then, a significant and diverse body of literature on the role of artists and art institutions in the gentrification of cities has mushroomed. Richard Florida's 2002 book, *The Rise of the Creative Class* happily affirmed the role of art as a tool of urban regeneration and provided a framework for the top-down instrumentalisation of art as a regenerating force by civic bodies and corporations, an argument which he has since rescinded, having seen how this vision supported economic segregation. In London, the instrumentalisation of 'creativity' by property developers has taken shape through myriad post-millennial initiatives, and criticisms of artists and art institutions as handmaidens to gentrification have proliferated almost as rapidly as the regeneration schemes themselves. Yet, within this discourse, hand-wringing self-criticism tends to dominate. Overall, not enough attention has been paid to the systemic relationship between property, race and class, which is the bedrock of capitalism and therefore of how cities develop under this system. Instead, there has been an over-emphasis on 'cultural capital', where individual consumption patterns and lifestyle choices are viewed as the agents of change, rather than as symptoms. Artists moving into a neighbourhood, luxury apartments, cereal cafes and organic grocers all signal varying stages within the story of how cities like London, New York and Los Angeles have seen huge rises in property prices and rents. But dwelling on these examples does not necessarily get us very far in terms of analysing and fighting against dispossession and the foreclosure of public space. Whilst areas like Boyle Heights in Los Angeles have recently mounted relatively successful anti-gentrification campaigns, these examples are few and far between.

Preceding spread Artist Stevey Scullion in his day-time job as SPACE maintainance staff and in his studio.

Members of the London Film Makers Co-op moving out of the Dairy in 1975.

In the art world, the discourse around art and gentrification is marked by such a degree of self-reflexivity that it often results in a peculiar kind of narcissism. Within the continuous restating of the formula artists = gentrifiers, there lies a capacity to lend the identity 'artist' a power and agency it rarely has in public life, aside from for those at the top of the food chain with a certain subject-hood. Moreover, anxiety among artists, art critics, curators and art institutions about their role in gentrification too often reinforces an exclusive and normative notion of artistic identity and practice. In 2014, the writer Daniel José Older succinctly summarised this problem in *Salon*.[2] Writing in response to a *New York Magazine* article entitled 'Is Gentrification All Bad?', which reproduced the standard narrative of artists as pioneers, Older insisted that the 'presumptive, unspoken' adjective that is missing in such debates is 'white'. In other words, when artists are inscribed as 'arriving' in a neighbourhood as agents of change, this implies that the poor, and often racialised, urban communities that are subject to the frontier effect of gentrification harbour no artists themselves. Older's argument brings into focus the limits of liberal narratives around art and gentrification. Not only does the standard story delegitimise cultural production that remains on the margins – whether by choice or exclusion – it also simultaneously serves to enshrine the identity of the artist in the tired old figure of the white, male genius, powerful in his capacity to transform a neighbourhood simply through the virtue of being there as an *artist*, rather than through other aspects of his subjecthood.

This points to the riven quality of the identity 'artist' and the unspoken hierarchies and exclusions that are operational within the force of the formula art = gentrification. Following on from Older's argument, how might we think more critically about contemporary identity formation within the art world and the relationship this has to lived experience in the cities which form the material base for that world? Are there contemporary possibilities of a collective identity formation around the designation 'artist' which do not simply indulge in the feedback loop of self-critique?

At the outset of the debate around art and gentrification at the end of the 1980s, the artist Martha Rosler embarked on what has become a seminal project within this discourse. Entitled *If You Lived Here*, Rosler worked alongside residents, activists and artists on a year-long project that dealt with issues of homelessness, public space and regeneration in New York City through a series of exhibitions and public programming. The project was based at the Dia Art Foundation's SoHo gallery space, and it thus involved a high degree of self-criticism and reflection due to Dia's implication in what Rosler describes as the 'real estate/art institution nexus'.[3] Following their expansion in the 1980s, Dia acquired a significant amount of property in Tribeca and SoHo, becoming deeply entangled in the forms of urban development Rosler's project sought to examine.

The collaborative orientation of the project affected the style of the storefront space on Wooster Street. The phrase 'Come on in – We're home' was stencilled in large red letters on the door, and ACT UP (AIDS Coalition to Unleash Power) displayed posters on the exterior of the building. Once inside the gallery, TV monitors showed films, photographs and paintings were displayed on the walls and paper-based materials were presented in filing cabinets and on pin boards. The space clearly sought to counter the standards of mainstream art world displays, and because of the project's purported function as a temporary site for analysing and responding to the housing crisis, the installation appeared more like a community centre or info-shop.

Once inside, visitors could spend an extended period of time browsing the material installed at each phase of the project, watching films or sifting through the leaflets which offered services, advice and notifications about political events relating to housing. The sign on the front door was the first signal that visitors were positioned less as viewers and instead thought of as entering a space in which they could interact with material in multiple ways, opening up the possibility of having different kinds of encounters with the subject of housing and homelessness. Different aspects of the exhibitions were also clearly targeted towards different demographics, perhaps most notably in Homeward Bound, which saw a self-organised coalition of homeless people taking up residence at Wooster Street, offering counselling as well as information about shelters, employment services and soup kitchens. The project was organised into three phases, with part one – 'Home Front' – taking up the theme of contested housing and directly addressing the relationship between art and gentrification. Printed on the wall of the exhibition was a statement by then Mayor, Ed Koch, stating 'If you can't afford to live here, mo-o-ve!' which summed up the attitude of the city's administration to community displacement by gentrification. Among other issues, Koch's support for artists' housing was discussed in the public forum entitled 'Artists' Life/Work', which formed part of the first exhibition, Home Front. In the early 1980s, the Koch administration began the Artists' Home Ownership Program, which enabled artists to buy units within 16 abandoned buildings in a dilapidated zone of the Lower East Side. Low-interest loans facilitated these purchases, and the applying artists were requested to form groups and prepare architectural plans for the rehabilitation of the buildings into live/work units at a low cost. The programme was eventually halted in 1983 as a result of local outrage at the city's desire to funnel $3m of public funds towards artists' housing, yet Koch's plans remained an important point of reference during the public forums.

If You Lived Here has become a kind of standard-bearer for how to approach the issue of art and gentrification from within the mainstream art world, and Rosler has continued to write extensively on the subject. Yet, the transcript of the 'Artists' Life/Work' event is instructive when considering an early example of the kind of self-aware, yet somewhat myopic, inertia that continues to characterise the dynamic between artists and gentrification, at least in part due to the incoherence of the identity 'artist'. Within the discussion, Jero Nesson, an artist who established a cooperative live/work space in Boston, pleaded the case for artists to professionalise their need for housing and studio space and work alongside local government. In contrast, Adrienne Leban, an artist from Manhattan, alongside Marilyn Nance, a photographer from Brooklyn, self-critically asked how artists could participate in struggles against displacement whilst knowing they form part of the problem. Joe Giordano, a painter employed in the Department of Cultural Affairs, advocated that artists form alliances and lobby for their interests as a group often marginalised by property speculation, despite their implication within this process.

These divergent positions indicate the lack of a common political touchstone for artists working in New York during the late 1980s and 1990s, as compared with various historical moments at which artists have temporarily organised politically, under the identity of artist as worker (for example, the Art Workers' Coalition, various artists' unions and, more recently, Working Artists and the Greater Economy (WAGE) in the United States). In Deutsche and Gendel Ryan's argument, authored just five years before Rosler's project, the l980s New York art world was characterised by the absence of a sustained collective politics. As they write, this was shaped by an atmosphere of hyper-individualism and the art world's market-led excitement over solipsistic, neo-expressionist painting which had come to supplant minimalism and conceptualism as the dominant genre being discussed in that moment.

Writing on the subject of gentrification more recently, Rosler remains intent on affirming that 'artists tend to want to lend themselves and their energy and abilities to social betterment and utopian dreaming, but not necessarily as participants within the sanctioned institutionalized frames. The artistic imagination continues to dream of historical agency'.[4] This clarifies one of the reasons why artists, and the art world more generally, have been situated as such a powerful force within contemporary debates on gentrification. If, as Rosler suggests, artists continue to dream of historical agency, the notion of artist-as-gentrifier has made this dream a reality, albeit in a dystopian, rather than utopian, framework. The notion offers a quality of agency because it links the individual experience of artists to their force as a social group. But, as Older has suggested, the unspoken truth of that social group's agency is always more to do with race, class and gender than being an artist. In the UK in 2017, perhaps these divisions and distinctions, which disallow any real coherence to the identity category 'artist', need to be reckoned with in relation to Brexit and the realities of the austerity years post-2010.

If the discussion during *If You Lived Here* evidenced the failures of a common position around housing for artists in New York almost 30 years ago, the reality of a post-Brexit London art world and its relationship to local, national and international concerns is even more riven. We might find a parallel with that moment in the late 1980s in the market hype around neo-expressionism, related to the re-assertion of London's position as a key site for the production, sale and display of contemporary art. This continuum begins with the yBa generation and has survived through the financial crisis and the austerity measures beginning in 2010. Since the Conservative-Liberal Democrat coalition came to power in 2010, public funding for the arts has contracted and university tuition fees have tripled. Yet, across London, small project spaces and galleries have continued to grow, primarily home to young artists, with the most successful ones often invested in the milieu of post-internet art, a genre which has been enormously hyped. In parallel with these market-friendly developments, the London art world experienced a kind of politicisation, with groups such as Arts Against Cuts and the Precarious Workers Brigade seeking to critique the art world's complicity with austerity. These trajectories have sometimes intersected, with many of the younger spaces in London projecting their associations with radical politics through programming and exhibitions. For example, galleries such as Arcadia Missa in Peckham convey a hyper-awareness of their role in gentrification, with their website asking visitors who are not familiar with the area to be mindful and support long-standing local pubs, restaurants and shops rather than 'Trojan horse' businesses. Yet the challenges of upholding such self-reflexive positions whilst maintaining a relationship to the market are significant, and they require responsibility from artists, institutions and others active in the art world. By invoking responsibility here, I am specifically not asking for an increase in professionalisation, which has become normalised as a path to success and respectability. Instead, if artists are to gain agency as a political force in the present – to 'lend themselves and their energy and abilities to social betterment and utopian dreaming' as Rosler suggests – they might do well to heed what Lippard wrote in 1970, in the context of the Art Workers Coalition. As she stressed, 'the majority of the artworld is afraid to take its bullshit out of the bars and into the streets, afraid of losing the toehold it got last year on the next rung of the ladder, but at the same time afraid that the ladder will have been burned, toppled or blown sky high'.[5]

Brexit and the rise of far-right populism are shaking the ladder of the liberal art world in more ways than one. Brexit has prompted concern from many in the art world over their own future, and one hopes – following Lippard – that it will simultaneously heighten awareness of how the careerist promise of future success is frequently complicit with an individualism that dehumanises others. Many in the art world responded to the Brexit vote with deep shock and a sense of anguish and betrayal, perhaps joining marches and draping themselves in EU flags or, at the very least, maintaining their pro-remain Facebook profile pictures, as if to preserve a time before this great loss.

Recently, Sven Lütticken described the art world's disbelief at the global rise of far-right populism – with Brexit as its crowning jewel in Europe and Trump in the US – as 'Wolfgang Tillmans

Syndrome'. In the run-up to the referendum on the UK's membership of the EU, photographer Tillmans launched a pro-EU poster campaign. Although many of the slogans warned directly of the relationship between Brexit and rising xenophobia and had a real value in doing so, others encapsulated everything about the so-called liberal, metropolitan elite as characterised by Leave voters. For example, one of Tillmans' posters read: 'My Father's Polish, My Mum's from Spain, I studied in Berlin, now live in the UK. It's never been a hassle to do so. And I don't want it to be'. The tone of this message captures the internationalism of the cultural sector, as marked by smooth, seamless transitions from one space to the next, and the politics that undergird this lifestyle, rooted in a preference for issues that might inconvenience career progression.

The sentiment conveyed in 'It's never been a hassle to do so. And I don't want it to be' could stand as a prompt for Prime Minister Theresa May's comment in her speech at the 2016 Conservative Party conference that 'If you believe you are a citizen of the world, you are a citizen of nowhere'. Writing in *The Towner*, the artist and writer Hannah Black provided a pithy response to May's cretinous statement: 'I am a proud non-citizen of this nowhere forged by the colonial and neo-colonial adventures of western Europe'.[6] Black's retort offers a means to contest the market-based internationalism that dominates the art world and has thus far shaped its response to Brexit, where the pain of losing EU membership can be seen to sit alongside attempts to align artists with the 'precariat', as well as the positioning of artists as victims of gentrification.

If debates around gentrification have sought to grant artists agency by enshrining their capacity to effect urban change, the Brexit moment should direct us to look more deeply into how that agency has always been unevenly distributed. The capacity for international travel to be 'hassle free' as less of a guarantee that comes with the identity 'artist' and more to do with the foundational ways in which our world is stratified. The question of what – if any – agency artists and cultural workers might gain as a collective in this moment is up for grabs. But in order to shift away from the mode that characterises the subjecthood of the 'creative' in debates around gentrification, perhaps the art world needs to reckon more fully whence this agency comes.

Notes

1 Rosalyn Deutsche and Cara Gendel Ryan, 'The Fine Art of Gentrification', *October,* vol. 31, Winter 1984, p. 94.

2 Daniel José Older, 'Gentrification's Insidious Violence: The truth about American cities', *Salon*, Tuesday 18 April 2014. Available at: tinyurl.com/njgv6tw

3 Martha Rosler, 'Fragments of a Metropolitan Viewpoint', in Brian Wallis (ed.), *If You Lived Here...: The City in Art, Theory and Social Activism* (Seattle: Bay Press, 1991), p. 40.

4 Martha Rosler, 'The Artistic Mode of Revolution: From Gentrification to Occupy', *e-flux*, Journal 33, March 2012. Available at tinyurl.com/y9fqznco

5 Lucy Lippard, 'The Artworkers Coalition: Not a History', *Studio International*, vol. 180, no. 927, November 1970, p. 174.

6 Hannah Black, 'Go Home', *The Towner*, 4 November 2016. Available at tinyurl.com/yaunn9cs

Fitzroy Road before SPACE moved in, 1975 →

Next spread View of Tower Bridge from St Katharine Docks with graffiti in the foreground.

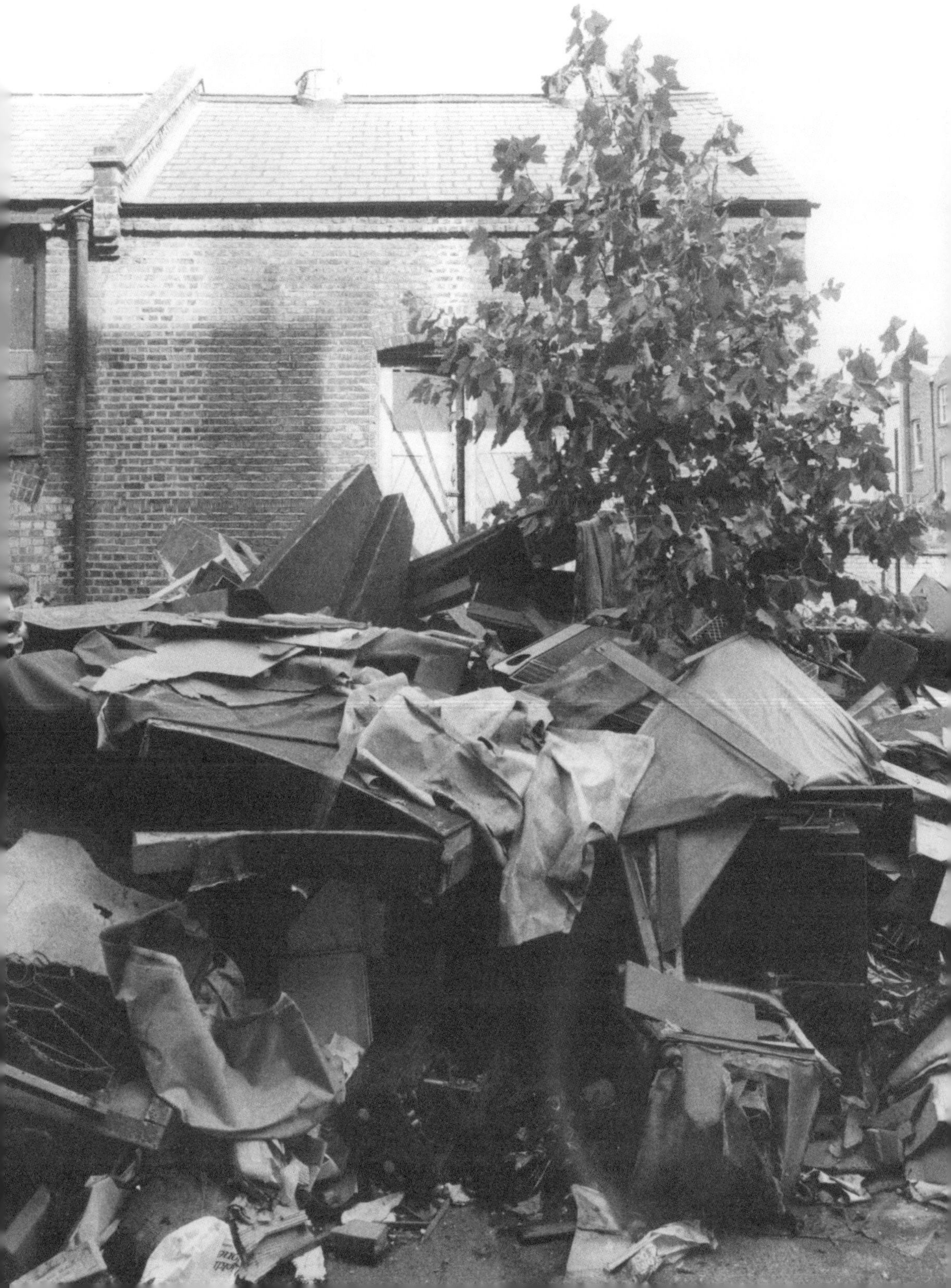

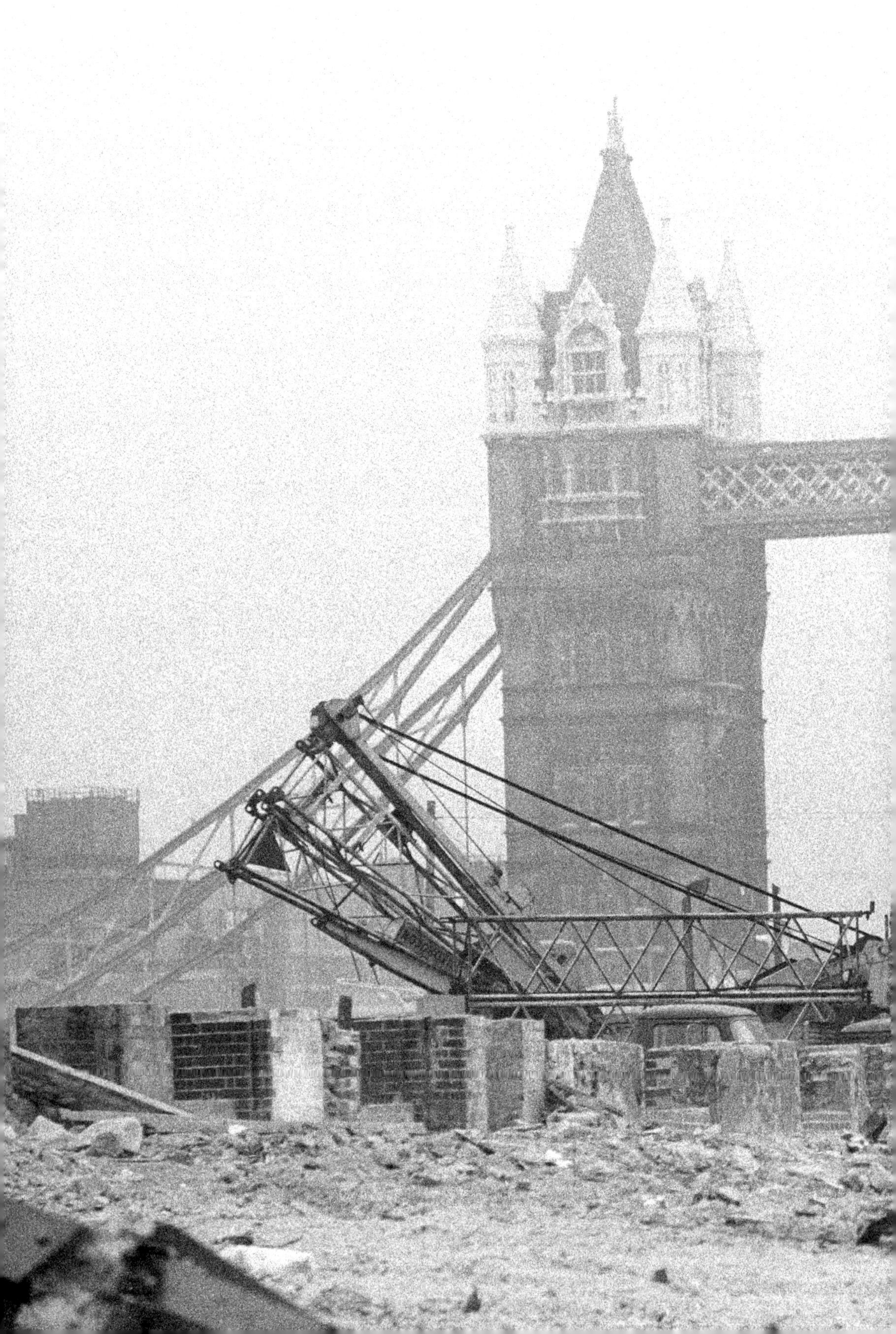

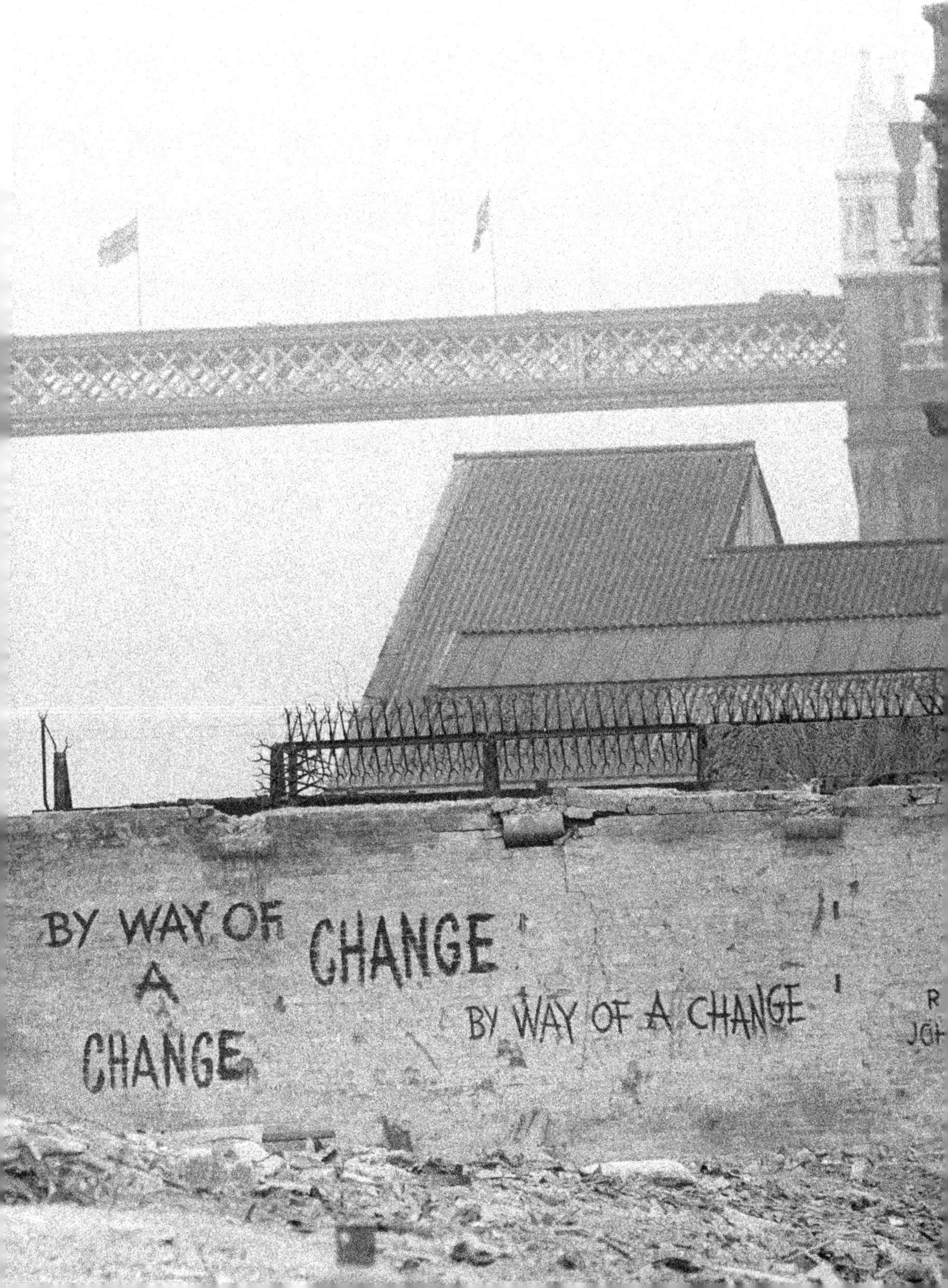
BY WAY OF
A
CHANGE
CHANGE
BY WAY OF A CHANGE

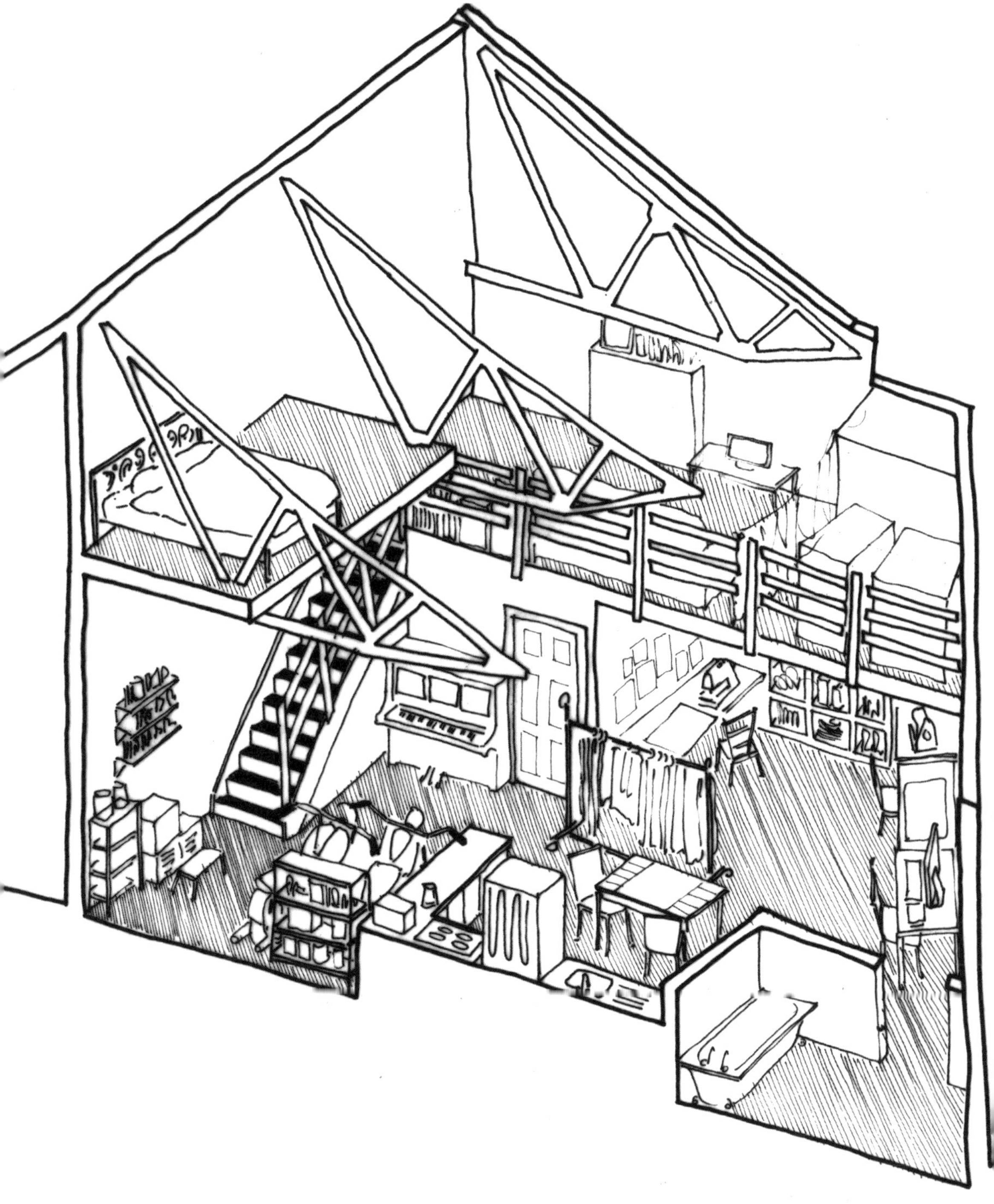

SPACE and the city

Mel Dodd

SPACE has a creative effect or *agency* in the city that is rich but hard to measure in conventional terms. The 800-plus art and design tenants in 19 studio buildings in London, and the multitude of programmes and exhibitions the organisation coordinates, present a complex matrix of operation which evades capture. SPACE's agency interweaves the built infrastructure of studio space provision with the soft infrastructures of organisational support and networks, creating strong spatialised creative foci which have positive ripple effects on the neighbourhoods (and wider city) in which they are situated. Demonstrating the value of these ripple effects is crucial when faced with the threat of rocketing land values in London and the constant disruption that this creates for organisations like SPACE.

'Creative clusters' and the 'creative city' are urban policy terms that have filtered through to the popular media and lost their precision and specificity, often replaced with a more generic and consumerist idea of a 'creative economy' with lifestyle benefits. As a consequence, the presence of creative clusters in city neighbourhoods is blamed for gentrification and displacement. Yet culture is a key driver for the economy, attracting high numbers of tourists and contributing £21bn to London's economy alone.[1] How can we be more precise in understanding the agency of SPACE, and other studio provider organisations and the creative clusters that they support, so that we can nurture and protect what they do?

It is important to remind ourselves of the value of artists in the city, especially in the contribution they make to new ways of thinking and new ways of living. There is a multiplicity of powerful research that outlines the contribution of artists and designers to innovation. One important measure is a 'willingness to try new things, and tolerance of ambiguity'. In *The Art of Innovation*, a research report by Oakley, Sperry and Pratt for NESTA (National Endowment for Science, Technology and the Arts UK), graduates of the University of the Arts London describe themselves as 'brokers, or people who can interpret across disciplinary boundaries' using

Drawing of Peanut Factory in Hackney Wick by Richard Brown.
Published in *Made In HWFI, The Live-Work Collectives* by Richard Brown, 2013

social networks to facilitate forms of social innovation.[2] A crucial part of this interpretative brokering is spatial and geographical proximity. The value of 'proximity, face to face interaction, and knowledge spillover' is that it promotes growth in a knowledge-based economy.[3] Artists are facilitated in their brokerage by the critical mass of people in their own area and by easy access to specialist providers and sub-contractors of the productive processes in which they engage (print, fabrication, production). *Art of Innovation* makes the critical observation that 'innovation is not usually for loners'.[4] Whilst artists often don't like the use of the word 'networking' to describe their activities, their statements reveal the importance of support structures – of being in touch with others through formal networks, like artists' studio groupings, as well as with friends and colleagues. One artist refers to this as 'ground networking'[5], reinforcing the qualities of face-to-face proximity and 'concrete' forms of spatial adjacency that require being in a place – being 'grounded' in the city – to really work.

A lack of detailed analysis of specific examples of cultural and creative activities in cities has resulted in imprecise interpretations of the ways in which creative clusters form and are sustained. As a result, top-down policy-driven cultural- and creative industry-led regeneration has often resulted in the raising of property values and rents, perpetuating the more superficial effects of cultural consumption and the promotion of city living. In these circumstances, gentrification arguably discredits the notion of creativity and, at its worst, connects creativity to problems of social displacement. An understanding of the threats to, and from, creative clusters, and further research into the idea that locally specific cultural and creative practices can resist the forces of gentrification, is therefore critical to the sustainability of these practices. As Pratt says, we need to recognise the 'value of acknowledging the subtleties of historical and locally specific practices of cultural and creative activities; only by taking such an analytic step can we understand the processes animating creative cities, and accordingly begin to develop a range of policy responses to them'.[6]

Interestingly, it has been found that the influence of key individuals – whether entrepreneurs, those in small organisations or artists – is often required to create and sustain local networks and facilities[7]. This is especially the case with smaller artist and designer studio organisations and larger community arts organisations, which are crucial in the way they provide ongoing and practical advocacy for artists and creative users. This type of 'creative agency' may be seen as a capacity to enable others to act creatively in the world and as a capacity for that agency to facilitate engagement in broader cycles of cultural production (beyond the individuals and organisations themselves).

In the case of arts organisations like SPACE, creative agency operates across a diverse range of scales and forms. This creative agency can facilitate the practical aspects of how an artist acts, produces and consumes objects, both in space (rooms, studios, galleries, the city), and over time (tenancies, residencies, tenures, exhibitions, events). It operates across specific locations (market, locale, historical and cultural territory) but also can be more ephemeral, enabling or indirect capacities such as educational support, financial support and the social and cultural structures and frameworks which encourage and drive creative productivity and facilitate the intrinsic and instrumental values of its production to be accessible to the rest of society.

These definitions of creative agency and cultural production make us think of a complex matrix or web of interactivities and enchainments, operating across the physical locations of production. Unpacking the constituent parts of this matrix can provide a more lucid picture of agency, illustrating the subtleties of locally specific cultural and creative agency. Such a matrix of creative productivity is arguably best represented through methods of communication that go beyond conventional measures and engage with techniques that can capture geography, space, occupation and time, using, for example, illustration, mapping and spatial model-making. Good examples one can draw on include Richard Brown's 2009 analysis, *Made in HWFI*[8], a study of Hackney Wick and Fish Island's artists' live/work spaces, which used detailed spatial drawings and diagrammatic family trees to illustrate the method through which occupation happened. This shows the ingenuity of the interiors of self-managed buildings and the temporal dimensions inherent in their cycles of use and occupation. Similarly, muf architecture/art's careful studies of the creative industries in HWFI[9] documented the location, scale and clusters of live/work studios and the typologies of yards and industrial buildings in which they were housed. In the 2009 report *Creative Potential: Hackney Wick and Fish Island* (commissioned by Design for London), muf documented the rich inter-relationship between studio spaces, occupied by artists, designers and galleries, and the supporting businesses that proliferate in response, from printers to financial consultants. This documentation was developed as a propositional strategy to support and sustain the area's creative network through the 'Design and Planning Guidance for Hackney Wick Fish Island', commissioned by the London Legacy Development Corporation in 2013. These examples capture some of SPACE's buildings as part of their analysis, locating and revealing their part in the interdependent spatial relationship of creative enclaves in the city.

Considering these methods of representation, a 2015 project by SPACE and researchers from Central Saint Martins (CSM) (funded by Creativeworks, London) began to think about ways of representing information that would allow the spatial and geographical qualities of SPACE's matrix of activity to be represented. The study trialled alternative methods for capturing the value of a creative enterprise, engaging in the collation of available evidence and deliberately representing diverse forms of value (intrinsic and instrumental) whilst seeking to synthesise this evidence through experimentation with visual and spatial forms of representation. The research used the idea of 'survey' to structure the process, where surveying was understood as a spatial activity of looking, rather than just a means of enumerating.

Although the metric analysis of artists' outcomes offers a powerful tool for measuring the economic value of SPACE as an organisation within the creative economy of London the project considered that engaging in the geographical, anthropological and spatial networks of production might be a powerful way to represent values of a different kind. This was also relevant in the context of recent policy research on artists' workspace provision undertaken by the Greater London Authority (GLA). These studies expose the vulnerability of artists' workspace in the capital, 51 percent of which is rented and subject to change-of-use or development threats. The GLA's reports conclude that affordable artists' workspace is a valuable but vulnerable asset for London, with the ambition being to look at ways to facilitate links with appropriate providers of the correct facilities, whether in new developments or existing buildings, to achieve the best value for the wider community.[10] Importantly, the GLA concluded that these initiatives should be considered alongside the potential for complementary local place making. It is well acknowledged by urban policy makers that the matrix of interactivities created by artists' workplaces extends in value beyond the buildings themselves and into the community beyond. As the GLA reports acknowledge and as is the case for SPACE's Triangle building in Hackney, artists' workspace provider enclaves are often the crux of a larger creative and cultural community that can generate new local investment, attract other businesses and create opportunities for improved public space.

The currency of concerns about vulnerability of workspace provides an opportunity to further develop understandings of the social and spatial ecologies of creative artists' workspace clusters through forms of survey mapping. The spatial surveys undertaken by SPACE and CSM collected information across four categories using the SPACE studio building at the Triangle on Mare Street as a core study site. Using a sample of SPACE tenants as volunteers, the research project conducted surveys of individual artists' studios spaces. This allowed an understanding of the spatial occupation of the workspaces themselves, which varied from individual units of sole occupancy to multi-occupancy spaces which operated as collectives, cooperatives or fully fledged collaborative practices. Structured interviews with sample artists established the working habits, productivity, income, employment, achievements and geographical reach of artists' work, their supply chain, participation and networks and their perceptions of the value of SPACE to their creative practice. In addition, we undertook daily (digital) tracking of artists' journeys to/from their studios and other venues while also logging artistic activities, key meetings and transactions. In addition to these four categories of spatial and geographical survey, we also undertook a building-wide tenants' questionnaire to collect data on production and outputs through exhibitions, commissions and events with geo-locatable information.

The obvious and unresolved challenge of this process was to find ways of synthesising and visualising rich and complex data that could accommodate the multiple scales and types of content derived from such a broad survey. Space, experience, journey and transaction all explain themselves through radically different forms of representation and, in so doing, are hard to show on the same piece of paper. Sectional line drawings of an artist's studio at a 1:20 scale, revealing daily routines, sit with some difficulty alongside geo-located walking routes in the city best described on a map at a 1:5000 scale. Similarly, a verbal transcript of an artist describing their recent work and exhibitions may need to be geo-located onto the geography of the places she navigates, to be meaningful. Qualitative surveys of space and daily occupation are necessarily disparate, open-ended and unfinished, the very opposite of quantitative data with its finite 'truths'. What qualitative data reveals may be a series of complex stories, rather than singular messages that can be easily digested, and herein lies the difficulty in communication of the value of organisations like SPACE to the city.

Critical messages emerged from the study, often in unanticipated ways. A Google map of central London captured the residential and studio locations of SPACE's artist tenants in yellow and brown, set against the location of their suppliers and exhibitions in red and blue. This clearly shows that artists and studio spaces are located in the North East of the city, whilst suppliers and galleries are in the South West. In this mapping, SPACE, as an organisation supporting artists' productivity in the east of the city, can be seen to be supplying the West End of London with cultural content through a one-way ripple effect. This chain of influence continues at global scale, and one of the key illustrative investigations sought to represent this ripple of productive outcomes from an individual's studio outwards, from building into neighbourhood, city and globe . Alongside the representation of certain artists' studio spaces, the study produced a drawn catalogue of SPACE buildings, representing them as physical environments of a certain scale, location, history and occupancy type.

In conclusion, understanding the creative agency or effect of an organisation like SPACE on a city like London is not possible through a simple set of figures or measurable data connected to economic values – although these are available and persuasive. The rationale of looking beyond economic value is crucial if we are to understand how artists' studio provider organisations like SPACE really work to nurture city neighbourhoods and places. This is important as a way of arguing against mainstream narratives in which artists' enclaves are perceived (in a negative way) to contribute to gentrification. As Journalist Matt Bolton claims, 'It seems that wherever artists go, rising property prices, cafes filled with seats from 1940s railway stations and low-level ethnic cleansing appears to follow: is art itself to blame?'.[11]

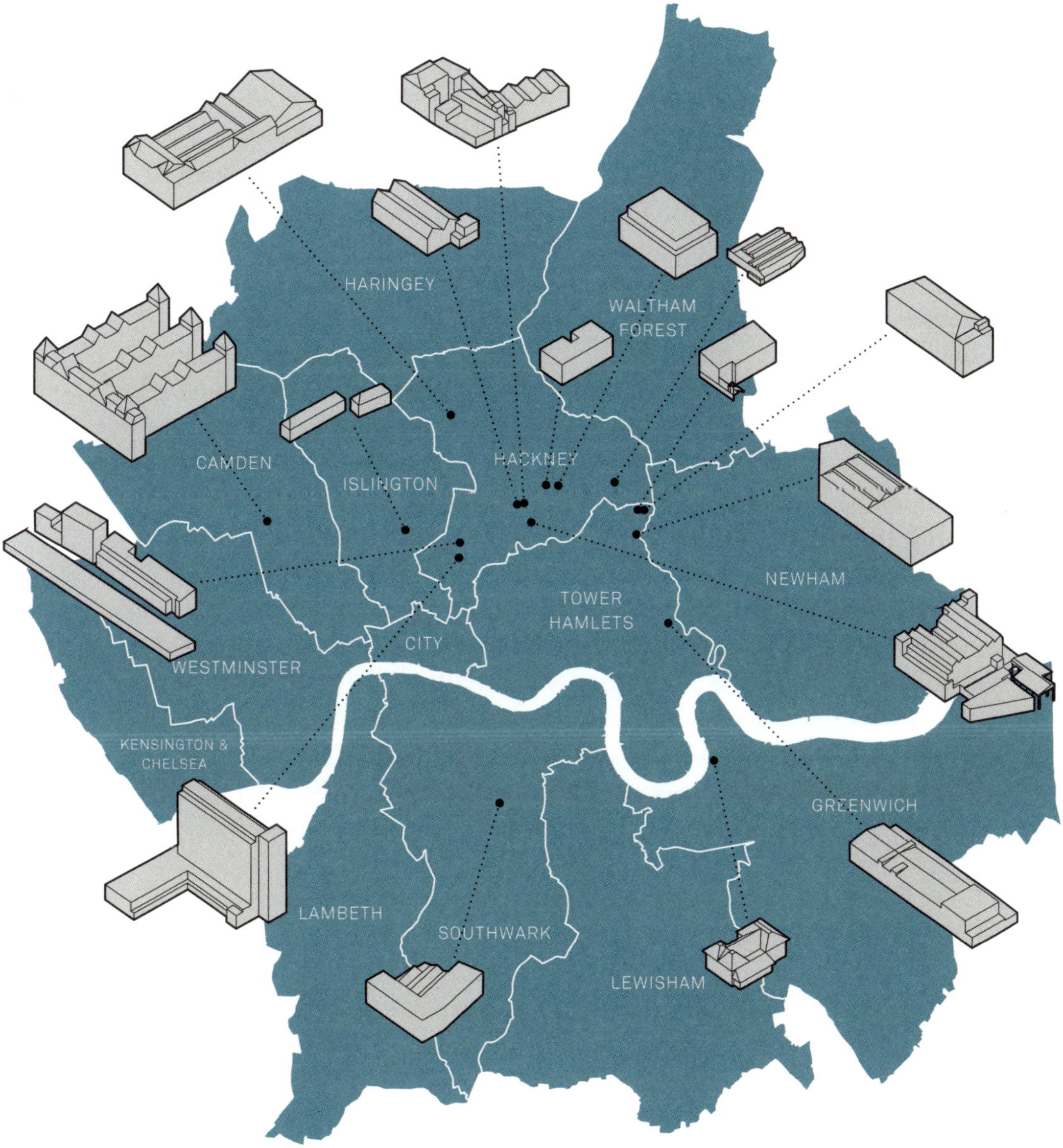

3D renderings of SPACE studio buildings in 2015
Drawings by Katherine Spence

As researchers and commentators understand, the capital's search for profit would exist regardless of culture, even if certain cultural processes like artists' enclaves do 'smooth' the journey in certain neighbourhoods. The underlying point is that we need to reject simplistic associations between the creative economy and economic development. As Pratt complains, 'the notion of creativity has a humanistic root, in the valuing of individual creativity and humanity, yet this has been powerfully re-articulated in recent years and linked to economic innovation and competitiveness'.[12]

Looking more closely at values creative organisations can bring to city life is vital. As we approach the end of the second decade of the 21st century, we need to re-balance city policy toward the intrinsic value of the cultural and creative field and the construction of new cultural identities and political discourses, understanding that, in the narrow field of economic value, we already have plenty of evidence that the cultural economy is playing a significant role in London. Policymakers seem to be starting to understand this, as evidenced by recent studies on artists' studio networks by the GLA and others and exemplified by more recent research on how important production and small-scale manufacturing is for city resilience. Most important of all, when seen from this perspective, organisations like SPACE act to resist the overwhelming forces of commodification and consumption in contemporary cities. We need to better understand and visualise their effects, because of the ways in which they might lead us toward new processes of political and cultural transformation.

Notes

1 Mayor of London, *Creating Artists' Workspaces.* Report (GLA, 2014). Contributors: Kirsten Dunne, Tobias Goevert, Levent Kerimol, Katherine Spence.

2 Kate Oakley, Brooke Sperry and Andy Pratt, *The Art of Innovation: How Fine Art Graduates contribute to Innovation*, NESTA 2008, p. 5.

3 Ibid, p. 16.

4 Ibid, p. 33.

5 Ibid, p. 34.

6 Andy Pratt, 'Creative cities: Tensions within and between social, cultural and economic development', in *City, Culture and Society*, 1, 2010 pp. 13–20.

7 Evans, G. 'From Cultural Quarters to Creative Clusters. Creative Spaces in the new urban economy', in *The Sustainability and Development of Cultural Quarters* (Stockholm: Institute of Urban History, 2009), pp. 32–59.

8 Richard Brown, *Made in HWFI: The Live Work Collectives*, 2013, published on Issuu.

9 Design for London, *Creative Potential: Hackney Wick and Fish Island* (London: muf architecture/art llp, 2009).

10 Mayor of London, Artists' Workspace Study: Report and Recommendations (GLA, 2014) Contributors Kirsten Dunne, Tobias Goevert, Levent Kerimol, Katherine Spence.

11 Matt Bolton, 'Is Art to blame for Regeneration?', *The Guardian*, 30 August 2013.

12 Andy Pratt, 'Creative cities', op. cit.

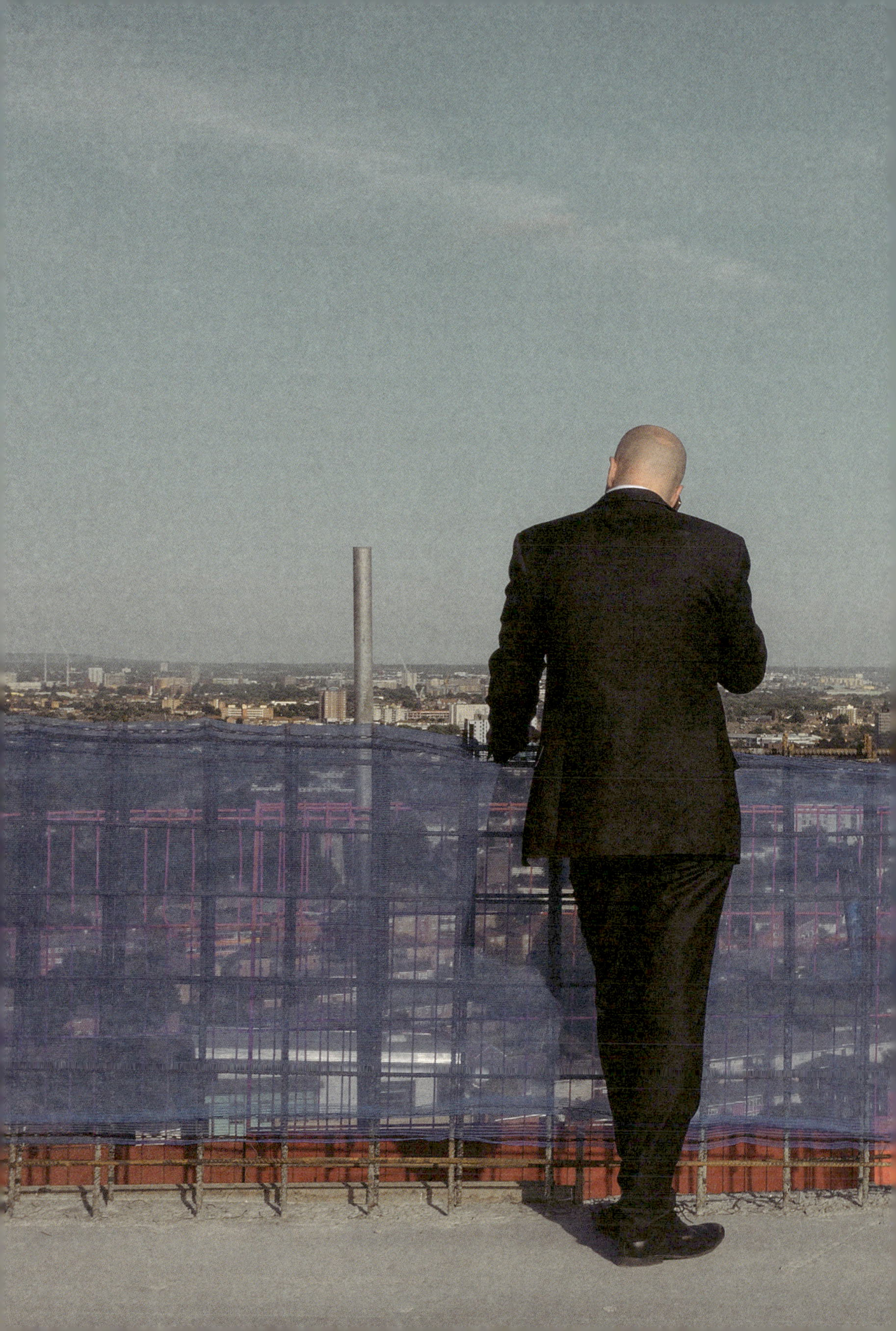

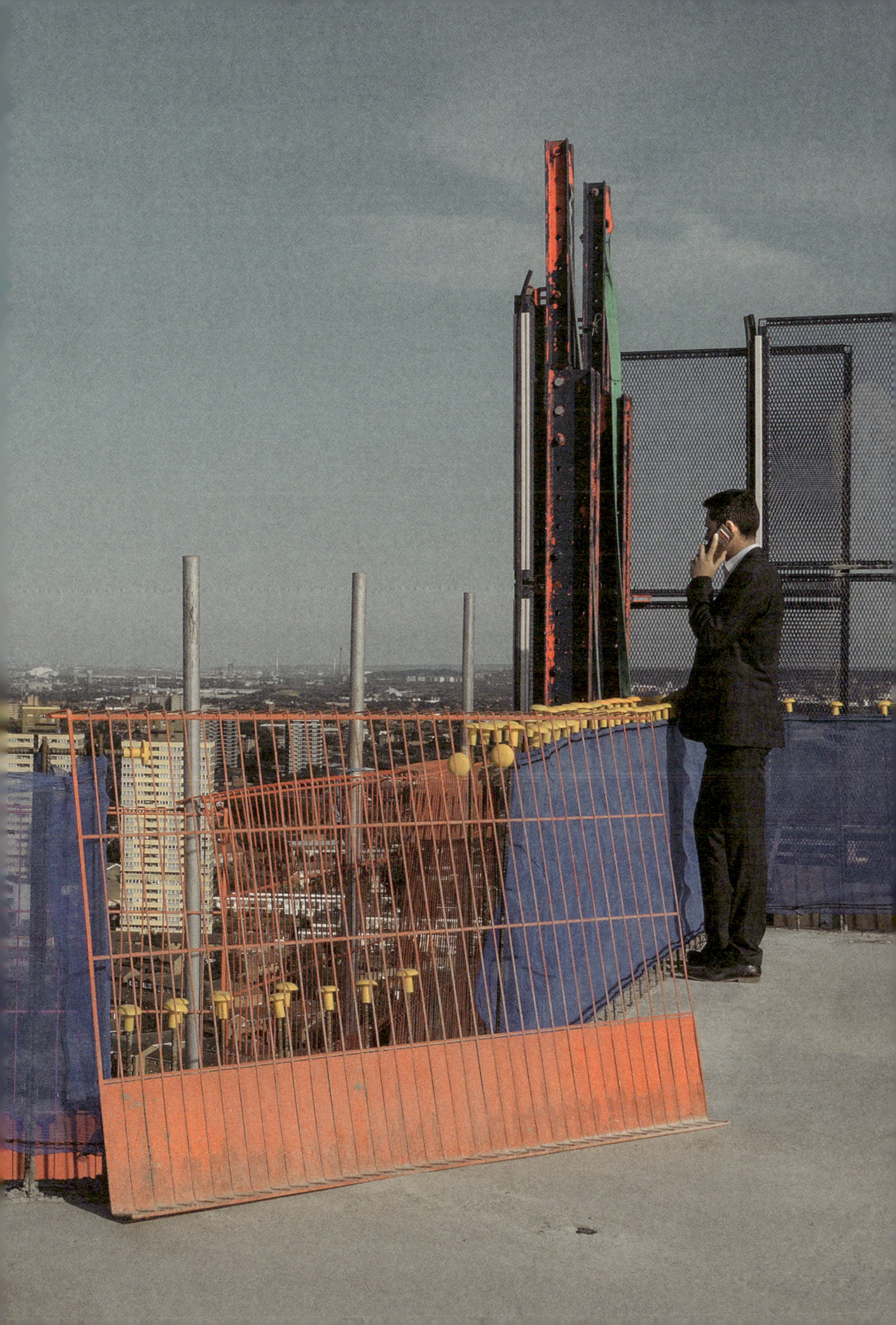

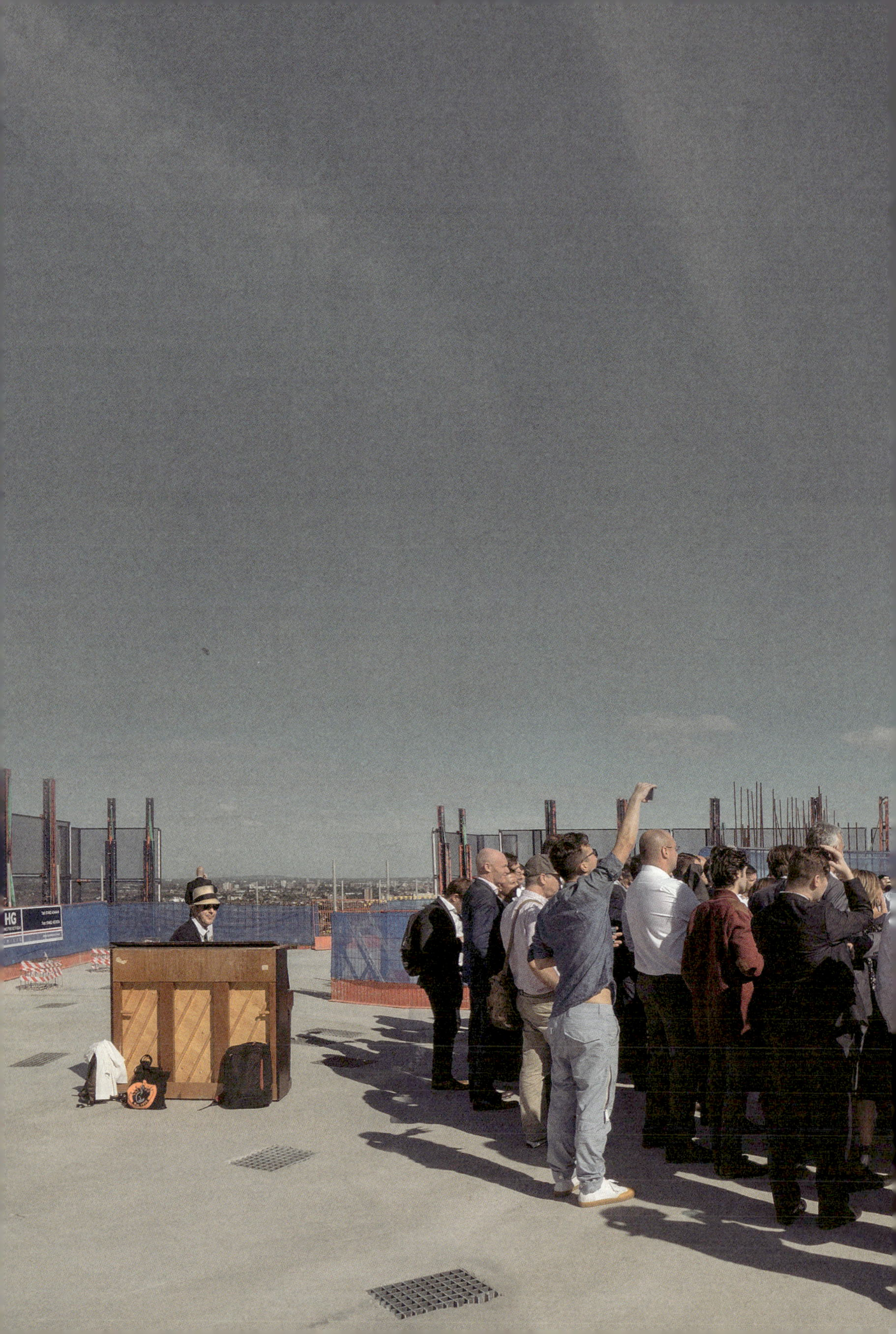

The growth of London and its consequences for artists' spaces

Rebecca Gordon-Nesbitt

The 50-year history of SPACE is also a history of regeneration in London. The organisation's Chief Executive, Anna Harding, has noted that 'Since 1968 SPACE has championed the role of artists in society – and in urban regeneration', the latter of which has been SPACE's 'worst enemy'.[1] This text examines the relationship between SPACE and urban regeneration over the past half-century, through specific partnerships – with a local authority, regeneration agency, housing association and private developer – and through the open market.

Local Authority: Greater London Council (GLC)

When SPACE was set up in 1968, construction in Inner London was largely centred on filling in residual spaces and vacant sites. The Port of London Authority was in the process of selling the bomb-damaged and derelict St Katharine Docks, built during the Napoleonic wars, to the GLC. SPACE attracted the support of Arts Minister, Jennie Lee, whose 1965 White Paper had specified that 'if a high level of artistic achievement is to be sustained and the best in the arts made more widely available, more generous and discriminating help is urgently needed'.[2] Early funding for the organisation came from the Arts Council of Great Britain (ACGB) (£3,000 from an untapped source for studio provision), Calouste Gulbenkian Foundation and from the participating artists, above and beyond the rental income. In 1968, sculptor Henry Moore won the Erasmus Prize, and convention dictated that he should give half of it to a deserving European cultural cause. After some delibera-tion, Moore donated between £5,000 and £6,000 to SPACE.

Preceding spread and opposite Topping out event at Aspire Point, Stratford. SPACE will have studios in the building in 2018.

Contemporaneous metropolitan coverage subscribed to the idea that art graduates needed a place to work, unencumbered by income generation and domestic life. Writing in *Canvas,* Marina Vaizey elaborated the potential of SPACE and AIR to overcome the twin challenges facing artists – lack of space in which to make, and make a living from, their work.[3] Outside the capital, critics were less forgiving. With a second-city snarl, Anthony Everitt observed in the *Birmingham Post* that 'young men in Jimmy [sic] Hendrix hairstyles and tight velveteen jeans can be seen strolling down the cobbled street', concluding that 'If this is life in the docks, then it is no wonder that our exports are doing badly'.[4]

The GLC lease ran until December 1970. By June 1970, it was clear that Taylor Woodrow – which had the redevelopment contract for the site – would soon commence demolition work as part of a £22m scheme. In the same month, *Hackney Gazette* reported the arrival by helicopter of Desmond Plummer, Conservative leader of the GLC, to a reception hosted by SPACE and his commitment to keeping an eye out for alternative premises. Collaboration with local authorities formed a central part of the organisation's early strategy.

Regeneration Agency: Olympic Park Legacy Company (now London Legacy Development Corporation)

Fast forward 35 years. The announcement in July 2005 that the 2012 Olympic Games would be hosted by London brought with it a wave of property speculation. The Olympic build was overseen by the public sector Olympic Delivery Authority (2006–14) and the private Olympic Park Legacy Company (OPLC, 2009–14), with many sites being acquired through compulsory purchase orders.

The legacy of the Games was contemplated in parallel with their planning, with the aim of securing the same life chances for people in the local area as in the rest of London. In November 2005 SPACE initiated a series of annual symposia, entitled Legacy Now, which aimed to steer policy on the Olympic legacy for East London by bringing together policy makers in government, Olympic bodies and the creative sector, with some success.

The Mayor of London had signed a memorandum of understanding with the Treasury, committing to repaying an initial £625m and an additional £300m of public money invested in the

Olympic Park.[5] It was agreed that a modest part of the former would be raised through council tax dividends and the route for raising the remainder would be left to the discretion of the Mayor, barring council tax and fare increases. The initial plan was for this amount to be repaid over 30 years. When the Coalition Government came to power in 2010, despite Hackney Council advocating phased repayment over a minimum of 25 years, the repayment process was accelerated. This flaw in national policy meant that the maximum quantity of land had to be sold for the highest possible premium, making it difficult to ensure that development was relevant to, and supportive of, the local community.

Harding has observed that 'Kick-starting regeneration is about creating opportunities for developers to exploit for profit. The release of industrial land through land assembly and compulsory purchase orders for regeneration is profit-motivated, not quality of life or community motivated'.[6] At the 2008 Legacy Now gathering, the artist Laura Oldfield Ford aptly described this as a 'corporate land grab, an attempt to privatise public space, and public housing'.[7] This reality was reflected in Oldfield Ford's work[8] and in Anja Kirschner and David Panos' 2008 film, *Trail of the Spider*, which took the westward expansion of the USA as a metaphor for the eastward expansion of London.[9]

While there are isolated examples of art enacting a critique of gentrification, a collaborative research project initiated by SPACE exploring the exploitation of 'creativity' for private gain noted that 'Sometimes the displacement and inequality embedded in such urban developments is camouflaged by art and culture'.[10] At a Creative Industries Federation event in September 2016, the incoming Minister for Digital and Culture, Matt Hancock, declared 'The hipster is a capitalist. Cultural rebirth, connectivity, and economic revival go hand in hand'.[11] Three years earlier, Feargus O'Sullivan had coined the term 'artwashing' to describe the process through which the 'work and presence of artists and creative workers is used to add a cursory sheen to a place's transformation'.[12] According to this explanation, artistic activity provides a seductive short-term narrative of creative triumph over blight, distracting attention from messier longer-term consequences wrought by the channelling of public funds into the private sector and the displacement of local populations – including artists – by more profitable businesses. Accordingly, O'Sullivan accuses artists of acting as 'human shields' for developers. Stephen Pritchard documents an even more insidious trope of aesthetic cleansing – that of socially engaged artists collaborating with local residents, gaining their trust and lulling them into a false sense of security.[13]

Reflecting on the Legacy Now events, Harding outlined the process whereby 'Canny landlords waiting to unlock the goldmine engage with the artist community to create interest and maximise profit. Cultural diplomacy greases palms. Arty tenants on short lets, some rent-free, animate spaces awaiting redevelopment – SPACE included at The White Building'.[14] In 2010, SPACE won a competition, run by the OPLC, to develop and manage a building in Queens Yard, White Post Lane, E9, named by SPACE The White Building. SPACE acquired a 10-year lease on the building from 2012 and sublet a café space to CRATE pizzeria and microbrewery, overlooking the canal, which has proven popular.

The White Building forms part of Hackney Wick and Fish Island, a landlocked area adjacent to the Olympic Park allegedly containing the highest density of artists in Europe, which began to be thought of as a 'major hub for London's creative sector'.[15] The project was intended as a significant part of the Olympic legacy, providing space and facilities for artists and creative organisations. The agreement between OPLC and SPACE made provision for 'creative activities designed to benefit the surrounding residential communities'.[16] As the Games approached, the OPLC transmuted into the London Legacy Development Corporation (LLDC), with a budget of £296m to transform the park. Incoming Executive Director of Regeneration and Community Partnerships, Paul Brickell, was committed to a process of community engagement he referred to as 'dents in the fence' – fissures in the fortifications being constructed around the Olympic site that could prefigure hopeful future activities and minimise the sense of exclusion.[17]

The White Building was set up as SPACE's centre for art and technology. OPLC invested in a design competition for emerging architects, won by David Kohn Architects, funded the design and fit-out of six studios, an event space and a large shared residency studio and underwrote the rent for five years. SPACE has delivered a renowned art and tech programme centred on residencies and a learning programme. Pupils from an inner-city boys' school learnt how to make boats from tin cans fuelled with sunflower oil pressed from seeds they had grown, while students at an academy in Hackney and a primary school in Tower Hamlets experimented with solar power. During the summer holidays of 2013 to 2016, 500 young people in transition from primary to secondary school attended summer schools at The White Building, using the Olympic Park as a classroom and bridging the inside and outside of the park. A group of retired men ('The Geezers') from Tower Hamlets excavated the history of the area, in conversation with an artist and oral historian, which culminated in an engaging film documenting both the project and changes they had witnessed.[18] Six years into SPACE's occupancy of The White Building, a break clause in the lease was invoked by the landlord, bringing this partnership to an end.

Housing Association: Community Housing Association (now One Housing)

In 2009, SPACE negotiated a 20-year lease with Community Housing Association (now One Housing) on 12 studios in a new-build mixed-use development at Timber Wharf, E2. The studios were located on the ground and first floors, with social housing above them, and SPACE raised fit-out social investment from The Shoreditch Trust. Two years later, eight railway arches opposite were added, accommodating a further 55 tenants. In the meantime, with the same housing association, a short-term tenancy was signed for 15 studios in Dean Street in the heart of Soho, and a 16-year lease was taken on 13 studios in Arlington, NW1.

In Dean Street, SPACE used a chapel and offices as studios in premises ancillary to a homeless hostel. Despite operating in a borough with high levels of homelessness, Westminster Council underwent a change of policy and withdrew its homeless initiatives and, in 2014, the building, including studios, was redeveloped to function as a hostel for backpackers called SoHostel.

Arlington House was established in 1905, at the behest of Lord Rowton, to provide lodgings for up to 1,000 men seeking work in the capital; George Orwell famously worked on *Down and Out in Paris and London* while living there. Managed for a time by Camden Council, the stately Victorian block was taken over by One Housing and underwent a £50m redevelopment completed in 2010.

It currently provides two-year tenancies on studio flats, for people on a low income with an affiliation to Camden, and half-board accommodation for 95 people at various stages on the 'journey from homelessness back to independent living'.[19]

SPACE successfully bid to form part of the social economy of the building, taking responsibility for a suite of artists' studios, one of which has been used for group creative activities since 2010 under the banner of the Creative Space. Weekday workshops, led by artist-tutors employed by SPACE, are open to everyone passing through the Camden Pathway, which addresses homeless need in the borough. A programme coordinator is provided by One Housing, and running costs of £24,000 are split equally between the two organisations.

Workshops encompass visual art, music, performance, fabric printing and creative writing and have led to the publication of a fanzine called *EMMA*, the formation of a band, the Arlingtones, and a presence at Notting Hill Carnival. Visits, enabling free access for homeless people, have been made to galleries and museums such as Tate, Whitechapel, the V&A and the Royal Academy. Two open studios are organised every year, with one forming part of Creativity and Wellbeing Week. Once a year, the programme culminates in an exhibition of artwork produced during workshops.

The primary objective of the Creative Space programme is to facilitate social connection, enticing residents to interact with others in the building. Beyond this, the workshops aim to unleash latent talent and interest in the arts, increasing confidence, skills and wellbeing. SPACE artists with studios at Arlington are supportive of the organisation's wider remit and, where appropriate, contribute to the Creative Space. Arlington staff are encouraged to attend at least one workshop a year, to better understand the impact of creative activity upon residents. Internal evaluation shows steady increases in participants' wellbeing, and residents leaving Arlington are reputedly reluctant to give up their involvement in the Creative Space.

Private Developer: Alumno

In 2017, SPACE took a 25-year lease on 12 studios at Havil Street, SE5. Southwark Council had accepted a proposal by Alumno, developer-operator of student housing, to regenerate the former

Southwark Town Hall.[20] Operating in an environment which makes securing planning permission for conventional student housing difficult, Alumno founder, David Campbell, understood he needed partners that would complement the student cohort.[21] Campbell is sympathetic to the fact that artists both kick-start regeneration and are the first to suffer from it, and finds their need for well-proportioned, dry, secure space relatively easy to accommodate. SPACE was involved in the early stages of the town hall redevelopment, becoming part of what Campbell describes as the 'strategy and narrative' of the building. This included a new home for Theatre Peckham, which sees New Peckham Varieties encouraging children and young people to take part in the performing arts. SPACE was represented alongside Alumno at pre-planning meetings with Southwark Council.

As well as occupying high-quality studios on the ground and lower-ground floors, SPACE manages a programme of open studios, providing access to artists for around 120 residents, many of whom are Goldsmiths arts students (undergraduates at Chelsea College of Art and Design were also involved in the design of the building's communal areas). In this sense, SPACE artists provide a living example of professional practice for those newly contemplating it. Alumno and SPACE also offer a bursary, in the form of a rent-free studio for a year, to an artist graduating from Goldsmiths. A similar development is emerging in Stratford, involving 445 student rooms and 20 SPACE studios plus graduate bursaries.[22]

Freehold: Haymerle Road SE15

In 1992, Lynn MacRitchie observed that, of all the artist-led organisations established in the 1960s and '70s, SPACE was the 'only one to have survived with its aims and methods almost intact', by which she meant the democratisation of making, funding, exhibiting and discussing art.[23] MacRitchie simultaneously bemoaned the lack of a unifying ideology around which artists could organise while paraphrasing the then-director, Eva Woloshyn's description of the organisation as a business that 'must be as dynamic and efficient as possible'.[24] At that time, MacRitchie was a SPACE trustee. At the Annual General Meeting held on 19 January 1994, the Council of Management was expanded to include eight to 12 trustees, half of whom were studio holders, and MacRitchie resigned. The main aim of the Council was to keep rent low for their fellow artist tenants. As a result, no reserves were accumulated to buy or repair property.

Each year since 2005, money has been set aside for property acquisitions, encouraged by the chair of the board of trustees from 2007–12, Alan Leibowitz, a property developer. In 2011, SPACE bought the freehold of a 1958 former pram factory at Haymerle Road, SE15, comprising 33,000 ft^2 of property – enough space for 89 tenants in 69 studios – with a mortgage. An immediate £400,000 fit-out, including the installation of solar panels on the rooftop to supply 40 percent of the building's electricity, was followed two years later by a £350,000 upgrade from a £1.26m Arts Council Capital grant.

The Haymerle Road site is currently being encroached upon on all sides, as part of the controversial Old Kent Road area regeneration, following Southwark Council's demolition of Elephant and Castle's Heygate Estate, the threatened destruction of homes on the Aylesbury Estate and a swathe of use change from heavy to light industrial. Developers are falling over themselves to build new high-rises, and the artists' enclave risks becoming a 'compromised haven' in the midst of hyper-gentrification.[25] While Southwark Council seems convinced of the merits of having artists' studios in the borough and is brokering discussions between SPACE and property developers (with the former on the council's approved list of studio providers), it stands accused of social cleansing by local activists. Indeed, its cabinet members, challenged with reconciling demands for housing and raising income for new transport infrastructure, seem to fit the description, drawn up by Southwark Notes, of 'those who pretend to act in our interests but are only ever about giving even more of what we've got away to those who already have too much'.[26]

Taking Stock

Early in its history, SPACE distinguished itself from commercial tenants on the basis of its flexibility. In areas slated for redevelopment, this fleet-footed approach granted access to impressive buildings that would otherwise have been impossible to secure.

A 1975 endorsement from the London Borough of Islington's Coordinator of Regeneration mentioned concerns about the 'wild and infectious misbehaviour one might be inviting into the neighbourhood' being allayed by the experience of working with SPACE.

The exponential development of London has made flexibility and sustainability incompatible when it comes to artists' studios. In spring 2014, the Greater London Authority (GLA), under the jurisdiction of Mayor of London, Boris Johnson, commissioned a survey of artists' workspace provision. This showed that only 17 percent of studio buildings in London were owned under freehold. By contrast, one third of SPACE tenants are currently in studios in which the organisation owns the freehold.

Spiralling property prices have a pronounced impact on rental values. In 2012, the average rent for light industrial units in Hackney was £12.21 per ft^2; by 2017, this had climbed to £32.50, an increase of 266 percent.[27] Added to this, business rates approximately doubled in April 2017; insurance costs climb all the time; legislation requires electrical upgrades and increasingly complex fire safety procedures, all necessary to ensure the welfare of artists. The GLA report predicted that 'as many as 3,500 artists are likely to lose their places of work in the next 5 years – 30% of the current provision', and called for action to protect this valuable but vulnerable asset.[28]

For SPACE, the priority remains keeping studio rents as low as possible. In a 1973 publication, the organisation complained about licence costs to artists increasing from 20 to 70p per ft^2; today they are £12.85 to £22.30 per ft^2, with amenities having improved in most cases. The organisation has ensured that its tenants will not face the kind of rent increases seen on the open market, by capping premiums to landlords at a maximum of 30 percent over five years on all recent leases. In this way, SPACE has achieved relative sustainability by exploiting pragmatic gaps in the almost impossibly commercialised fabric of one of the world's most expensive cities.

Notes

1 Anna Harding, 'Legacy Now: SPACE's engagement in Olympic Legacy', in Hilary Powell and Isaac Marrero-Guillamon (eds.), *The Art of Dissent: Adventures in London's Olympic State* (London: Marshgate Press, 2012), p. 264.

2 Jennie Lee, *A Policy for the Arts: The First Steps* (London: Her Majesty's Stationery Office, February 1965), p. 5.

3 Marina Vaizey, 'S.P.A.C.E. Ltd.', *Canvas*, vol. 4, no. 10, February 1970.

4 Anthony Everitt, 'An Artists' Haven in a Disused Dockland Warehouse', *The Birmingham Post*, 6 September 1969.

5 Olympic Funding: Revised Memorandum of Understanding between the Government and the Mayor of London, June 2007 tinyurl.com/yaflsh2z

6 Anna Harding, op. cit., p. 269.

7 Ibid, p. 268.

8 See, for example, Laura Oldfield Ford, Olympic Drift: Making Way for the Games, 8 August 2012: tinyurl.com/y8ujjubq

9 Anja Kirschner and David Panos, *Trail of the Spider*, 2008: vimeo.com/51777155

10 ShinJoung Yeo and Toby Miller, *Artists in Tech Cities* wp.me/p6HU2I-ak

11 Matt Hancock, Minister for Digital and Culture Creative Industries Speech, 9 September 2016, available at: tinyurl.com/hv4mb9d

12 Feargus O'Sullivan, The Pernicious Realities of 'Artwashing', available at: tinyurl.com/y7zm8nhg

13 colouringinculture.org

14 Anna Harding, op cit., p. 270.

15 Agreement between Olympic Park Legacy Company and Art Services Grants Limited (Operating as SPACE), 3 January 2012.

16 Ibid.

17 Gillian Evans, *London's Olympic Legacy: The Inside Track* (Springer, 2016).

18 The film, *The Geezers On Tour In Hackney Wick*, was produced by Hi8us with SPACE. youtu.be/JQI5p_JtSzc

19 tinyurl.com/y8wqz3uq

20 tinyurl.com/y9r2lgfl

21 David Campbell in conversation with the author, 23 August 2017.

22 tinyurl.com/q3n7ksy

23 Lynn MacRitchie, 'Air and Space', *Art Monthly*, 156, 6 (May 1992), p. 7.

24 Ibid.

25 ShinJoung Yeo and Toby Miller, op. cit., p. 11.

26 southwarknotes.wordpress.com

27 Co-Star analysis 2017 provided by a SPACE trustee.

28 Munira Mirza, 'Foreword' in Artists' Workspace Study: Report and Recommendations (London: Greater London Authority, September 2014), p. 5.

Artists inside a perspex box at St Katharine Docks studio →

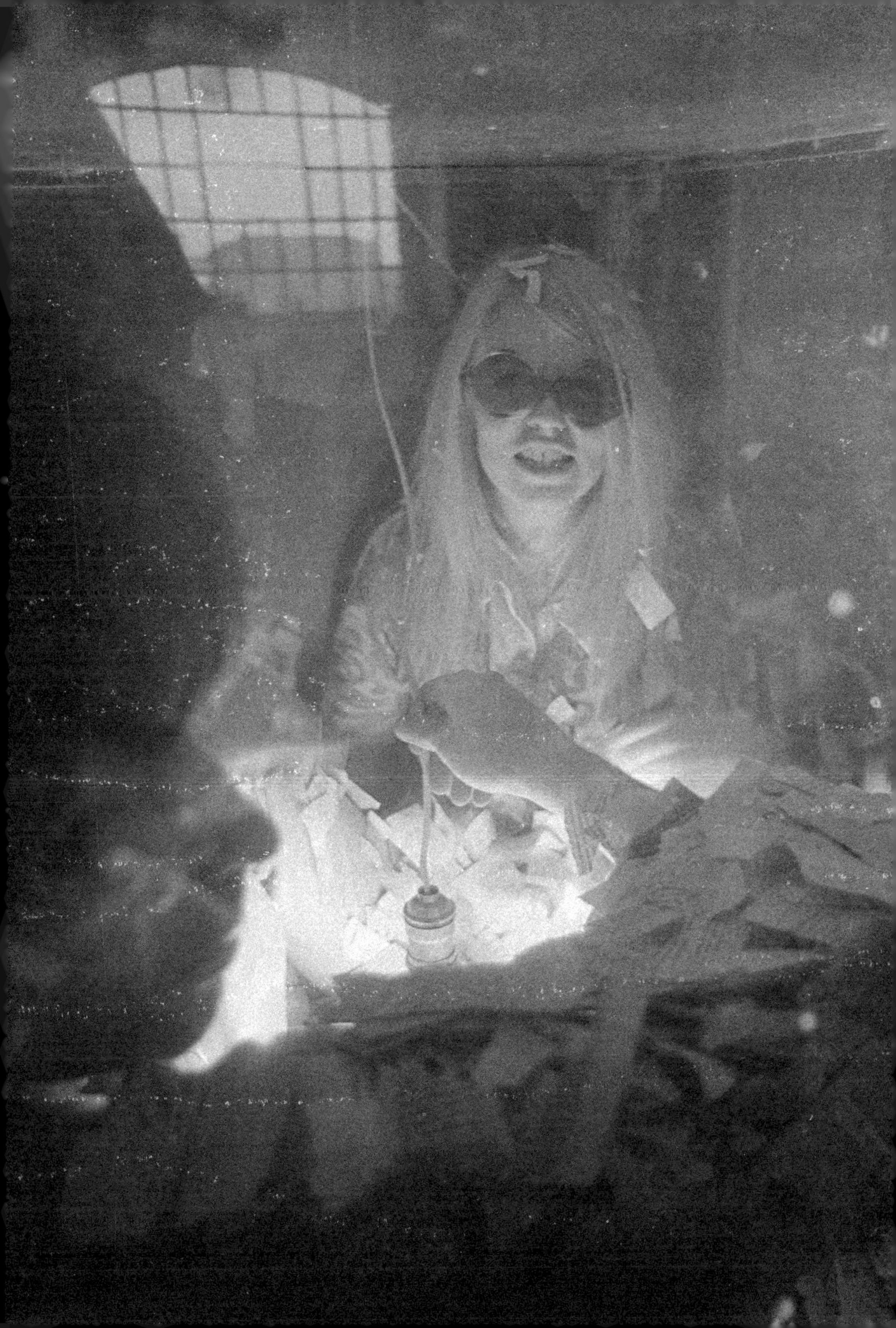

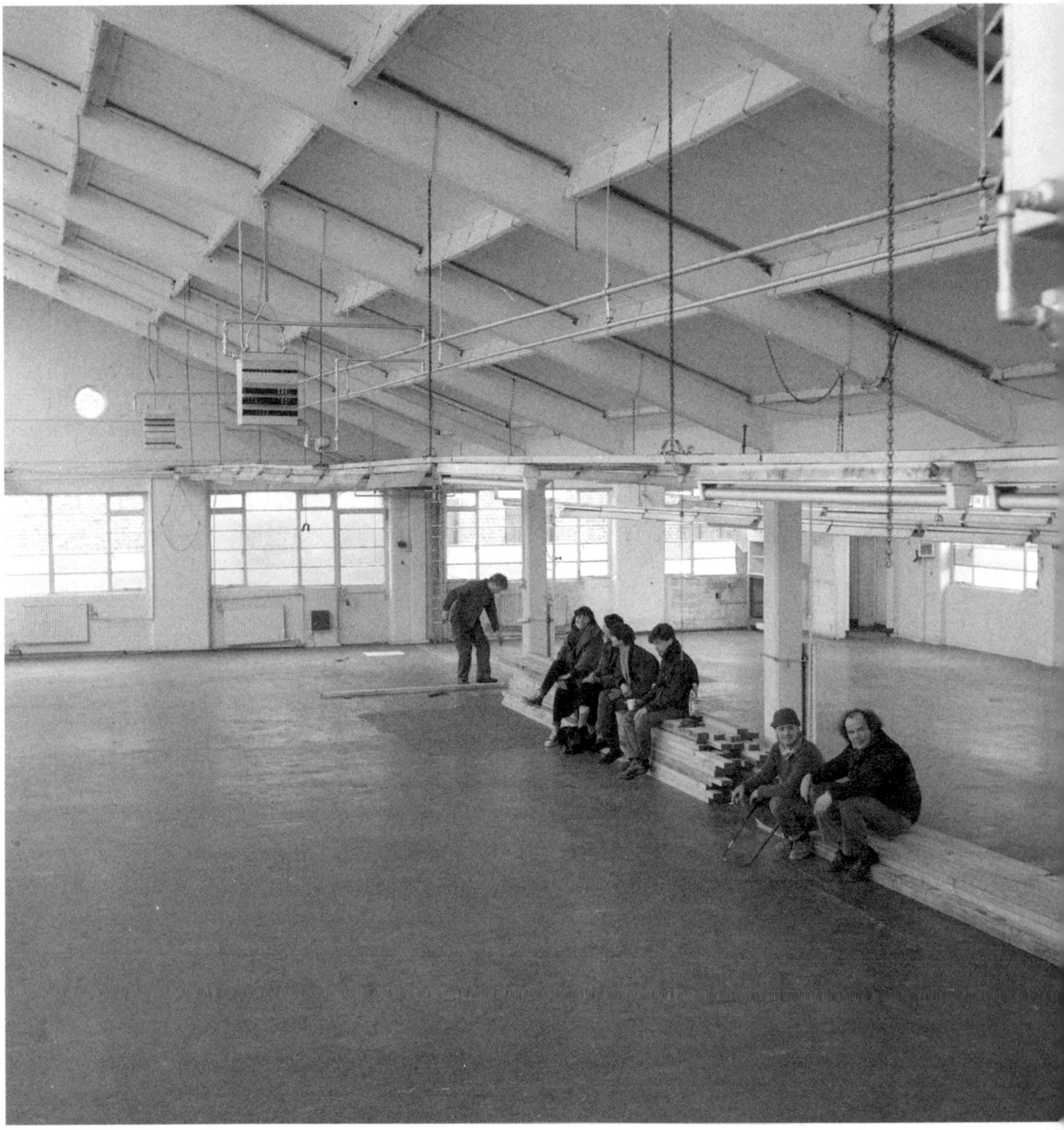

Artists in Victor House putting up partitions for studios in 1985.

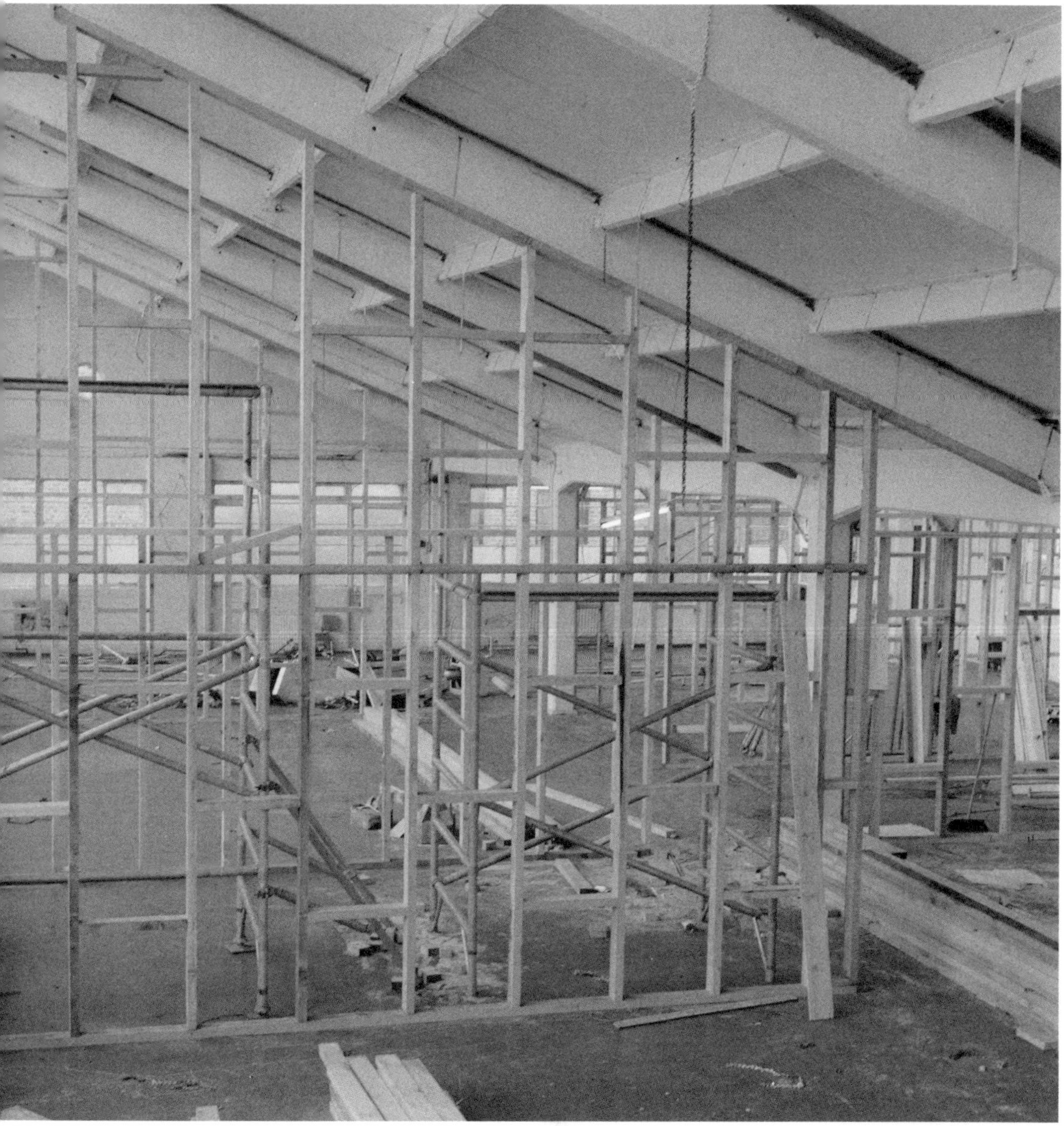

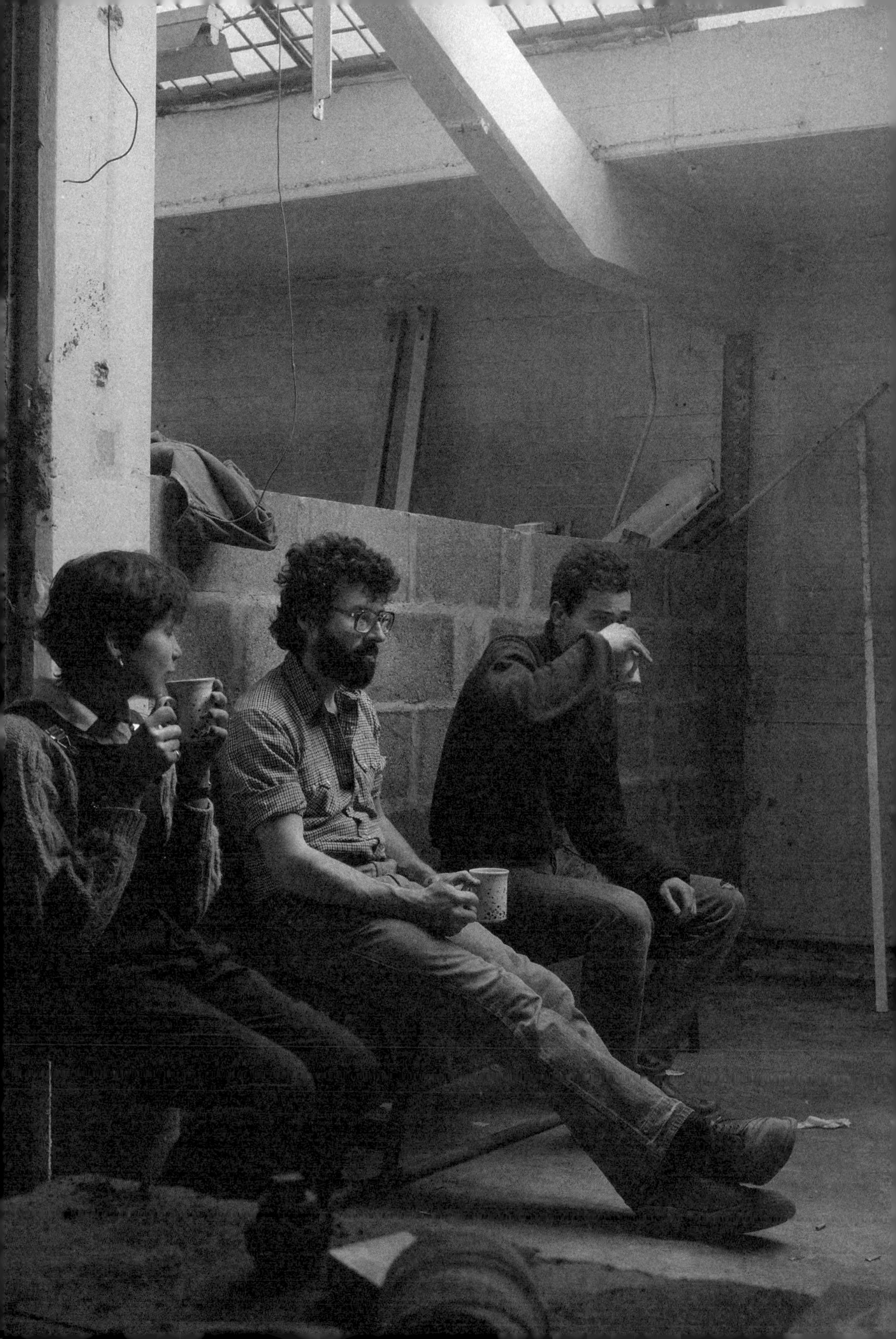

DIY

David Morris

What is DIY? Shifting across activities and histories, re-appropriated and redefined, it is a cipher for a changeable set of ethics and ideals. The past five years have seen a flurry of books about self-organised and artist-led initiatives – Institution for the Future; Self-Organised; Artist-Run Spaces; Institutions by Artists; Artist-Run Europe – and the bookshelves on the wider meanings of DIY weigh heavier, with recent titles on community gardening, urbanism, activism, fashion, skateboarding, interior design, music, science, hacking, knitting and craft, plus related terms like DIWO (do-it-with-others) and FUBU (for-us-by-us). DIY defies useful analysis. This may be deliberate.

A DIY morphology could include things like: action and immediacy; localism and proximity; small scale; available (or 'poor') materials; the hand-made; self-authorisation and autodidacticism; affirmative incapacity ('mess-thetics'); anti-authority and sociality. There is also something to do with taste. Lucy Lippard's writings on hobbyism and craft in the early '70s address this point, considering everyday practices of embroidery, knitting, craft and the existing conditions of the art world against a utopian horizon wherein every maker may set their own standard. DIY taught me what I know, and this text is written in the spirit of maintenance: not to throw the whole thing out and start again (too much a grand gesture) but to take apart, rearrange or renovate where necessary.

In the 1950s, do-it-yourself was already a movement. A 1952 edition of US magazine *Business Week* declared the 1950s the 'age of do-it-yourself', and, throughout that decade, DIY displays were the focus of industrial and consumer exhibitions, many widely-read magazines and a popular UK television show (*Do It Yourself*), part of a domestic boom set off by the 1951 Festival of Britain. The shift into a wider ethos becomes more apparent in the middle '60s, via self-build instructions for geodesic domes (R. Buckminster Fuller's plans for a build-your-own Sun Dome on the cover of *Popular Science* magazine in 1966) or the *Whole Earth Catalog* ('For a publication whose purpose is to egg on the conjuring and living

Artists having a tea break during Victor House renovation, 1986.

of new forms, the *Catalog* is rather a traditional instrument, no more radical than Sears Roebuck or Consumer Reports, merely attuned to a new market, the sub-economy of dope and rock'). In its beginnings, DIY appears as a modulation between suburban hobbyism and radical world-building, between home improvement and makeshift utopia.

SPACE's founding in 1968 was DIY in both these ways. Converting the warehouses at St Katharine Docks (and many buildings since) into artists' studios was a major feat of self-organised property renovation, the result of extensive work by many pairs of hands, with some artists expected to construct their own studio spaces, learning through doing. It was also a means for a group of artists in London to 'find their own salvation', in the words of Tony West, one of SPACE's original Council of Management, with a mood on the pragmatic side of utopian: 'I went to the ministry of housing and local government to find out what had been done about artists' studios, and their records showed nothing at all ... the artists just cannot find a space to work'. As co-founder Peter Sedgley reflected on the first years of SPACE, once the two-year lease on the original warehouses was up, 'the value is it happened, it will lead to other things. One can't really assess what one is doing. You feel it's right, just do the thing ya gotta do'.

Do-it-yourself was the product of a growing consumer economy on both sides of the Atlantic, driven by property ownership and an expanding middle class, and it also lent itself to the backlash. In *DO IT! Scenarios of the Revolution* (foreword by Eldridge Cleaver), Jerry Rubin writes: 'Do. Do. Do. The movement gets its unity around tactics. We become a community through collective action. [...] Fuck programs! The goal of revolution is to abolish programs and turn spectators into actors. It's a do-it-yourself revolution, and we'll work out the future as we go'.

From dumping dollars onto the trading floor of the New York Stock Exchange in 1967 and running a pig ('Pigasus') for the 1968 presidential race to his later reinvention as a businessman and Wall Street trader, Rubin came to symbolise a certain idea of 1960s–70s radicals-turned-neoliberal pioneers. This idea has become a reactionary one, but it's easy to see how a DIY ethic parallels 'creative class' values of entrepreneurship, hyper-individualism, gentrification and advanced capital accumulation. Even worse, consider the following remark from the newly elected Richard Nixon's address to the nation on the subject of the Vietnam War in November 1969 (my emphasis): 'We Americans are a *do-it-yourself* people. We are an impatient people. Instead of teaching someone else to do a job, we like to do it ourselves. And this trait has been carried over into our foreign policy'.

Capitalist, imperialist, violent and impatient. But also: communal, utopian, modest, transformative. How to untangle these DIY-lectics?

*

The 'do-it-yourself times into which the metropolitans were moving' around the time of SPACE's founding are depicted in Nigel Fountain's *Underground: The London Alternative Press 1966-74*. His description of a 1966 'All Night Rave' to launch the underground newspaper International Times projects subterranean links towards the rave continuum of the 1980s–90s as well as the first emergence of youth culture in the 1950s, noting the early entry of the word 'raver' into the British lexicon as a result of 'some mild disorder' among teenagers at the 1960 Beaulieu Jazz Festival. As George McKay explains in his book *DiY Culture* (sharing its initials with free party collective DiY Sound System), this DIY is characterised by 'a youth-centred and -directed cluster of interests and practices around green radicalism, direct action politics, new musical sounds and experiences [...] a combination of inspiring action, narcissism, youthful arrogance, principle, ahistoricism, idealism, indulgence, creativity, plagiarism, as well as the rejection and embracing alike of technological innovation'.

Nostalgia for the 1960s is a toxic force, as the following generation knew already ('Never trust a hippy!'), but the shifting contours of DIY allow some continuities to be drawn. Worth highlighting are para-educational and radical social spaces such as the Antiuniversity, the London Free School, the Mangrove or Dialectics of Liberation – all of which drew energy from, and coexisted with, everything else for which 'the 1960s' is known or notorious. The flyer for the 1966 rave listed 'STRIP – TRIPS – HAPPENING – MOVIE – POP – OP – COSTUME – MASQUE – DRAG BALL / bring your own poison, bring Flowers and Gass filled balloons'(sic). It began at 11pm, featured Bob Cobbing and London Film-Makers' Co-op showing William Burroughs' *Towers Open Fire* and Kenneth Anger's

Scorpio Rising, live bands, jelly sculptures, light shows and so on. Also present was Yoko Ono, who appeared on stage during a set by Soft Machine and invited the audience to touch one another. In the same year, Ono was producing works such as do it yourself dance piece ('SWIM IN YOUR SLEEP / GO ON SWIMMING UNTIL YOU / FIND AN ISLAND'), which formed part of the 13-day festival Do It Yourself Fluxfest Presents Yoko Ono and Dance Co. Ono has been credited with pioneering the do-it-yourself artwork (see *The do-it-yourself artwork*, edited by Anna Dezeuze) beginning with her 1961 work *Painting to Hammer a Nail*:

> Hammer a nail into a mirror, a piece of glass, a canvas, wood or metal every morning. Also, pick up a hair that came off when you combed in the morning and tie it around the hammered nail. The painting ends when the surface is covered with nails.

A year later, as part of a score entitled 'Read music: do it yourself', Nam June Paik instructed La Monte Young to 'read all the white pages very slowly / (more than three seconds) You should not just 'read' / as a normal reading matter but 'really' 'do', / or try to do or at least imagine to / do all the events yourself'. Do it yourself was a motto of several artists within the international Fluxus network, not only Ono and Paik but also its central node, George Maciunas. At that time, Maciunas was renovating ex-industrial New York lofts into affordable coop artists' studios, the model that would inspire Bridget Riley and Peter Sedgley's establishment of SPACE. Do-it-yourself appears here as a technique of transformative, experimental manual-artistic labour; the work of DIY is part renovation, part participation – just as Ono's painting is completed by whoever is holding the hammer – realised through cooperative forms of art-action, dance and musicality.

The poster for the 1966 rave in London also listed 'STEEL BAND'. (In the various reminiscences about this event, there is little further information, except that they were there.) At that time, steel pan music was a new art form – close in age to the amplified blues with which it shared the stage – invented when musicians began to experiment with the resonant and rhythmic qualities of scrap metal, biscuit tins, dustbin lids and automobile brake drums. With roots in the bamboo orchestras of Port of Spain, Trinidad, themselves part of cultural resistance to the colonial British through the 19th century, steel pan found its contemporary form through the adaption of oil canisters in the 1940s (dumped by the US army, who established a military base in Trinidad in 1941). This coincided with a period of anti-colonial unrest as well as a flourishing cultural scene, including the emergence of a group of intellectuals around the journal Beacon including Ralph de Boissière, Albert Gomes, Alfred Mendes and CLR James. In his major study of Carnival, Errol Hill describes the moment: 'War clouds hung in the air. Trinidad youth responded by producing a revolution in musical sound.'

Steel pan invented both an aesthetic and a technology – it is the twentieth century's only new acoustic instrument, and with a political orientation. In a study of the steel band movement, Stephen Stuempfle writes that steel pan players

> belonged to that sector of society that Trinidadians refer to as grass-roots: the working class, the marginally employed and the unemployed. Their bands were based in different neighbourhoods and villages and intense rivalries ensued as they developed their new instruments. The grass-roots basis of the music and the violent clashes in which bands sometimes engaged evoked much hostility from the middle and upper classes and even from many members of the grass-roots class itself. Essentially the new music was perceived as a threat to the social order…

The new music was a 'downtown' rival to the more respectable calypso. Lloyd Bradley notes that 'Steel pan was seen as trifling, a DIY ghetto extension of Port of Spain's violent street gangs, while calypso's associations with jazz and nightclubs were judged the height of sophistication'. DIY or no, by the 1950s it gained wider acceptance as part of the decolonial independence movement. Among the first performances of steel pan music in Britain was that by the Trinidad All Steel Percussion Orchestra (TASPO), at London's new South Bank complex, beginning a six-week tour as part of the 1951 Festival of Britain. The steel had oxidised on the crossing from Trinidad, and, in contrast to the Festival's imperial pomp, the group chose to play their instruments rusty – an affirmation of materials and impaired fidelity but above all a trick on the audience, who were astonished.

At this point, the meaning of DIY starts to unravel. Alongside the 1951 exhibition, which inaugurated the do-it-yourself market for a generation of post-war consumers, one of the newest musics then in existence entered a new phase. Members of TASPO remained in London following the tour; they played gigs, taught steel pan to others and formed new groups. In the late '50s, members of the band became involved in the London Caribbean Carnival, precursor to the Notting Hill Carnival, inaugurated by Trinidad-born activist Claudia Jones and the West Indian Gazette (founded by Jones and Amy Ashwood Garvey) as a popular response to a climate of racist attacks and intimidation. In Carole Boyce Davies' intellectual biography of Jones, *Left of Karl Marx: The Political Life of Black Communist Claudia Jones*, she notes Jones' spirit of 'working with what she had available' in the formation of Carnival in London, as well as the politics of 'taking space' – as fundamental to the event as music, dance and costume. In the recollection of Sterling Betancourt, one of the original TASPO members, it was the steel band led by Russell Henderson Band that broke the barriers of a children's fete (organised by community activist Rhaune Laslett as part of the London Free School), and reorientated Carnival to the streets.

Carnival returns the narrative to the familiar origin story of DIY in late 1970s punk – perhaps the clearest articulation of basic DIY principles ('This is a chord; this is another; this is a third. Now form a band'; 'It was easy, it was cheap – go and do it!'). Punk drew both politics and poetics from Carnival. According to Paul Gilroy, 'The street carnival, with its bass-heavy sound systems pumping out the new militant 'rockers' beat of reggae as the half bricks and bottles flew overhead, demonstrated to the punks the fundamental continuity of cultural expression with political action'. The punk story is multiple – between 1976 and '78, it appears in Istanbul, São Paulo, Mexico City, Tokyo, Stockholm and Warsaw – as punk and scholar of Iranian intellectual history Golnar Nikpour explains:

> [...] punk emerges like an explosion at a particular historical moment in a number of places and then lives many lives enmeshed in colonial and neo-colonial power structures and capitalist economies. I would argue until the end of time with anyone who told me that Bad Brains invented hardcore and that Olho Seco was some

> sort of imitation or secondary instantiation. This is not just a conceit of a bitter person of colour who wants something to call her own, or a multiculturalist 'we all have our own culture' kind of intervention - it is one that takes seriously the Marxian rejoinder that capitalist processes produced global economies from their inception, and that these processes have something to do with the unfolding of social worlds and histories. The linkages aren't always causal or obvious, but they cannot be ignored.

Steel an' Skin's 1979 recording *Afro Punk Reggae (Dub)* connects some of these threads. The band, founded by community activist Peter Blackman with a group of London-based musicians, began in 1975 with the help of Beryl Gilroy as a project of black education. With workshops and performances in schools across the UK, as well as in prisons, psychiatric institutions and festivals, the group also set up three autonomous drum, dance and drama groups in other cities. With around a hundred new groups coming into existence in the mid '70s, steel pan was by now a movement, cultivated in part so there would be more players to participate in Carnival. The oil economy makes the pattern more complex still. Members of Steel an' Skin also played in the 20th Century Steel Band, which, in 1977, travelled to Lagos to participate in FESTAC '77, the great Pan-Africanist festival underpinned by Nigeria's booming oil economy. The latter group was sampled repeatedly by Grandmaster Flash (also later Doug E Fresh, Soul II Soul and Jennifer Lopez); and in the Bronx at that same time, in the beginnings of hip-hop, the same 55-gallon oil drums that formed the basis of steel pan were being transformed again into bass speakers for block party sound systems.

The 1966 appearance of steel pan at the 'All Night Rave' is a historical loop, a political aesthetics much older than Fluxus experiments and do-it-yourself counterculture, a counter-counterculture erupting within its formative moments. The larger, deeper cultural politics of steel pan eclipse the idea of DIY, but – youth-orientated, collective, ingenious, transformative – fit its conditions of possibility; a new art-form for a new political project. A recent exhibition at the Black Cultural Archives took up this lineage, linking the self-determining, -authoring and -authorising circuits of pirate radio and sound systems, via calypso, to the Florence Mills Social Parlour, the social space, restaurant and club established by Amy Ashwood Garvey and Sam Manning in the mid 1930s that provided a meeting point for intellectuals and Pan-Africanists – all under a sign of DIY Culture. Steel pan also connects to an ongoing and still-radical (counter)culture. (For a test of contemporary relevance, compare present-day Carnival to the stale spectre of endless 1960s tributes, rehashes and reunions.) Steel bands are traditionally un-notated, unstandardised and leaderless, with techniques and pieces learned mutually through trial and error. A different DIY, or a technology for its undoing; complexly anti-imperial, popular, contagious, resonant, malleable, alchemic. As Errol Hill wrote in 1972: 'The period of experimentation and consolidation is not over.'

Because DIY is something to be taken apart another way again. In the assessment of the drummer in the band playing behind Yoko Ono at the 1966 rave, 'In the end the culture we were involved in was an Anglo-American cultural narcissism revamped, and if you look at it from the point of view of world culture it actually reflected the power structure, the extraordinary media power of the English-speaking West'. What makes sense at one moment in one small part of the world will not make sense everywhere. And there might be other, better, ways to think about it. With reference to artist-organised initiatives in Indonesia, Grace Samboh told me: 'The way our society works does not leave us space nor time to move alone. (This might need a longer conversation.) So, most likely things are done together. Some people call it DIWO. But, these terms... unlike Coca Cola, which is definitely an imported culture, the fact that we have always to rely on each other and do things together have been in our culture since forever, maybe even before that'.

Something to be salvaged from DIY is its mess – a conceptual messiness that allows it to be reformulated, allows links across actions and histories. Its uses across a wide field also carry potential for breaking the enclosures within that field – the overlaps between DIY and conversations and practices of commoning seem more than coincidence. A resistance to generalisation also appears to be part of DIY's DNA. Considering the irreducible particularity of innumerable micro-endeavours and the practical difficulty of locating resemblances between wildly different disciplines, initiatives and activities, it is bound to be heterogeneous and blurred, which gives scope for manoeuvre. At the time of writing the need for multiple alternatives appears urgent. And perhaps it is a good moment to move past talk of 'alternatives' towards more expansive possibilities – the present is not sustainable and any futures will require many hands and a lot of rebuilding.

A theory is exactly like a box of tools, Gilles Deleuze and Michel Foucault said, but DIY is not a theory exactly. It is more like an attitude to the present, an action-ism with whatever is available, with different results at any given time. Although DIY has an 'I' at its centre, its 'I' is not individual; its 'it' is an action that is collective and constructive. In *Living a Feminist Life*, Sarah Ahmed writes that 'Feminism is DIY: a form of self-assembly', and that 'A collective is what does not stand still but creates and is created by movement'. As a collective endeavour, DIY creates and is created by movement; it is what you do with it, a concept that invites action. Nothing to explain, nothing to understand, nothing to interpret – the 'it' is in the doing. Do it!

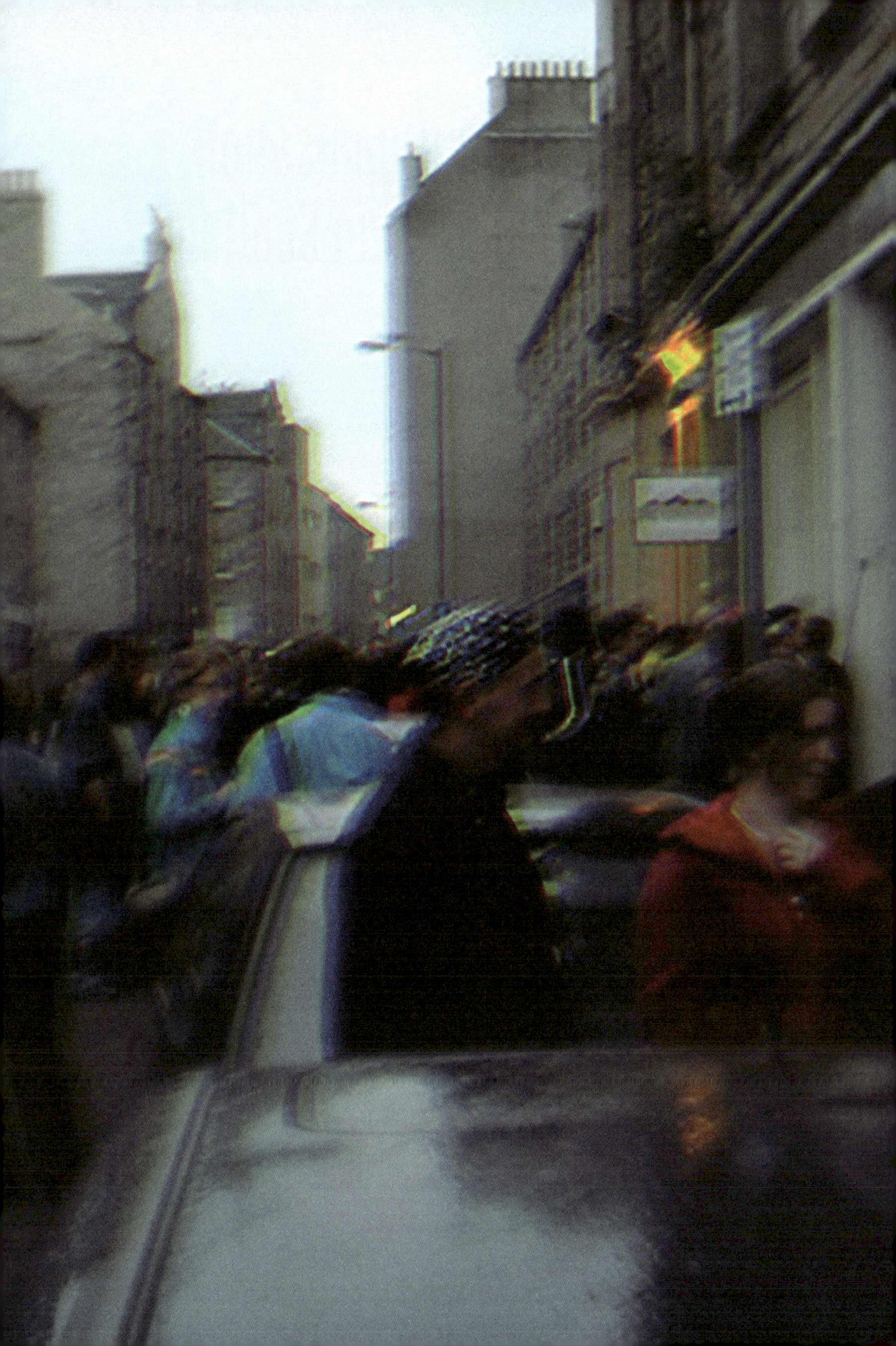

The Unlearning Organisation: cultural devolution in Scotland 1967–2017

Neil Mulholland

As I write, self-determination is paramount to the agendas of both the Scottish and British Governments. The May 2017 local authority elections and the UK General Election in June, however, concern radically incompatible conceptions of self-determination. Tory self-determination is indistinguishable from the authoritarian nationalism of Pax Britannica (1815–1914). It promises a companionless return to neorealist international relations; the anarchical system of sovereign states enshrined by the Treaty of Westphalia (1648), from which the then United Kingdom of Scotland and England and its Empire grew.[1] In Scotland, self-determination embraces the post-World-War-II Pax Europaea: fluid states of interdependence, asymmetric layers of authority, each of which share sovereignty with the others. The signature of the Treaty of Rome, just over 60 years ago, determined that neomedieval international cooperation would supersede the anarchic neorealism that had led to numerous European wars.

The Scottish National Party (SNP) Government (2007–) and the broader YES Scotland independence campaign have largely consolidated Pax Europaea's neomedievalist vision of interdependent self-determination over the past few years. But this vision is part of a movement that has much broader and deeper cultural roots across Britain and the Anglosphere. Indeed, SPACE is a key player in the story of what Michael Gardiner called The Cultural Roots of British Devolution.[2] At this moment in time, it is crucial we remember that the values of interdependent self-determination embodied by SPACE run entirely counter to the authoritarian nationalism of the Tories.

Street view on the night of the Embassy's first show in their East Crosscauseway gallery (June 2004). The exhibition 'Bishop's Move' featured artists based in Manchester. Photo: Neil Mulholland

We can begin to understand something of the significant role SPACE has played in the development of the global infrastructure for contemporary art by observing that its inception came at a pivotal point in the governance of the arts in Britain. In 1967, public subsidy of the arts in Scotland was devolved from the Arts Council of Great Britain (ACGB, 1945–94) in London to Edinburgh, when the Scottish Arts Council (SAC) replaced the ACGB's Scottish Committee (1947–67).

SAC was a largely autonomous branch of ACGB Colonial Office in London. It championed Scotland's national interests in Scotland, while loyally following John Manyard Keynes' arm's length/'few but roses' vision for the ACGB (ironically Keynes had vociferously opposed administrative devolution of the arts to Scotland). Like its ACGB overlord, SAC espoused an Arnoldian view of culture as unitary and idealist. A Cultural NHS, SAC inherited something of the Committee for Encouragement of Music and the Arts (CEMA, 1940–46) welfare-state meliorism, situating its surgeries closer to its patients, directly hosting exhibitions in galleries and community centres scattered in Scotland's most sparsely populated areas. The subsidiary approach was a bitter-sweet victory for cultural nationalism in Scotland. Scotland's 'artistic traditions' would be determined by branch managers of the Keynesian project, its vernaculars officially sanctioned by the (much more refined) British Union State.

The foundation of SAC directly coincided with a period of heightened political nationalism in Scotland that was flamed by the international counterculture of the late '60s. Younger artists rejected the conservatism of Scotland's old artist-initiated academies such as The Royal Scottish Academy in Edinburgh (1826–), The Royal Glasgow Institute of the Fine Arts (1861–), and The Society of Scottish Artists (1891–). Instead, they established their own, more participatory, citizen-led organisations such as the Glasgow League of Artists (founded 1968).[3]

Such organisations took two distinct forms:

1. Sites and Systems of Distribution: Artist-run Initiatives (ARIs)

In the late 19th century, Scottish industrialists established numerous private galleries, a number of which were instrumental in nurturing European modernism. By the '50s, Scotland had grown conservative in social attitudes, so much so that the Conservative and Unionist Party won a majority of Scottish votes in the 1959 election. The ambitious collectors who had bankrolled Scottish modernism, such as the art dealer Alexander Reid and the publisher Walter Blackie, were not being replenished. The dominant system of distribution came in the moribund form of Scotland's old artist-initiated academies (which monopolised Scotland's four art schools). This Académie Française approach was not particularly conducive to avant-gardism. With no dealers or patrons stepping into this fray, contemporary artists were compelled to establish their own galleries and advocate on behalf of their peers. Hence, from 1957 to 1966, Scotland witnessed the rise of what would become foundational independent artist-run initiatives (ARIs): 57 Gallery (1957), Jim Haynes Paperback Bookshop and Gallery (1959), Traverse Theatre (1963) and Demarco Gallery (1966), all in Edinburgh, and Charing Cross Gallery (1963) in Glasgow. The Edinburgh ARIs, notably, all shared an interdisciplinary commitment to the arts: visual art, writing and theatre. They prefigured the post-industrial, neomedieval discourses on self-determination that would dominate Scottish International magazine (1968–74) and which should be considered an integral part of the ARI counter-culture. Collectively, such ARIs initiated what was a global shift from modernism towards what we still call 'contemporary art'.

2. Systems of Production: Studios and Workshops

Post-war Scottish modernism was diasporic; most ambitious artists migrated. Without fabrication facilities, artists were unable to work and so left Scotland to establish viable working studios elsewhere. By the end of the '60s, the more overtly countercultural ARIs had reconnected Scottish artists with the world, affirming a global community of purpose. Dialogues were established with international peers, including the founders of AIR, SPACE and Acme in London and The Institute for Art and Urban Resources (PS1) in New York, and tactics and strategies for self-determination were shared. In Gallowgate, Docklands, Queens, Hackney and Leith, the post-Fordist downturn of the early '70s heralded the rise of the studio loft. In 1977, artists organised in Scotland's nascent industrial wastelands, building the affordable, and democratically accountable, Working Artists' Studio Provision Scotland (WASPS) in Edinburgh, Aberdeen, Dundee and Glasgow. WASPS perfectly complemented Edinburgh Printmakers (1967–), Glasgow Print Studio (1972–), Peacock Printmakers, Aberdeen (1974–) and Dundee Printmakers Workshop (1977–98). Large-scale fabrication finally arrived with the foundation of the Scottish Sculpture Workshop in Lumsden in 1979.

Studios, workshops and ARIs were reciprocally intertwined. Artists practised in studios and workshops, exhibited and wrote about each other's work. As new sites and systems of distribution multiplied, demand grew for new sites and systems of production. The systems of production (studios and workshops) supplied the systems of distribution (ARIs). As the number and scale of ARIs grew, capacity was built for more artists to live and work in Scotland. Both forms of organisation were eager to gain the vital financial support of the new SAC.

SAC, however, had different long-term plans for the visual arts, preferring to establish and run its own galleries: Travelling Gallery, Edinburgh Charlotte Square Gallery, Glasgow Blythswood Square Gallery. Most of these galleries were in the salubrious 'salon' style of the Scottish National Gallery of Modern Art, which had resided at Inverleith House since 1960, and the private galleries of Dundas Street (Edinburgh) and St Vincent Street (Glasgow). While Scotland's ARIs nurtured dynamic participatory democracies, SAC administered with the cold dead hand of the British civil service.

Unlike the National Galleries of Scotland (NGS), SAC galleries were distributed but not devolved; they were all run directly from Charlotte Square in Edinburgh. In this sense, the embryonic Scottish patron state took a very long time to establish a more arm's length relationship with its benefactors, the perception in London being that there were no worthy arts benefactors in Scotland, that SAC had to invent, incubate and manage them. This patronising and agonistic attitude was, in hindsight, folly.

One of the most significant galleries in mid 20th century Scotland had emerged a decade prior to SAC: the 57 Gallery. Co-founded by a group of painters led by John Houston, this became 'New 57', based in Rose Street from 1961 to 1974, before resettling above SAC Gallery Edinburgh (the upstairs floor of what is now the Fruitmarket Gallery). 57 Gallery's constitution established a highly influential model of having an unpaid committee of six who were able to serve no more than two years as directors. They formed a committee for the contemporary visual arts and supported lay members of their organisation, who all paid a small fee to cover the ARI's running costs. They were accountable to the collective's members. To avoid conflicts of interest, the directors could not exhibit or promote their own work. This model has been copied across Scotland by Collective (Edinburgh), Transmission (Glasgow), Generator (Dundee), Embassy (Edinburgh), and it has spread to Catalyst (Belfast) and 126 (Galway) in Ireland. It is, by now, such an established form of collective artistic endeavour that we may call it a DIY doxa. While this form of participatory democracy is by no means exceptional to Scotland, Scotland is internationally celebrated for its dogged pursuit, and so is all too often naïvely mythologised as a Shangri-la by artists living elsewhere.

The doxa was, and remains, important for four reasons:

Firstly, it is a fluid palimpsest rather than a fixed 'statute'. Voluntary committee-run constitutions are based on precedent, but they are all a little different. Each ARI copies, then rewrites the constitution of a previous ARI. The constitution develops, adjusts to fit its situation, and flourishes. The doxa, therefore, is not absolute; it is an adaptive, elective affinity.

Secondly, the doxa invites a form of cultural amnesia that is germane to contemporaneity. ARIs that consent to being governed by the DIY doxa completely change their DNA every three years. The constitutional founders are quickly forgotten, thus mitigating against the formation of embodied institutional memory. Rapid volunteer turnover ensures that the doxa is not constantly subjected to institutionkritik; it remains 'hidden'. The precarity this ensures is seen to nourish and enhance cultural innovation. The effects on artistic programming, the intense dynamism of production, are what is most visible, and attractive, to audiences. This is a self-fulfilling prophecy that accounts for the further palimpsests of the doxa.

Thirdly, the doxa is a powerful ethical code that binds, and offers a form of self-empowerment to, local artistic communities. The doxa is virulent among younger contemporary artists because it is a means of defining and maintaining social relations and status through the act of reciprocal participation ('gift-bonding').

To receive recognition from your artistic peers consigns you to counter-gifting within your own network. The DIY doxa, therefore, operates – initially at least – as a localised system of establishing value among peers within a specific community of practice.

Finally, and following on from the previous point, providing that artists gift their output to the local commons, they are free to use its open resources. Thus, distinct communities of practice (local variants of the DIY doxa) are reciprocally tied to one another via a transnational commonwealth of networks. This commonwealth, simultaneously, offers a decentralised solidarism that transcends the unitary power of the art world's established public and private bodies.

The DIY doxa, then, functions as a shared ethic, one that has underwritten the values of much contemporary artistic practice since the late 1960s. Its viral nature has ensured that it continues to unbundle territories, facilitating exchange with internationalist ARIs around the world. The development of this doxa is a key reason why, in the 1970s, Tom Nairne's Scottish International Institute could anticipate a future neomedieval Scotland that was, simultaneously, internally decentralised and externally globalised.

In the late '60s, such values were often at odds with those sanctioned by the state and with those of the art market. The former is more overtly mandated by top-down arts policy, while the latter is negotiated between retailers and consumers. The DIY doxa, by contrast, was prosumerist; the producers were their own audience. However, this doxa was, and remains, a financial ouroboros, a potlatch or inextinguishable debt; the only way artists can escape cyclical self-subsidy is to access state subsidy or the art market. Given that Scotland's contemporary art market had been dilapidated, securing state support for this grassroots infrastructure became the overriding preoccupation.

It is no coincidence that this concurred with rising pressure on the British Government to devolve more political office to Scotland. Conceding to the ACGB's Scottish Committee's long-running campaign to run SAC in Edinburgh was an opportune sop to cultural nationalism that ensured political office remained in Whitehall. Devolution meant that, in Scotland, two conflicting, and overlapping, forms of artistic governance came to coexist: the DIY doxa of grassroots self-determination and the British model of 'devolution': limited delegated authority temporarily granted by a centralised authority. In the early '70s at least, emerging artists tended to identify with the former, more established academicians with the latter. While the two distinct forms of artistic governance frequently conflicted, they were, and remain, interdependent. Over the past 50 years, for every soupçon of self-determination won by artists, there has been a concession of autonomy in exchange for 'stability'. For every attempt made by SAC to canonise contemporary art, there has been a maverick independent intervention. By way of illustration, I will now turn to a few dates in the history of the devolution of the visual arts in Scotland since the advent of SAC: 1971, 1979, 1992, 1999 and 2014. In each instance, I will sketch the struggle playing out between the international DIY doxa and the Keynesian model of devolution granted, with great reluctance, by the British Union State.

1971

The rise of the ARI collectivist doxa overlapped with the slow establishment of SAC's Glasgow Arts Centre. SAC began curating a room in the Glasgow Lady Artists' Club in Blythswood Square in 1967. It mainly exhibited touring exhibitions, dispatched by the ACGB, to educate provincial Scots. Blythswood Square was a slice of Cork Street 'civilisation' in deepest darkest Glasgow. (It had a Cona Coffee Maker and served egg and cress sandwiches.) In 1971, the Lady Artists' Club declared bankruptcy, so SAC bought the building from them for £35,000. On 9 February 1971, SAC held a 'talk-in' there. The Glasgow League of Artists proposed to requisition the building as a rentable gallery and printmakers' workshop for local artisans and act 'democratically' as its 'advisory committee' (i.e. to establish the New 57 doxa in Glasgow).

SAC, instead, decided to invite a live-in director to take care of the building and to programme events for Glasgow in Glasgow. They appointed the visionary International Times editor and playwright Tom McGrath, who also found time to write plays and establish the Tron theatre while directing what, in 1974, became Third Eye Centre. McGrath patronised younger Scottish artists while bringing a wide array of intermedia into Third Eye's programme, developing this along similar lines to the European-Joseph-Beuys-Postminimalist lineage that, by 1970, had many artist advocates in Edinburgh. He introduced Glasgow to photo/video community studios, muralism and American forms of social practice informed by field trips to New York and Chicago. Such forms of artistic activity was actively discouraged by the academicians teaching in Scotland's four art schools.

In spite of this confident self-determination, the textbook Keynesian attitude at SAC remained that Scotland had suffered from a modernist bypass and their role was to give it a crash course. The Second Earl Haig of SAC wrote to McGrath regarding his proposed inaugural programme of 1974 that 'there should be no difficulty in enabling Glasgow viewers to have the opportunity of absorbing and learning some of the main trends. Apart from Rennie McIntosh [sic.] there doesn't seem to be any items in your list which cover this sort of thing. Joan Eardley and Stanley Spencer, though good artists, are not part of any of the main movements which I have in mind'.[4]

Thus, the blinkered monoculturalism of the Bloomsbury Group continued to patronise and suppress Scotland's contemporary artists. When SAC part-funded ARIs, such as New 57, it did so reluctantly. Compared to its own venues and those run by Richard Demarco, New 57 received a pittance. This was not because Demarco's ARI was more effectively networked but because Demarco – as an accountable quasi-commercial gallerist in the Cork Street tradition – represented forms of continuity and advocacy recognisable to SAC. In this sense, SAC supported organisations that mirrored ACGB's Bloomsbury values. It dismissed the movement among younger artists in '70s Scotland to embrace the reciprocal nature of art's gift economy as an expression of the customary solidarism of the 'Scots Cellar'.[5] This risk aversion did not pay off. It was New 57, Transmission and Collective, not Demarco or the NGS, that spearheaded what became Scotland's first home-grown international art movement since Art Nouveau, the New Image.

1979

SAC Director Alexander Dunbar had high hopes that the devolution referendum of 1979 would make SAC directly answerable to Edinburgh's New Parliament House. He wrote: 'My guess is that the Government will decide that the arts will be devolved to Scotland, partly because it makes sense and goes with related functions, and partly because both main parties are so scared of giving Scotland real economic power that they will compensate by giving Scotland everything except real economic power'.[6] However, an ACGB-inspired lack of trust in artists (and, more generally, in the ability of Scots to directly govern their culture) intensified throughout the 1970s and, with the failure of the first Scottish Referendum to deliver devolution, into the '80s.

In the late '70s, SAC increased pressure on New 57 to appoint and pay an 'accountable' director and ratify a more linear management structure. By the early '80s, New 57 were in talks to merge with SAC-run Fruit Market Gallery in Edinburgh to form the independent Fruitmarket. In 1984, part of the New 57 committee, led by Jim Birrell, narrowly voted to merge. Dissenting New 57 members were supported by Iain Patterson, who, in the same year, formed Collective on the basis of the original '57 constitution. Fruitmarket quickly appointed a director and abandoned its artist committee forever, proving the Collective group's mistrust legitimate.

When McGrath departed Glasgow, artists in the city were given fewer opportunities to exhibit as Third Eye attempted to be more 'international' (which meant a return to imported touring exhibitions). Artistic disgruntlement led to consultation with members of New 57 in Edinburgh, and this, in turn, birthed Glasgow's Transmission Committee for the Visual Arts in 1983. Throughout the '80s, it was Transmission that negotiated Glasgow's entry into the international art world; Third Eye shivered in its shadow.

1992

Ten years later, SAC civil servants attempted to strong-arm Transmission and Collective to appoint a paid 'accountable' director. They withdrew funding from both ARIs in a bid to make them acquiesce. Collective, with high rents and little support from Edinburgh Council, was forced to appoint a director in 1992. Transmission held out, and, during the 'Scotia Nostra' period of the early 1990s[7] in which its international reputation skyrocketed, it won its battle with SAC. In the early '00s, Collective replaced its committee with a board, the preferred structure of SAC. Ironically, while SAC was still insisting on top-down accountability, ACGB was being disbanded. In 1994, SAC was devolved to the Scottish Office, thus gaining a greater degree of authority.

Transmission's small victory over SAC, and the recognition this bestowed upon them from the international art world, demonstrated the power of the commonwealth; this provided a largesse greater than any individual or organisation could return to it. Throughout the 1990s, artists based in Scotland consistently practised the DIY doxa, establishing their own infrastructure and only seeking public support after having built a considerable international reputation. Notably in Glasgow, Patricia Fleming established a range of studio and exhibition projects through her FUSE programme that were pivotal to the rise of Glasgow as an international visual arts centre. She did this on a shoestring, exploiting John Major's changes to Unemployment Benefits to the benefit of her peers.

1999

By the time the Scottish Parliament reconvened in 1999, SAC had been devolved for 32 years and free of the ACGB for five years. The end of the millennium did not herald any further cultural devolution of arts governance within Scotland; on the contrary. Most of the 1999 Scottish Election manifestos (excepting that of Labour) were critical of arm's-length bodies (ALBs). Keynes' arm's-length model was first revoked by the 1999 Lib-Lab Scottish Executive who were determined to make SAC an executive body of government. The number of Scottish ALBs has since been purposefully and substantially reduced. One ALB that was axed was SAC, disbanded in 2010.

The zombie brainchild of New Labour, Creative Scotland (CS) is a different beast – a patron state that rejects Arnoldian conceptions of culture and one that is far less accountable to the public. CS makes no distinction between different art forms seeking Open Project Funding, nor does it distinguish between individual artists and large organisations. For example, CS's current 10-Year Plan, Unlocking Potential Embracing Ambition, places a great deal of emphasis on the 'learning organisation'; on enabling audiences to establish the parameters of social practice and their own creative hubs, while actively developing their own infrastructure.

Superficially, this sounds like an endorsement of an anthropological, democratic and devolved approach to culture. However, CS has heightened SAC's centrist managerial approach. Only the foundational discourse differs in its totalising instrumentalism. So, where SAC recognised distinct and specific artistic practices (and privileged a highly developed, if rather naturalised, modernist theory of 'practice'), CS is concerned with entirely generic corporatisms such as 'development needs', 'advocacy' and 'influencing'. The cult of personalities and impresarios that dominated SAC in the '70s has been superseded not by transparent 'systems', but by the cult of quantitative 'evidence-based' managerialism. SAC saw the visual arts (and artists) as wild things that needed to be sensibly nurtured (infantilised) if they were to blossom. CS, by contrast, imagines the visual arts to be, incontestably, part of the cultural industries, the key objective of which is 'culturepreneurial' wealth creation.[8] CS has thus economised culture rather than encultured the economy. Its goal of 'enabling audiences' (rather than artists or arts organisations), is a familiar euphemism for enthroning consumer choice.

Buried deep within the DNA of CS, and the New Labour project from which it arose, is structuration theory. According to Anthony Giddens' account of structuration, everyone must become their own system. Certainly, as I have outlined here, the international development of contemporary art since the late '60s may be understood as a history of artists forming a wide range of formal and informal organisations. Partly as a means of survival and partly for artistic reasons, artists have de-centred themselves in favour of very broad meshworks.

Structuration is a rich and complex theory, and, in the right hands, can help us understand how ARIs might be catalysts for genuine cultural devolution (as opposed to mere 'creative economics'). However, in a largely rudderless instrument of governance such as CS – one oblivious to its own origins and goals – it has proven disastrous. (It is notable that the Creative England experiment was swiftly abandoned by Labour's Department for Culture, Media and Sport.) The role of centripetal organisations such as CS and the NGS – arguably incompatible with a structuration-based approach to culture – remains unquestioned by the Scottish Government, despite the fact that everything that is vital and celebrated about art in Scotland since the late '60s has emerged from self-devolved organisations and infrastructures.

2014

In spite of the CS debacle, the YES Scotland campaign was very visibly supported by artists in Scotland. This attests to its cell-like organisational approach, which drew both systemically and ethically upon the DIY doxa. National Collective – the cultural movement for Scottish independence during Scotland's Referendum from December 2011 to September 2014 – explicitly established this connection, signing up more than 4,000 members across the country. While the YES campaign ultimately lost the referendum to the Unionist NO vote, it decisively won the cultural crusade, embedding the DIY doxa into a mainstream national imaginary that has long included constitutional solidarism (Scots are sovereign, not the Scottish Parliament).

Meanwhile, offering no alternative to the viral DIY doxa, authoritarian British nationalism amplifies neorealist fantasies of territorial order, strength and stability. Luckily, artists in Scotland, as elsewhere in the world, continue to establish their own 'learning organisations' and forms of self-governance as they have consistently over the past 50 years (e.g. The Edinburgh Annuale, Open House Glasgow).

Advocates of Scottish independence – such as the SNP, Green Party and Common Weal – have drawn much sustenance from Nordic models of social democracy. They would be as well served by examining why the DIY doxa impetus continues to gather a groundswell of support in contemporary Scottish cultural politics, and they will learn much from the ever-evolving forms it takes. The question of how a centripetal statelet such as Scotland (independent or not) might dissolve its national arts bodies in order to redistribute public resources towards self-evolving organisations and user-generated infrastructures in the arts is a thornier one. As The Jimmy Reid Foundation has demonstrated, in policing and local government, Scotland is now less devolved that it was before 1999. The fact that Scotland's patron state for the arts (CS) is also more singular and centralised now than it was in 1994, some years prior to political devolution, is no cause for celebration. History clearly demonstrates that the Union State's preoccupation with centralisation – under the ACGB and in SAC's early years – failed to nurture emerging artistic practice.

There is little point in Scotland running its own affairs if it uses its powers merely to establish tartanised versions of the British Union State's administrative apparatus – a Unionist-Nationalist trope that runs consistently from the early 19th century through Scotland's arts organisations: RSE, RSA, NGS, SAC... Devolution in the arts means fully entrusting them to interdependent communities of practice and communities of interest, something that ARIs such as SPACE have long embodied constitutionally. Culture is the infinite diversity of absolute opacities. Total noise in the channel. It has no centre as such; it is a Republic of Static.

Notes

1 Hedley Bull, *The Anarchical Society* (New York: Columbia University Press, 1977).

2 Michael Gardiner, *The Cultural Roots of British Devolution* (Edinburgh: Edinburgh University Press, 2004).

3 An artist-led organisation that pursued more socially-engaged and political work than the SSA. It was also active in setting up studio spaces.

4 Dawyck Haig, Letter to Tom McGrath, 20 August 1973. (Third Eye Centre Archive, CCA/Glasgow School of Art).

5 FM McNeill, *The Scots Cellar: Its Traditions and Lore* (Edinburgh: Reprographia, 1973).

6 Alexander Dunbar, *Devolution and the Scottish Arts Council* (Edinburgh: SAC, 19 February 1975), p. 16. (Third Eye Centre Archive, CCA/Glasgow School of Art).

7 Moira Jeffrey, *Generation: 25 Years of Contemporary Art in Scotland* (Edinburgh: National Galleries of Scotland and Glasgow Life, 2014).

8 Anthony Davies and Simon Ford, 'Art Futures', *Art Monthly* 223, 1999, p. 9–11.

Michael Michaeledes, *Lions Gate*, 1968 →

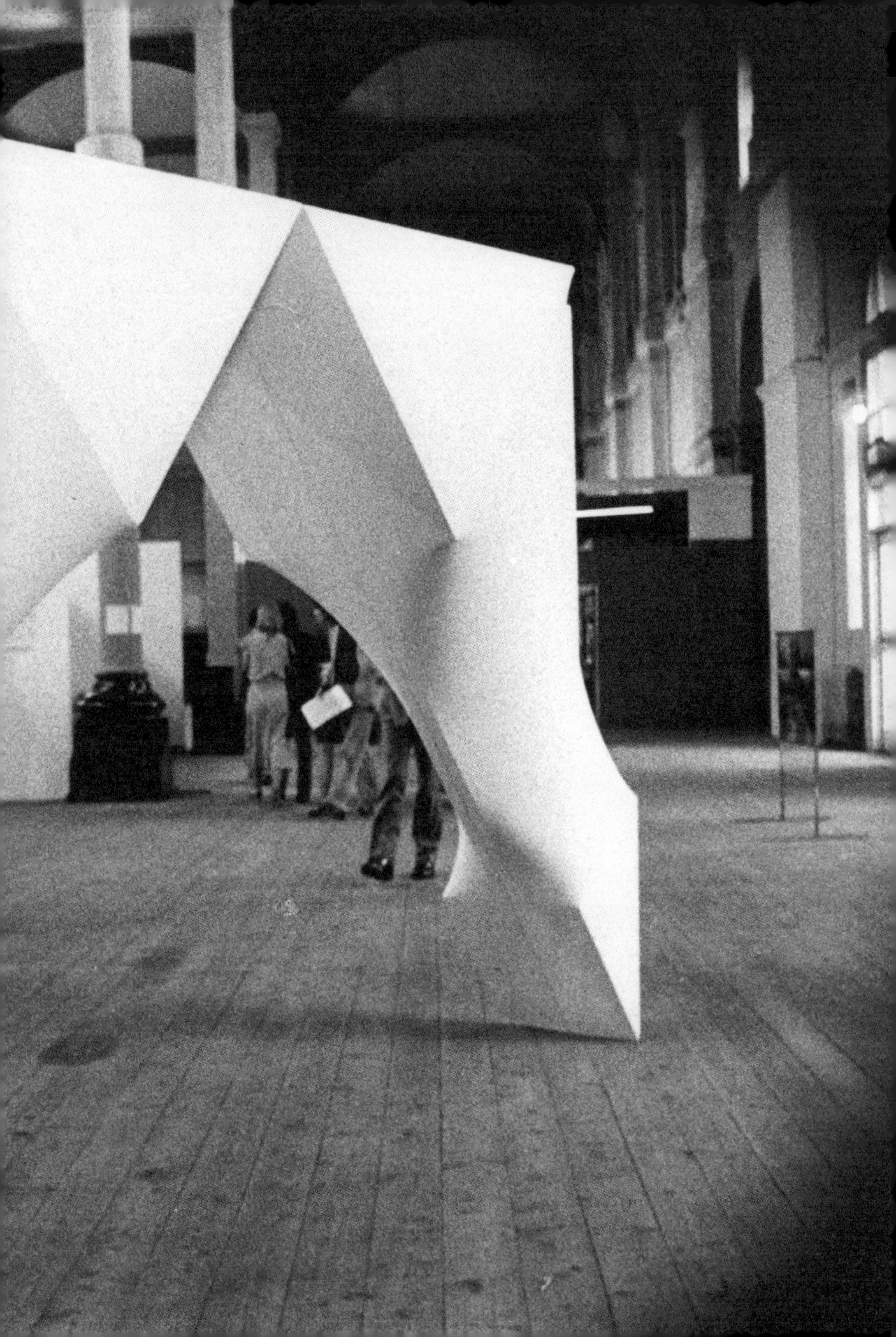

The space consists of a circle that travels in time

J&K / Janne Schäfer and Kristine Agergaard

The notion of time travel is at the heart of artist duo J&K's commissioned project to celebrate the 50-year anniversary of SPACE. This method of artistic excavation was used to look 50 years back to 1968 when SPACE was founded, and 50 years forward to 2068. Artists that were involved with the organisation at its beginnings, as well as current and past SPACE studio artists, met with J&K in-person to partake in conversations and guided time-travel meditation sessions. Situated within early studio sites, both active and departed, visions of the past and future were excavated and recorded. The resulting text and exhibition present an abstracted narrative of the past and future in which SPACE is the shuttle for a time travel experiment and a conduit for projecting a future for the role of art.

Log of Collective Time Travel Excavations (◀□ 1968 / ▶ 2068)

0. Entrée (Intermediate state)

◀□▶ It was very dark, water flowing underneath. I was a pupa, I was other than myself. Deeply curled up, not awake, not conscious. The pupa is not yet born but you are alive.

I. Roof (Everything becomes soft)

◀□ I am standing on a roof, it is sunset, there is a feeling of freedom.

◀□ People were lying around on old rugs. Everything should become soft, it was all about making soft environments, liberate the body and roll around. Occupy areas to lie down.

◀□ People were moving like panthers and animals.

◀□ There was a black dog. It was very sociable, milling around the people, everyone seemed to know it. I definitely seemed to be contained in some kind of body but I couldn't interact with people the way they were, I was an ethereal visitor. It was night, it was dark.

II. Wiring (Human control)

▶ There was something that was categorically different. It felt like everything was so human. There was no chance, no randomness. Everything was mapped out and controlled, will-dominated.

▶ Down in the basement there was a lot of equipment, maybe some subterranean infrastructure that was high-tech. This darkness below, this obscurity in the underbelly seems to have some intelligence about it. It's not this kind of horrendous darkness. Cool and quietly this infrastructure is wiring away, leaving everyone tranquil in the light upstairs.

III. Boiler Room (Looking for Scotty)

◀□ I landed through a machine. There was a guy who showed me where we were on the machine, it was a bit like a radar, but with knobs, like a mechanical iPad.

◀□ It's quite dark and dank, with many tunnels. Feels very neglected, like if nothing has happened here for a while. I am looking for a guy called Scotty but I don't know who he is but I got his name: Scotty is the man I'm looking for. He's got the future, he has the plan.

IV. Garden (Paradisiacal construction)

▶ There is a huge garden, growing fields, warm and harmonious, everyone is working in the garden.

▶ They were working with plants, they were very concerned about food production, so they had all these biggish lab containers with very green plants, spinach or something, inside. They were occupied with that, very serious about it, about the planet, about food production. And then there was an erotic scene, all of a sudden they were having sex. That was another thing they were very concerned with, in a very serious way, sexual expression and food production.

▶ A biosphere. Paradisiacal.

▶ It was an empty room with water running through it, it was part open, part closed. There were windows and steps outside, and gravel, water running through the gravel. Very natural, green. An inside outside.

▶ It felt like a sanctuary, like a tranquil place to be. It just felt calm and social in a very serene kind of way. What happened to all the artists, maybe everyone was tranquil and asleep?

V. Park (Luminous poison)

▶ The first question I asked myself was, would it be apocalyptic? It was absolutely not, it's not a kind of dystopian place, it's a really connected place. Everyone was spiritually connecting. I was thinking of the mushrooms, spectral luminous connections between people, very immaterial. Then I was out with the trees again and I just had this vision that each of them was like a shrine. Everyone was out there worshipping the trees, they'd become centres of spiritual energy.

▶ It was like this horrible pea green, rather poisonous yellow colour. There weren't any buildings and I couldn't really approach anyone. They were moving like panthers as if they were bushes, but they weren't bushes. It was as if no one really had a place in this ugly poisonous coloured society.

VI. Basement (Becoming Animal)

◀□ I was in a room, a bit squalid, smelly, it smelt of dope, greasy hair, cotton faded trousers.

◀□ There was a strong feeling of young male energy trying for some creative endeavour here. There was also the squirrel. It was quite a dark and gloomy building but the squirrel was a sudden bright flash from the outside world, coming into somewhere that felt like it was quite an intense place, for all kinds of reasons. It wasn't where animals normally were.

◀□ A guy with black eyeliner was doing sound experiments, a pre-punk kind of character. He pretended to be experimental but actually he was quite a sad being, lost somewhere in the basement. He was all about experimenting with himself, becoming something else. Then the dog told me it was about becoming more animalistic, being one with the animal.

◀□ I had sex with the dog, it was licking, orgiastic, sensual.

VII. Piping (Going with the flow)

◀□ Water was flowing through a massive pipe, I see a man dressed up as a zoo guard in khaki shorts, in an old fashioned way. He says: "I'm the water gate guy".

◀□ There were huge paintings, canvasses, and the paint was dripping down to the floor and dripping off under the floor into a waterfall of oil paint.

◀□ The stream goes faster and deeper until I reach this open cave where I get out. There had been human presence there in the past but there was no one there now. There were steps and an altar place, a little pool of organic life. I picked up a small frog and gave it a kiss. I put the frog in my pocket. I was dressed in a white tunic and sandals.

VIII. Floor (Pulsating vibration)

◀□ Everything had a sort of vibration about it. There was a buzzing in the materiality of the building and the park. Everything was very soft and organic. There was a lot of life pulsating and throbbing in the material itself.

◀□ Quick glimpses, like the sun is flickering through the original wooden floor, permeated by formations of luminous grass, snake-like formations of grass up and down, hair-like, stiff hard grass, like you find on the beach, with light coming from inside of it.

IX. Lift (Flying experiment)

◀□ I am climbing on steep walls, the space has transformed into this climbing wall.

◀□ There were some very large pieces of yellow fabric, like air balloons. I realised there was an experiment going on that was connected to the body. Somehow there was this connection between the hollow spaces in the body and a flying experiment.

◀□ I am seeing everything from a bird's perspective. There was the sensation that everything was quite derelict and crumbling apart, that all the buildings were being taken apart and were overgrown, and there was this lush feeling. It was difficult to judge whether it had just all fallen apart and was a post-apocalyptic urban scenario or whether it was the purpose to change everything to a more natural setting.

▶ There is a futuristic lift in an urban space. There are sprawling squares in the urban landscape. A strong sense of organic forms, big shapes of dense green growth, goose-bumpy surfaces with mossy growth, egg-like, foamy bits like you find on the beach. Weird texture, squidgy stuff. Urban sprawl exploded by a dark green hole, these big shapes of green surfaces, like jelly fish, with very long tentacles. Inside myself and the lift and the tentacles were part of the same, the feeling of light and luminosity.

X. Bathroom (Preservation of time)

▶ An orange Californian sunset, a path way with pebble stones, a bus shelter, an open structure made from wood, some people sitting there, naked.

▶ They are filling all their time with pleasure. There is a concern about the regulation of pleasure and the ability to control how much pleasure you need at a certain moment and when you don't need it.

▶ A lot of people had shaved heads. There was also something about babies being quite forbidden and there was a connection between the shaved heads and adolescence.

▶ The attitude to themselves was total: their health and well being was what made sure they lived as long as possible. That took up all of their lives, the preservation of time.

XI. Off site (Communicating with other beings)

◀□▶ Along the sides of the canal there is invisible plexiglas, like perspex walls around the whole perimeter. I sit down and suddenly the perspective through which I was looking at everything separates from the person that was experiencing the thing, so suddenly I am there also with a guy dressed in white and he sits down. There is a blue flame and all the light turns very blue.

▶ A blue colour, very shiny and very bright. We are going to leave the planet, we are going to be on another planet.

▶ It was like we were here ourselves communicating with people from other planets. I had this feeling of trying to communicate with other beings.

▶ There was a sense of curiosity, and almost as if someone was taking photographs of the presence that had arrived into the future so there was still a creative interest here in something that had come from the past. There were bright flashing lights, and it was like I was caught in the light of the attention, as a mysterious presence that came, that people were examining from the future.

XII. Studio (The space consists of a circle that travels in time)

▶ Life now is art, art is life. It is all about living out the art in this life-art way, we are co-creating this place.

▶ Art was a cerebral activity. People were still working and doing activities but the idea of art was something else, some form of meditation maybe. There was no need to construct objects and look at them on walls. That is over.

▶ The future space also consisted of a circle that could travel in time. People there were sitting like us here. We were dreaming that future together and creating it. The art creation was a ceremonial practice connected to the first way of making art—being in a ceremony, a collective co-creation.

► It was like a museum and there were people walking around like tourists. There was a guided tour. I was one of the waxwork sculptures, I felt people walking in and looking at me, and you. It was both of us. It felt like a preservation of radical ideas, the anniversary of something, the revolution. A celebration of something that had happened before.

The Log of Collective Time Travel Excavations (◀□ 1968 / ▶ 2068) has been compiled by J&K from time travel experiments made with Thorbjørn S. Andersen, Mariana Bassani, Nicholas Brooks, Gina Buenfeld, Persilia Caton, Charlotte Cullinan, Karen Davies, Chris Dorley-Brown, Emma Douglas, Fiona Furness, Cecilie Gravesen, Anna Harding, Peihang Huang, Christine Jakobson, Mark Molloy, Hugh Mendes, James Moore, Nisha Nishikawa, Valentina Orrù, Jane Ostler, Mildred Rambaud, Julien Sebban, Graham Stevens, Fritz Stolberg, and Andrea Zucchini.

Thanks to Keith Albarn, Flick Allen, Chris Dorley-Brown, Adam Hart, Robin Klassnik, Shirley Read, Michael Rhodes, Peter Sedgley, Graham Stevens and James Faure Walker for their insights into SPACE's history and visions for the future.

SPACE information

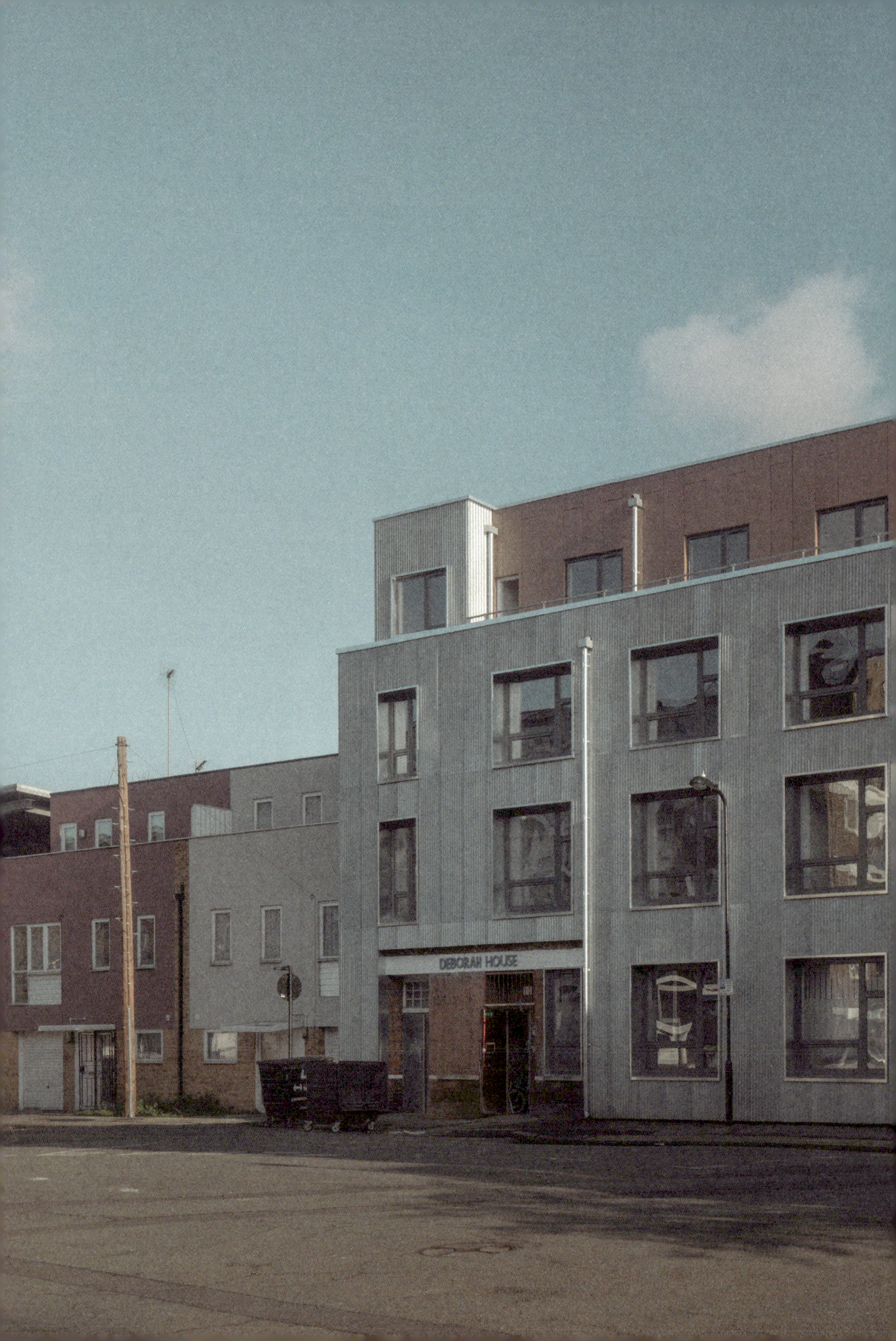
DEBORAH HOUSE

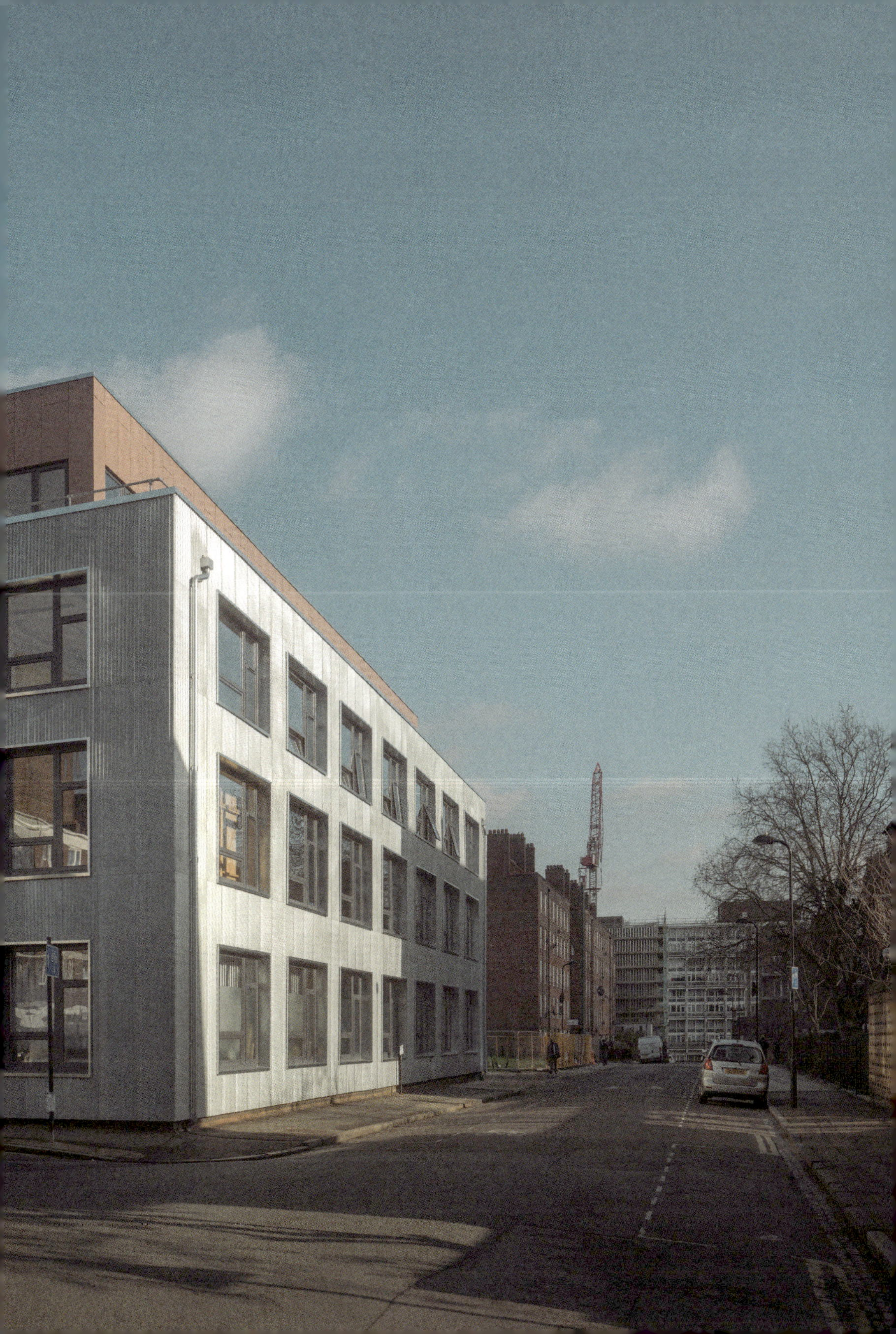

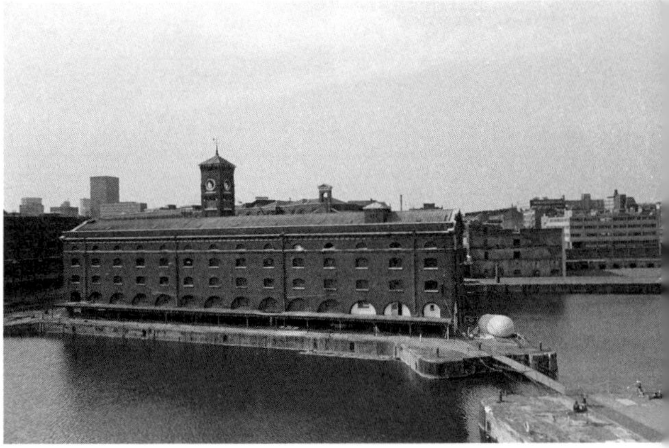

1968-70 St Katharine Docks, E1W

1968

1969

← Deborah House, leased from 1988 freehold purchased 2010, refurbished 2013.

Timeline of studio sites

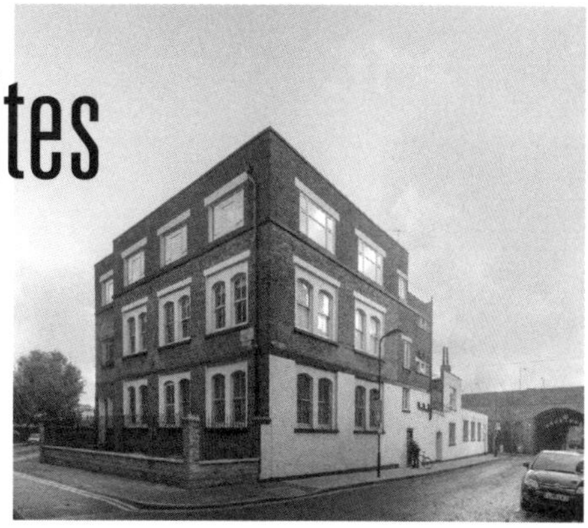

10 Martello Street, E8

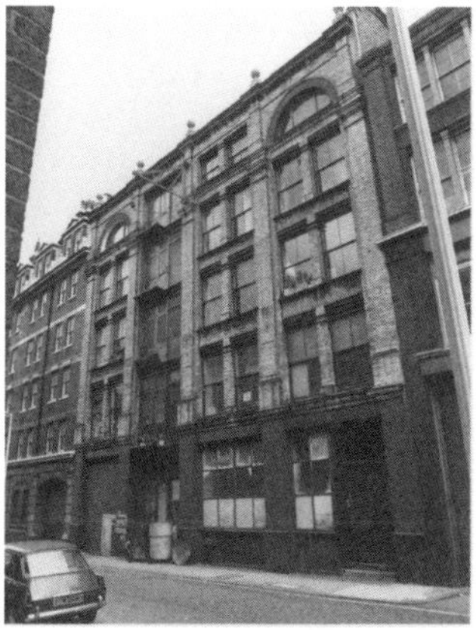

124–130 Tabernacle Street, EC1

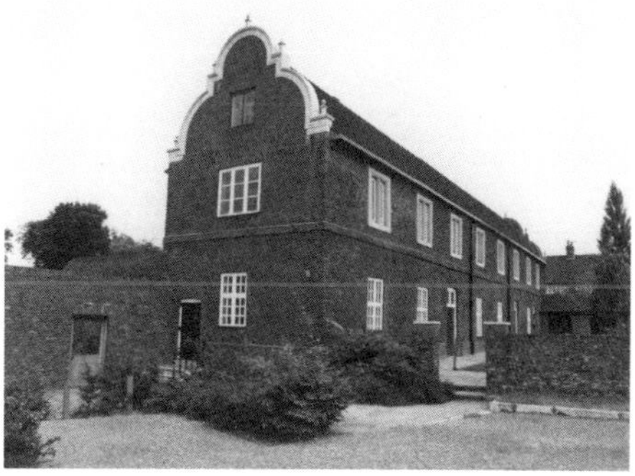

Charlton House Studio SE7

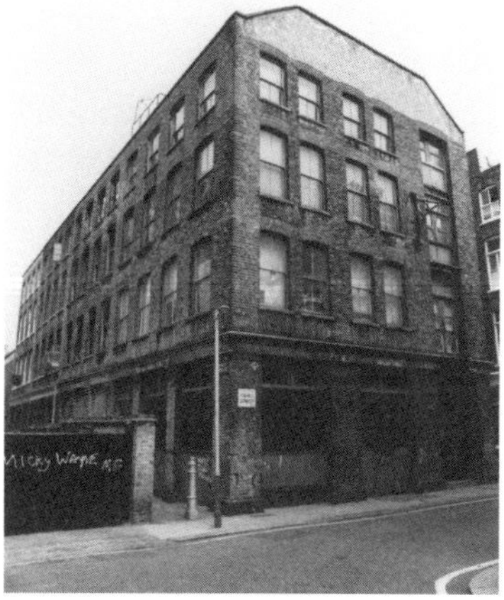

1 Cahill Street, EC1

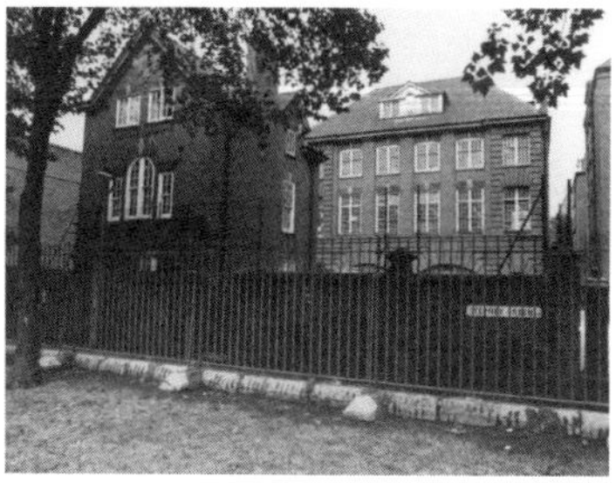

71 Stepney Green, E1

1971 – ongoing Martello Street

1971-86 Tabernacle Street

1971-86 Charlton House Studio

1971-85 Stepney Green

1971-78 Cahill Street

1970–2002 Columbia Road

1970

1971

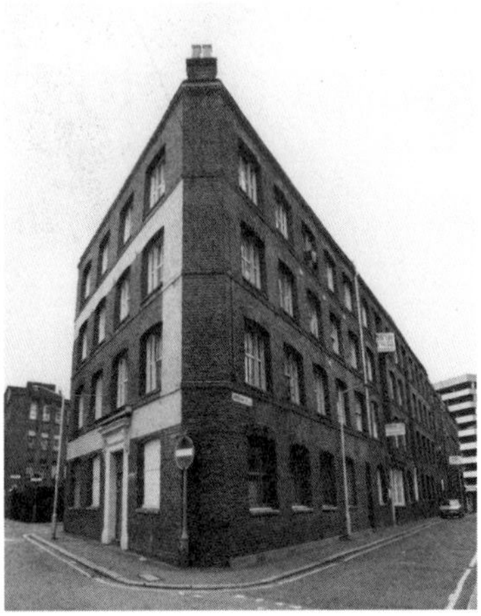

18 Phipp Street, EC2

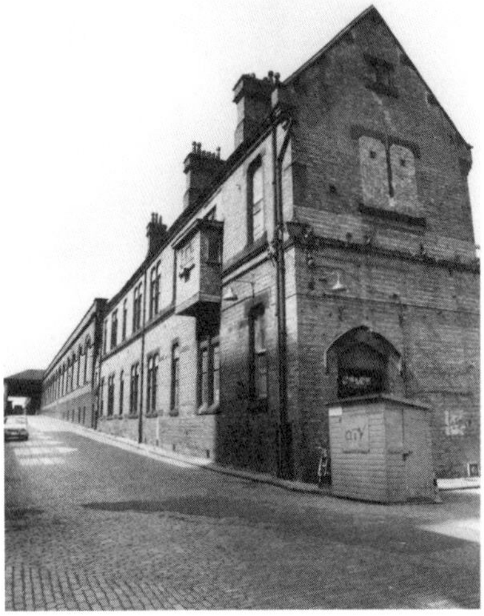

Somers Town Depot, 98 Euston Road, NW1

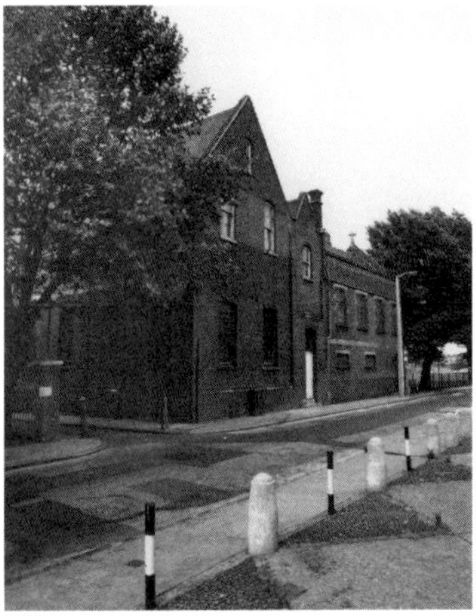

St Patrick's School, Buxton Street, E1

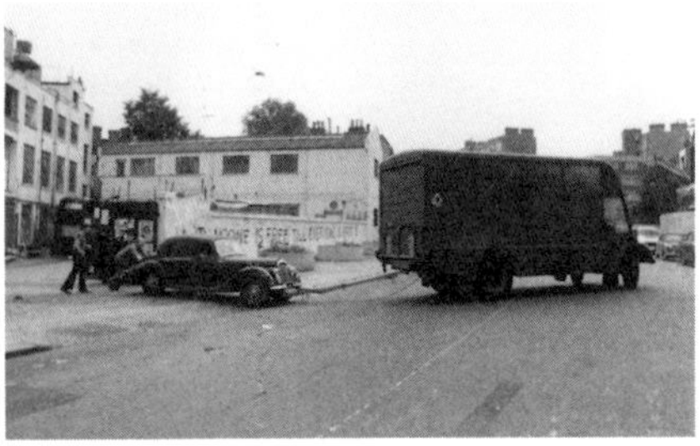

The Dairy, 15 Prince of Wales Crescent, NW1

1972-? Phipp Street

1972-80 Buxton Street

1972-75 Somers Town Depot

1972-75 The Dairy

1972

1973

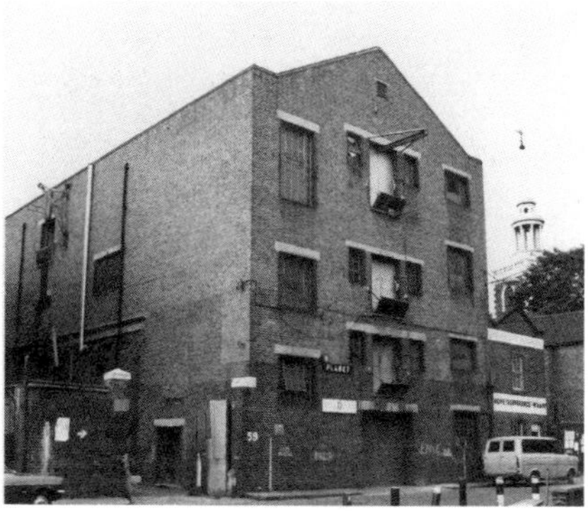

Bombay Wharf, 59 St Marychurch Street, SE16

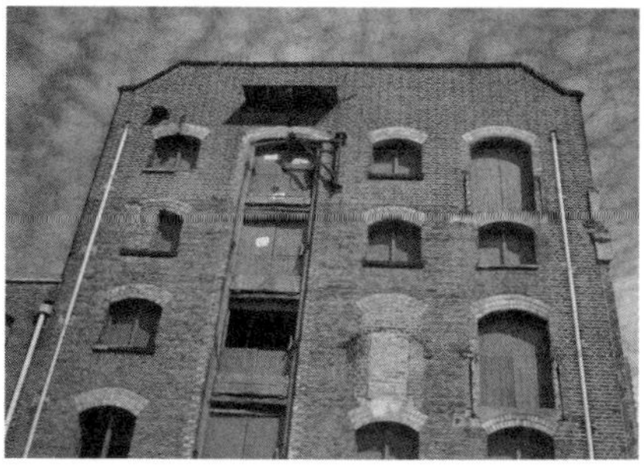

New Crane and Metropolitan Wharves
82 Wapping Wall, E1

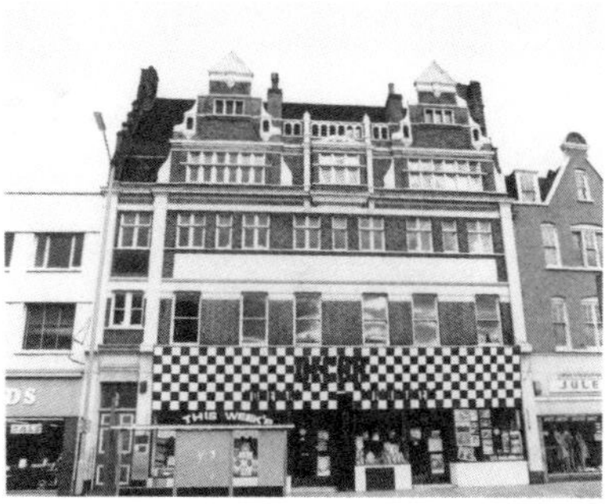

Deptford Studios, 8–12 Deptford High Street, SE8

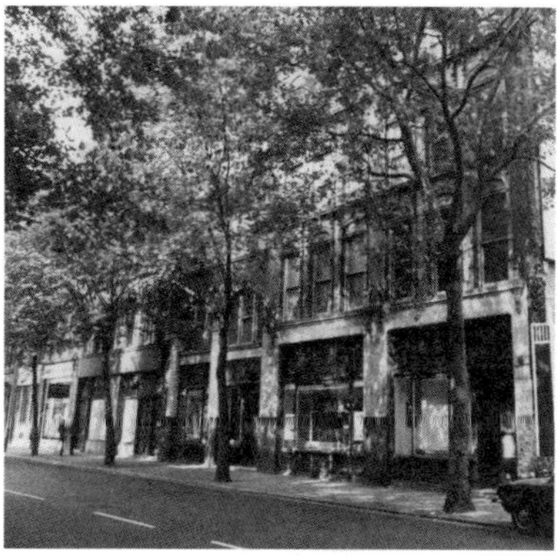

125–129 Shaftesbury Avenue, WC2

1975-78 Deptford Studios

1975-78 Shaftesbury Avenue

1975-77 Fitzroy Road

1974-92 Bombay Wharf

1974-86 New Crane and Metropolitan Wharves

1974-82 Lots Road

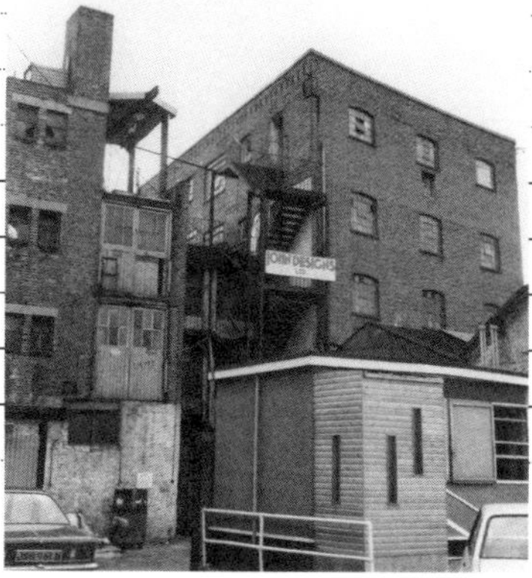

79–89 Lots Road, SW1
(became independent of SPACE in 1982)

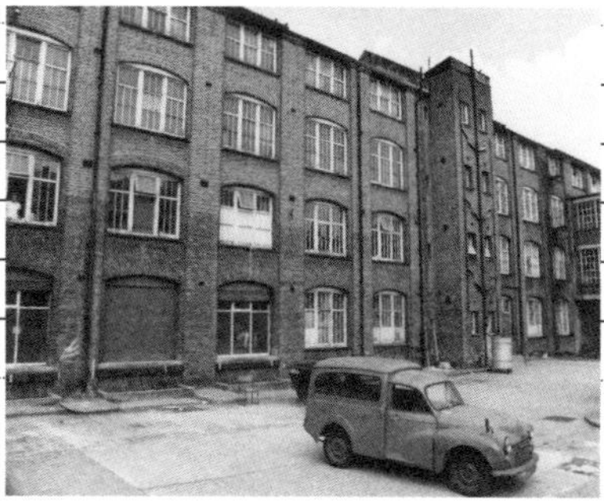

44 Fitzroy Road, NW1

1974

1975

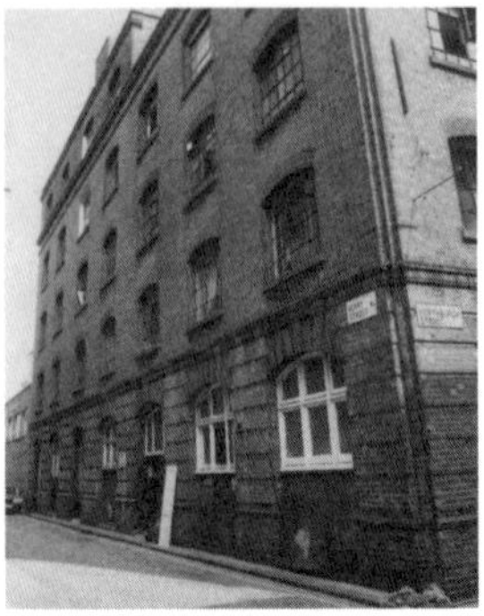

8 Berry Street, EC1

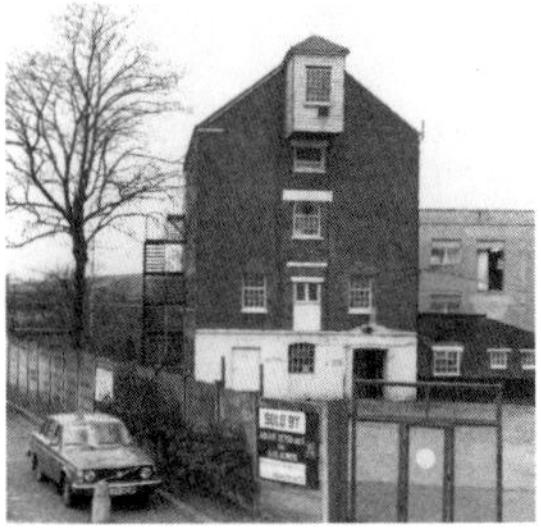

Old Mill, Molesworth Street, SE13

1978-90 Berry Street

1978-89 Old Mill

1978-84 Boot Street

1976-86 Essex Road Baths

Deptford Studios

Shaftesbury Avenue

Fitzroy Road

Cahill Street

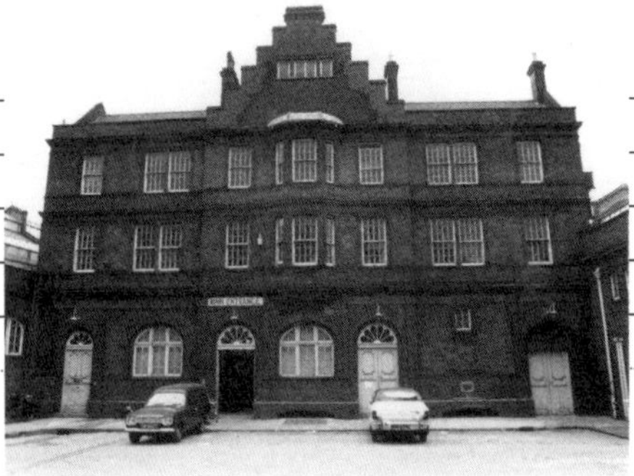

Essex Road Baths, Greenman Street, N1

1976 1977 1978 1979

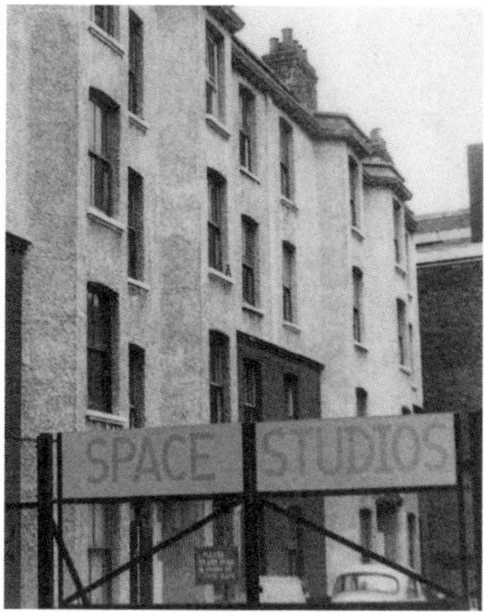

Norfolk House, Brookmill Road, SE8

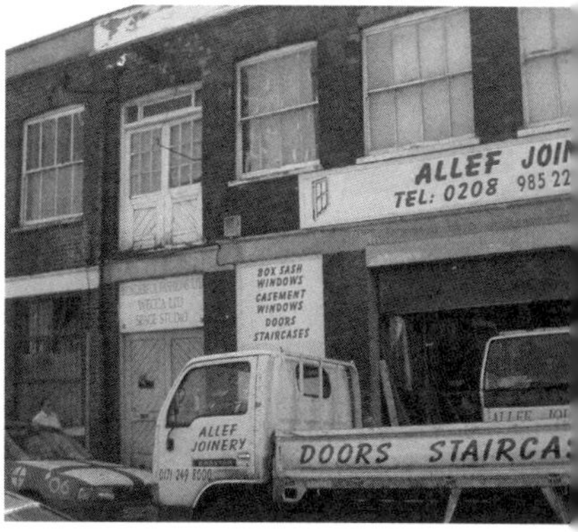

16 Belsham Street, E9

1981 – ongoing Belsham Street

1981–2001 Milborne Street

1981 Leigham Court Road

1980-91 Norfolk House

1980-85 Surrey Docks

Buxton Street

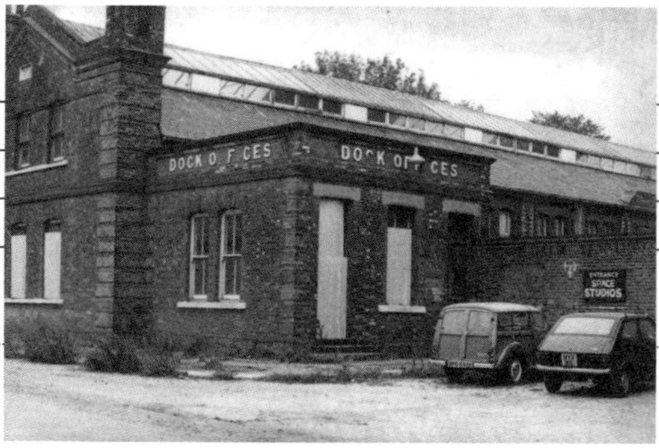

Dock Manager's Office, Surrey Docks, Lower Road, SE16

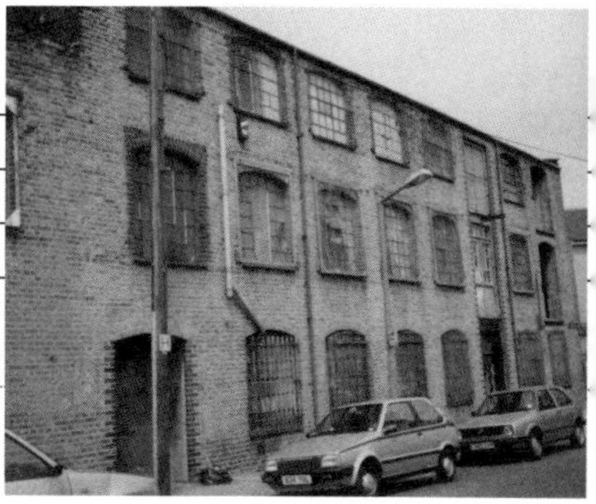

15 Milborne Street, E9

1980

1981

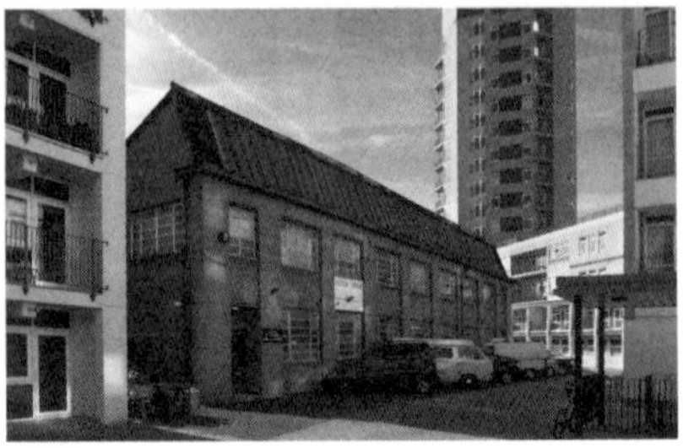

Victor House, 282a Richmond Road, E8

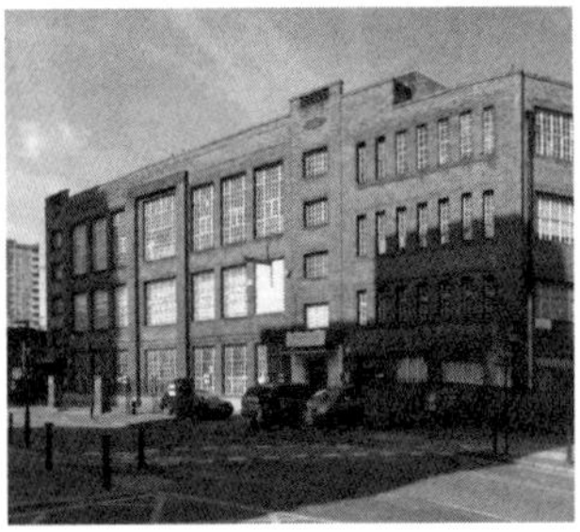

Richmond Road, E8

1986 – ongoing Azof Street

1985 – ongoing Victor House

1985-91 Vandy Street

1984–2009 Winkley Street, E2

1983 – ongoing Britannia Works

1982–2008 Richmond Road

Leigham Court Road

Surrey Docks

Boot Street

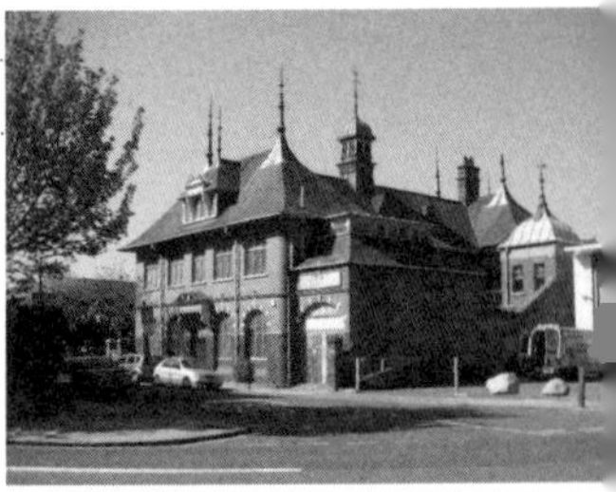

Rothbury Hall, Azof Street (1st Fl), SE10

New Crane and Metropolitan Wharves

Lots Road

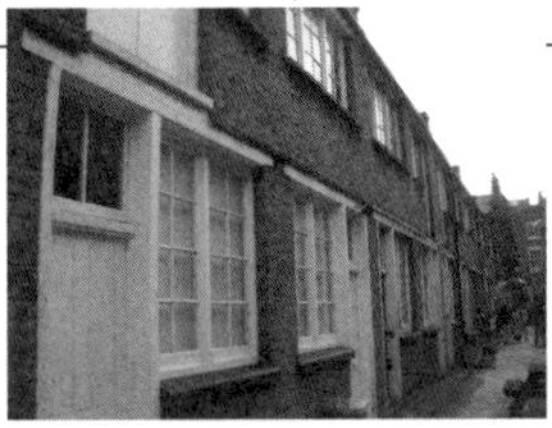

7 Winkley Street, E2

Tabernacle Street

Charlton House Studio

Stepney Green

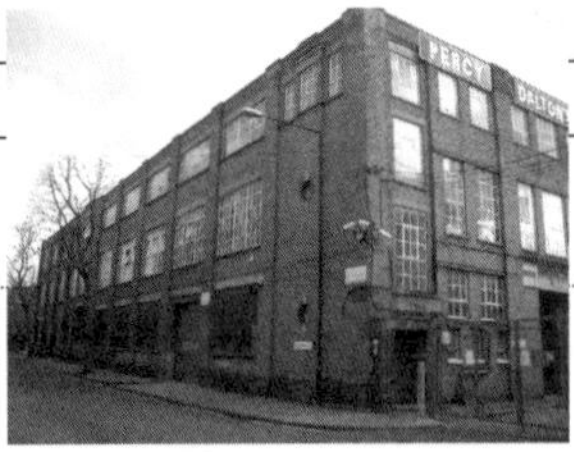

Britannia Works, Dace Road, E3

1982 1983 1984 1985 1986 1987

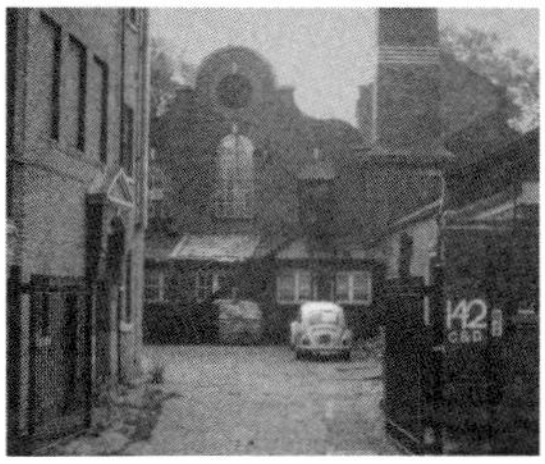

1992-99 Eastway Baths

1992-93 Carrington House

1990-99 Lea Bridge Road, E9

1988 — ongoing Deborah House

Norfolk House

Berry Street

Old Mill

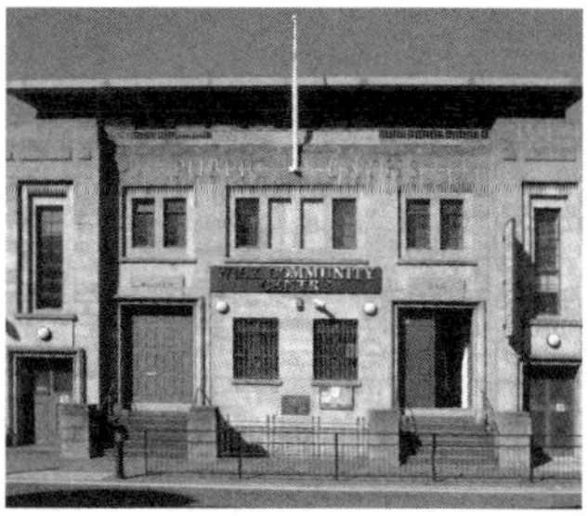

Eastway Baths, E9

Bombay Wharf

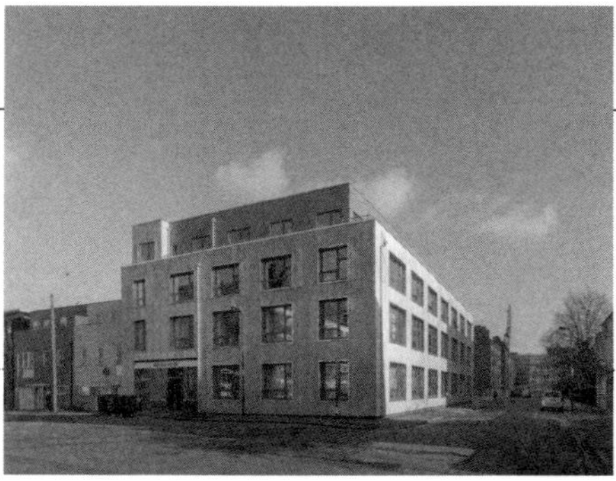

Deborah House, Retreat Place, E9

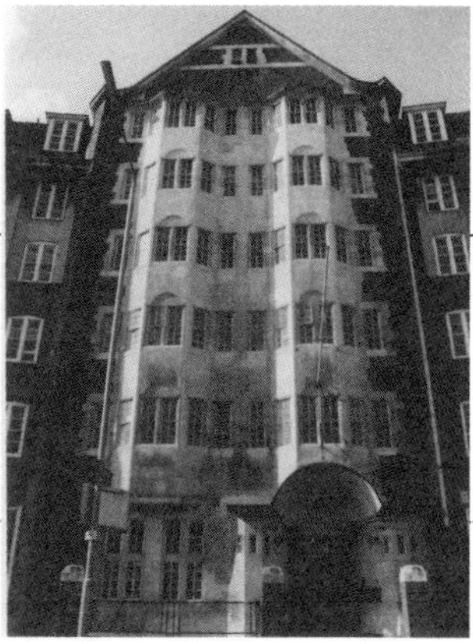

Carrington House, SE8

1988 1989 1990 1991 1992

1996 – ongoing Sara Lane

1993 – ongoing Eastway Laundry

1993–2012 Vauxhall Street Studios

Carrington House

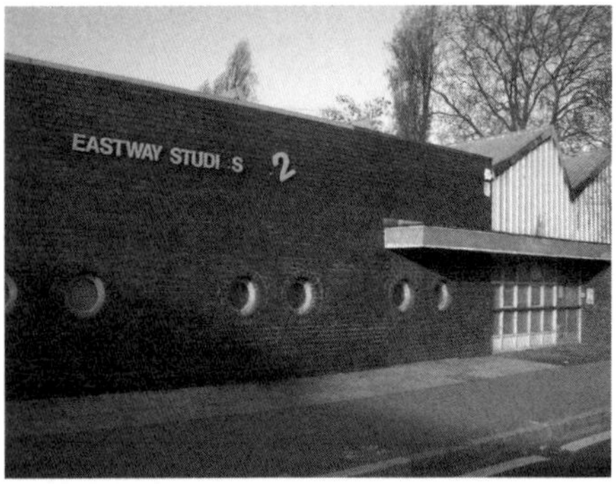

Eastway Laundry, E9

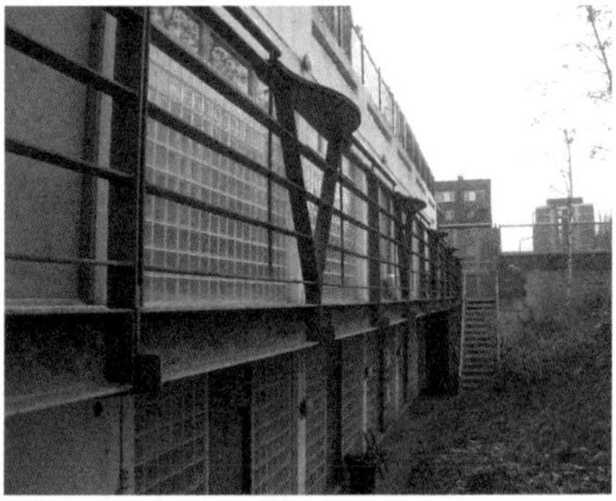

Sara Lane, N1

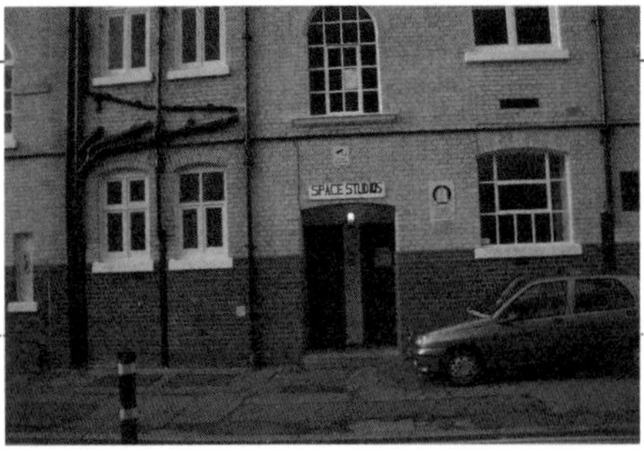

Vauxhall Street Studios, SE11

1993 1994 1995 1996 1997 1998

Eastway Baths

Lea Bridge Road

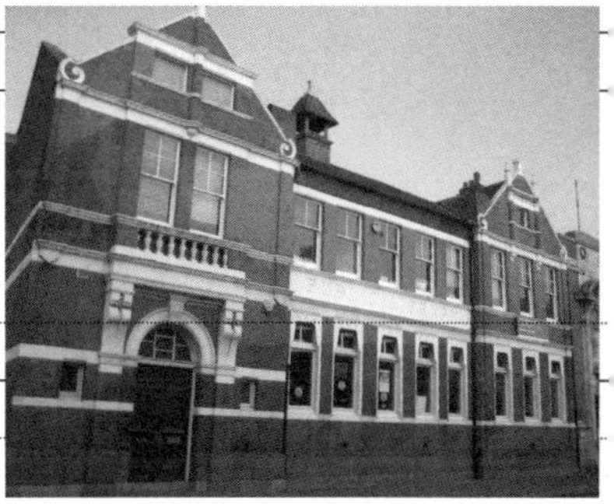

Stoke Newington Library, N16

Milborne Street

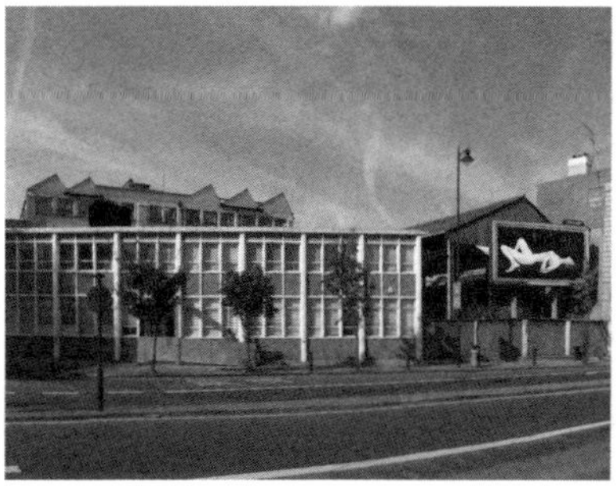

The Triangle, E8

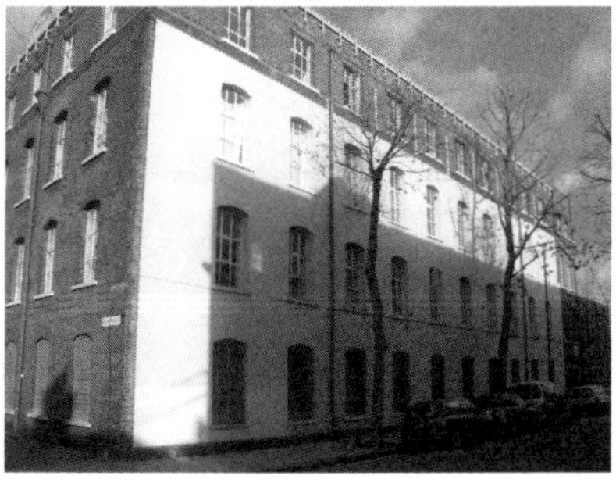

Bridget Riley Studios, Dace Road, E3

2002 — ongoing Stoke Newington Library

2002 — ongoing The Triangle

2002-07 Success House

2001-06 Baron's Place

1999 — ongoing Bridget Riley Studios

1999–2010 Morning Lane

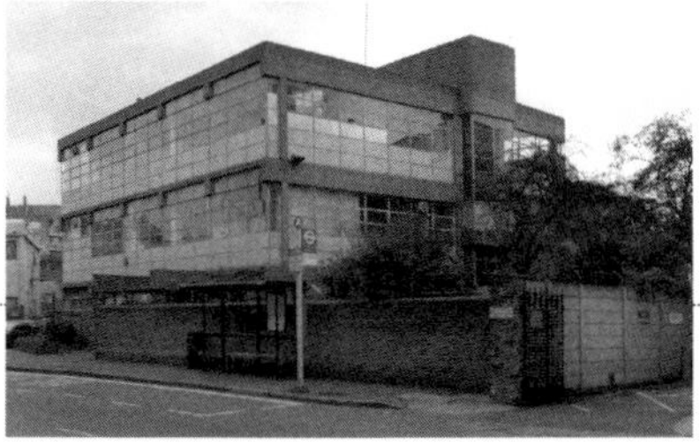

209a Morning Lane, E9

Columbia Road

1999 2000 2001 2002

Richmond Road

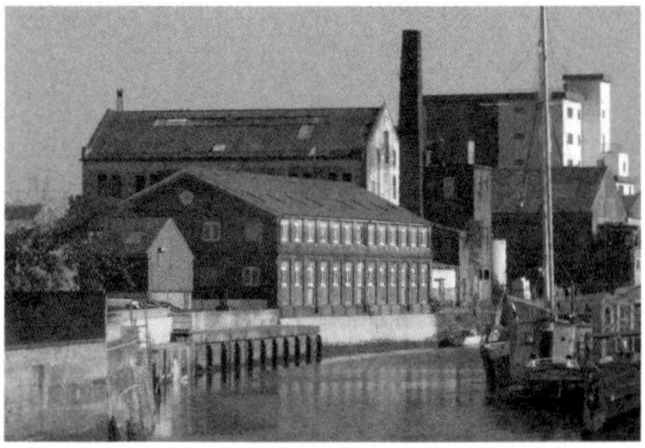

Barking Malthouse, Abbey Road, IG11

2008 – ongoing Timber Wharf

2007-12 Barking Malthouse

Success House

Baron's Place

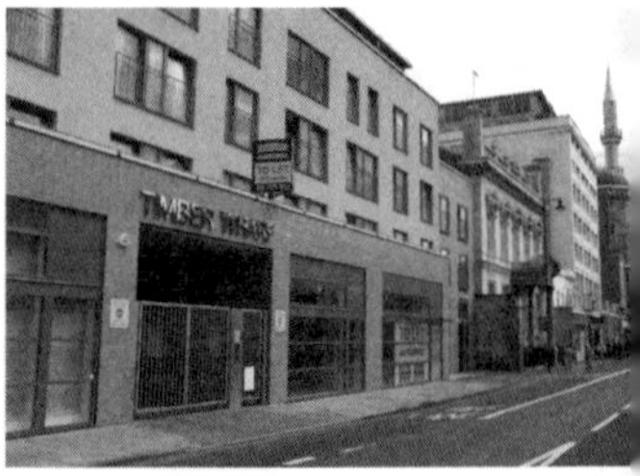

Timber Wharf, E2

2003 2004 2005 2006 2007 2008 2009

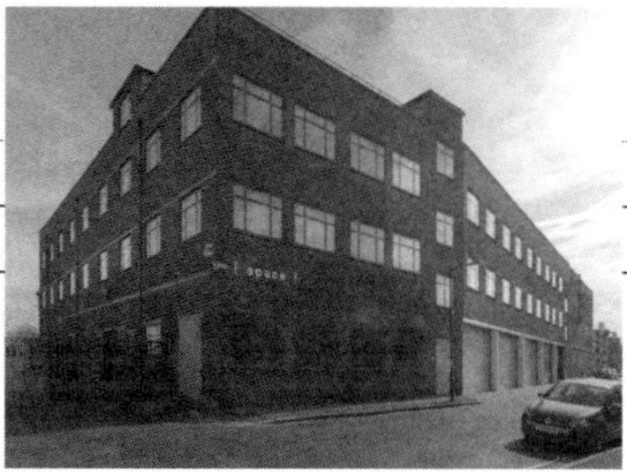

Haymerle Road, SE15

Vauxhall Street Studios

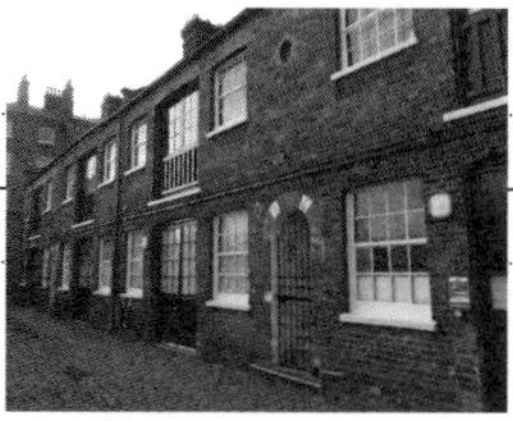

Peabody Yard, N1

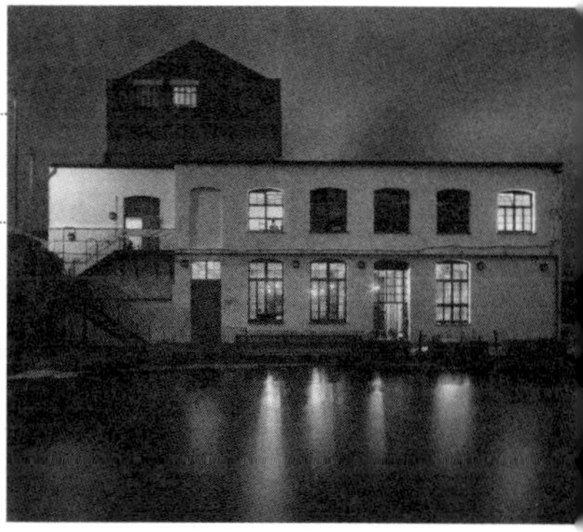

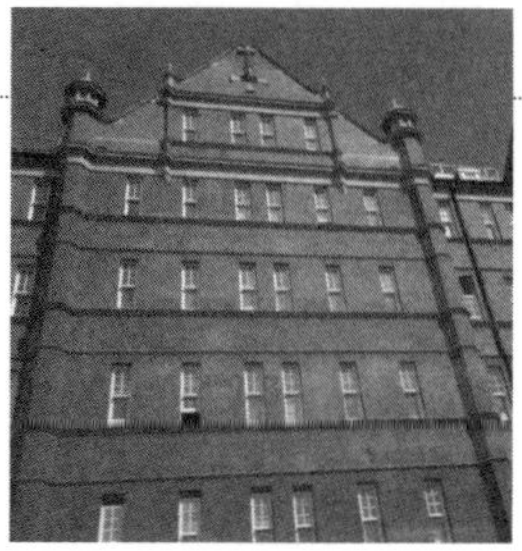

Arlington, NW1

2012-17 The White Building, E9

2011 — ongoing Haymerle Road

2010 — ongoing Peabody Yard

2010 — ongoing Arlington

2010-14 Dean Street

Morning Lane

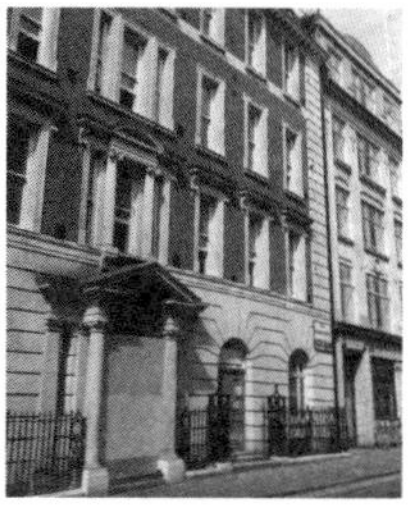

Dean Street, W1

2010

2011

2012

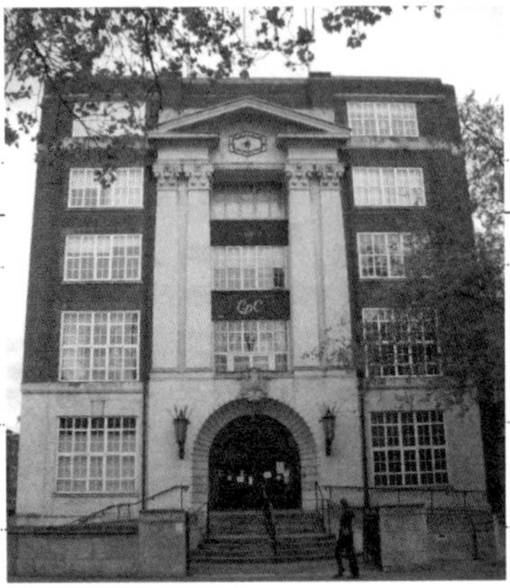

Havil Street, SE5

2017 – ongoing 37 Queen Street

2016 – ongoing Havil Street

2014 – ongoing Brickfield Studios

The White Building

Dean Street

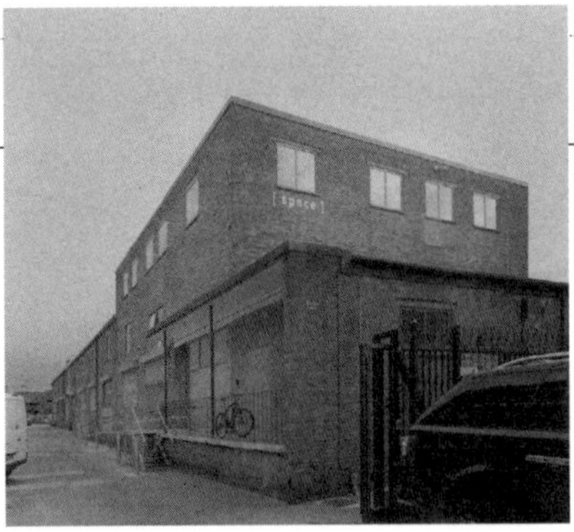

Brickfield Studios, E3

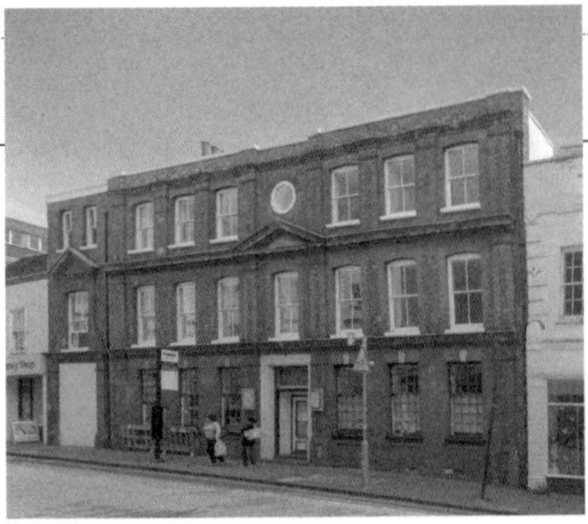

37 Queen Street, Colchester CO1

2013 2014 2015 2016 2017

1996 – ongoing Sara Lane

1993 – ongoing Eastway Laundry

1988 – ongoing Deborah House **(Freehold)**

1986 – ongoing Azof Street

1985 – ongoing Victor House

1983 – ongoing Britannia Works

1981 – ongoing Belsham Street

2016 – ongoing 37 Queen Street

2016 – ongoing Havil Street

2014 – ongoing Brickfleld Studios **(Freehold)**

2011 – ongoing Haymerle Road **(Freehold)**

2010 – ongoing Peabody Yard

2010 – ongoing Arlington

2008 – ongoing Timber Wharf

2002 – ongoing Stoke Newington Library

2002 – ongoing The Triangle

1999 – ongoing Bridget Riley Studios

1971 – ongoing Martello Street

2018

List of SPACE studio artists 1968-2018

Antoni Abad · Baffour Abbabio · Erica Abbiss-Biro · Lisa Abbott · Douglas Abercrombie · Katharina Abildgaard Lupnova · Erica Abiss-Biro · Margherita Abozzo-Heuser · Peter Abrahams · Marius Abramczuk · Tomma Abts · Caroline Achaintre · Larry Achiampong · Myriam Achour · Tom Ackers · Grace Adam · Olivier Adam · Victoria Adam · Pauline Adams · Laura Adamson · Linda Adcock · Louise Adolphsen · Seung Ae Lee · Felicitas Aga · Ann Agee · Matt Ager · Esfandiar Ahmadi · Do'wan Ahmet · Sarah Ainslie · Dan Ainsworth · Peter Ainsworth · Sharon Aivaliotis · Deborah Akam · Penny Akester · Kate Alcock · Christian Aldridge · Sue Aldworth · Jose Alfredo · Theodora Alfredsdottir · Emily Allchurch · Bill Allen · Eddie Allen · Flick Allen · Julie Allen · Tim Allen · Anthea Alley · John Allin · Edward Allington · Guy Allott · Hermione Allsopp · Hamad Alomar · Ricardo Alvares · Timothy Alves · Frida Alvinzi · Nadia Alzapiedi · Sylvia Ambrogi · Francesca Amfossi · Maria Amidu · Kim Amis · Roy Amiss · Clare Amos · Bevan Anderson · Sawako Ando · Wil Ando · Michael Andreae · Euphrosyne Andrews · Amy Angold · Lawrence Anifalaje · K. Anis · Laura Ansell · Axel Antas · Rosie Antrobus · Tony Antrobus · Matthew Appleton · Rasheed Araeen · Reza Aramesh · Arc Theatre · Nick Archer · Antonio Argenio · Athanasios Argianas · Fernando Arias · Dana Ariel · Suesal Arieli · Saleem Arif Quadri · Annika Aril · Bridget Armstrong · Dominique Armstrong · Ake Arnerdal · Paula Arntzen · Simon Aronson · Peter Arris · Artangel · Sophie Arup · Rebecca Ash · George Ashbolt · Michael Ashcroft · Jonathan Ashworth · Soraya Aslam · Harriet Aston · Bruce Atherton · Patricia Atienza Ramirez · Conrad Atkinson · Julia Atkinson · Max Attenborough · Tony Attile · David Austen · Trisha Austin · Andres Ayerbe · Michael Azu · Chike Azuonye · Rachel Babares · Jo Bacon · Kate Baden Fuller · Julien Bader · Brian Baderman · Polly Bagnall · Claire Baguet · Yasmin Baig · Rachel Bailey · Robin Baillie · Katy Baird · Andy Baker · Anthony Baker · Bryan Baker · Carol Baker · Charlie Baker · Chris Baker · Jonathan Baker · Jules Baker · Sarah Baker · Sharon Baker · Sam Bakewell · Tamar Balakjian · Suzie Balazs · Dave Baldwin · Didi Baldwin · Martin Ball · Billy Ballard · Fay Ballard · Michael Ballard · Nick Ballon · Neil Bally · Russell Bamber · David Bangs · Peter Banks · Sarah Banks · Cuillin Bantock · Stephen Banville · Rachel Barbaresi · Helen Barff · Mark Barker · Johnathan Barker · Lucy Barlow · Phyllida Barlow · Hugh Barnden · Jane Barnes · Jeanette Barnes · Lesley Barnes · John Barrat · Ian Barratt · Ruth Barter · Vivienne Bartlett · Hannah Barton · Jordan Baseman · Elton Bash · James Basham · Mati Basis · David Batchelor · Meridy Bates · Roger Bates · Guy Batey · Diann Bauer · Josh Baum · Edward Baure · Olivia Bax · Shiraz Bayjoo · Joel Beach · Philippa Beale · Katriona Beales · Carla Beard · Flisan Beard · Kevin Beasley · Michael Beasley · Basil Beattie · Beaumont & Bampton · Richard Beck · Haidee Becker (Kenedy) · Vanessa Beckles · Sarah Beddington · Sarah Beeby · Andrew Beeching · Kim Beer · Eldina Begic · Alexandra Bell · Alison Bell · Janet Bell · Mark Bell · Umberto Bellardi Ricci · Jane Belli · Hermelinda Bellido · Carole Bellon · Sara Bellon · Caspar Below · Kate Belton · Louis Benassi · Zoe Benbow · Jose Benitez · Clare Bennett · Daniel Bennett · Julie Bennett · Kiera Bennett · Kim Bennett · Peter Bennett · Amanda Benson · Kjetil Berge · Dee Berridge · Anne Berrington · Josh Berry · S. Beth · Veronica Bethell · Simon Betts · Tony Bevan · Lorraine Bewick · Chris Bianchi · Teresa Bianchi · John Bicknell · Rosalind Bieber · Susan Billington · Pat Binder · Esmond Bingham · Marina Binns · Rebecca Binns · Howard Birch · Martin Birch · Laura Bird · Simon Bird · Gonçalo Birra · Steve Bishop · Nanna Bjornsdottir · Robin Blackledge · Su Blackwell · Devin Blair · Louise Blair · Robert Blair · Louise Blaire · Rose Blake · Tim Blake · Hedevig Blakstad · Henry Blanch · Jenny Blanchard · David Blanco · Annaabel Blanes · Katrina Blannin · Slavomir Blatton · David Blazer · Christopher Bledov · Chris Bledowski · Sarah Blee · Rut Blees Luxemburg · Sean Blem · Ruth Blench · Adam Blencowe · Ulrika Blide · Maurice Blik · Claudia Blume · Nita Bocking · Ludovik Boden · Sarah Bohannon · Isha Bohling · Jane Bolden · Juan Bolivar · Delyth Bolt · Thomas Bolwell · Julian Bond · Kate Bond · Alex Booker · Matthew Booth · Katiushka Borges · Jill Borten · Christine Boshier · Madeleine Botet de Lacaze · Katerina Botsari · Jenny Boulter · Roger Bourke · Katarzyna Bourlatchka · El Bourmistrov · Ron Bowen · Day Bowman · Gabriella Boyd · Jamie Boyd · Carmel Boylan · Erika Braccini · J. Brades · Jyll Bradley · Simon Bradley · Stuart Bradshaw · Jacqueline Bradshaw-Price · William Bragg · Jon Braley · Robert Bramwell-Jones · James Brand · Paul Brandford · Clive Brandon · Dean Brannagan · Maria Brannan · Leanda Brass · David Bratby · Ian Breakwell · Ruth Breckell · Marc Breen · John Bremner · Cecily Brennan · Joady Brennan · Marie Brenneis · Piero Bresson · Lyndan Brewer · Martyn Brewster · Cecile Briand · James Bridgman · Louise Brierley · Jack Briggs-Miller · Kate Bright ·

Patrick Brill · Mel Brimfield · Sharon Brindle · Joanna Brinton · Maya Brisley · Stuart Brisley · Anne Bristow · Dan Britt · Sarah Brittain-Edwards · Jon Britten · Robert Britten · S. Broadbent · Cleo Broda · Leora Brook · Andy Brooke · Alan Brooks · James Brooks · Jason Brooks · Adam Broomberg · Michael Broughton · Ray Brouitt · Angela Brown · Celia Brown · David Brown · Glenn Brown · Hannah Brown · Hogan Brown · James Brown · Jemima Brown · Jessica Brown · Martin Brown · Norman Brown · Rebekah Brown · Tessa Brown · Marianne Browning · Jane Bruce · Jill Bruce · Marion Bruce · Anna Bruder · Camilla Brueton · Bianca Brunner · Jo Bruton · Jill Bryan · Sheila Bryan · Andrew Bryant · Emma Bryant · Bucket + Slater · C. Buckley · Zbigniew Buday · Sebastian Buerkner · Michael Buhler · Sarah Buist · Steve Bunn · Anna Bunting-Branch · Claire Burbridge · Jake Burchell · Gina Burdass · Frances Burges · Ruth Burgess · Yuma Burgess · Henny Burnett · Valerie Burnett · Joan Burr · Tom Burr · David Butler · Joanna Butler · Joanna Buxton · David Byers · Rebecca Byrne · Gareth Cadwallader · Chris Cairns · Charlie Calder-Potts · Paul Calderwood · Jennifer Caldwell · Zoe Callaghan · Kit Callahan · Renee Callahan · Ruth Calland · Sheena Calvert · Juno Calypso · Emma Cameron · Helen Cammock · Janet Campbell · Natasha Campbell · Louise Camrass · Anthony Canavan · Rob Canning · Mark Cant · Gill Capewell · Giannina Capitani · Joe Carcary · Gary Card · Carlotta Cardana · Faye Carey · Matthew Carey · Rupert Carey · Rachel Carey-Thomas · Jon Carmichael · Gillian Carnegie · Anika Carpenter · Benedict Carpenter · Merlin Carpenter · Amy Carr · Nichola Carre · Kate Rose Carrick · Ann Carrington · Helen Carroll · Paul Carter · Luis Carvalho · Isabela Castelan · Beatriz Castro · Brian Catling · Rachel Cattle · Barbara Cavanagh · Ergin Cavusoglu · Carolina Caycedo · Marco Cecere · Lydia Cecile Gifford · Mary Cefai · Jolanta Cerniauskiene · Rocio Chacon · Chamberlain & Shillingford · Louisa Chambers · David Champion · James Champion · Oliver Chanarin · Nigel Chandler · Alice Channer · Cos Chapman · Alex Chappel · Photis Charalambou · Soti Charalambou · Sophie Charalambous · A. Jacques Charoux · Jim Cheatle · Jonathan Cheifetz · Belinda Chen · Ting-Chun Chen · gordon cheung · Marco Chiandetti · Matt Chick · Nicolas Chiffe · Alessandra Chila · John Chilver · Alex Chilvers · Yoonsuk Choi · Gayle Chong Kwan · Jessie Chorley · Kelly Chorpening · Kal Chottai · Lubna Chowdhary · Petros Chrisostomou · Christopher Christophorou · Andreas Christou · Elenor Church · Martin Church · Citizen News & Media · Jon Clair · James Clancey · Fabia Claris · Jane Clark · Amanda Clarke · Ami Clarke · Ece Clarke · John P. Clarke · Leigh Clarke · Richard Clarke · Robert Clarke · Trevor Clarke · Melanie Clifford · Genevieve Closuit-Rousson · Anne Cloudesly-Thompson · Prunella Clough · Shelagh Cluett · Judith Clute · Giulietta Coates · Marcus Coates · John Cobb · Maurice Cockrill · Sineid Codd · Gian Codemo · Andy Cohen · Revital Cohen · Richard Cohen · Paul Coiling · Gary Colclough · Paul Coldwell · Andy Cole · Martin Cole · Miranda Collett · Phoebe Collings-James · Dave Collins · Michael Collins · Susan Collins · R. Collishaw · Stephen Colson · Brigit Connolly · Martin Conreen · Herve Constant · Prokopi Constantinou · Daisy Cook · Dean Cook · Karen Cooke · Justin Coombes · Daniel Coombs · Julian Cooper · Frances Copeman · John Copnall · Matt Copson · Paul Corcoran · Michael Corkrey · Victoria Cornwell · James Cotterill · Robin Coulson · Ian Coulson Thorpe · COUM · Melanie Counsell · Emma Cousin · Richard Cousins · Graca Coutinho · Marion Coutts · Ben Cove · Keith Coventry · Richard Coward · Alice Cowling · Jason Cox · Julia Crabtree · Zak Crafer · Andrew Craig · Kit Craig · Richard Crawford · Martin Crawley · Amelie Crepy · Rebecca Cresswell · Paula Crickard · Fiona Crisp · Eleanor Crook · Alison Cross · Diana Cross · John Crossley · Erin Crowe · Mark Croxford · Juan Cruz · Sophie Cundale · Tim Cunliffe · Fiona Curran · Robert Currie · Blue Curry · Gary Curson · Joan Curtis · Layla Curtis · Gillian Cutbill · Kate Cuzner · David Cyrus Smith · Peter D'Alessandri · Nathalie d'Arbeloff · Andy D'Cruz · Marie d'Elbee · Pedro da Costa Felgueiras · Ania Dabrowska · Malcolm Dakin · Sandra Dakin · Annabelle Dalby · S. Dale · Dexter Dalwood · Paul Dash · Anne Davey · Mary Davey · Paul Davey · David David · Enrico David · Karen David · Claire Davies · Rebecca Davies · Cliff Davis · Deborah Dawkin · Laurence Dawson · Robert Dawson · Rufus Dayglo · Jonathan Dayman · Victor de Circasia · Cyril de Commarque · Jules de Goede · Penny de Haas Curnow · Tony de Jasay · Nathalie de Laval · Ercilia de Marco · Cathy De Monchaux · Colette Morey de Morand · Charles de Paula · Venka de Rooij · Dolores de Sade · Brian Deaghton · Ben Deakin · Judith Dean · Mick Dean · Timonthy Dean · Tom Dearie · Bernard Debaillie · Tobi Deeson · Pierre Degen · Michele del Campo · Sebastien Delahaye · Anita Delaney · Lalu Delbracio · Robin Deller-Thompson · Melita Denaro · Peter Denmark · Stuart Denyer · Stafford Derek · Nicolas Deshayes · Silke Dettmers · Alex Deutsch · Paulina Deutsch · Emma Dewing · Helen Dey · Cristiano Di Martino · Pedro Diablo · Joan Diamantis · Clara Dias · William Dick · Mark Dickens · Sophie Dickens · Gail Dickerson · Nelly Dimitranova · Rebecca Disney · Adam Dix · Roger Dixon · Zoran Djorjevic · Peter Dockley ·

Karin Dolk · Kaye Donachie · Elise Doney · Paul Donnelly · James Dooley · Jean-Philippe Dordolo · Alex Dordoy · Chris Dorley-Brown · Anthony Dorrell · Adam Doughty · Emma Douglas · Sarah Douglas · Freya Douglas-Morris · Angie Dove · Clare Dove · Michelle Dovey · Luke Dowd · Natalie Dower · Marysa Dowling · Theresa Dowling · Abigail Downer · Ross Downes · Rachel Downey · Ian Downing McIntyre · Jonathan Doyle · Shaun Doyle · Milena Dragicevic · Alex Drew · Smadar Dreyfus · Crate Drinks · Janaina Drummond · Yvonne Drury · Alex Du Preez · Melissa Duarte · Aniela Dublaszewska · Tamara Dubnyckyi · Monika Duda · Fiona Duffelen · Debbie Duffin · Chris Duffy · Fritz Duffy · Joe Duggan · Paul Duggan · John Dugger · Flora Duley · Alberto Duman · Hamish Dunbar · Jim Dunkley · Alison Dunlop · Francoise Dupre · Rowan Durrant · Steve Dutton · James Dyer · Ursula Dyson · Krystyna Shackleton Dzieszko · Paul Eachus · Elizabeth Eamer · Betty Earle · Ewan Eason · East London Printmakers · Colin Eastwood · Zachary Eastwood-Bloom · Linda Eaves · Tatiana Echeverri Fernandez · Sadie Edginton · Frances Edmonds · Ben Edwards · Iain Edwards · John Edwards · Sue Edwards · Michael Edwards · Nina Ehni · Alex Eisenberg · Gazmend Ejupi · Andy Ekins · Husam El Odeh · Yosra El-Essawy · Catherine Eldridge · Paul Elliman · Stuart Elliot · Caroline Elliott · Belinda Ellis · Liz Ellis · Nigel Ellis · Sharon Elphick · Julian Emens · Joseph Emilien · Schieppatt Emilo · James Emmerson · Annabel Emson · Eden Endfield · Hanne Enemark · Teresa Eng · Anne Helen English · Rose English · Sarah Entwistle · Ellis Erryl · Thomas Estes · Barbara Etter · David Everleigh Evans · Garth Evans · Gethin Evans · Kristina Evans · Matthew Evans · Tom Evans · William Evans · Adrian Everitt · Adrian Everitt · Ruth Ewan · Luci Eyers · Fab · Sean Fairman · Stella Fajerson · Ayan Farah · Rima Farah · Nooshin Farhid · Andrew Farley · Tessa Farmer · Michael Farrell · Julia Farrer · John Fassolas · James Faure-Walker · Nicholas Fay · Chloe Feinberg · David Fenwick · Heidi Ferid · Anne Ferris · David Ffyske · Jim Fielding · London Fields Film & Video · Tim Fink · James Finlay · Anne Finlayson · Andrea Finn · Rose Finn-Kelcey · Berit Fischer · Andrea Fitzpatrick · Chris Fitzpatrick · Paul Flannery · Robert Flather · Martin Fletcher · Tom Flint · Chloe Flynn · Gabriel Flynn · Jerry Flynn · Roisin Fogarty · Ehlana Foley · Gareth Foote · Anthony Ford · Becky Ford · Tony Ford · Ben Ford-Smith · S. Fordham · Adam Forman · Katarina Forss · Noel Forster · Alison Forsyth · J. Fortnum · Susan Fortune · Ruth Fosker · Lorraine Fossi · George Foster · Marcus Foster · Tim Foster · Simon Foster-Ogg · Hannah Fothergill · Lilah Fowler · Jon Fox · Neal Fox · Kayser Foyz · Annete Frances-Robinson · Anthony Francis · Errol Francis · Lucien Francis · Michael Frangou · Sean Frank · John Frankland · Peter Fraser · Megan Frazer · Gary Freedman · Anna Freeman Bentley · Chloe Fremantle · Bruce French · Rebecca French · G Fresco · Felix Friedmann · Andrew Friend · Robin Friend · Alex Frost · Luke Frost · Mia Frostner · Holly Froy · Maya Fujiwara · Aya Fukami · Anna-Lena Fuller · Matthew Fuller · Gordon Furn · Zach Furniss · Marenka Gabeler · Belinda Gaffney · Ramirez Galindo · Neil Gall · Ken Gallagher · Munro Galloway · Rock Galpin · Susan Gamble · Tony Gammidge · Ryan Gander · Laura Gannon · Rachel Gannon · Katherine Gardner · Rachel Garfield · Charles Garrad · Rose Garrard · Steven Gee · Daniele Genadry · Alex Gene Morrison · Ana Genoves · Nick Gentry · Arlette Kim George · Jack George · Gery Georgieva · Kyriaki Gerontaki · Herrera Gianino · Adam Gibbons · Jeff Gibbons · Alex Gibbs · Tom Gidley · Jane Gifford · Alice Gilbertson · Emilie Giles · Adam Gillam · Faith Gillespie · Liam Gillick · Heidi Gilmour · Charles Gimpel · Sarah Girard · Frode Gjerlow · Vasiliki Gkotsi · Robert Glowacki · David Gluck · Judith Goddard · Monica Godwin · Sarah Gold · Rupert Goldberg · David Goldenberg · Jane Goldsmith · Mike Goldwater · Priscilla Golush · Martin Gomez · Rachel Gomme · Diana Gonsalves · Nat Goodden · Simon Goode · Jane Goodwin · Emma Goosey · David Gopsill · Jenny Gordon · Virginia Gordon · Peter Gore · Kasia Goria · Lara Gorlach · J. Gosling · Oliver Gosling · Nick Goss · Luke Gottelier · Lachlan Goudie · Alex Gough · Jackie Gough · Polly Gould · Ted Gould · Romen Gouveia · James Graham · Paul Graham · Christian Grandjean · Simon Granger · Ed Gray · Joel Gray · John Gray · Nicholas Gray · Greatbatch + Cousins + Sherrif · Ronald Greaves · Alan Green · Amy Green · Paul Green · William Green · Aron Greenwood · Diana Greenwood · Karen Gregory · Zed Gregory · Berit Greinke · Barbara Greisman · Abby Grewcock · Charlotte Grierson · Peter Grieve · Huw Griffith · Andrew Griffiths · David Griffiths · Kevin Griffiths · Kim Griffiths · Richard Grimes · M Grimes · Damien Grist · Jon Groom · Thijs Groot Wassink · Robert Grose · Michael Grossbard · Colin Grove · Julia Groves · Maty Grunberg · Michael Guida · Kim Gum Rye · Kimberley Gundle · Sally Gunnett · Kim Gunter · Ayan-Yue Gupta · Ajay Gupte · Gonkar Gyatso · Kwabena Gyedu · Tom Hackney · Rob Hadingham · Kirsten Hadley · Penny Hadrill · Ole Hagen · Janey Hagger · Carley Hague · Kat Hahn · Susan Haire · Jon Hale · Matthew Hale · Benjamin John Hall · Christopher Hall · Julia Hall · Sarah Hall-Craggs · Dido Hallett · Sam Halstead · Fiona Hamley · Sarah Hammond · Mark Hampson · Germaine Hampton · Jin Han Lee · Yoko Hand ·

Roger Hands · Markus Hansen · Ross Hansen · Ross Hansen · D'Este Hanson · Jane Hanson · William Hardie · Christina Hardinge · Anne Hardy · "K · " Hare · Rachael Harlow · Mark Harrell · C. Harrington · Jessica Harrington · Catherine Harris · Chris Harris · Louise Harris · Hayley Harrison · Lucy Harrison · Will Harrop · Adam Hart · Andrew Hart · Emma Hart · Philip Hartigan · Alex Hartley · Rupert Hartley · Grit Hartung · Graham Harwood · Kay Harwood · Camey Hashe · Rana Hassanieh · Vicky Hawkins · Vincent Hawkins · Peter Hawksby · Matthew Hawtin · Katherine Hayes · Sara Hayes · D. Hayhurst · Jack Haynes · Nicole Hazelton · Tim Head · Timothy Healy · Claude Heath · Daniel Heath · Jennifer Hegarty · Alexander Heim · Sara Heitlinger · Ingolv Helland · Jeff Hellyer · Charly Helyar · Alun Hemming · William Henderson · Miles Henderson-Smith · Francis Henry · Alex Hermon · Caroline Heron · Susanna Heron · Pascal Hervey · Fabienne Hess · Yoav Hessayon · Leonard Hessing · Guy Hetherington · Hannah Hewetson · Coco Hewitt · Charles Hewlings · Rosalind Hibbins · Justin Hibbs · Beth Higgins · Jene Highstein · Giles Hill · Harriet Hill · Tony Hill · Susan Hiller · Rhys Himsworth · Neil Hinchley · Chup Hinton · Daniel Hirschmann · Thomas Hjelm · Natasha Hoare · Diana Hobson · Henry Hobson · Monroe Hodder · Gemma Hodge · Nicola Hodge · Ed Hodgkinson · Clive Hodgson · Jennifer Hodgson · Jordan Hodgson · Paul Hodgson · Linda Hoetink-Geary · Jonathan Hogg · Pam Hogg · David Holland · Kate Holliday · Andrew Holligan · Steve Hollins · Ali Holloway · K. Holloway · Marianne Holm Hansen · Emma Holmes · Robert Holyhead · Nancy Honey · Kang Hong Chen · Jane Hoodless · Lisa Hook · John Hooper · Hilary Hope Guise · Georgie Hopton · Zil Hoque · Jefford Horrigan · Nick "Horrocks · " · Hamish Horsley · Brenda Horsman · Sophie Horton · Katie Horwich · Amanda Houchen · Howard · Anni Howard · John Howard · Rachel Howard · D. Howel-Evans · Kazuko Howlin · Lesley Howling · Jeanne Hoyle · Andy Hsu · Peihang Huang · Graham Hudson · Amy Hughes · Catherine Hughes · Louie Hughes · Rachelle Hughes · Rowena Hughes · Tom Hugues · Mustafa Hulusi · Jane Humphrey · Tom Humphreys · Georgina Hunt · Gerry Hunt · Kay Hunt · Roderick Hunt · Alexis Hunter · Linzie Hunter · Tom Hunter · Mick Hurd · Mary Hurrell · Nigel Hurst · Israel Hurtado Cola · Cedric Huson · Louisa Hutchinson · John Hutton · Lisa Huxley-Blythe · Jungyoon Hyen · Max Hymes · Jonathan Hynd · Helen Iacovou · Alice Ibsen · Shona Illingworth · John Imhasly · Gillian Ingham · Rachel Inman · Jeff Instone · Albert Irvin · Dennis Irving · Kaoru Ishii · Isabel Ivars · Jim Jack · Kevin Jackson · Sandra Jacobs · Ann-Marie James · Anna James · Anne James · Annette James · Lisa James · Rebecca James · Nicholas James Snelling · Benjamin Jamie · Maggie Jamieson · Velika Janceva · Robert Janz · Kapil Jariwala · Thomas Jarvis · Catherine Jauslin · Zarja Jazbinsek · Nick Jeffrey · Simon Jeffries · Alana Jelinek · Chris Jennings · Maggie Jennings · Andrea Jespersen · Peter Jessett · James Jessop · Li Jia · Juan Jimenez · Laurie Jo Wright · Jovica Jocic · Jasper Joffe · Annie Johns · C Johnson · Arvid Johnson · Ben Johnson · Claudette Johnson · Ezra Johnson · Michael Johnson · Pete Johnson · Tom Johnson · Alexis Kim Johnson · Rachel Johnston · John Johnstone · Evy Jokhova · Abigail Jones · Alison Jones · Bernard Jones · Chris Jones · Christian Jones · Darren Jones · Dennis Jones · Ian Jones · Justin Jones · Lucy Jones · Mark Jones · Nick Jones · Peter Jones · Philip Jones · Sally Jones · Sioned Jones · Tim Jones · Louisa Jordan · Melissa Jordan · Tam Joseph · Clair Joy · Susie Joyce · Ben Judd · Heidi Jukes · Louise Julian Joseph · Sue Juncal · Yeondoo Jung · Sarah Jury · Silia Ka Tung · Jo Ann Kaplan · Mark Karasick · Joan Karmen · Kerstin Kartscher · Alaa Kassim · Miranda Kaula · David Kay · Emma Kay · Mary Kay · John Keane · Paddy Keane · Verity-Jane Keefe · Stine Keinicke · Jim Kelly · Roger Kelly · Peter Kemp · Alistair Kendry · Peter Kennard · Rudi Kennard · Jonathan Kennedy · Katie Kennedy · Rosie Kennedy · Dan Kennedy-Martin · Andrew Kenny · Mike Kenny · Ana Kerin · Ingrid Kerma · Bernadette Kerrigan · Sophie Ketley · Annie Kevans · Joan Key · Soojin Khan · Waszem Khan · Richard Kidd · Neill Kidgell · John Kilday · Seeun Kim · Dan Kimerling · Adam King · Gerald King · Joe King · John King · Lucia King · Sue King-Brewster · Stephanie Kingston · Will Kippax · Kyle Kirkpatrick · Linda Kitchen · Roger Kite · Michael Kitterhing · Marie-F Kittler · Joel Kitzmiller · Robin Klassnik · Christoph Klauke · Kevin Knight · Max Knight · Michael Knight · Sophie Knight · Karen Knorr · Stuart Knowles · Kurt Kochercheidt · Halbo Kool · Serena Korda · Katrin Koskaru · Derek Kotz · Tania Kovats · Robbie Kravitz · Gereon Krebber · Florian Kremb · Aliki Krikidi · Matthew Krishanu · Alec Kronacker · Chris Ku · Suzanne Ku · Barbara Kukovec · Nicholas Kulkarni · Denise Kum · Chila Kumari Burman · Rannva Kunoy · Rita Kunzler · Kyriacou · Yvonne Kyriakides · Matthew Kyte · Matthew La Croix · Bruce Lacey · LADA · Lagoudakis · Walter Lam · Walter Lam · Rachel Lamb · Maxine Lambert · Yu-Chieh Lan · Christopher Landoni · Cathryn Lane · Kate Lane · E. Lane · Jonathan Lane-Smith · Andreas Lang · Liane Lang · Rembert Langham · Daniel Langlois · Tim Laskey · Jessica Latowicki · Fabio Lattanzi Antinori · Jim Latter · Scott Lattimer · Andrea Laubmann · Keith Law · Nicola Lawler · Ben Lawley ·

Erin Lawlor · Marinella Lawrence · Debbie Lawson · Mark Lawson Bell · Dana Lazarus-Cass · Suzanne Le Blanc · Chloe Le Drezen · Angus Leadley Brown · Thomas Kevin Leahy · Simon Leahy-Clark · David Leapman · Richard Learoyd · Rebecca Leathley · Su Leaver · Mark Leckey · Andrew Lee · Jeffrey Lee · Jungwoo Lee · Rama Lee · Rona Lee · Sophie Lee · Dean Leigh · Ute Leiner · Lawrence Lek · Patricia Lennox-Boyd · Dante Leonelli · Camille Leproust · Ann-Marie LeQuesne · Linda Leroy · Sarah Leslie · Harry Levene · Lucy Levene · Sophie Levi · Alastair Levy · Barbara Levy · Garth Lewis · Jonathan Lewis · John Lewis · Philip Lewis · Anna Liber-Lewis · Heather Libson · Peter Liddell · Mark Liebenrood · Adam Lieber · Linda Lieberman · Sarah Lightman · Covalec Limited · Shi-Chi Lin · Yu Lin Kang · Ian Lindsay-Edwards · Simon Ling · Wai Ling Cheung · Su Ling Wang · Simon Linington · Simon Linke · Tony Linkson · Matthew Linley · Claudia Lipsey · Eva Lis · Robert Lisney · Caroline List · Steve Littman · B. Lloyd · Hilary Lloyd · Peter Lloyd Bennett · Brad Lochore · Hew Locke · Isabella Lockett · James Lockett · Andrew Logan · Glen Logan · Peter Logan · Lorena Lohr · John Loker · Cathy Lomax · Jo Longhurst · Nicola Lorini · Duncan Loudon · Josh Love · Mark Lovell · James Low · Brighid Lowe · Colin Lowe · Dan Lowe · Anna Livia Lowendahl-Atomic · Gian Paul Lozza · Sophie Luard · Jose Luis · Jude Lunn · Alice Lunt · Juliet Lushington · Maria Lusia Rocco · Vibeke Luther · Jonathan Lux · Max Lyons · Anna Lytridou · Julie Macara · Rosie Maccurrach · Ruth MacDonald · Catherine MacGregor · Kate Mackeson · James Mackinnon · Jane Mackintosh · Kenny Macleod · Jo Madden · Agata Madejska · Jim Madge · Lee Maelzer · Jeremie Magar · Alan Magee · Keith Magnum · Hanan Magou · Nevine Mahmoud · Evariste Maiga · Joshua Mainprize · Emily Jane Major · Mary Jo Major · Cornelius Makkink · Herman Makkink · Steve Malies · Sophia Malig · Oliver Malin · Julius Malkin · Keith Mallinson · Helen Mallison · Philippe Malouin · Sean Maltby · Mutalib Man · Phineas Manasseh · Cartin Mandy · Nina Mankin · Priscilla Manthey · Karl Manwaring · Susan Marcangelo · Alex March · Antonio Marguet · Arkem Mark Walton · Persefoni Marlaka · Josh Marriot · Michael Marriott · Darren Marshall · Sam Marshall · Chris Marshall · Helen Marten · Anabel Martin · Barry J. Martin · Graham Martin · Kelly Martin · Anna Masing · Don Mason · Jill Mason · Paul Mason · Robert Mason · Will Mason · Nigel Massey · Nick Masters · Nerys Mathias · Lucie Mathiszig · Tetsu Matsumto · Nao Matsunaga · Peter Matthews · Tom Matthews · S Maxen · Zoe Maxwell · Phil Mayer · Ursula Mayer · Guy Mayman · Benito Mayor Vallejo · Caroline Mayow · Alice Mazzilli · Kiki Mazzucchelli · Elizabeth McAlpine · Nick McAuley · Lauren McCalmont · Caroline McCarthy · Tom McCarthy · Mandy McCartin · Miki McCarty · Trisha McCauley · Philip McCluney · Emma McClure · Gareth McConnell · Dan McDermott · John McDonald · Lindsay McEwan · Alan McFetridge · Eline McGeorge · Sarah McGinity · Martin McGinn · R. McGoldrick · Adam McGowan · Bernard McGuigan · Fergus McHardy · Sophie Mcilwain · James McKay · Ian McKeever · Jordan McKenzie · James McKinnon · Jessica McKinnon · Jessie McLaughlin · John McLeod · Mark McPadden · Nick Mead · Sacha Meaden · Lyn Medcalf · Andrea Medjesi-Jones · Kerri Meehan · Sneh Mehta · Ivy Mei · Sarah Meidan · Fleur Melbourn · Chris Mellor · Nathaniel Mellors · Alex Menace · Hugh Mendes · Tobias Menzies · Shaheen Merali · Fiona Merchant · James Merifield · Brian Merry · Stephanie Mesenge · Romain Meunier · Bill Meyer · Sarah Miatt · Sean Michael · Michael Michaelides · Ann Michie · Marilyn Middlemiss · Cedric Migroyan · Diana Mikula · Heidi Miller · Jeremy Scott Miller · Rosalind Miller · Clair Miller · Elizabeth Millership · Charles Mills · Simon Mills · William Mills · Peter Milne · Lisa Milroy · Chris Milton · Vanessa Mitter · Jan Mladejovsky · Abi Moffat · Gorka Mohamed · Mark Molloy · Marian Monas · Michael Monk · William Monk · Arlette Monkewitz · Ian Monroe · Guillermo Monroy · S. Moodie · Brendan Moore · Douglas Moore · Lindsay Moran · Sonia Morange · Denese Morden · Annabelle Moreau · Giovanna Morellan · Barry Morgan · Eleanor Morgan · Kathryn Morgan · Peter Morgan · Stephen Morgan · Sue Morgan · Paul Moriarty · Vicky Morley · Neil Morley · Mark Morley-Smith · Jon Morrell · Katie Morris · Nicole Morris · Sarah Morris · Paul Morris · Laura Morrison · Nicole Morrison · Paul Morrison · Patrick Morrissey · John Mortimer · Katrina Mortimer · Emerald Mosley · Amanda Moss · Gabrielle Motola · Tony Mott · Andrew Mottershead · Batilde Moutou · Jordene Moydell · Clem Moyes · Omeima Mudawi · Yin Mui Tang · Robert Muir · Malkhaz Mukhiguly · Martina Mullaney · Dean Mullings · James Mullord · Ann Mulrooney · David Munns · Jonathan Munro · Shane Munro · Rosie Munro Kerr · Jost Munster · Matthew Murphey · John Murphy · Matthew Murphy · Paul Murphy · Nancy Murphy Spicer · Murray · Bethany Murray · Frances Murray · Helen Amy Murray · Graham Murtough · Matthew Musgrave · Gary Mwagg · Adriette Myburgh · Martin Myers · Noel Myles · Miriam Nabarro · Marina Naja · Freya Najade · Mark Nash · Janet Nathan · Martin Naylor · Roy Naylor · Paul Neagu · Clare Neasham · Nika Neelova · Mike Nelson ·

Stephen Nelson · Nicola Nemec · Hannah Nerl · Alison Neville · S Nevin · Christian Newby · Charles Newington · Avis Newman · Hayley Newman · Peter Newman · Matthew Newsome · Ferris Newton · John Henry Newton · Keh Ng · Lay Ngo Koay · Sam Nias · Colin Nicholas · Simon Nicholas · Ian Nichols · Brian Nicol · Annabel Nicolson · Anushia Nieradzik · Steve Niner · Guy Noble · Paul Noble · Peter Noble · Mitsuru Nomura · Claudia Norman · Nils Norman · Carlos Noronha Feio · Paul Norton · Richard Norton · Norton + Jalees · Kat Nowak · Vincent Nowak · Nick Nowicki · Ralf Nuhn · Fabian Nyblom · Helene Nymann · Kevin O'Brien · Maureen O'Connell · Darren O'Connor · Fergus O'Connor · Matt O'Dell · Hugh O'Donnell · John O'Donnell · Suzanne O'Driscoll · Thomas O'Kane · Shirley O'Neill · Catharine O'Shea · Elizabeth O'Sullivan · Megumi Ochi · Nick Offer · Richard Oginz · Markn Ogue · Jenny Okun · Saskia Olde Wolbers · Laura Oldfield Ford · Jill Olenski · Stephen Olinski · Ken Oliver · Clara Oloriz Sanjuan · Reni Olsen · Zero One · Jemma Ooi · Jane Opher · Owen Oppenheimer · Bridget Orlando · Chris Orr · Janet Orrock · Maria Teresa Ortoleva · Bill Osment · Benjamin Osterberg · Jane Ostler · Carlien Oudes · Lydia Ourahmane · Gail Outhwaite · Oxenburgh · Russell Oxley · Hiroko Ozeki · Denizhan Ozer · Linda Packer · Greg Page · Sirpa Pajunen-Moghissi · Cliff Palmer · Liam Palmer · Mary Palmer · Magnus Palsson · Annabelle Pangborn · Nicholas Pankhurst · Eva Papadopoulou · Frixos Papantoniou · Annarita Papeschi · Emma Park · Jinyong Park · John Parker · Selma Parlour · Dan Parnell · Daniele Parolin · Stephanie Parr · James Parr · Richard Parrington · Simon Parris · John Parry · Jacqueline Parsons · Johanna-Maria Parv · Urvesh Parvais · Andy Parvitt · Ana Maria Pascescu Stewart · Maria Pask · Jaimini Patel · Neil Patersonn · Eliza Patten · Richard Patterson · Simon Patterson · Jennifer Pattison · Richard Paul · D. Paul-Wright · Juhan Pawmiscland · Tracey Payne · Guillermo Paz · Fabian Peake · Catherine Pearson · Milly Peck · Rosie Pedlow · Reggie Pedro · Michael Peel · Joseph Pelling · Simon Pemberton · Alexander Pemberton · Sue Pembridge · Terry Pendle · Richard Penna · Lisa Penny · Penzold · Andrew Pepper · Thomas Percival · George Percy · Ana Pereira · George Perendia · Indika Perera · Irene Pérez Hernández · Enrique Perezalba Red · Peter Peri · Paige Perkins · Jeff Perks · Roxane Permar · Roman Perona · Tracy Perrett · Eileen Perrier · Sarah Perritt · Julian Perry · Maurice Perry · Zoran Peshich · Claire Pestaille · Jean Petrie · Daniel Pettitt · Luke Petty · Ben Petzold · Julia Peyton Jones · Harry Philbrick · Simon Philipps · Cat Phillipps · Maurice Phillips · Jason Phillips · Robert Phillips · Heather Phillipson · Annette Philo · Nathan Philpott · Simon Phipps · Amalia Pica · Picchu · Matthew Pick · Julie Pickard · Roy Pickering · Cherry Pickles · Duncan Pickstock · Jessica Piddock · Paul Pieroni · Sebastiaan Pieter Groenen · Jason Pietracatella · H-Dieter Pietsch · Rui Pignatelli · Beverley Pile · Johnny Pinchard · Austen Pinkerton · Tom Piper · Philomene Pirecki · Alex Pitt · Kathryn Place · Ana Placencia · Sam Plagerson · Cristina Planas · Richard Plank · Mary Plant · Veronica Planton · Sarah Platt · Chris Plytas · Peter Podworski · Jenny Polak · Mia Pollak · Jill Pollard · Fred Pollock · Alison Poltock · David Porritt · Michael Porter · Neil Porter · Portugal Prints · Albert Potrony · John Potter · Malcom Potter · Jan Poul · Chris Poulton · Beth Pountney · Shirley Pountney · David Powell · Julia Powell · Amelia Power · Katherine Power · Sista Pratesi · Michelle Prazak · Lawrence Preece · Elizabeth Price · Joanna Price · Keith Price · Ariane Prin · Mark Prince · Nicola Probert · Joe Proietti · Oleg Prokofiev · Dan Proops · Kitta Protgieter · Laure Prouvost · Ben Pruskin · Susan Pryke · Tero Puha · Kristina Pulejkova · Emma Pune · Simon Purins · Dovile Puzinaite · E. Pyne · Frances Quesnel · Lucia Quevedo · Robert Quick · Jane Quinn · Malcom Quinn · Federico Radaelli · Susan Rae · Michael Raedecker · Micol Ragni · Ana Rajcevic · Sitraka Rakotonainina · Charlotte Raleigh · Ram & Fab · Roger Rama · Patricia Ramirez · Carole Ramoya · Alexander Ramsay · Alan Ramsay · Sherriffs Ranald · Nick Rands · Julie Rankin · Nicolas Ranko · Sam Ratcliffe · Heidrun Rathgeb · Matthew Raw · Tessa Rawcliffe · Mark Read · Shirley Read · John Reardon · Henry Recces · Paul Redfearn · Keith Redhead · Anne Redmond · Sam Reeles · Ben Reeves · Keith Reeves · Ktty Reford · Luc Regis · Paula Rego · Erik Rehl · Benjamin Reichen · Clunie Reid · Denise Reid · Mari Reijnders · Sadie Renwick · Alex Ressel · Magali Reus · Sam Reveles · Graham Revell · Rocio Reyes-Cortez · Mark Reynolds · Olivia Reynolds · Michael Rhodes · Joseph Richards · Lois Richards · Matthew Richardson · John Richert · Olivier Richon · Madeline Ridgeway · Christian Rieben · James Rielly · Heather Rigg · Richard Rigg · Marko Righo · Bridget Riley · Paul Riley · Anders Rindom · Peter Rippon · Ernesto Rivera · Carole Robb · Helen Roberston · Joanne Roberts · Michael Roberts · Perry Roberts · Richard Roberts · Shantha Roberts · Claire Robertson · Ian Robertson · Valerie Robertson · Annette Robinson · David Robinson · John Robinson · Neal Rock · Polly Rockberger · Marie Rodgers · Sylvia Rodgers · Alida Rodrigues · Suzanne Roles · Lewis Ronald · Annabel Rooker · Jeffrey Roper · Rebecca Roscorla · Juliet Rose · James Rosenthal · Sheila Ross · Arabella Ross · Naneen Rossi · Eva Rothschild · Helen Rousseau ·

Carl Rowe · Julia Rowlands · George Rowlett · Salvatore Rubbino · Philip R.J. Ruben · Gerda Rubinstein · Julieta Rubio · Cameron Rudd · Luke Rudolf · Ken Runciman · Jon Rundall · Maria Luis Ruocco · Mark Rushton · Steve Rushton · Bruce Russell · Caroline Russell · Henry Russell · Lynda Russell · Marlowe Russell · Michael Russell · Peter Russell · Robert Russell · Axelle Russo-Heath · Iain Rutherford · David Ryan · Ryszard Rybicki · Natalie Ryde · Andrew Ryder · David Ryle · Helen Sachs · Chris Sacker · Deborah Sadler · Georgio Sadotti · Julian Sainsbury · Louise Sakula · Andrew Salgado · Mike Salter · Rebecca Salter · Adrian Samson · Daniel Samson · Michael Samuels · Fernando Sancho · Natalie Sanders · Jon Sanders · Margarida Sardinha · Emily Jo Sargent · Hrair Sarkissian · Cosmo Sarson · Atsuko Sasaki · Anne-Marie Saunders · Coleman Saunders · Marsha Saunders · Peter Saunders · Helen Savage · Terence Scales · Terry Scales · Tim Scales · Ann Scannell · Fraser Scarfe · Henry Schalk · Andreas Schmidt · Martina Schmueker · Michael Schnorr · Frank Schofield · Heather Schofield · Maaike Schoorel · Zsofia Schweger · Gavin Scobie · Anthony Scott · Ben Scott · Cameron Scott · Celia Scott · Michael Scott · Rebecca Scott · Jeremy Scott-Miller · Colin Scull · Stevey Scullion · Sean Scully · Bridget Searle · Tom Seaton · Andrew Sect · Piers Secunda · Peter Sedgley · Tom Sedgwick · Naomi Sekandi · Howard Selina · Diana Sellars · Deanna Sellars · Stella Semple · Lorraine Sempliner · Sandy Sempliner · Jacques Senechal · Stephen Setford · John Seth · Lou Sexty · Krystyna Shackleton-Dzieszko · Rob Shaer · Nigel Shafran · Lilly Shahravesh · Eleanor Shalken · Jessica Shamash · Daniel Shanken · Alli Sharma · Binod Sharma · Iain Sharpe · Lain Sharpe · Kenneth Sharpe · Michael Shaughnessy · Michael Shaw · Rose Shawe-Taylor · Chen Sheng Tsang · John Shennan · Rob Sherwood · Ilric Shetland · Stephen Shiell · Sly Shillingford · Yinka Shonibare · John Short · Joanna Short · Martin Shortis · Sarah Shoughi · Boady Shouls · Jamie Shovlin · Cyrus Shroff · Tim Siddall · Kathryn Siegel · Susannah Silver · Abigail Simmonds · Linda Simmonds · Francesca Simon · Marianne Simonin · DJ Simpson · Kevin Sinnott · Welsh Siobahn · Walid Siti · Susanne Siverland · Pam Skelton · Charles Skinner · Eric Skuggevik · Veronica Slater · Constance Slaughter · Souheil Sleiman · Rebecca Sloan · Grant Smaldon · David Small · Alison Smart · Kevin Smeeing · Pablo Smidt · Adam Smith · Alison Smith · Amanda Smith · Angela Smith · Barry Smith · C.M Smith · Charlotte Smith · David Smith · Desmond Smith · Lesley Smith · Lou Smith · William Smith · Lorraine Snape · Robert Sollis · David Somerville · Yinan Song · Annalisa Sonzogni · Enver Sopi · Martacarmela Sotelo · Eliza Southwood · Karen Souza · Marcela Spadaro · Simon Spain · Martin Spanyol · Aerial Sparks · Felicity Sparrow · David Sparshott · Julia Spicer · Jackson Sprague · Sue Spring · Marianne Spurr · Kate Squires · Monika Srodon · Marty St. James · Geoff Staden · Patrick Staff · Daiana Stanescu · Peter Stanley · Siobhan Stanley · J. Stansfield · Fergal Stapleton · Kay Stark · Helen Starr · Katie Starr · Maz Staruch · Jeffrey Steele · Vicky Steer · Lucy Steggals · Jemima Stehli · William Stein · Eva Stenram · Ben Stephenson · Veena Stephenson · Dunn Steve · Chris Stevens · Paula Stevens-Hoare · Susan Stevenson · Andrew Stewart · Frances Stewart · Harriet Stewart · Kerry Stewart · Rebecca Stewart · Maria Stewart Wilson · Dilys Stinson · James Stirling · Lisa Stockham · Ben Stockley · Heidi Stokes · Karen Stokes · Mirribell Stolzenberg · Denise Stonebridge · Laurence Storey · Samantha Stork · Catherine Story · Olivia Strange · Richard Strange · Elizabeth Strath · Naomi Strauss · Graeme Strutt · Michael Stubbs · Phoebe Stubbs · Caroline Styles · Glenn Sujo · Anthony Sullivan · Lisa Sullivan · Angela Summerfield · John Summers · Phillip Summers · Arin Sunaryo · Priya Sundram · Mari Sunna · Mark Surridge · Ben Sutton · Trevor Sutton · Peter Sutton · Yuji Suzuki · Sharon Swaine · John Swarbrick · Kelly Sweeney · Ben Swift · Matthew Swift · James Swinson · Anne Sykes · Jodi Symmonds · Judith Symons · Gordon Synn · Borbala Szanto · Katarzyna Szczotarska · Dorothy Szulc · Rebecca Taber · Richard Taffs · Yuhei Taichi · Tomoko Takahashi · Taryn Takahashi · Akane Takayama · Takahiko Takemoto · Jennifer Talbort · Anne Tallentire · Dafna Talmor · Swapna Tamhane · Jack Tan · Andreas Tana · Yosuke Tanaka · Sanne Tang · Ying Mui Tang · Bridget Tapp · Stuart Targett · India Tatham-Banks · Corinne Taylor · Diana Taylor · Gary Taylor · Justin Taylor · Michael Taylor · Sue Taylor · Wendy Taylor · A. Teale · David Tebbs · Paul Tecklenberg · Sally Temple · Sally Temple · Michiel ten Bohum · Thorwald ter Kulve · Kate Terry · Hannah Terry · Nasser Teymourpour · Alice Theobald · Katharina Thiel · Rajesh Paul Thind · Deborah Thomas · Lex Thomas · Mark Thomas · Philip Thomas · Dominic Thomas · Dolly Thompsett · Andrew Thompson · Carolyn Thompson · Debbi Thompson · Jenny Thompson · John Thompson · Mimei Thompson · Niall Thompson · Jesper Thomsen · Tony Thornton · Torey Thornton · Ian Thorpe · Jo Thorpe · Stephen Thorpe · Jim Threapleton · Caragh Thuring · Zhu Tian · Tom Tiffin · Andrew Tighe · John Tildesley · Joe Tilson · John Timberlake · Sharon Ting · Adele Tipler · Akane Tkayama · Martin Toft · Mitsuru Tokutomi · Katharine Tolladay · Joel Tomlin ·

Jannine Tompkins · Paul Tonkin · Caroline Topley · Robert Toplis · Catherine Tough · Rebecca Tough · Polly Townsend · Frankie Tracey · Michael Tracey · Emily Tracy · Daniel Treacy · Stephen Treherne · Agnes Treplin · Charles Trevelyan · Tony Tribe · Maria Trimikliniotis · Rebecca Truscott-Elves · Pippa Tuck · Chris Tucker · Ann Tuckwell · David Tuckwell · Nick Tudor · Katherine Tulloh · Silia Ka Tung · Susan Turcot · Brett Turnbull · Bruce Turner · Louise Turner · Sophie Turner · Philip Turner · Nick Turvey · Leanne Turvey · Ben Twiston Davies · Sally Tyley · Barbara Tyrrell · Simon Tyszko · Chinedu Umenyilora · Sally Underwood · James Unsworth · Peter Upward · James Urquhart · Martin Usborne · Gill Usher · Usher & Burberry · Michelle Ussher · Robert Uszkurat · Ufuk Uyanik · Covadonga Valdes · Sheena Vallely · Tuur Van Balen · Manja Van de Worp · Janneke van der Hagen · Be Van der Heide · Lennaart Van Oldenborg · Nigel van Wieck · Therese Vandling · Lisa Vandy · Miranda Vane · Floyd Varey · Pandora Vaughan · Marc Vaux · Raisa Veikkola · Marta Velasco · Leo Verhoeven · Cristina Vezzini · Camille Vic-Dupont · Anna Vickers · Wendy Vincent · Ib Vindbjerg · Julia Vogl · Stephanie Von Reiswitz · Carl Von Weiler · Roy Voss · K.M Wade · Lorna Wadsworth · Johnny Waeridge · Lee Wagstaff · Jala Wahid · Dedalus Wainwright · Julian Wakelin · Peter Waldron · Charlotte Wales · Brendan Walker · Caroline Walker · Haggle Walker · Pam Walker · Peter Walker · Owen Wall · Christofer Wallentin · Simon Waller · Prue Waller · Mark Wallinger · Jo Walter · Stephen Walter · Robi Walters · Ian Walton · Alice Walton · Ian Walton Smith · Tim Walton Smith · Ms A Walton Smith · Andrew Walworth · David Wamer · Suling Wang · David Ward · Eddie Ward · Michael Ward · David Warner · Rebecca Warren · Pat Warren · Crispin Warwick · Johnny Wateridge · Simon Waters · Richard Wathen · Bill Waton · Christine Watson · Fiona Watt · Jill Watton · Ronwen Watts · Ania Wawrzkowicz · Matthew Webber · William Webber · Gavin Weber · Klaus Weber · Ruth Weinberg · Andy Weir · Harley Weir · Louise Weir · Weis · Weis · Willem Weismann · Matt Welch · Stuart Welch · Michael Wenyon · Graham Westfield · Craig Westlake · Benjamin Westoby · Teresa Weston · Oliver Westover · Imogen Wetherell · Rose Wetherell · Andy Whamond · Anthony Whishaw · Jon Whitaker · Delia Whitbread · Anastasi White · Douglas White · Endel White · Rhonda Whitehead · Dan Whiteson · Rosalind Whitman · Ed Whittaker · John Whittaker · Lee Whittaker · Amanda Whittle · Louise Whittles · Andy Wicks · Jessica Wiesner · Alison Wilding · Simon Willems · Suzy Willey · Andrew Williams · Ben Williams · Dominic Williams · Julian Williams · Keith Williams · Laura Williams · Lucy Williams · Michael Williams · Nevina Williams · Philip Williams · Tracey Williams · Aaron Williamson · Joby Williamson · Jonathan Williamson · Victor Willing · Jo Wilmot · Tom Wilmott · Anne Wilson · Camilla Wilson · Edmund Wilson · Gerard Wilson · Jane Wilson · Laura Wilson · Louise Wilson · Paul Wilson · Rachel Wilson · Sarah Kate Wilson · Scott Wilson · Richard Wincer · Sam Wingate · Gerd Winner · Steve Winney · Paul Winstanley · Sam Winston · Christopher Winter · Jonny Winter · Keef Winter · Lucie Winterson · Caroline Wirth · Carol Wiseman · Jane Wisner · Emma Withers · Rachel Withers · Joanne Woffinden · Jo Wonder · Brian Wood · Ciaran Wood · Sarah Wood · Trevor Wood · Wilfrid Wood · Ben Woodeson · Sarah Woodfine · Belinda Woods · Christopher Woods · Clare Woods · Beth Woodward · Harvey Woodward · Joanna Woodward · Malcolm Woodward · Mary Lee Woolf · Tom Woolner · Public Works · Gary Wragg · Aaron Wright · E. Wright · Freya Wright · Lisa Wright · Victoria Wright · William Wright · Patricia Wynn Davies · Zadie Xa · Zhang Xing · Kentaro Yamada · Henry Yang · Yard Theatre · Ekatarina Yaschuk · Maria Yaschuk · F. Yocum · Shizuka Yokomizo · Felicity Youett · Ainslie Yule · Maria Zahle · A. Zakiewicz · Claire Zakiewicz · Neil Zakiewicz · Xing Zhang · Toby Ziegler · Jamie Zubairi · Andrea Zucchini · Cristian Zuzunaga

Contributor biographies

Mel Dodd is an architect and academic, and currently Programme Director of Spatial Practices at Central Saint Martins. Her teaching, practice and research interests focus on the relationships between social and political infrastructures, and built environments, included in her book *Live Projects: Designing with People* (RMIT Press, 2012).

William Fowler is a writer, film historian and musician. He is Curator of Artists' Moving Image, BFI National Archive and the co-founder and co-programmer of The Flipside at BFI Southbank. His seasons and restoration projects at the BFI have included *GAZWRX: the films of Jeff Keen*, *Queer Pagan Punk: Derek Jarman* (the largest ever Jarman retrospective) and *This Is Now: Film and Video After Punk*, the latter of which is currently touring internationally through LUX. He contributed chapters to, and co-edited, *The Edge is Where the Centre is: David Rudkin and Penda's Fen*. He programmes the monthly BFI strand Experimenta and has, since 2013, been the co-programmer of Experimenta in the London Film Festival. He regularly gives talks and presents films.

Larne Abse Gogarty is the Terra Foundation for American Art Postdoctoral Teaching Fellow at the Humboldt Universität, Berlin (2016–2018). She completed her PhD at University College London in 2015. Her primary research interests lie in modern and contemporary art with an emphasis on American performance, sculpture and social practice, Marxism, race and gender. She is currently working on her first book, provisionally titled *The Art of Living: Social Practice and State Formation in American Art*. She has also begun a new project on Chicago artists' groups between 1945 and 1975. She regularly writes criticism for *Art Monthly* and elsewhere, and is on the editorial collective for *Cesura//Acceso*, a journal for music, politics and poetics.

Rebecca Gordon-Nesbitt for a decade from the mid 1990s worked as a curator in the UK and the Nordic countries, and has since been conducting research into the socio-economic conditions of artistic practice. Her book on the cultural policy of the Cuban Revolution was published in 2015, and a selection of her other writing is available at shiftyparadigms.org. Based at King's College London, Rebecca has researched and drafted a report for the All Party Parliamentary Group on Arts, Health and Wellbeing, exploring the health and wellbeing benefits of arts engagement throughout life, which was launched in Parliament in July 2017 and is available at artshealthandwellbeing.org.uk/appg-inquiry.

Anna Harding has been Chief Executive at SPACE since 2005. After her MA she worked as a volunteer at the AIR Gallery in 1985. She then worked at the Whitechapel Gallery, John Hansard Gallery Southampton, Hayward Gallery and Camerawork London before becoming Director of Kettle's Yard, University of Cambridge, 1989–92. She set up the MA Creative Curating at Goldsmiths where she was programme director from 1995 to 2003. She has published several books including *Curating: The Contemporary Art Museum and Beyond* (Art & Design, 1997); *Potential: Ongoing Archive* (Artimo, Amsterdam, 2000); and *Magic Moments: collaboration between artists and young people* (Black Dog, 2006).

J&K – Janne Schäfer and Kristine Agergaard. The artist duo has been working together since 1999. Working with cultural history and museum collections to reframe history, their practice has continually interrogated the work of art and the creative process as invaluable contributions to the fabric of our world and our understanding of it. Their performative interventions into public and institutional spaces result in sculptural and mixed media installations. J&K have exhibited extensively in Europe, notably in Denmark and Germany, with solo presentations in museums such as: National Gallery of Denmark, Copenhagen; Pergamonmuseum, Berlin; KUNSTEN Museum of Modern Art, Aalborg, and Overgaden Institute for Contemporary Art, Copenhagen. The artists have extensive experience working in the public realm.

Robert Kudielka is Professor Emeritus for Aesthetics and Theory of Art in Berlin. In 1967, he first came to London as a freelance art critic and worked from 1969 to 1974 as German correspondent for *Studio International*. The present piece was published in 1971, under the title 'SPACE. Eine Antwort auf die Situation der Künste in London heute' in the catalogue of the SPACE exhibition, London Now in Berlin.

Courtney J Martin is the Deputy Director and Chief Curator at the Dia Art Foundation. Prior to Dia, she was an assistant professor in the History of Art and Architecture department at Brown University; assistant professor in the History of Art department at Vanderbilt University; Chancellor's Postdoctoral Fellow in the History of Art at the University of California, Berkeley; a fellow at the Getty Research Institute; and a Henry Moore Institute Research Fellow. In 2015, she received an Andy Warhol Foundation Arts Writers Grant. She also worked in the media, arts and culture unit of the Ford Foundation in New York.

Alicia Miller has worked for more than 20 years in the contemporary visual arts, in various capacities, including positions as Associate Director at San Francisco Camerawork, Head of Education and Public Events at the Whitechapel Gallery and the Axisweb Associate in Wales. She has been a board member of both the Chisenhale Gallery, London, and Ffotogallery, Cardiff. Her writing has been published in *Art Monthy*, *Art Review*, *Contemporary*, *Flash Art*, *Sculpture Magazine*, *Source* and many others. She is particularly interested in artists' role in gentrification and the spaces of the city and has extensively researched the early history and organisational development of SPACE.

David Morris is a writer, editor, researcher and sometime DIY musician. He is co-editor, with Sylvère Lotringer, of *Schizo-Culture: The Event, The Book* (Semiotexte/MIT, 2014); and, with Margarita and Victor Tupitsyn, *Anti-Shows: APTART 1982–84* (Afterall Books, 2017); and is an editor at *Afterall*. He is based in London.

Neil Mulholland is Chair of Contemporary Art Practice and Theory at Edinburgh College of Art and Dean of Postgraduate Studies for the College of Arts, Humanities and Social Sciences, The University of Edinburgh. He works with artists to develop speculative and theory-fiction approaches to writing, paragogy and artistic research. He collaborates with Norman Hogg (Concordia University, Montréal). As the Confraternity of Neoflagellants, they have fictioned the artistic field and method of *neomedievalism.* With Dan Brown, Curator of Research at Edinburgh Sculpture Workshop, Neil co-directs Shift/Work, a paragogy that reconfigures workshop-based artistic learning to generate open educational resources. Neil is also founding member of Atelier: Making Research Material Across the Arts and Social Sciences and co-editor of their journal *Visual Culture in Britain* (Routledge).

Naomi Pearce is a writer and producer living in Glasgow. She is co-founder of the Woodmill, an artist-led studio and gallery project based in Bermondsey, South London, from 2009 to 2014. Recent projects include 56 Artillery Lane at Raven Row, London (co-curated with Amy Budd). She is co-editor of *A-OR-IST* journal and a current AHRC-funded PhD candidate in Art at the University of Edinburgh (supervised by Maria Fusco and Dr Elizabeth Reeder).

Shirley Read is a curator, writer and oral historian working in photography. Her books include *Exhibiting Photography* and *Photographers and Research* (with Mike Simmons). She has been interviewing photographers for the *Oral History of British Photography*, a sound archive held by the British Library, since 1994.

Bridget Riley was born in 1931. She spent her childhood in Cornwall during the War and began painting when she was 14, going on to study life drawing at Goldsmiths. Her first solo exhibition took place in 1962 and she has continued to exhibit in the UK and internationally ever since. She has been awarded many prestigious awards and honours for her work in the field of painting, including Honorary Doctor of the Universities of Oxford, 1993, and Cambridge, 1995. Bridget Riley lives and works in London, Cornwall and the South of France. In 1968, she was a founder member of SPACE.

Peter Sedgley was born in 1930 in London and educated in Building and Architecture at the School of Building, Brixton. He worked as an architectural assistant from 1950 to 1960, and in 1961 trained as a radar mechanic in the RAF. Since 1962, he has worked as an autodidact in painting, kinetic art and light sculpture installations. He has received art and architectural commissions and awards, has exhibited widely and has been represented in international collections, including: the 9th Mainichi International Biennale, Tokyo, Japan, prize-winner of Education Ministers Award, 1966; Founding member of AIR and SPACE, 1968–72; Stipendiat of German Academic Exchange Service, Berlin Artist Programme, 1970; and the 42nd Venice Biennale, Art and Science, 1986. Peter Sedgley continues to work in Berlin and Worthing, Sussex.

Ana Torok is a curator and art historian based in New York City, specializing in conceptual and time-based media practices of the 1960s and 1970s. Her research interests include cultural representations of workers and labor-related issues, as well as the relationship between art practice and bureaucracy. While at the Courtauld Institute of Art, her MA thesis concerned the Institute for Art and Urban Resources, led by Alanna Heiss, and their work in founding P.S.1 and organizing its inaugural exhibition in 1976. She is currently a Curatorial Assistant at the Museum of Modern Art and has worked in the curatorial departments of the Solomon R. Guggenheim Museum and the Whitney Museum of American Art, while organizing exhibitions independently.

Andrew Wilson is senior curator of modern and contemporary British art, and archives, at Tate Britain. He co-curated the 2017 retrospective of David Hockney at Tate Britain and tour to Centre Pompidou, Paris, and Metropolitan Museum of Art, New York. He is developing a retrospective exhibition of Patrick Heron at Tate St Ives for 2018; he is concurrently preparing a spotlight display at Tate Britain examining the aftermath of the events of May 1968 that will open in May 2018. He is the author of *Richard Hamilton: Swingeing London 67 (f)* (London: Afterall Books, 2011).

Bibliography SPACE 1968-75

Dalya Alberge, 'At the sharp East End', *The Independent,* 4 December 1990, p. 27.

Barbara Armstrong, 'A Studio Community for Impoverished Artists', *Leeds Student*, 6 November 1970, pp. 6–7.

Cyril Barrett, 'St Katherine's Dock', *Hibernia*, 28 August 1969, p. 19.

AM Bell Macdonald, 'Old Dock for Arts', *The Times*, 6 July 1969.

Misha Black, 'Old Dock for Arts', *The Times*, 3 July 1969.

Harry Brack, 'What should we do with St. Katharine dock?', *The Evening Standard,* 8 April 1969.

Su Braden, 'A.I.R.R.A.R.I.P?S.P.A.C.E.D.', *Time Out*, 24–30, September 1971, pp. 20–21.

Guy Brett, 'Underneath the arches and down at the docks', *The Times*, 17 November 1970.

Donald Brook, 'UK commentary on 'London Now' Berlin Arts Festival', *Arts Review*, 10 August 1971, pp. 87–91.

Sibyl Burgess, 'Arts Scene', *Lincolnshire Chronicle*, 31 August 1973, pp. 11.

Dennis N Cole, 'Old Dock for Arts', *The Times,* 4 July 1969.

Ian Dunlop, 'Life at the Depot two years later', *The Evening Standard*, 29 September 1969.

Ian Dunlop, 'Colour and size make Bridget's art different', *The Evening Standard*, 21 July 1969, p. 7.

Gloria Emerson, 'Once a London Warehouse, Now an Artist Studio', *The New York Times,* 15 May 1969, p. 40.

Anthony Everitt, 'An artists' haven in a disused dockland warehouse', *The Birmingham Post*, 6 September 1969

Anthony Everitt, 'S.P.A.C.E. ... at the Midland Group Gallery, Nottingham', *The Birmingham Post*, 7 June 1971.

Anthony Everitt, 'Come into the indoor garden room, Maud!', *The Birmingham Post*, 19 August 1972.

Anthony Everitt, 'S.P.A.C.E. exhibition ... at the Wolverhampton Art Gallery', *The Birmingham Post*, 6 August 1971.

Anthony Everitt, 'Ikon's new policy is a break from tradition', *The Birmingham Post,* 13 January 1972.

Julian Exner, 'Londoner Hafen fuer Kuenstler: Altes Speicherhaus als Ausweg aus der Atelierraumnot *Frankfurter Rundschau*, 14 March 1970.

Andrew Forrest, 'popa at moma', *Art & Artists*, June 1971.

Peter Fuller, 'Review of Julian Cooper and Robert Graham exhibition', *Connoisseur*, October 1971.

Edward Gage, 'SPACE spectacular', *The Scotsman Edinburgh*, 25 October 1971.

Nigel Gosling, 'An abstract workshop', *Observer*, August 1971.

Michael Granger, 'Mutation Phenomena III: Evidence of Thought', *Art & Artists*, November 1969.

Robert Hughes, 'Grapevine' *Harper's Bazaar,* 1969.

Gerry Hunt, 'After Spectrum' *Art & Artists*, August 1971, pp. 12–14.

John H Holloway, 'International Science-Art News (Art et Science: Nouvelles de L'Etranger)', *Leonardo* 2, no. 4, October 1969, p. 450.

Elinor Kennedy, 'Space project: 1970', *The Kentish Independent*, 21 January 1970.

Robert Kudielka, 'London Now in Berlin, Akademie der Künste, Berlin', *Die Welt*, 26 March 1971.

Edward Lucie-Smith, 'A future of the visual arts', *The Times*, 1968.

Edward Lucie-Smith, 'Studios in the docks', *The Times,* – 1969.

Lynn MacRitchie, 'AIR & SPACE', *Art Monthly*, May 1992, pp. 6–9.

John McEwen, 'What is SPACE?', *Greater London Arts*, no. 54, August 1972.

Edwin Mullins, 'Space for artists', *The Sunday Telegraph*, 2 February 1969

Cordelia Oliver, 'SPACE in Aberdeen', *The Guardian Manchester Edition*, 19 October 1971.

Paul Overy, 'Watch this space', *Listener*, 13 February 1969.

William Packer, 'Wapping Artists Open Day', *The Financial Times*, 4 July 1981.

Hilary Pyle, 'Computered colour steals SPACE show', *The Sunday Independent Dublin*, 15 August 1971.

Bryan Robertson, 'Space in time', *Spectator*, 7 February 1969.

Bryan Robertson, 'Old Dock for Arts', *The Times*, July 1969.

Bryan Robertson, 'Demure walls', *Spectator*, 13 September 1969.

Bernard Rudd, 'Old Dock for Arts', *The Times*, 9 July 1969.

Bernard Rudd, 'Old Dock for Arts', *The Times*, 5 July 1969.

John Russell, 'A space to watch', *The Sunday Times*, 2 February 1969.

John Russell, 'First options', *The Sunday Times*, 14 June 1970.

C.S, 'Report on the reports', *Art & Artists,* April 1971.

Peter Schmitt, 'Swinging, Confusing London', *The Daily Telegraph*, 27 March 1971.

Peter Sedgley, 'Art Information Registry', *Studio International*, vol. 180, no. 924, July–August 1970.

Peter Sedgley, 'Facts about arts grants', *The Evening Standard*, 7 October 1969.

Peter Sedgley and Heinz Ohff, 'My Kinetic Artworks and Paintings (1971–1982)', *Leonardo* 15, no. 3, Summer 1982, p. 184.

Michael Shepherd, 'Free as the AIR', *The Sunday Telegraph*, 2 November 1975.

Michael Shepherd, 'AIR and SPACE', 1975, p. 639.

Rosemary Smith, 'Watch this Space for the fine arts: London charity gives painters and sculptors room to create', *Evening News*, 11 July 1978.

Caroline Tisdall, 'Review: Peter Hide', *The Guardian,* 12 October 1971.

Caroline Tisdall, 'Letting AIR into art', *The Guardian*, 30 March 1972.

Peter Townsend, 'A Proposal to Provide Studio Workshops for Artists', *Studio International*, vol. 177, no. 908, February 1969, pp. 65–67.

Tessa Traeger, 'Spotlight section', *Vogue*, September 1970.

Marina Vaizey, 'S.P.A.C.E. Ltd.', *Canvas,* vol. 4, no. 10, September 1970.

Marina Vaizey, 'Lord Eccles, Paymaster-General: A New Minister of the Arts', *Arts Review*, 29 August 1970.

Marina Vaizey, 'Artists' Market', *The Financial Times*, 6 October 1973.

Keith Vaughan, 'No threat', *The Times*, 7 July 1969.

David Wilcox, 'London dock scheme comes under fire'.

David Wilcox, 'Doubts over new homes deal at the docks', *The Evening Standard*.

'Portrait of the artist as a young woman', *The Observer Review*, 1 August 1971, p. 2.

'Young artists angry about patronage', *The Times*, 9 June 1969.

'The future of London Docks', *Wapping on Thames News*, Summer 1970.

'Artists at work in St Katharine's Docks', *The Times*, 7 July 1969.

'News', *Arts Review*, 11 February 1969.

'Art of charity', *The Sunday Times*, 28 November 1971.

'The remorseless Riley follows up her declaration of intent', *Antiques Weekly*, 2 August 1969.

'A bit of artistic license down in dockland', *The Daily Mirror*, 30 January 1969.

'Brush with Council', *Evening News*, 12 February 1969.

'Artists Will Be Taking Over St. Katharine's Dock Warehouse', *East London Advertiser,* 31 January 1969.

'Warehouses as artists' colony', *The Guardian*, 31 January 1969.

'Room and View', *The New York Times*, 16 March 1969.

'St Katharine Dock', *Studio*, July/August 1969.

'Moore space', *The Guardian*, 2 January 1970.

'News', *The Sunday Times*, 4 January 1970.

'News', *The Times*, 22 September 1969.

'The Glasshouse', *Arts Review*, 20 December 1969.

'Artists take over St K warehouse block', *The Port*, 27 March 1969.

'The Need for Studios', *Country Life*, 22 March 1973.

'In Search of Space', *Greater London Arts*, no. 70, December 1973.

'Space for art', *Marylebone Mercury*, 25 May 1973.

'Space probe', *Leicester Mercury*, 4 June 1971.

'It will attract the stock-broker class: Local residents oppose flats and marina plan', *East London*, 20 March 1970.

'Investing in Leisure: Finding room for artists', *Municipal and Public Services Journa*l, 11 May 1973, pp. 679–80.

'Accommodating the Artist', *Estates Gazette London*, 20 June 1970.

'It's all very hush hush…', *The Daily Mail*, 19 September 1967.

'Art Finds a Place in the Docks', *The Daily Telegraph London*, 19 January 1970.

'Rapportage: S.P.A.C.E.', *Art & Artists*, April 1969.

'Artists banned', *The Birmingham Post*, 10 October 1968.

'A mistake resulted in artists' ban', *The Birmingham Post*, 11 October 1968.

'Service for artists', *Wood Green Herald*, 4 September 1970.

'Blow-up: Graham Stevens discusses air structures', *Art & Artists*, May 1972, pp. 43–45.

'Artists' Plea for a Rates Cut Rejected', *South London Press*, 7 February 1969.

'Londoner's Diary: Crisis looms over 120 artists', *The Evening Standard*, 8 July 1970, p. 16.

'Bridget Riley', *The Evening Standard*, 5 November 1969, p. 23.

'A friend at court for the E.1 artists?', *The Evening Standard*, 5 August 1969, p. 4.

'No rates reduction: Row over artist converting Southwark prison', *South London Observer*, 13 February 1969.

'Op yours for £4,000', *The Observer Review*, 25 May 1969.

'Minister to Visit Warehouse Studios', *Hackney Gazette*, 9 May 1969.

'They come from SPACE', *East London Advertiser*, 30 July 1971.

'Colour Village drew 1,300 to park', *Sunderland Echo*, 21 August 1972.

'They're cashing in on us, says the docks artist', *Evening News*, August 1969.

'Artists to be moved from St. Katherine's Docks', *Hackney Gazette*, 19 June 1970.

'Museum petition', *Western Morning News*, 3 February 1970.

'Suffolk man hopes to build up Norwich artists' community', *Eastern Evening News*, 3 December 1969.

'Depot Art', *The Evening Standard*, 14 October 1969.

'Spectacular scheme for St Katharine Docks: Wapping Objection to Hotel Site', *Hackney Gazette*.

'Artists to be moved from St Katherine's Docks', *Hackney Gazette & North London Advertiser*, 19 June 1970.

'Art in the Docks', Hackney Gazette & North London Advertiser, 8 July 1969.

'Empty Factory: Site for Arts Research', *Marylebone Record*, 4 July 1969.

'Insight into the work of 'action space'', *East London Advertiser*, 10 October 1969.

'Blow-Up... A big romp for the kids', *South Wales Echo*, 29 March 1971.

'Dockland studio', *The Times Educational Supplement*, 16 May 1969.

'Art show by SPACE men (and women)', *Bromley Times*, 2 August 1973.

'Space programme', *Greater London Arts*, no. 70, August 1971.

'The first arrivals from the Thames: London Now in Berlin', *Telegraf*, 25 March 1971.

'Confusion and Shame', *Spandauer Volksblatt*, 28 March 1971.

'London Now in Berlin', *Telegraf*, 28 March 1971.

'Frozen Action', *Telegraf*, 28 March 1971.

'How SPACE Helps Out (and In) the Artists', *House & Garden*, May 1973, p. 109.

Acme and SPACE, *Help Yourself to Studio Space* (London: Arts Council of Great Britain, 1975).

Photography credits

We have attempted to contact all copyright holders, who are acknowledged where possible, any omissions will be amended in future editions.

Photos © Douglas Smith, 1968-70
19, 22, 24-25, 28, 31, 36-37, 39, 58-59, 86-87

Photos © Andrew C. Tweedie, 1967-74
44-45, 46-47, 48-49, 50, 96, 99, 101, 103, 188-189, 213

Photos Andrew C. Tweedie, 1968-70. © GASACT
20-21, 56-57, 60-61, 62-63, 66, 167

Photos © Shirley Read
124, 126, 128, 129, 130-131, 134-135, 136-137, 178, 187

Photos © Christian Dorley-Brown
164, 170-173, 176-177, 200-201, 202, 214-215, 216, 252-253

Acknowledgements

We decided that, in the spirit of SPACE, self-publishing was appropriate, with distribution provided by Cornerhouse Publications. *Artists in the City: SPACE in '68 and beyond* has been developed with the tireless support of Editorial Assistant Christine Jakobson. I am also grateful for assistance from Ana Torok and Helen Brewer. I would like to thank all the authors, artists and photographers who have generously contributed, and to Letty Mooring, Shirley Read and Peter Sedgley who provided important archival material. The studio sites timeline was researched by Alicia Miller. Thanks also to Hugh Gilbert, Peter Dockley, Adam Hart, Bryan Kneale, Graham Stevens and Wendy Taylor for reminding me of the irreverent spirit of SPACE, and to The Henry Moore Archive for access to correspondence. Also to the late Chris Wainwright, who as SPACE Chair of Trustees gifted me ten days a year for personal research from which this project results.

Funding for the publication was generously provided by The Bridget Riley Art Foundation, Cockayne – Grants for the Arts and National Portfolio Organisation funding from Arts Council England.

Courtney J. Martin's essay 'The Studio and the City: S.P.A.C.E. Ltd. and Rasheed Araeen's Chakras' was originally published in *The Studio Reader: On the Space of Artists*, edited by Mary Jane Jacob and Michelle Grabner, University of Chicago Press. 2010, pp. 302-310. © 2010 by The School of the Art Institute of Chicago and is republished here with kind permission of the author and University of Chicago Press.